3

LAID-BACK CAMP

contents

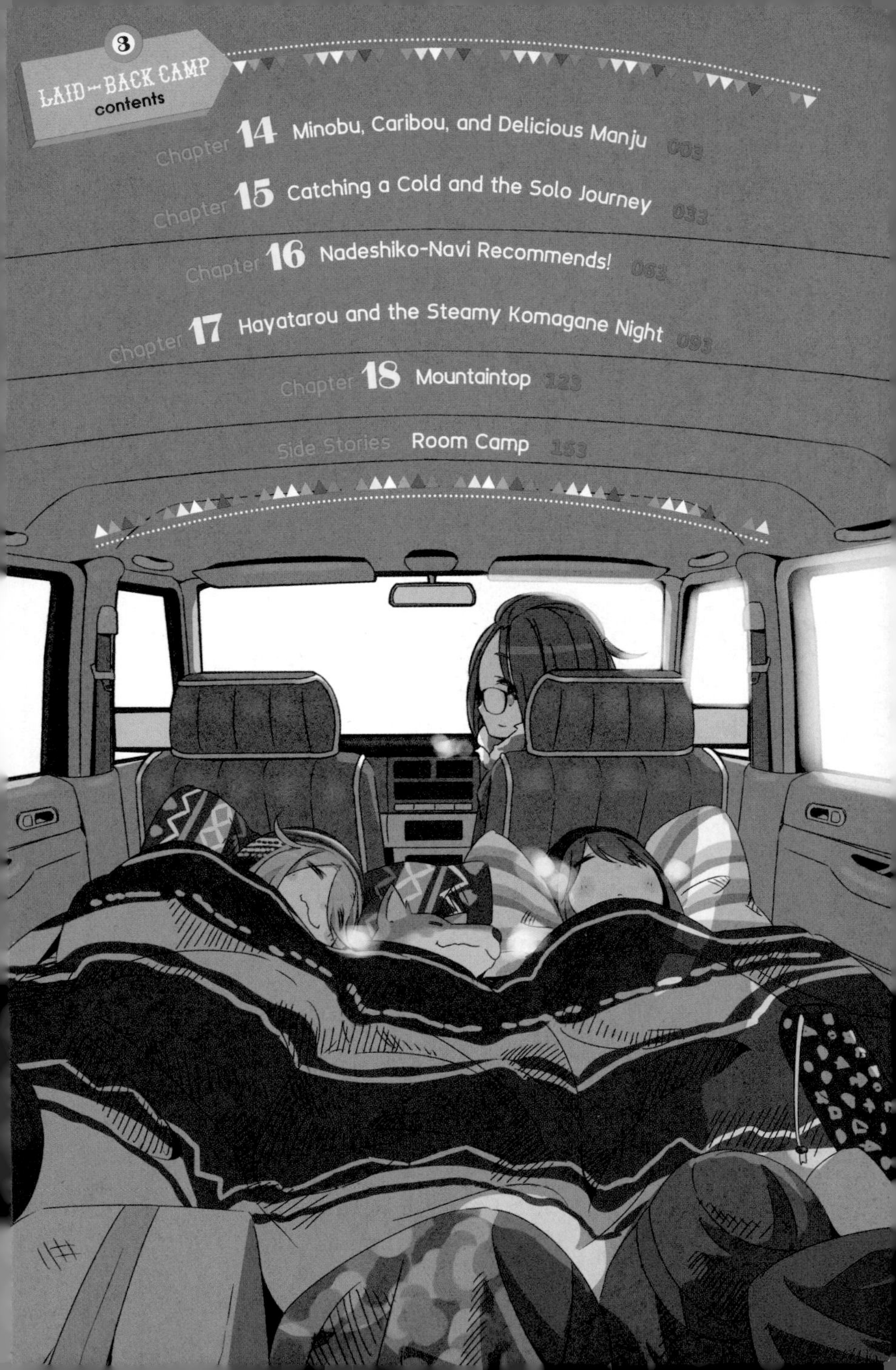

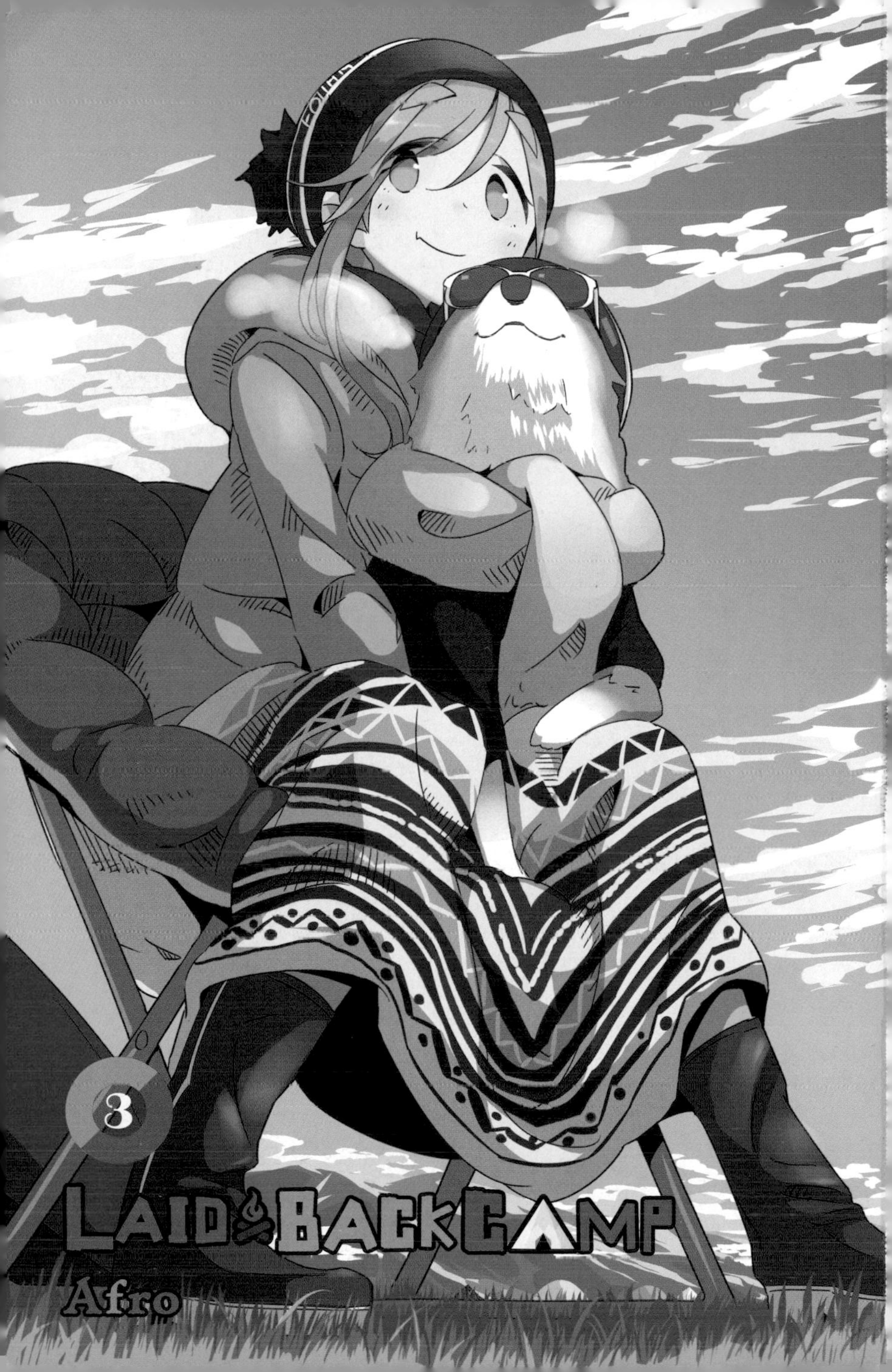
3
LAID BACK CAMP
Afro

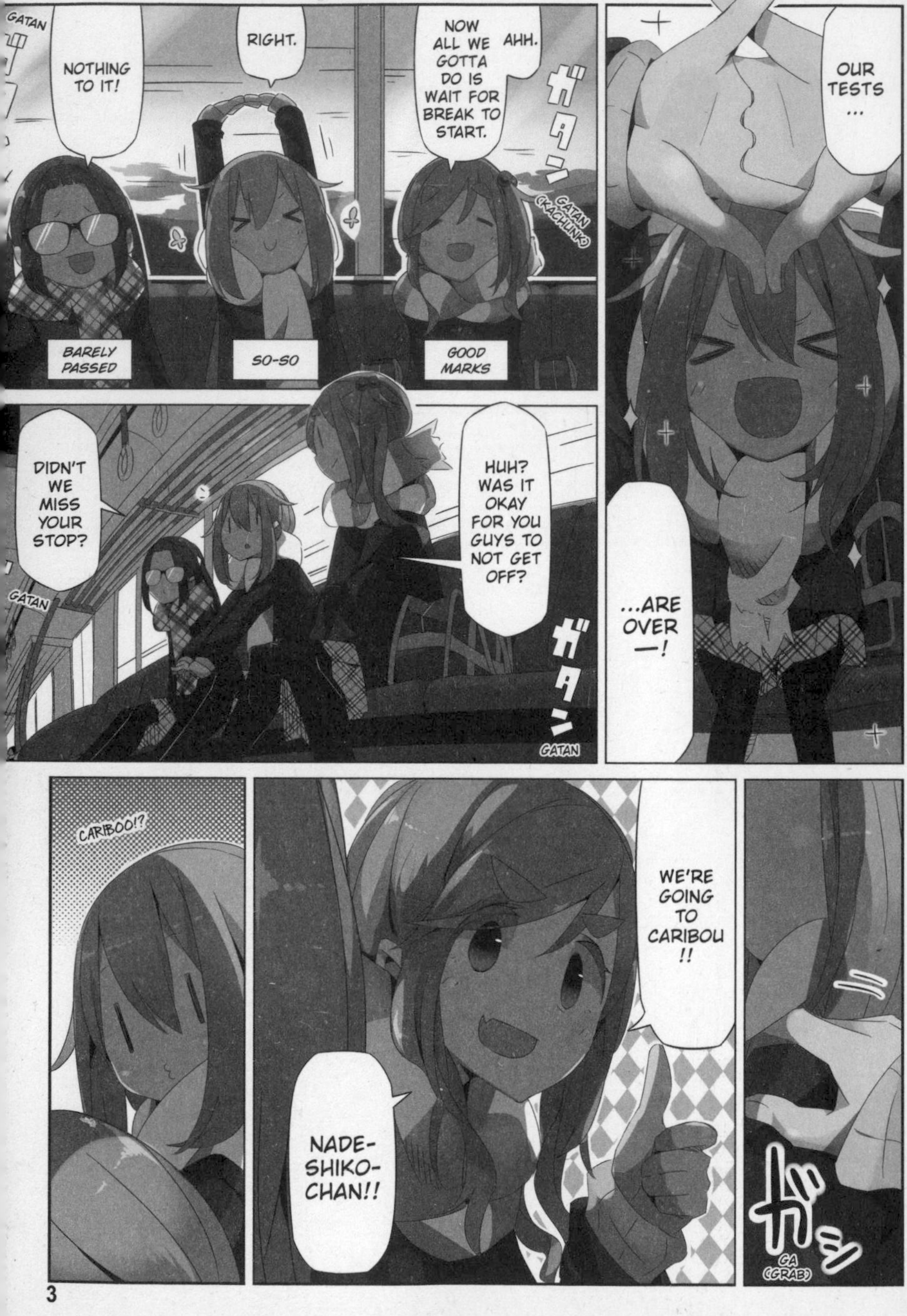
OUR TESTS ...
...ARE OVER—!
AHH.
GATAN (KACHLINK)
NOW ALL WE GOTTA DO IS WAIT FOR BREAK TO START.
RIGHT.
NOTHING TO IT!
GATAN
GOOD MARKS
SO-SO
BARELY PASSED
HUH? WAS IT OKAY FOR YOU GUYS TO NOT GET OFF?
GATAN
DIDN'T WE MISS YOUR STOP?
GATAN
GA (GRAB)
WE'RE GOING TO CARIBOU !!
NADE-SHIKO-CHAN!!
CARIBOO!?

Chapter 14
MINOBU, CARIBOU, AND DELICIOUS MANJU

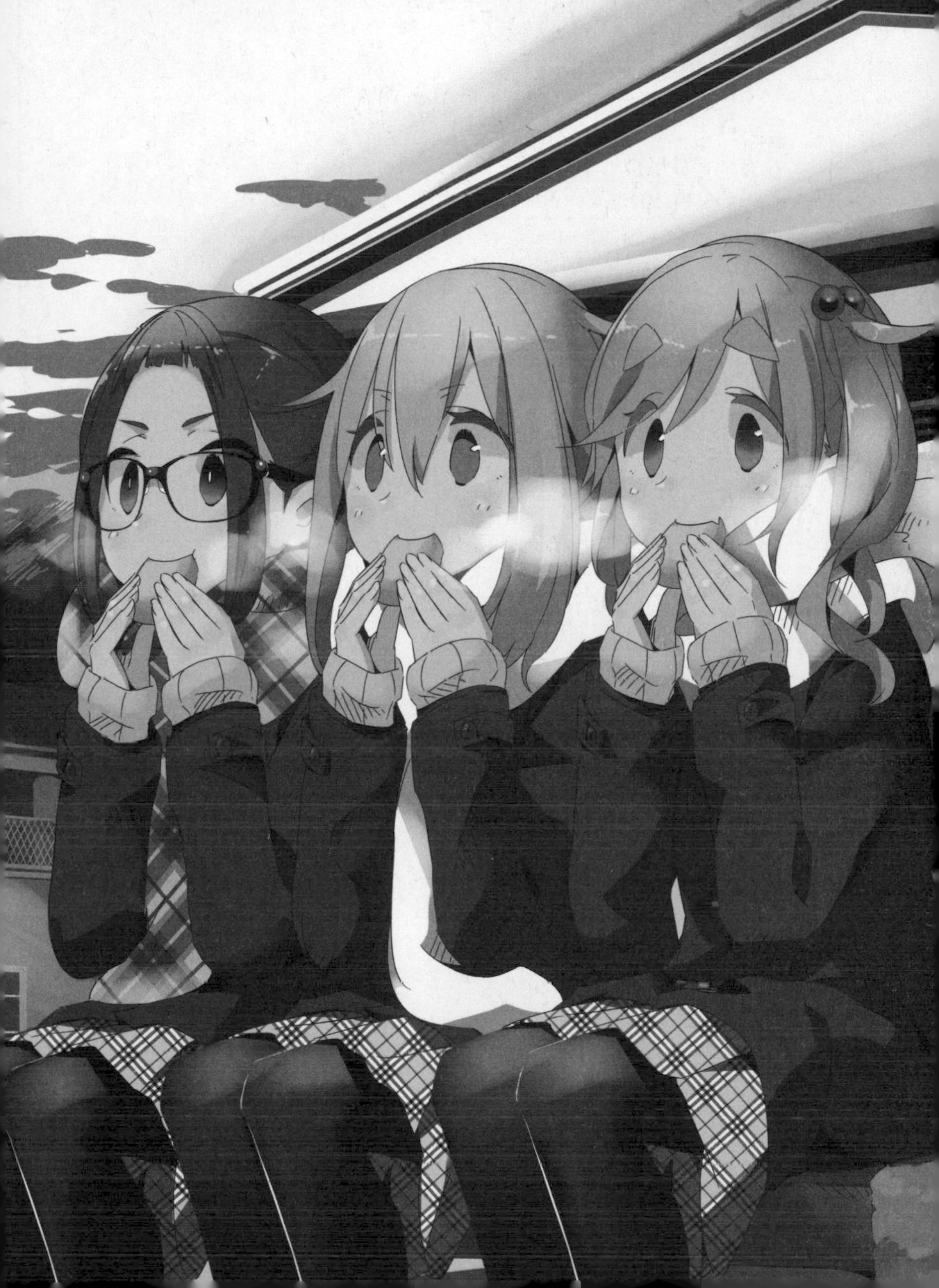

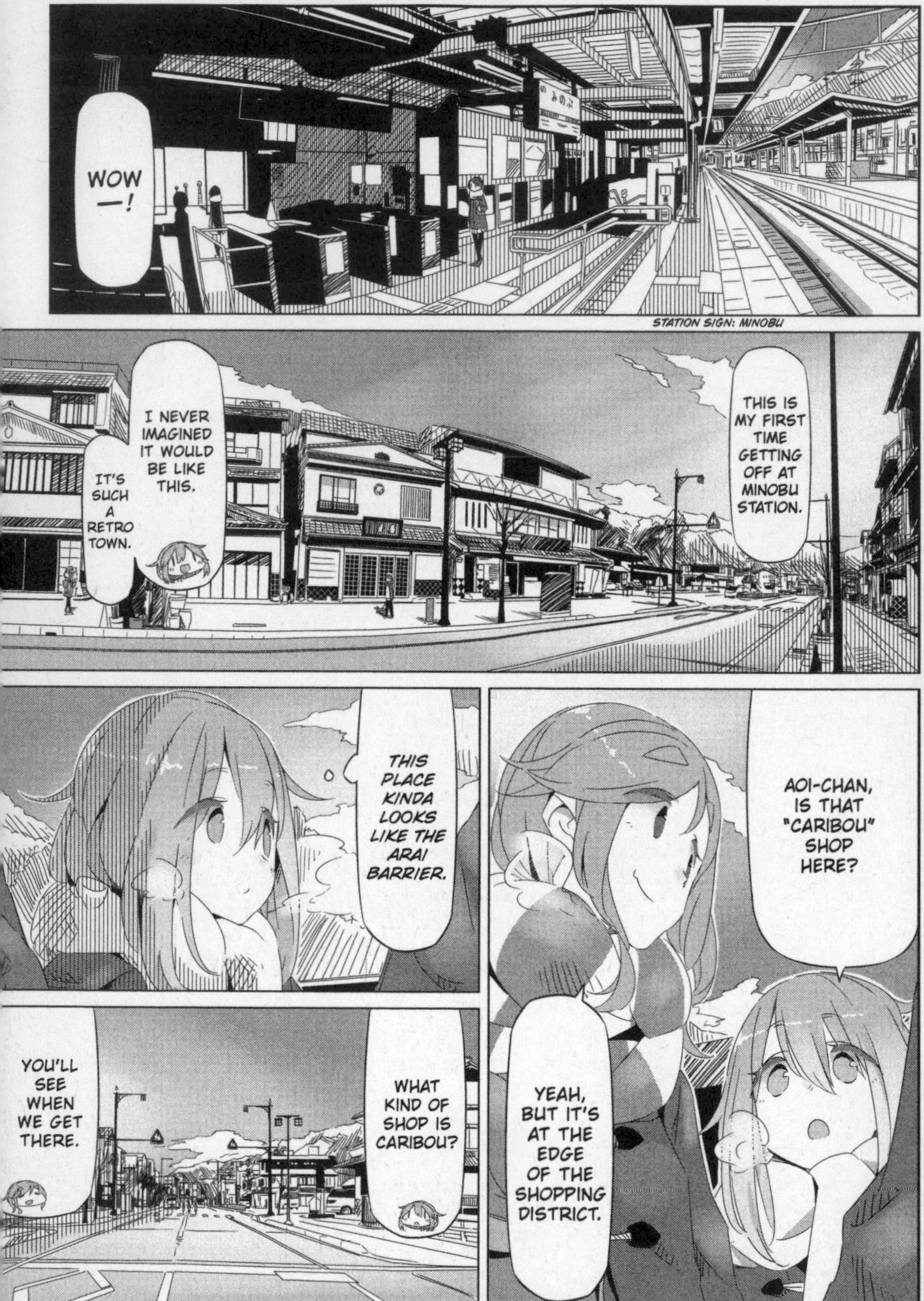
WOW—!
STATION SIGN: MINOBU
THIS IS MY FIRST TIME GETTING OFF AT MINOBU STATION.
I NEVER IMAGINED IT WOULD BE LIKE THIS.
IT'S SUCH A RETRO TOWN.
AOI-CHAN, IS THAT "CARIBOU" SHOP HERE?
YEAH, BUT IT'S AT THE EDGE OF THE SHOPPING DISTRICT.
THIS PLACE KINDA LOOKS LIKE THE ARAI BARRIER.
WHAT KIND OF SHOP IS CARIBOU?
YOU'LL SEE WHEN WE GET THERE.

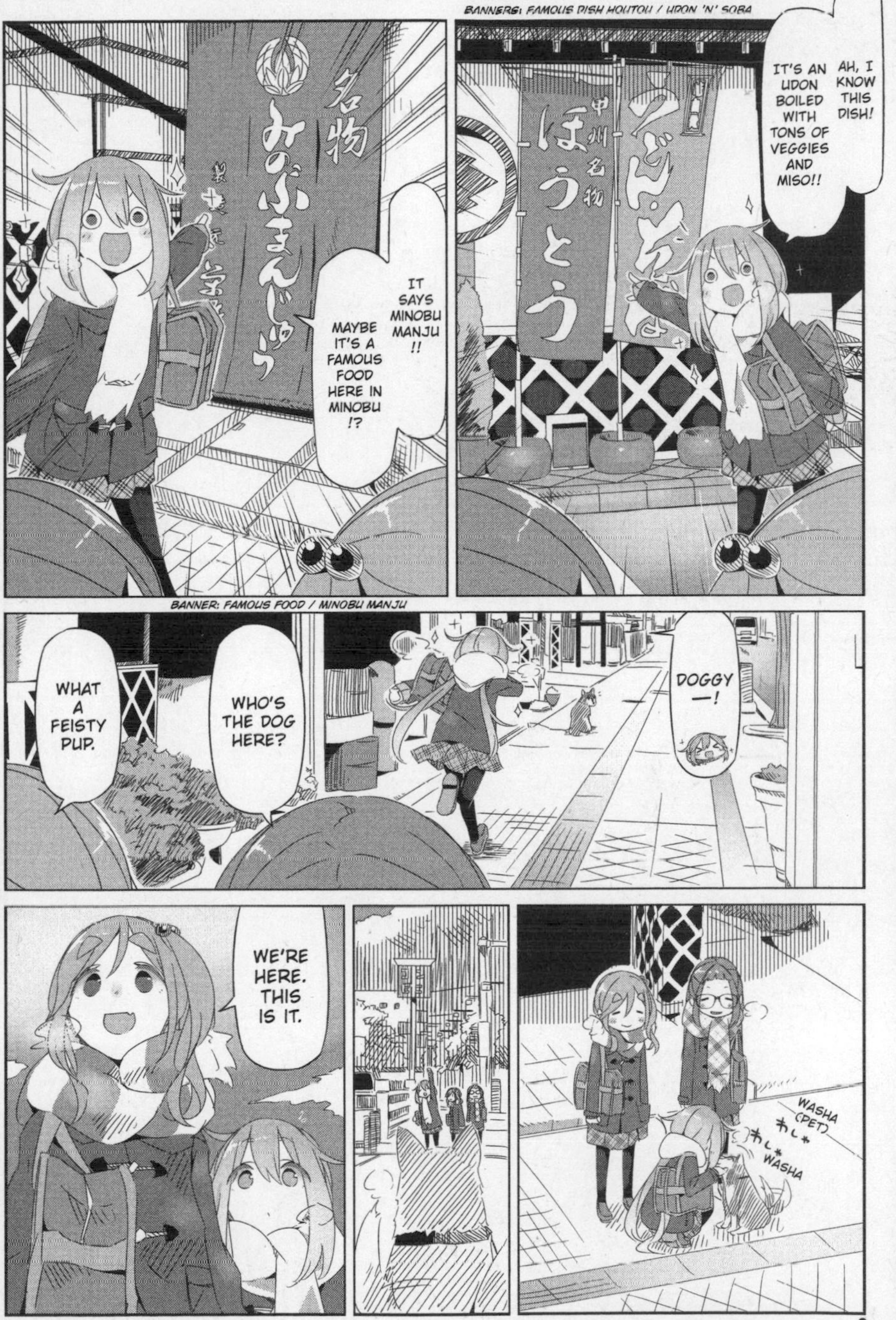
BANNERS: FAMOUS DISH HOUTOU / UDON 'N' SOBA
甲州名物
ほうとう
AH, I KNOW THIS DISH!
IT'S AN UDON BOILED WITH TONS OF VEGGIES AND MISO!!
名物
みのぶまんじゅう
IT SAYS MINOBU MANJU!!
MAYBE IT'S A FAMOUS FOOD HERE IN MINOBU!?
BANNER: FAMOUS FOOD / MINOBU MANJU
DOGGY—!
WHO'S THE DOG HERE?
WHAT A FEISTY PUP.
WASHA (PET)
わしゃ
WASHA
WE'RE HERE. THIS IS IT.

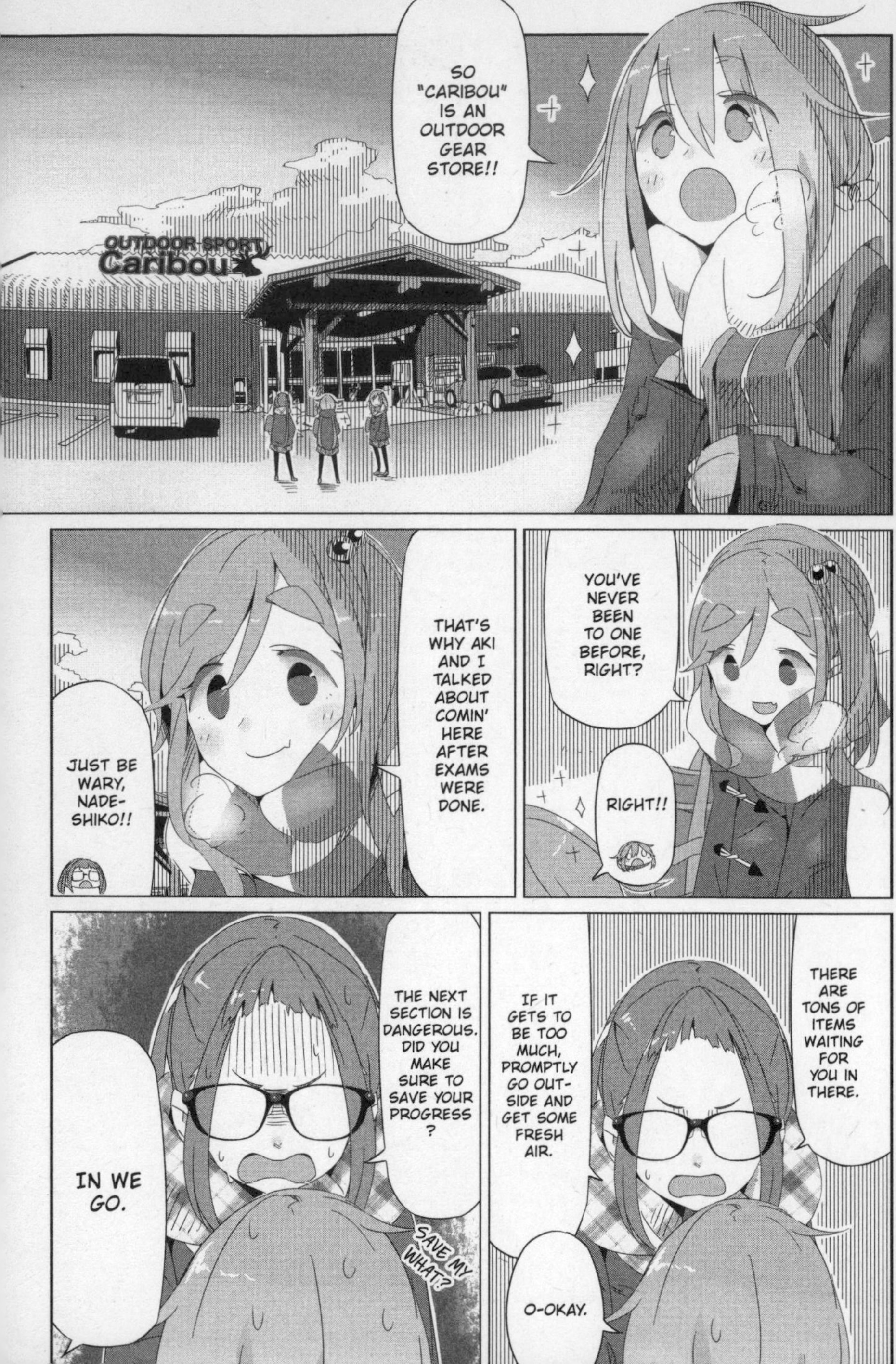
SO "CARIBOU" IS AN OUTDOOR GEAR STORE!!
OUTDOOR SPORT Caribou
YOU'VE NEVER BEEN TO ONE BEFORE, RIGHT?
RIGHT!!
THAT'S WHY AKI AND I TALKED ABOUT COMIN' HERE AFTER EXAMS WERE DONE.
JUST BE WARY, NADE-SHIKO!!
THERE ARE TONS OF ITEMS WAITING FOR YOU IN THERE.
IF IT GETS TO BE TOO MUCH, PROMPTLY GO OUT-SIDE AND GET SOME FRESH AIR.
O-OKAY.
THE NEXT SECTION IS DANGEROUS. DID YOU MAKE SURE TO SAVE YOUR PROGRESS?
SAVE MY WHAT?
IN WE GO.

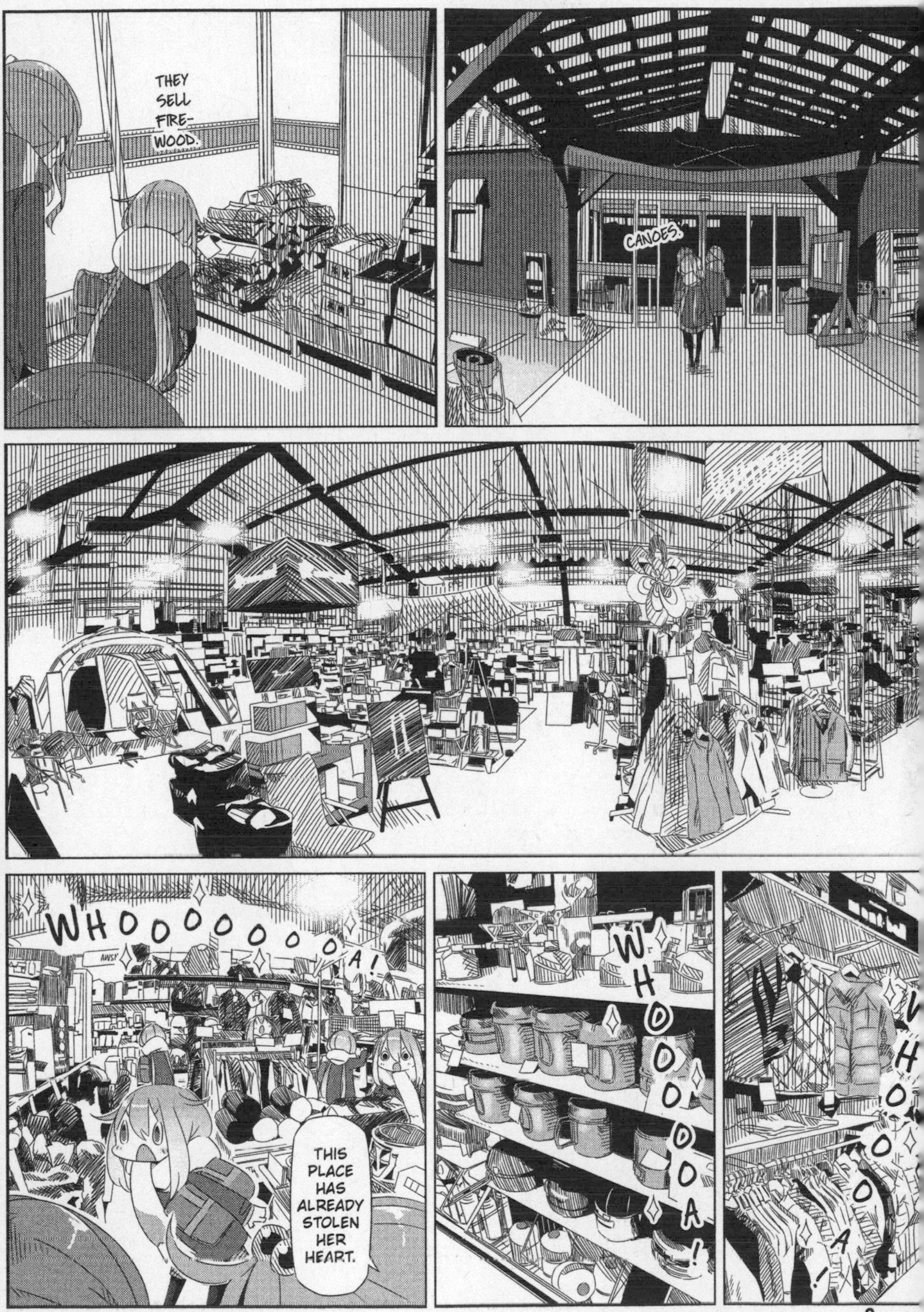
CANOES!
THEY SELL FIRE-WOOD.
WHOOOA!
WHOOOOOA!
WHOOOOOOOA!
THIS PLACE HAS ALREADY STOLEN HER HEART.

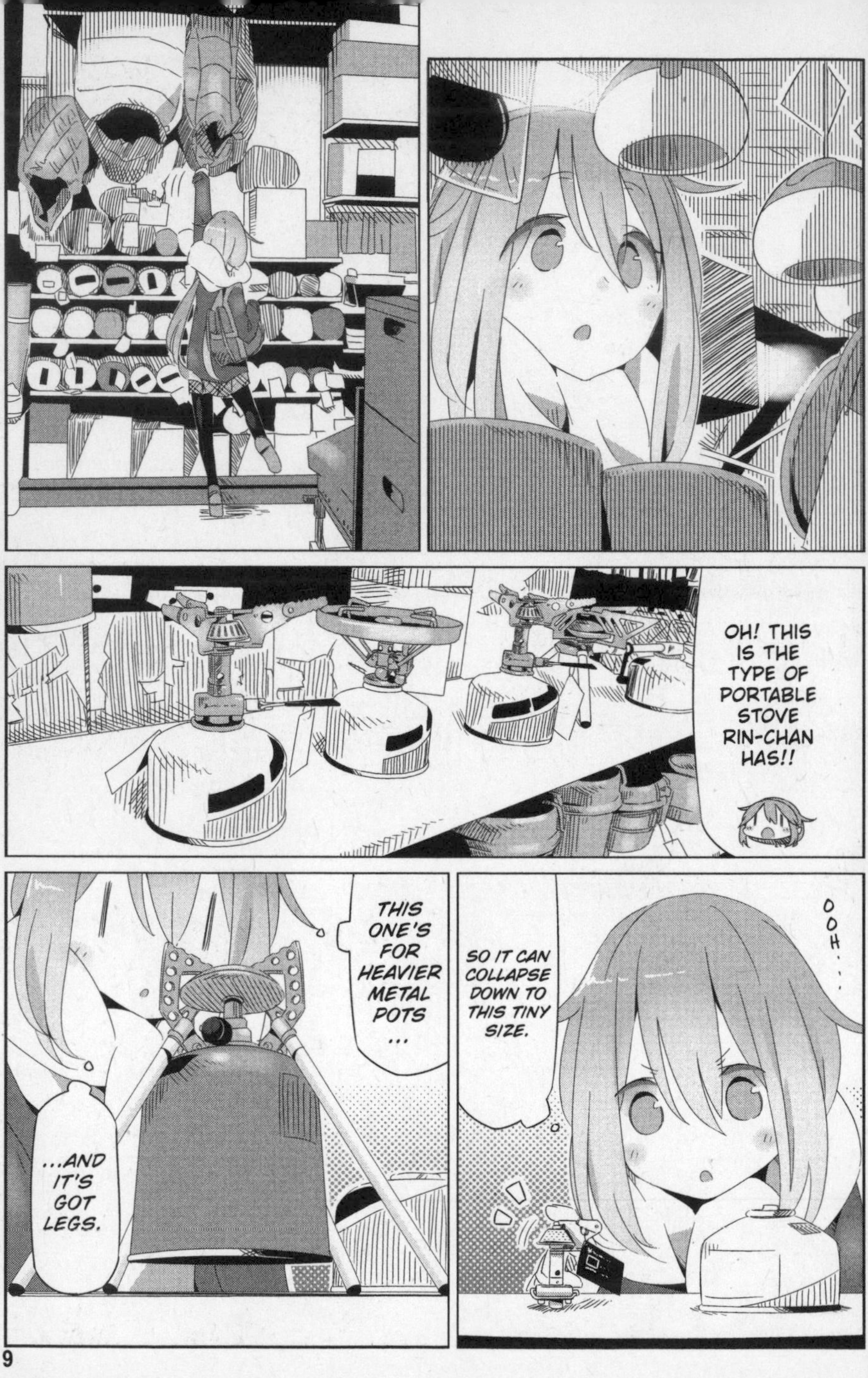
OH! THIS IS THE TYPE OF PORTABLE STOVE RIN-CHAN HAS!!
OOH...
SO IT CAN COLLAPSE DOWN TO THIS TINY SIZE.
THIS ONE'S FOR HEAVIER METAL POTS ...
...AND IT'S GOT LEGS.

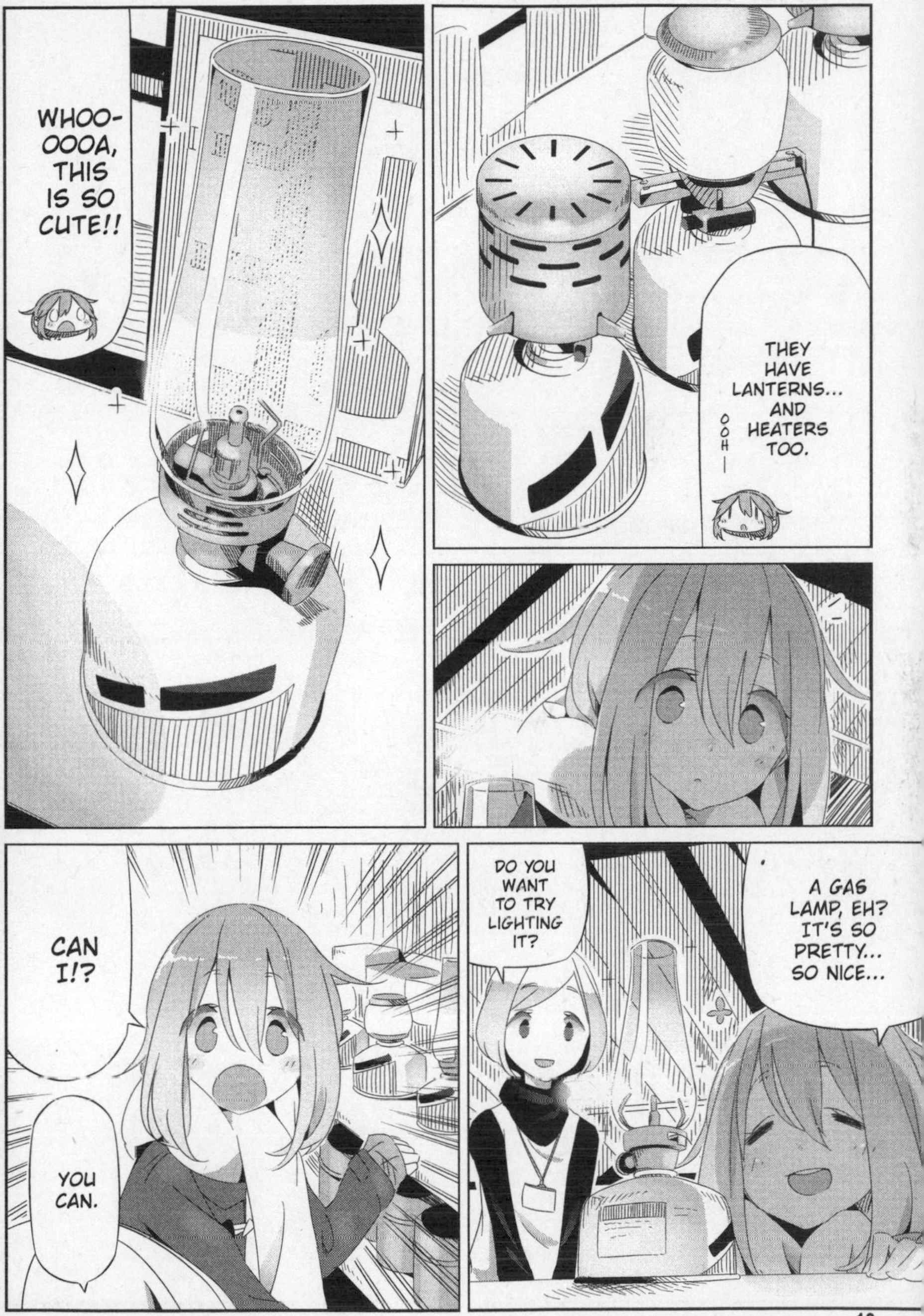
THEY HAVE LANTERNS... AND HEATERS TOO.
OOH—
WHOO-OOOA, THIS IS SO CUTE!!
A GAS LAMP, EH? IT'S SO PRETTY... SO NICE...
DO YOU WANT TO TRY LIGHTING IT?
CAN I!?
YOU CAN.

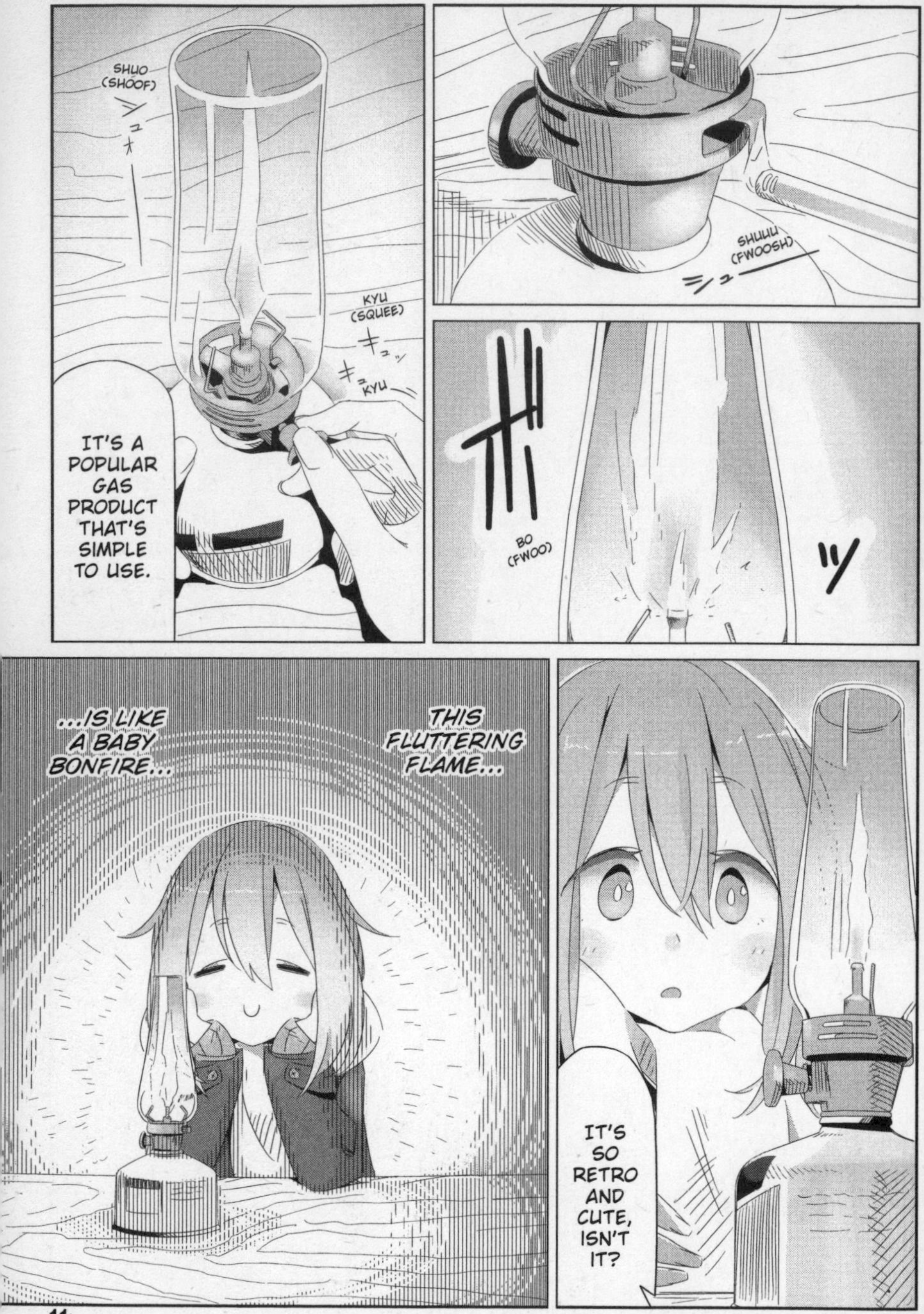
SHUUU (FWOOSH)
BO (FWOO)
SHUO (SHOOF)
KYU (SQUEE)
KYU
IT'S A POPULAR GAS PRODUCT THAT'S SIMPLE TO USE.
IT'S SO RETRO AND CUTE, ISN'T IT?
THIS FLUTTERING FLAME...
...IS LIKE A BABY BONFIRE...

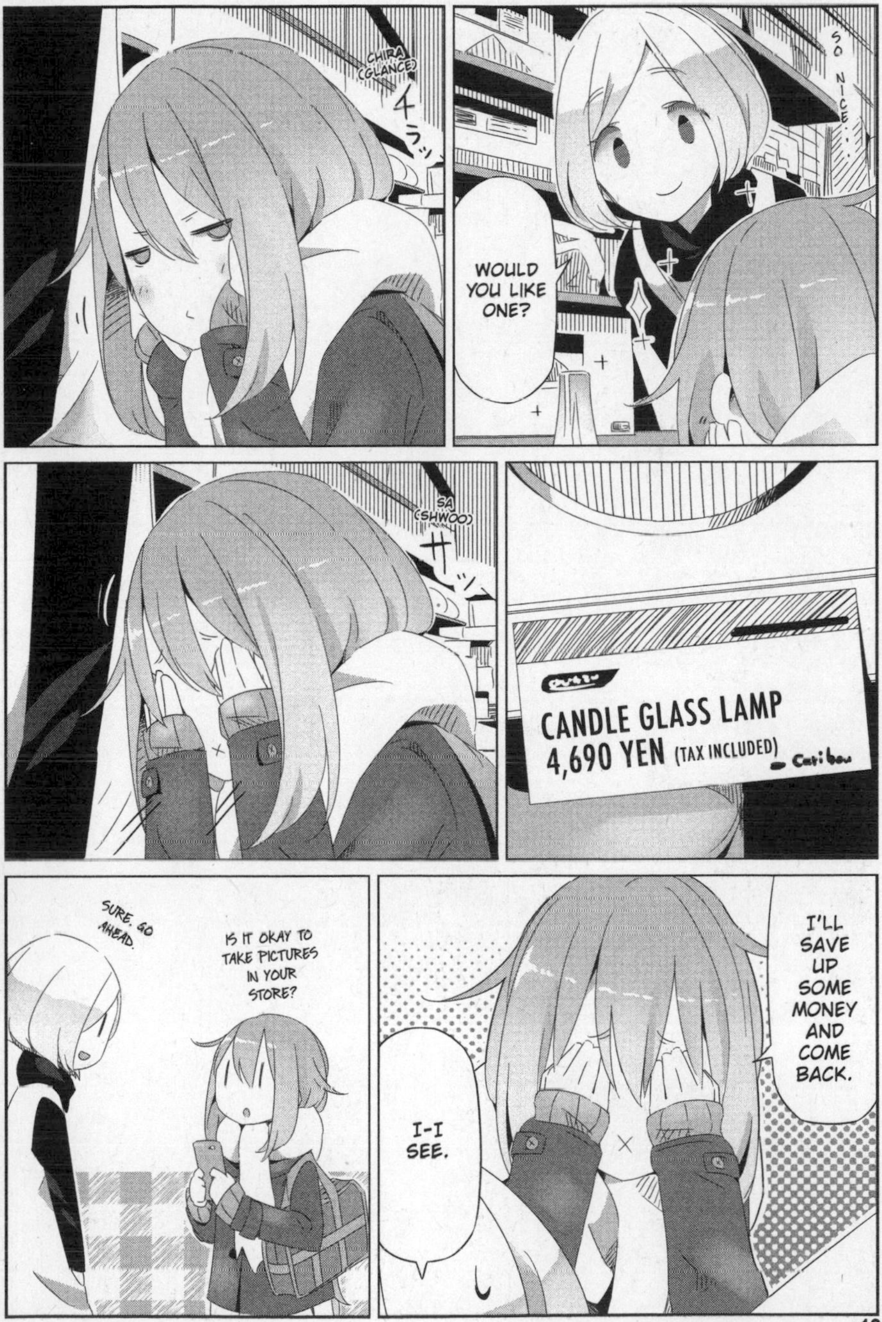
SO NICE...
WOULD YOU LIKE ONE?
CHIRA (GLANCE)
チラッ
CANDLE GLASS LAMP
4,690 YEN (TAX INCLUDED)
SA (SHWOO)
サッ
I'LL SAVE UP SOME MONEY AND COME BACK.
I-I SEE.
IS IT OKAY TO TAKE PICTURES IN YOUR STORE?
SURE. GO AHEAD.

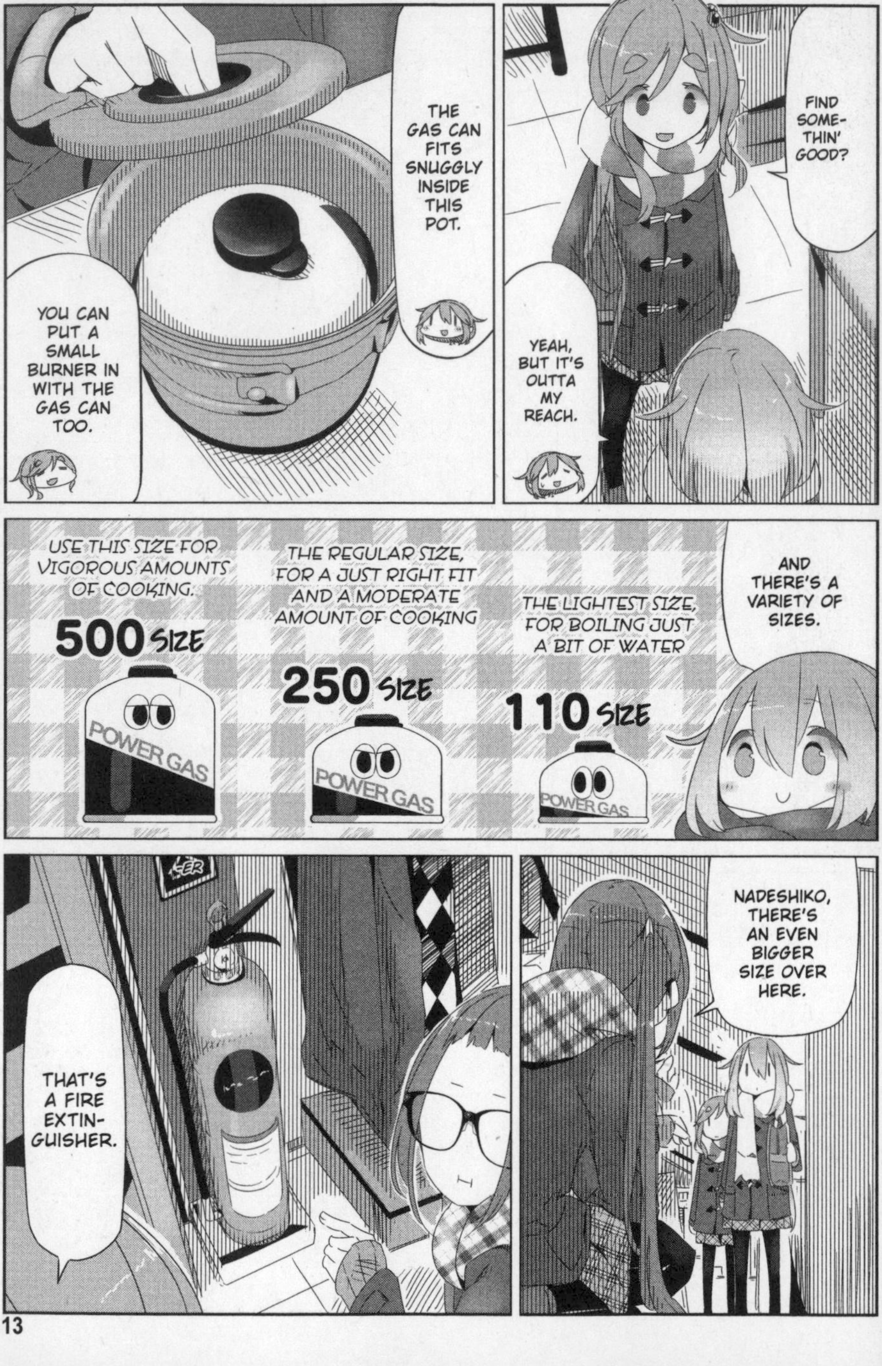
FIND SOME-THIN' GOOD?
YEAH, BUT IT'S OUTTA MY REACH.
THE GAS CAN FITS SNUGGLY INSIDE THIS POT.
YOU CAN PUT A SMALL BURNER IN WITH THE GAS CAN TOO.
AND THERE'S A VARIETY OF SIZES.
USE THIS SIZE FOR VIGOROUS AMOUNTS OF COOKING.
500 SIZE
POWER GAS
THE REGULAR SIZE, FOR A JUST RIGHT FIT AND A MODERATE AMOUNT OF COOKING
250 SIZE
POWER GAS
THE LIGHTEST SIZE, FOR BOILING JUST A BIT OF WATER
110 SIZE
POWER GAS
NADESHIKO, THERE'S AN EVEN BIGGER SIZE OVER HERE.
THAT'S A FIRE EXTIN-GUISHER.

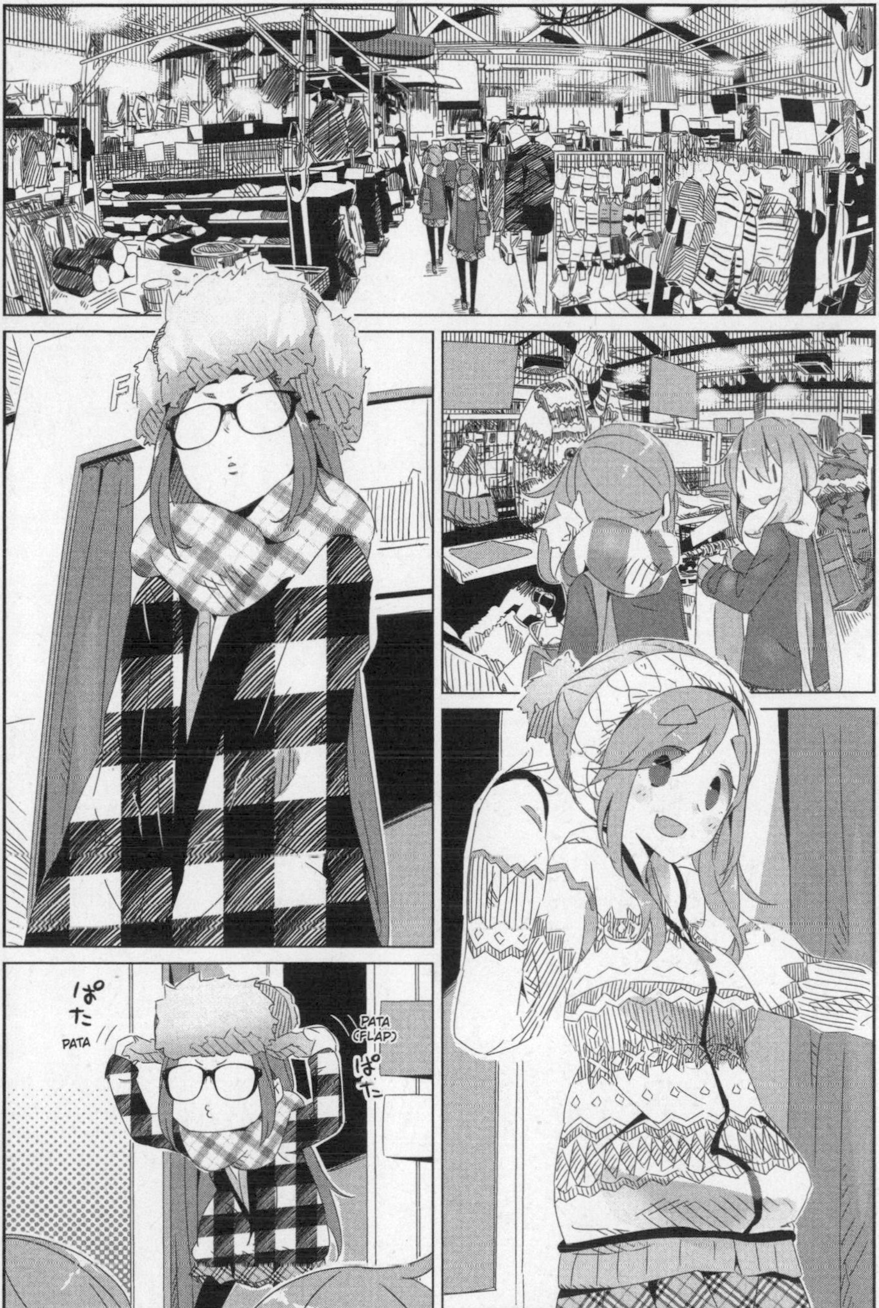
ぱた
PATA (FLAP)
ぱた
PATA

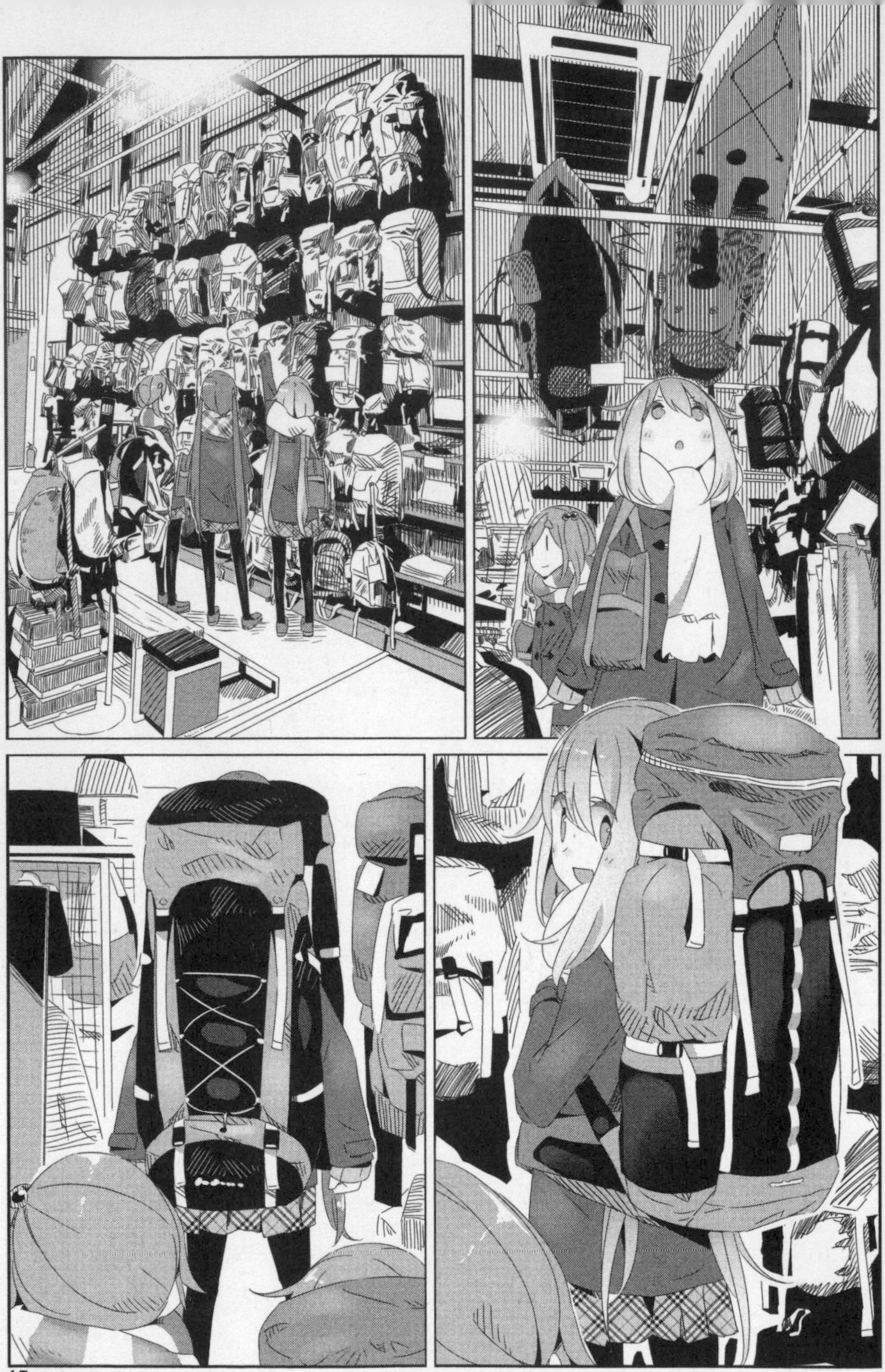

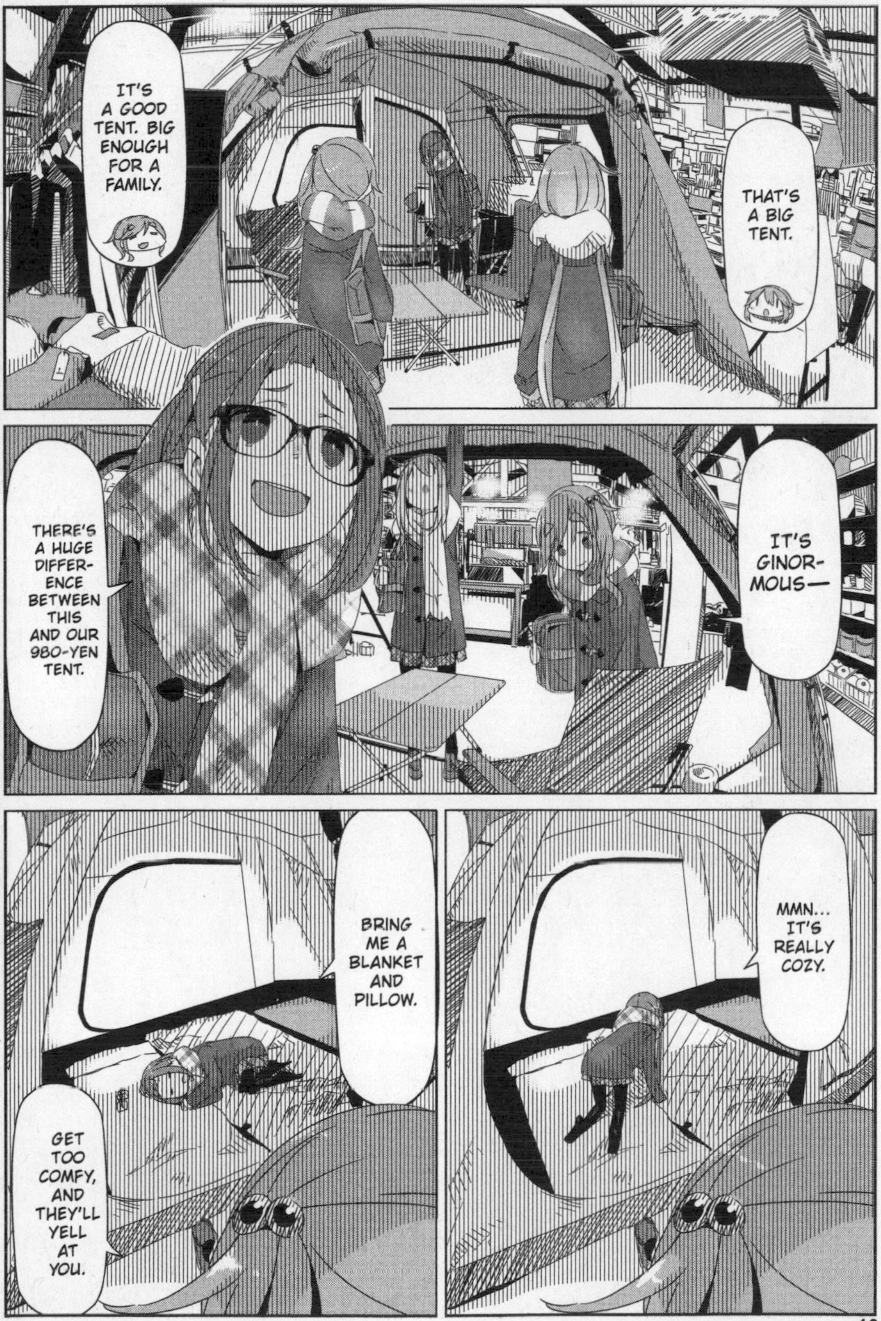
THAT'S A BIG TENT.
IT'S A GOOD TENT. BIG ENOUGH FOR A FAMILY.
IT'S GINORMOUS—
THERE'S A HUGE DIFFERENCE BETWEEN THIS AND OUR 980-YEN TENT.
MMN... IT'S REALLY COZY.
BRING ME A BLANKET AND PILLOW.
GET TOO COMFY, AND THEY'LL YELL AT YOU.

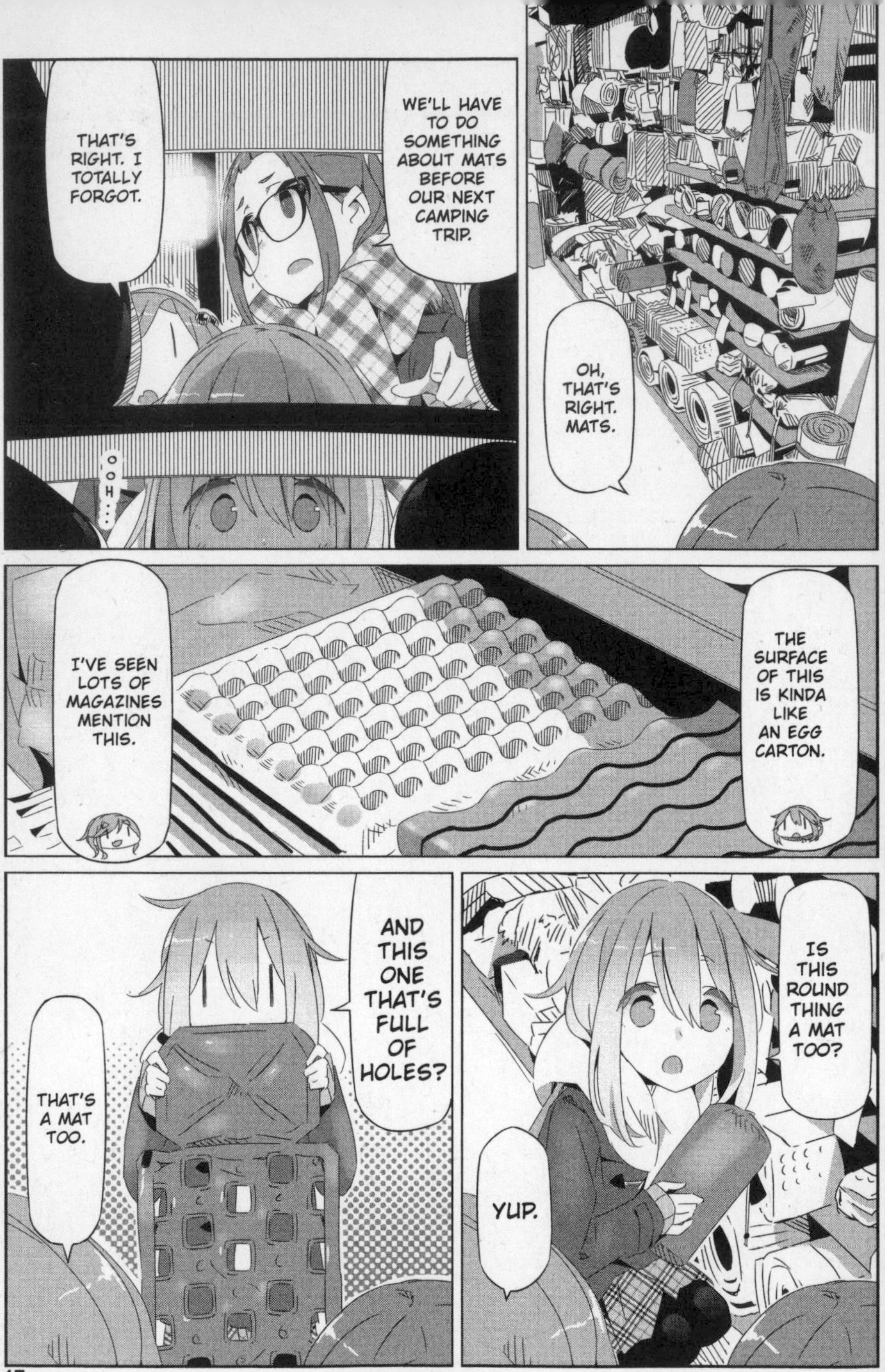
OH, THAT'S RIGHT. MATS.
WE'LL HAVE TO DO SOMETHING ABOUT MATS BEFORE OUR NEXT CAMPING TRIP.
THAT'S RIGHT. I TOTALLY FORGOT.
OOH...
THE SURFACE OF THIS IS KINDA LIKE AN EGG CARTON.
I'VE SEEN LOTS OF MAGAZINES MENTION THIS.
IS THIS ROUND THING A MAT TOO?
YUP.
AND THIS ONE THAT'S FULL OF HOLES?
THAT'S A MAT TOO.

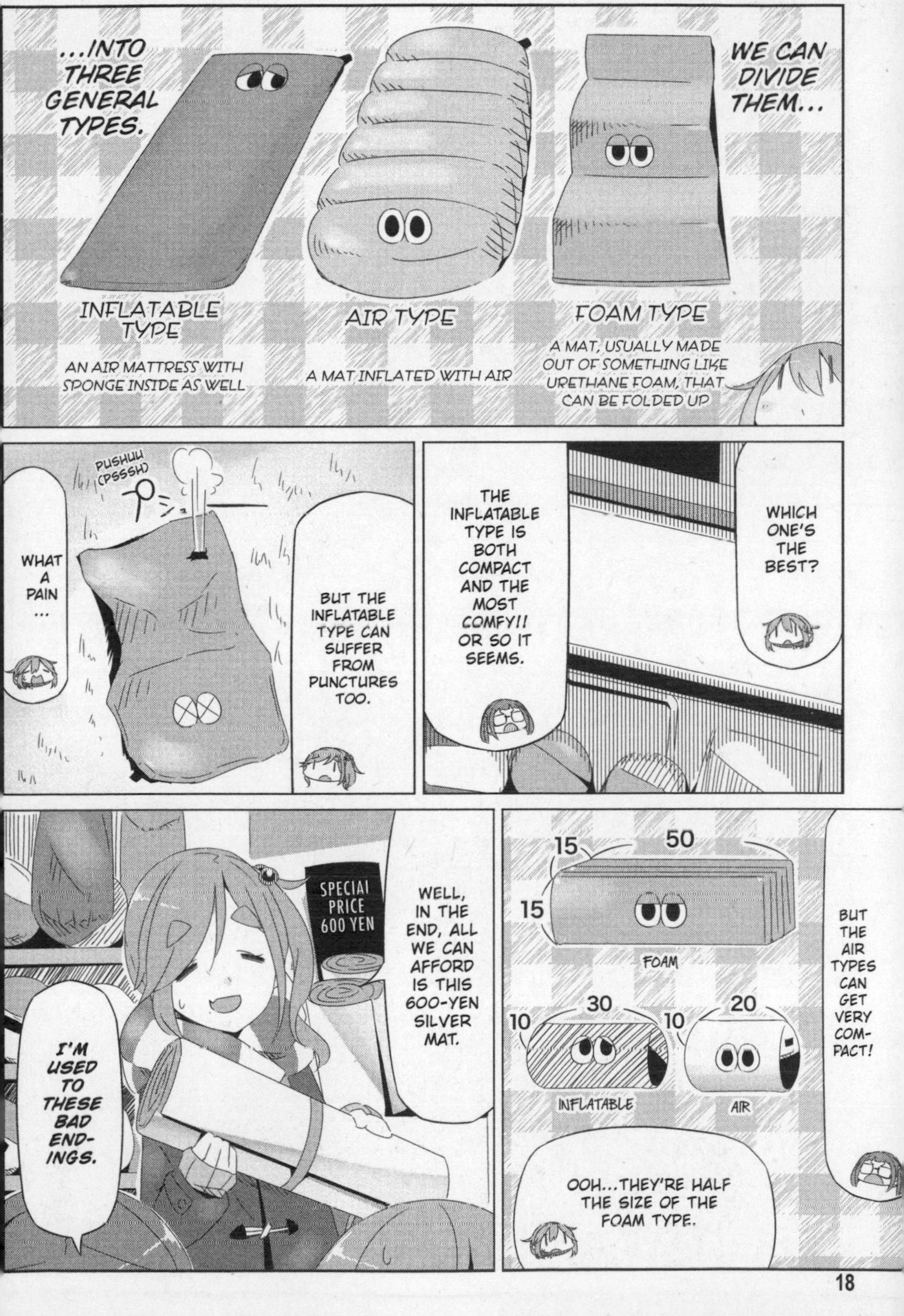
WE CAN DIVIDE THEM...
...INTO THREE GENERAL TYPES.
FOAM TYPE
A MAT, USUALLY MADE OUT OF SOMETHING LIKE URETHANE FOAM, THAT CAN BE FOLDED UP
AIR TYPE
A MAT INFLATED WITH AIR
INFLATABLE TYPE
AN AIR MATTRESS WITH SPONGE INSIDE AS WELL
WHICH ONE'S THE BEST?
THE INFLATABLE TYPE IS BOTH COMPACT AND THE MOST COMFY!! OR SO IT SEEMS.
BUT THE INFLATABLE TYPE CAN SUFFER FROM PUNCTURES TOO.
PUSHUU (PSSSH)
WHAT A PAIN ...
BUT THE AIR TYPES CAN GET VERY COM-PACT!
15
50
15
FOAM
30
10
INFLATABLE
20
10
AIR
OOH...THEY'RE HALF THE SIZE OF THE FOAM TYPE.
SPECIAI PRICE 600 YEN
WELL, IN THE END, ALL WE CAN AFFORD IS THIS 600-YEN SILVER MAT.
I'M USED TO THESE BAD END-INGS.

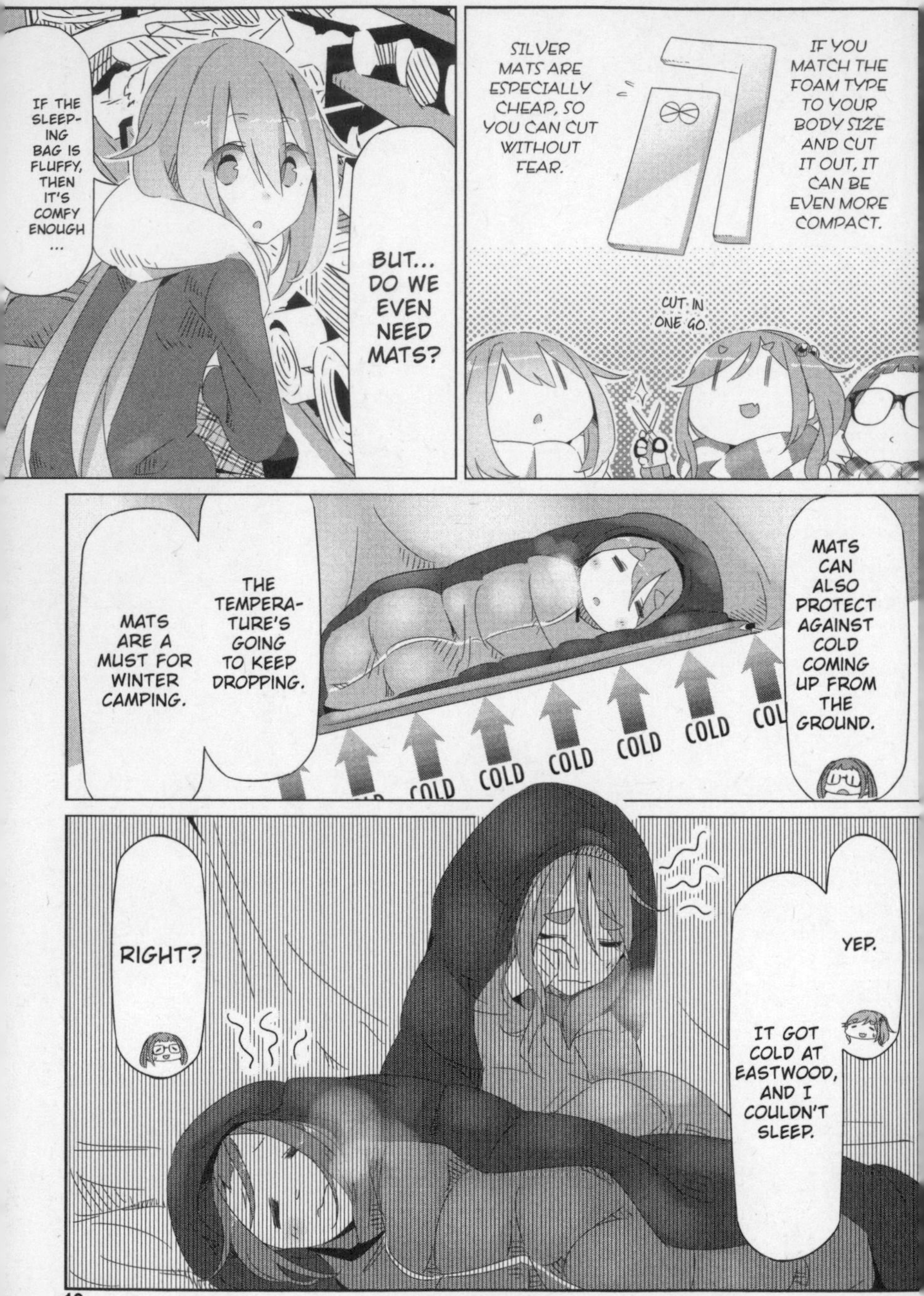
IF YOU MATCH THE FOAM TYPE TO YOUR BODY SIZE AND CUT IT OUT, IT CAN BE EVEN MORE COMPACT.
SILVER MATS ARE ESPECIALLY CHEAP, SO YOU CAN CUT WITHOUT FEAR.
CUT IN ONE GO.
BUT... DO WE EVEN NEED MATS?
IF THE SLEEPING BAG IS FLUFFY, THEN IT'S COMFY ENOUGH...
MATS CAN ALSO PROTECT AGAINST COLD COMING UP FROM THE GROUND.
COLD
COLD
COLD
COLD
COLD
COLD
THE TEMPERATURE'S GOING TO KEEP DROPPING.
MATS ARE A MUST FOR WINTER CAMPING.
YEP.
IT GOT COLD AT EASTWOOD, AND I COULDN'T SLEEP.
RIGHT?

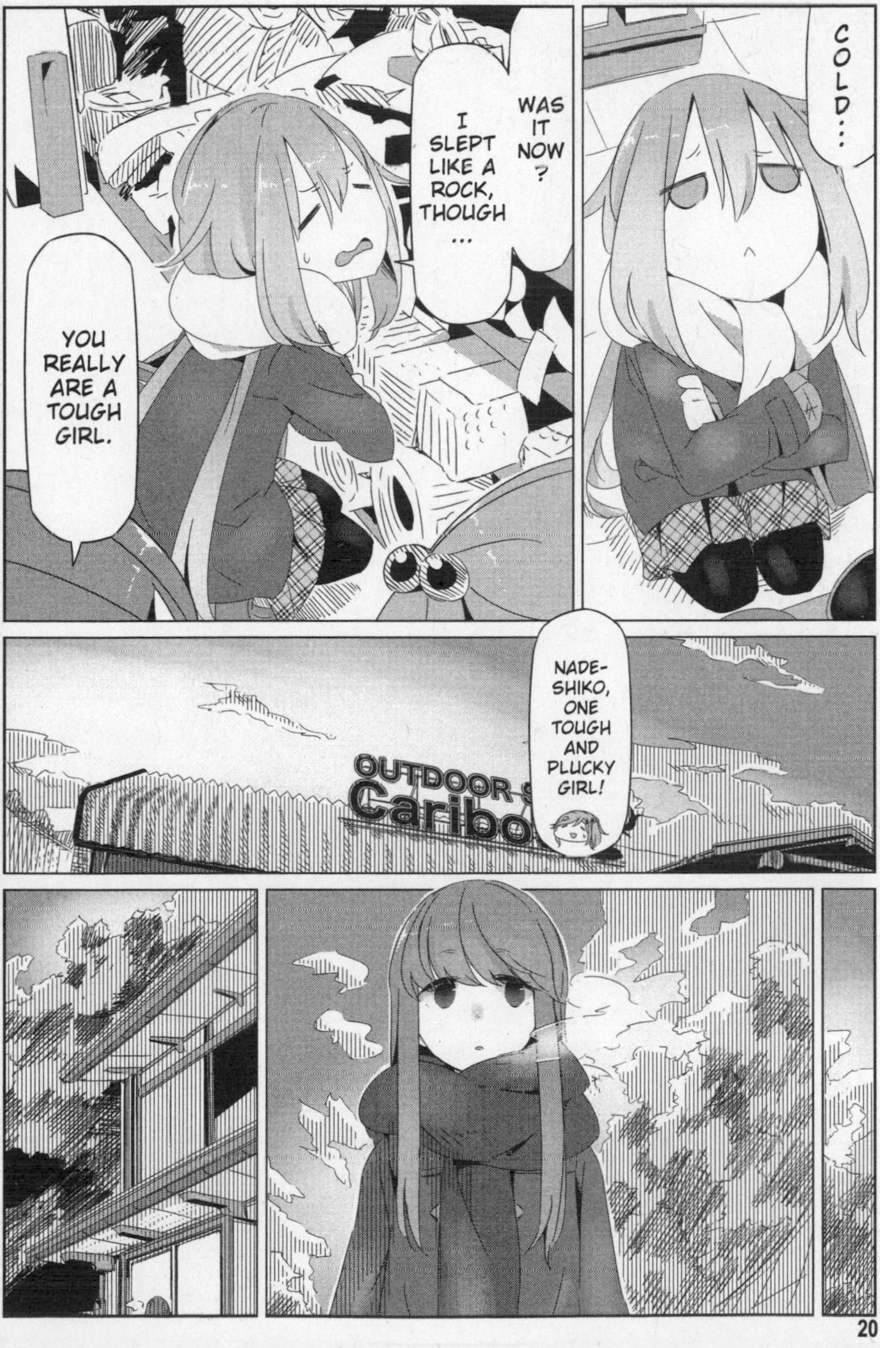
COLD...
WAS IT NOW?
I SLEPT LIKE A ROCK, THOUGH...
YOU REALLY ARE A TOUGH GIRL.
NADE-SHIKO, ONE TOUGH AND PLUCKY GIRL!

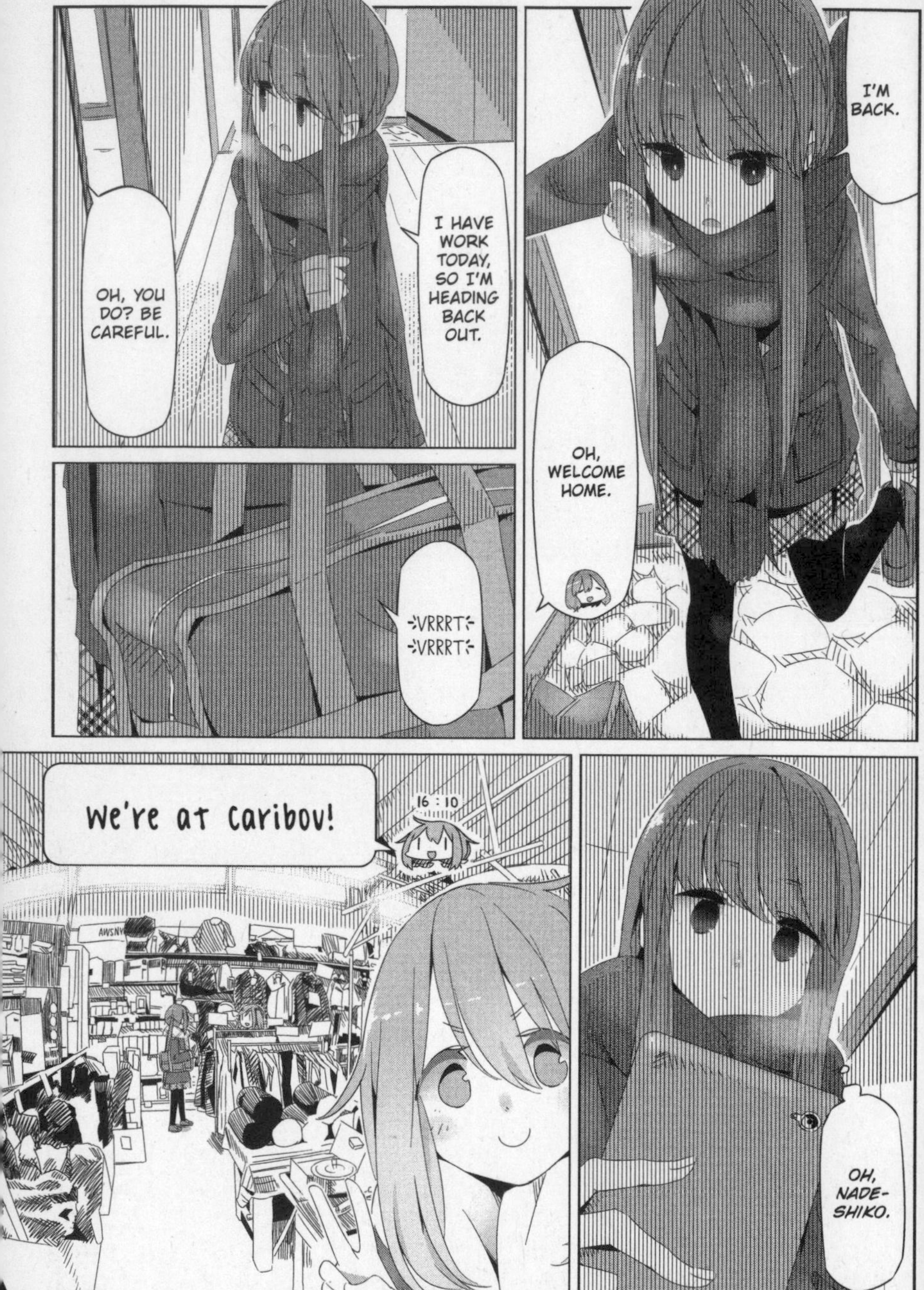
I'M BACK.
OH, WELCOME HOME.
I HAVE WORK TODAY, SO I'M HEADING BACK OUT.
OH, YOU DO? BE CAREFUL.
-VRRRT- -VRRRT-
OH, NADE-SHIKO.
16 : 10
We're at Caribou!

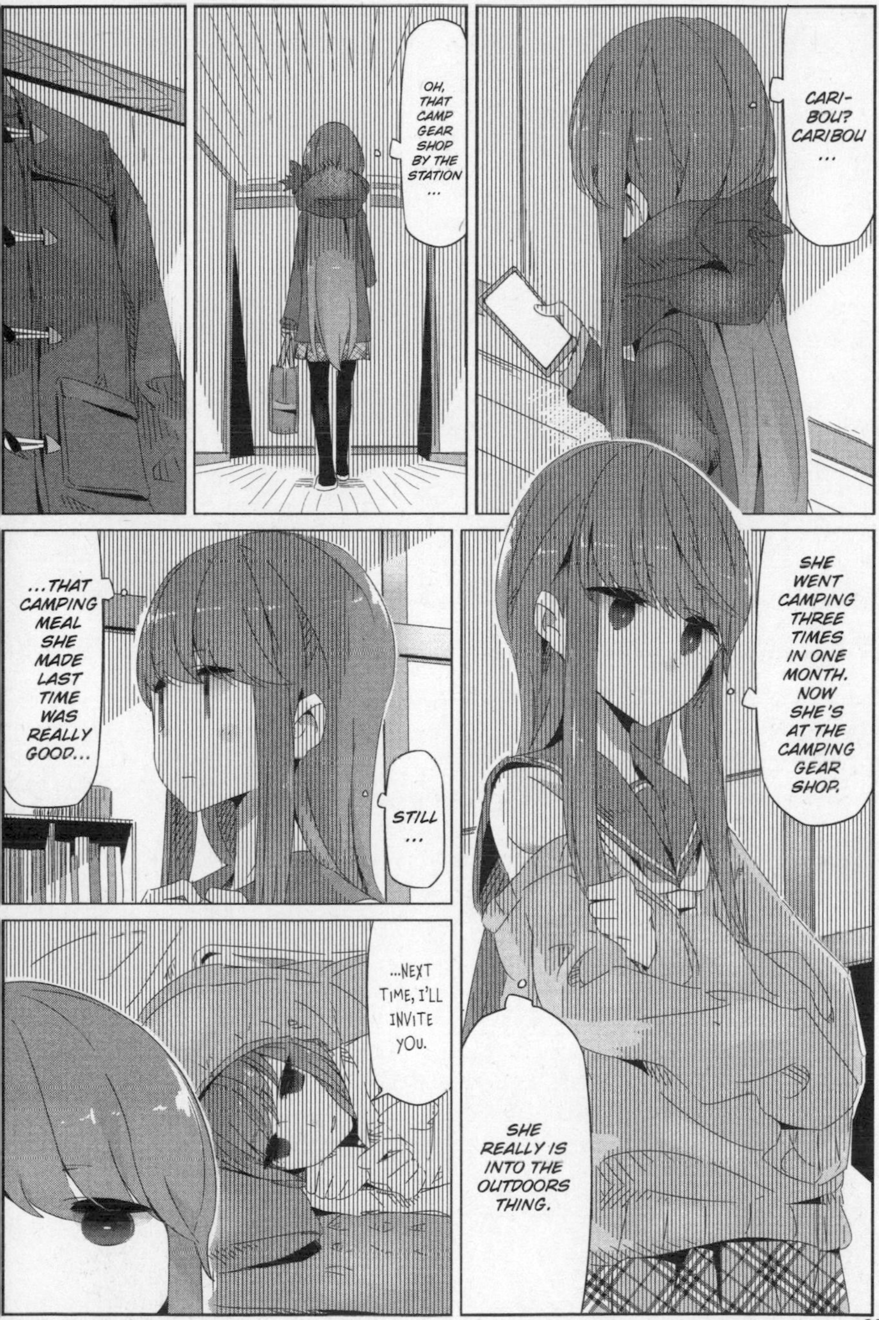
CARI-BOU? CARIBOU ...
OH, THAT CAMP GEAR SHOP BY THE STATION ...
SHE WENT CAMPING THREE TIMES IN ONE MONTH. NOW SHE'S AT THE CAMPING GEAR SHOP.
SHE REALLY IS INTO THE OUTDOORS THING.
...THAT CAMPING MEAL SHE MADE LAST TIME WAS REALLY GOOD...
STILL ...
...NEXT TIME, I'LL INVITE YOU.

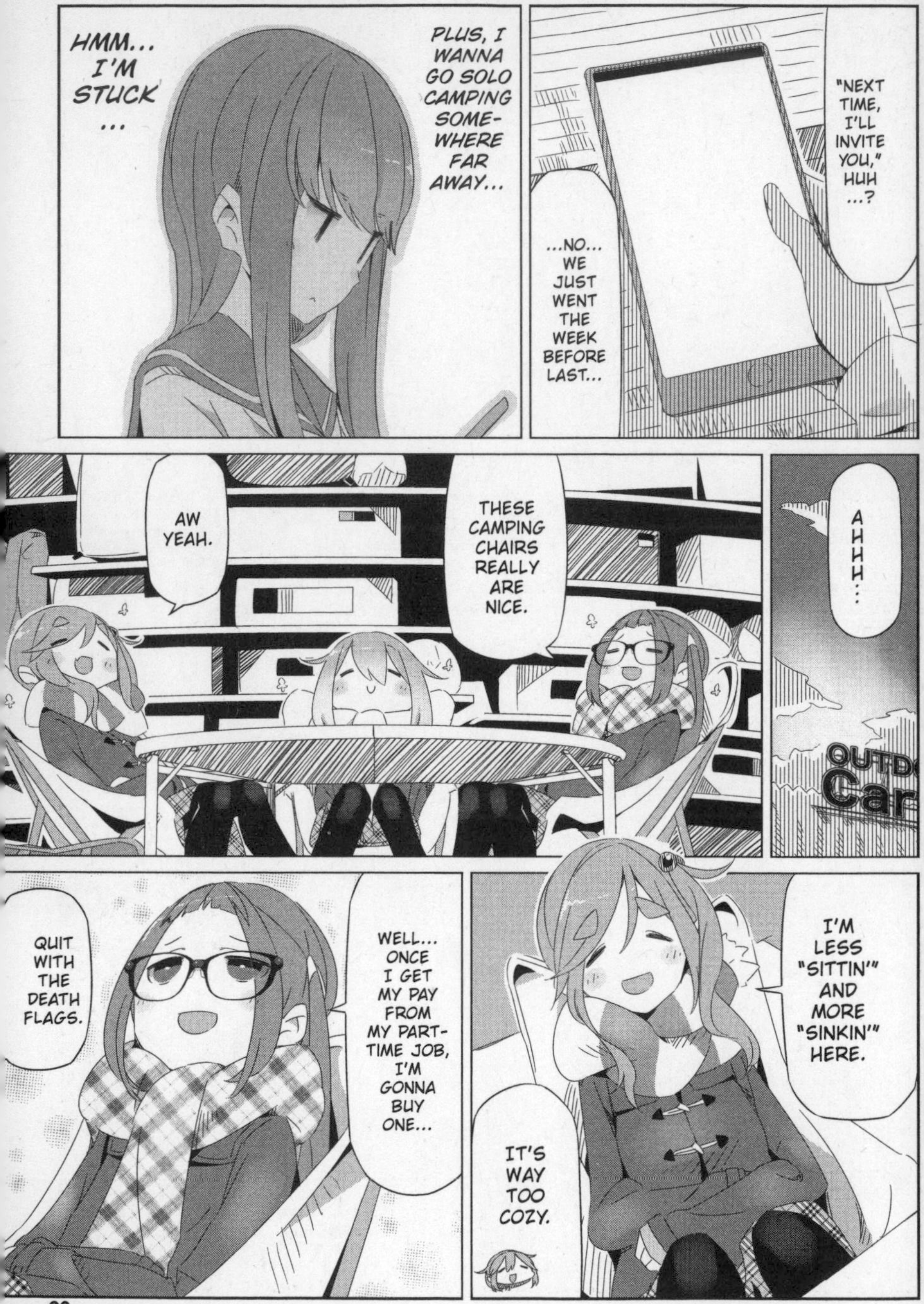
"NEXT TIME, I'LL INVITE YOU," HUH ...?
...NO... WE JUST WENT THE WEEK BEFORE LAST...
PLUS, I WANNA GO SOLO CAMPING SOME-WHERE FAR AWAY...
HMM... I'M STUCK ...
AHHH...
THESE CAMPING CHAIRS REALLY ARE NICE.
AW YEAH.
I'M LESS "SITTIN'" AND MORE "SINKIN'" HERE.
IT'S WAY TOO COZY.
WELL... ONCE I GET MY PAY FROM MY PART-TIME JOB, I'M GONNA BUY ONE...
QUIT WITH THE DEATH FLAGS.

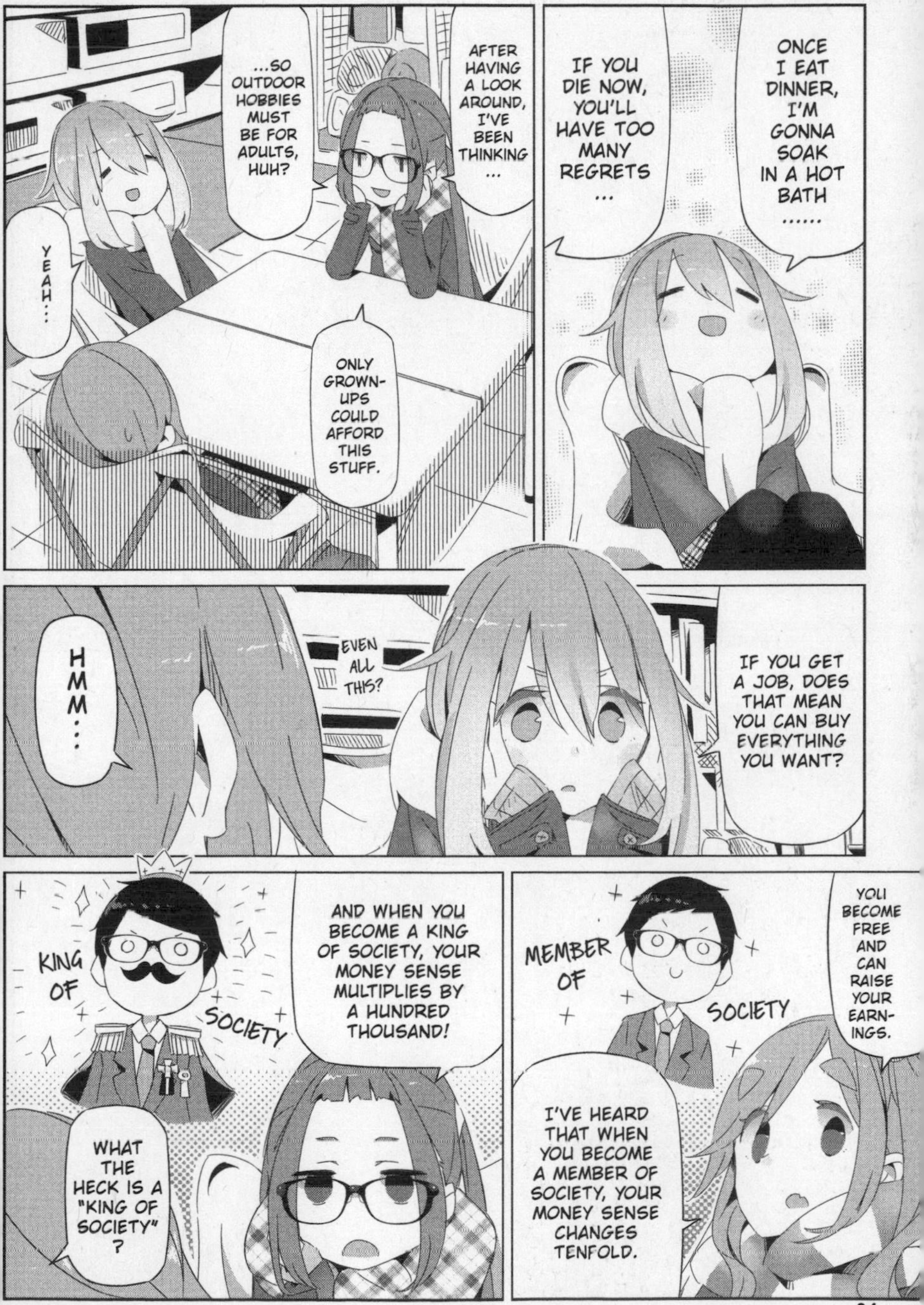
ONCE I EAT DINNER, I'M GONNA SOAK IN A HOT BATH ......
IF YOU DIE NOW, YOU'LL HAVE TOO MANY REGRETS ...
AFTER HAVING A LOOK AROUND, I'VE BEEN THINKING ...
...SO OUTDOOR HOBBIES MUST BE FOR ADULTS, HUH?
YEAH...
ONLY GROWN-UPS COULD AFFORD THIS STUFF.
IF YOU GET A JOB, DOES THAT MEAN YOU CAN BUY EVERYTHING YOU WANT?
EVEN ALL THIS?
HMM...
YOU BECOME FREE AND CAN RAISE YOUR EARNINGS.
MEMBER OF SOCIETY
I'VE HEARD THAT WHEN YOU BECOME A MEMBER OF SOCIETY, YOUR MONEY SENSE CHANGES TENFOLD.
AND WHEN YOU BECOME A KING OF SOCIETY, YOUR MONEY SENSE MULTIPLIES BY A HUNDRED THOUSAND!
KING OF SOCIETY
WHAT THE HECK IS A "KING OF SOCIETY" ?

SIGNS: ZEBRA / SAKE NO YAMAMOTO MINOBU STORE

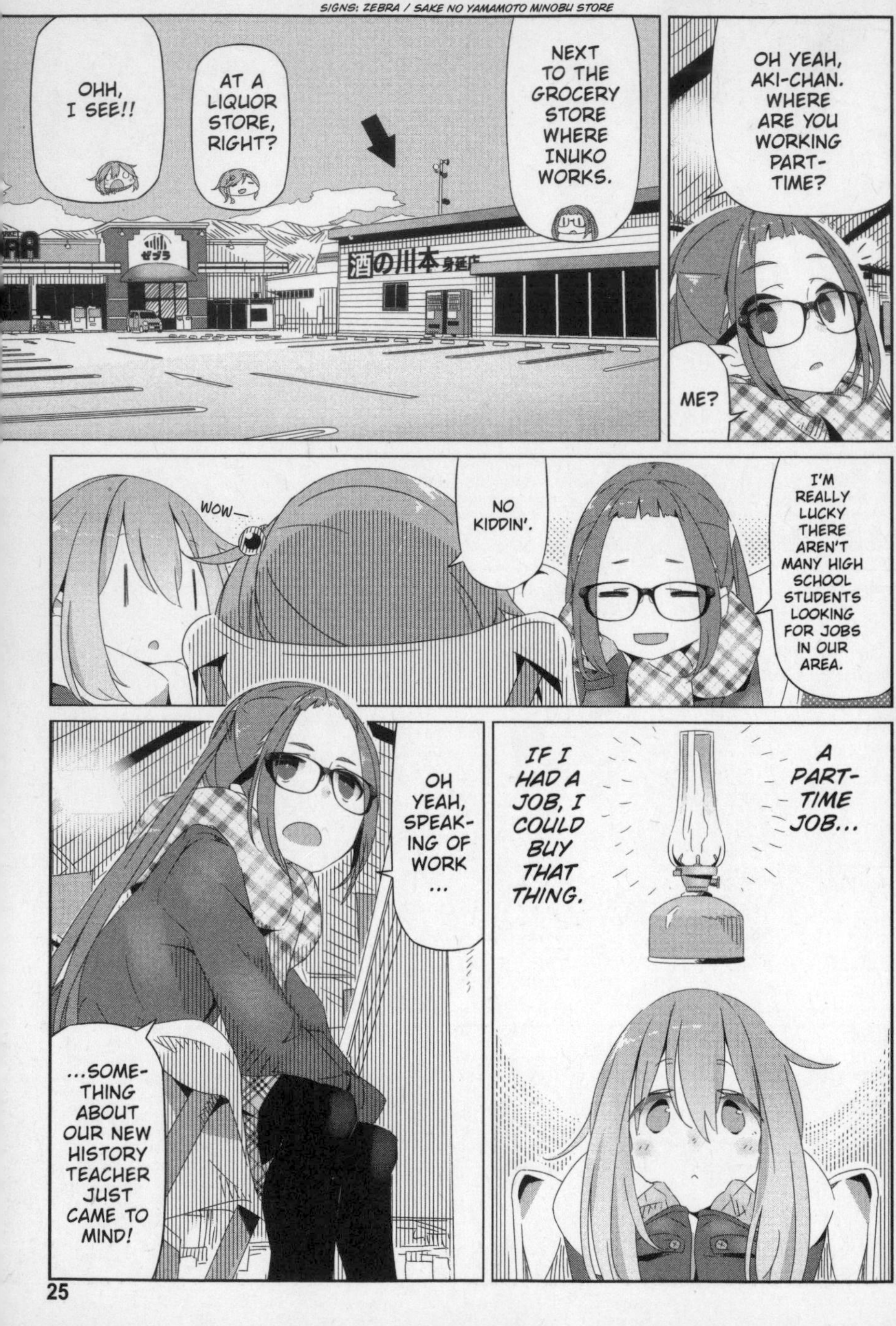

OH YEAH, AKI-CHAN. WHERE ARE YOU WORKING PART-TIME?
ME?
NEXT TO THE GROCERY STORE WHERE INUKO WORKS.
AT A LIQUOR STORE, RIGHT?
OHH, I SEE!!
酒の川本 身延店
ゼブラ
I'M REALLY LUCKY THERE AREN'T MANY HIGH SCHOOL STUDENTS LOOKING FOR JOBS IN OUR AREA.
NO KIDDIN'.
WOW—
A PART-TIME JOB...
IF I HAD A JOB, I COULD BUY THAT THING.
OH YEAH, SPEAKING OF WORK...
...SOMETHING ABOUT OUR NEW HISTORY TEACHER JUST CAME TO MIND!

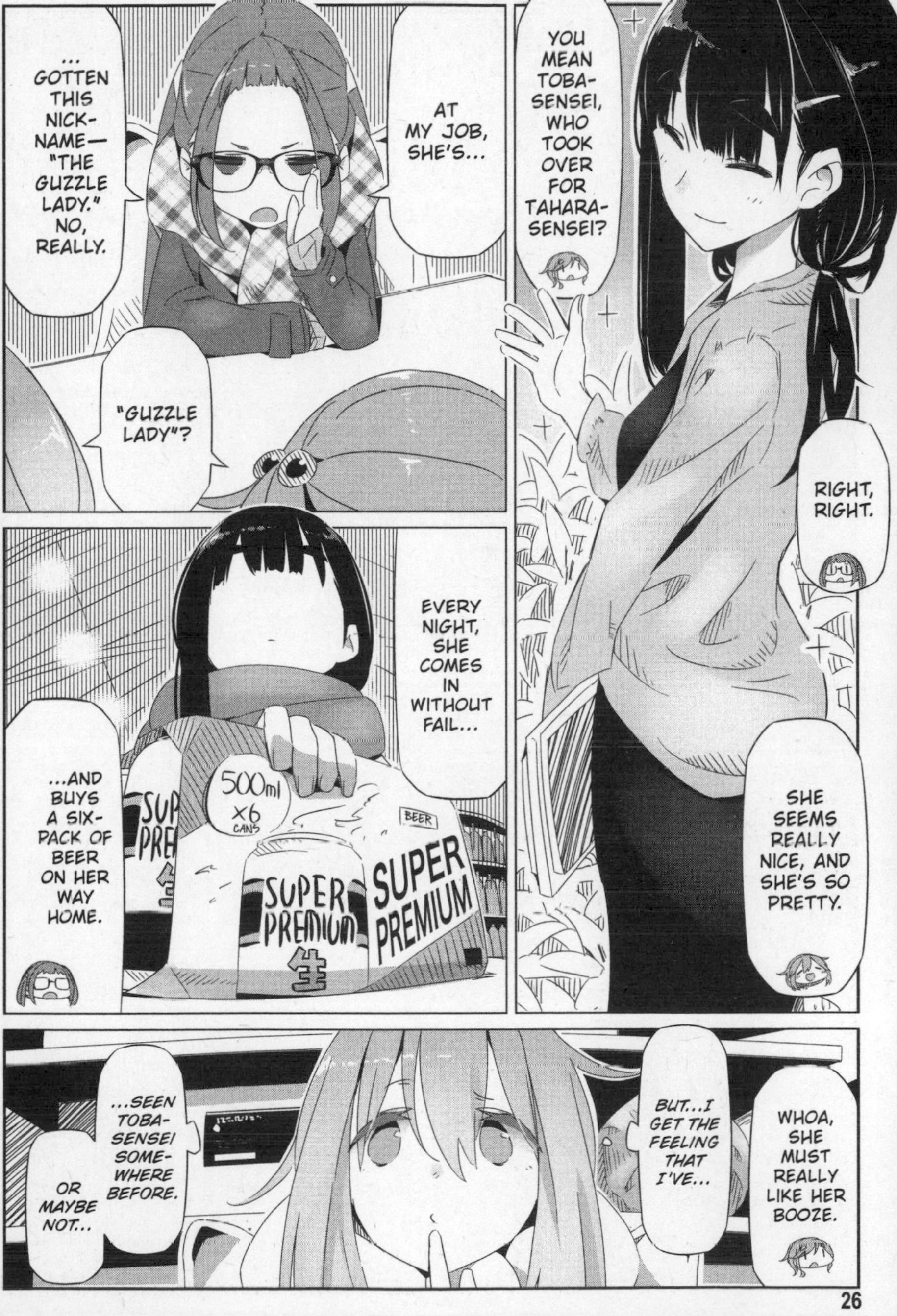
YOU MEAN TOBA-SENSEI, WHO TOOK OVER FOR TAHARA-SENSEI?
RIGHT, RIGHT.
SHE SEEMS REALLY NICE, AND SHE'S SO PRETTY.
AT MY JOB, SHE'S...
...GOTTEN THIS NICKNAME—"THE GUZZLE LADY." NO, REALLY.
"GUZZLE LADY"?
EVERY NIGHT, SHE COMES IN WITHOUT FAIL...
...AND BUYS A SIX-PACK OF BEER ON HER WAY HOME.
500ml ×6 CANS
BEER
SUPER PREMIUM
SUPER PREMIUM 生
WHOA, SHE MUST REALLY LIKE HER BOOZE.
BUT...I GET THE FEELING THAT I'VE...
...SEEN TOBA-SENSEI SOMEWHERE BEFORE.
OR MAYBE NOT...

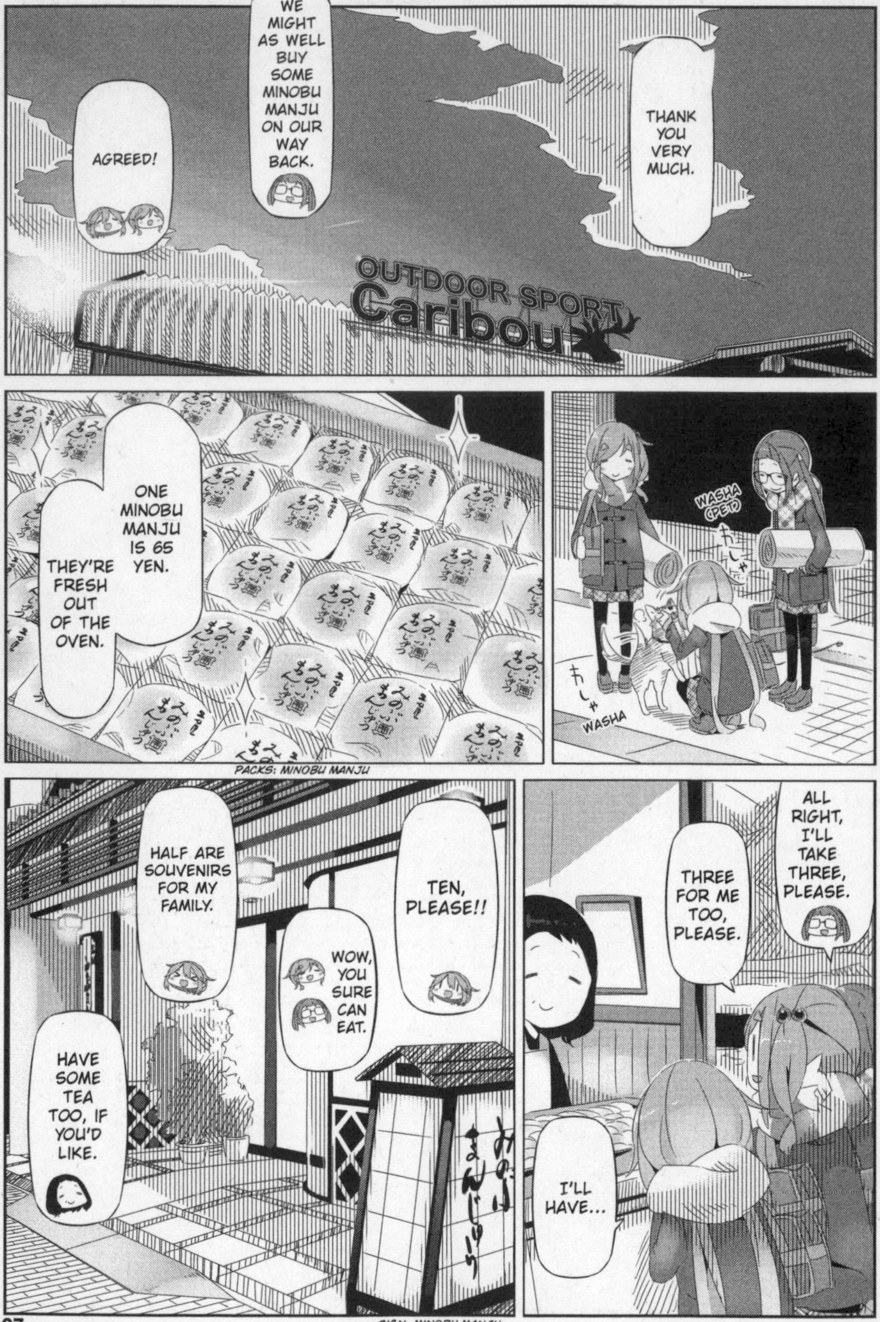
THANK YOU VERY MUCH.
WE MIGHT AS WELL BUY SOME MINOBU MANJU ON OUR WAY BACK.
AGREED!
OUTDOOR SPORT
Caribou
WASHA (PET)
WASHA
ONE MINOBU MANJU IS 65 YEN.
THEY'RE FRESH OUT OF THE OVEN.
PACKS: MINOBU MANJU
ALL RIGHT, I'LL TAKE THREE, PLEASE.
THREE FOR ME TOO, PLEASE.
I'LL HAVE...
TEN, PLEASE!!
HALF ARE SOUVENIRS FOR MY FAMILY.
WOW, YOU SURE CAN EAT.
HAVE SOME TEA TOO, IF YOU'D LIKE.

SIGN: MINOBU MANJU

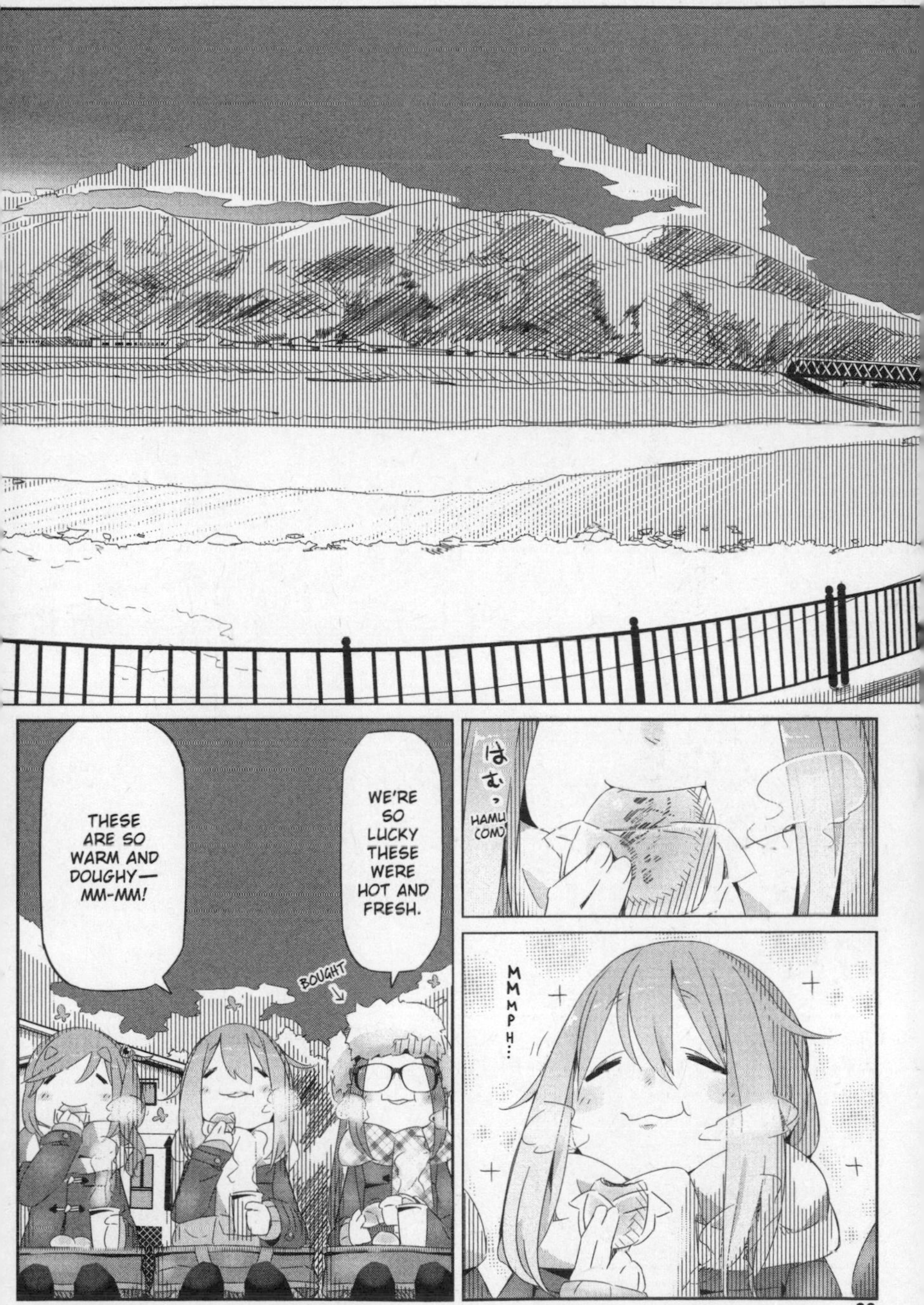
はむっ
HAMU (OM)
MMMPH...
WE'RE SO LUCKY THESE WERE HOT AND FRESH.
BOUGHT
THESE ARE SO WARM AND DOUGHY— MM-MM!

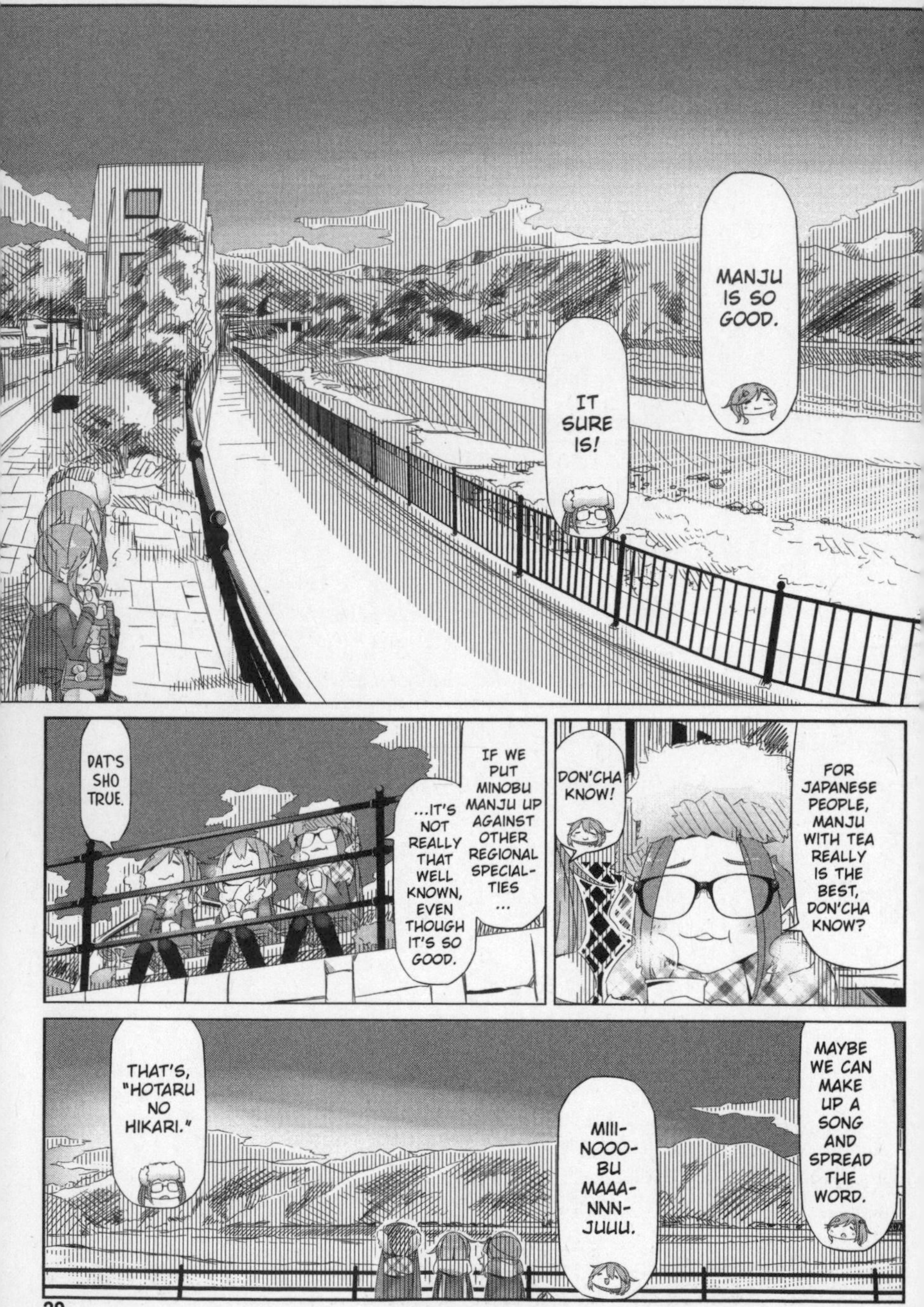
MANJU IS SO GOOD.
IT SURE IS!
FOR JAPANESE PEOPLE, MANJU WITH TEA REALLY IS THE BEST, DON'CHA KNOW?
DON'CHA KNOW!
IF WE PUT MINOBU MANJU UP AGAINST OTHER REGIONAL SPECIAL-TIES ...
...IT'S NOT REALLY THAT WELL KNOWN, EVEN THOUGH IT'S SO GOOD.
DAT'S SHO TRUE.
MAYBE WE CAN MAKE UP A SONG AND SPREAD THE WORD.
MIII-NOOO-BU MAAA-NNN-JUUU.
THAT'S, "HOTARU NO HIKARI."

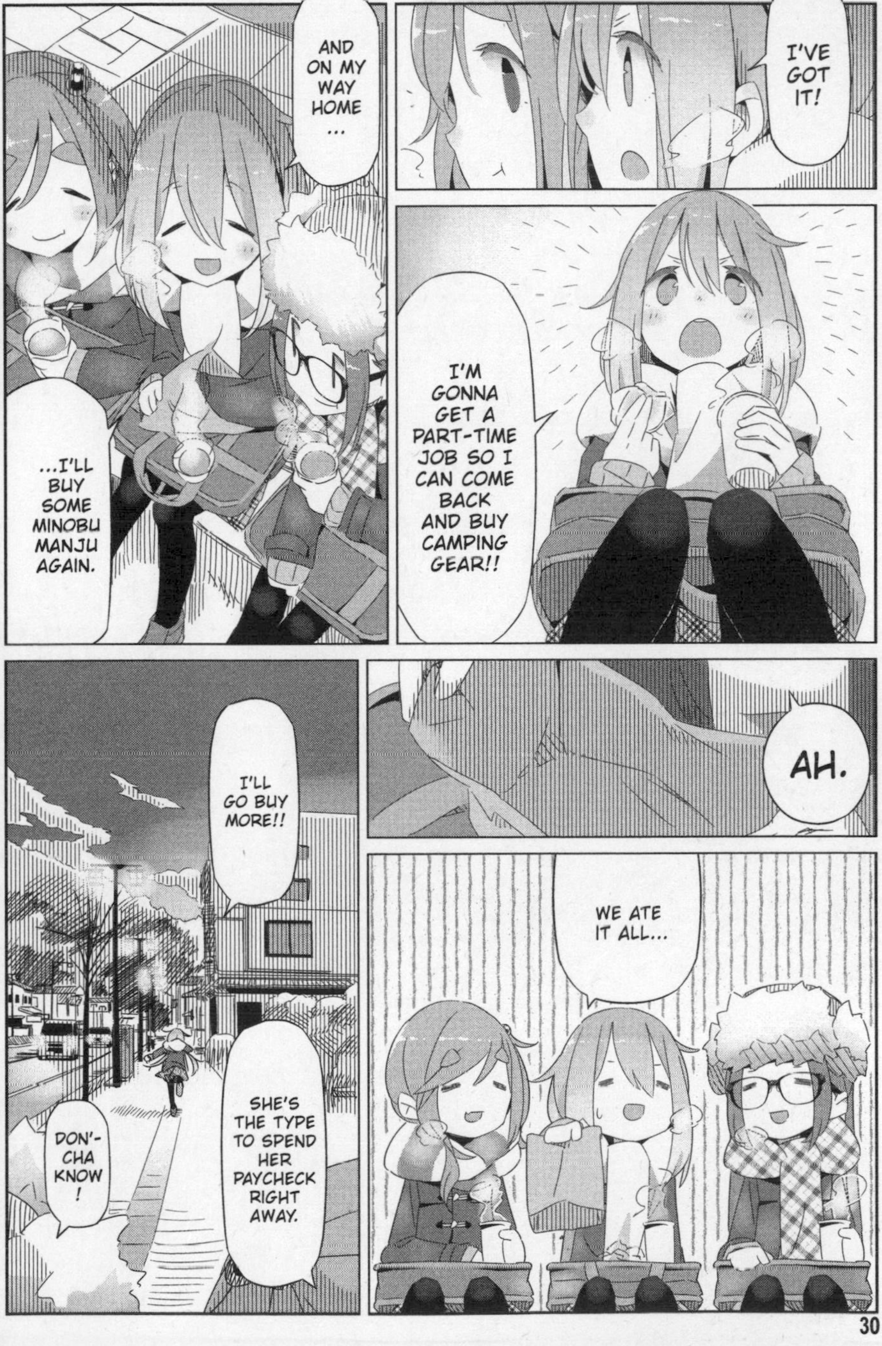
I'VE GOT IT!
I'M GONNA GET A PART-TIME JOB SO I CAN COME BACK AND BUY CAMPING GEAR!!
AND ON MY WAY HOME ...
...I'LL BUY SOME MINOBU MANJU AGAIN.
AH.
WE ATE IT ALL...
I'LL GO BUY MORE!!
SHE'S THE TYPE TO SPEND HER PAYCHECK RIGHT AWAY.
DON'-CHA KNOW!

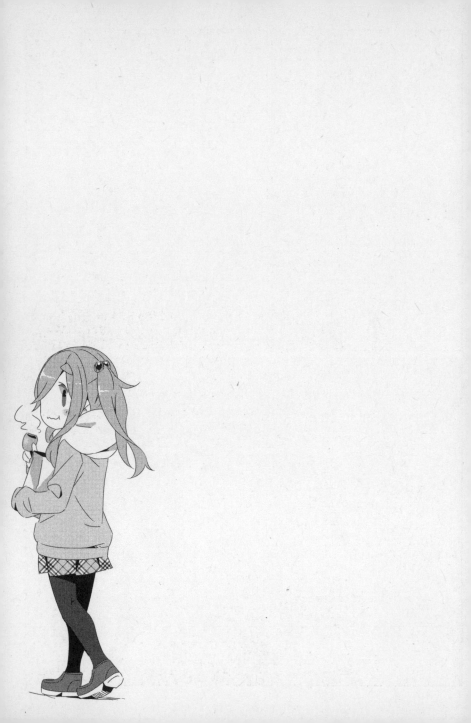

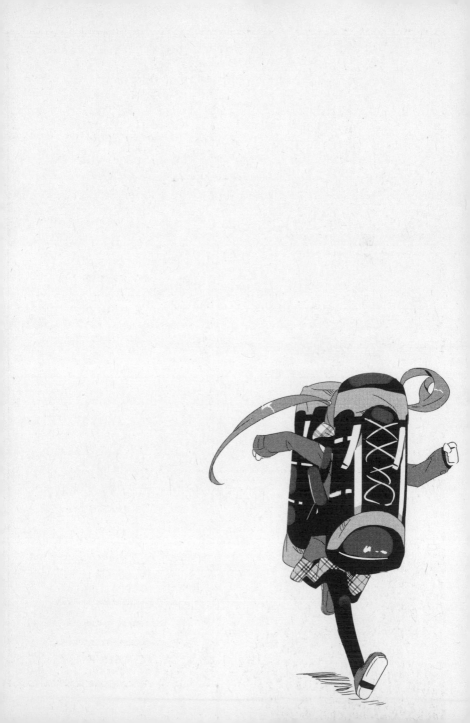

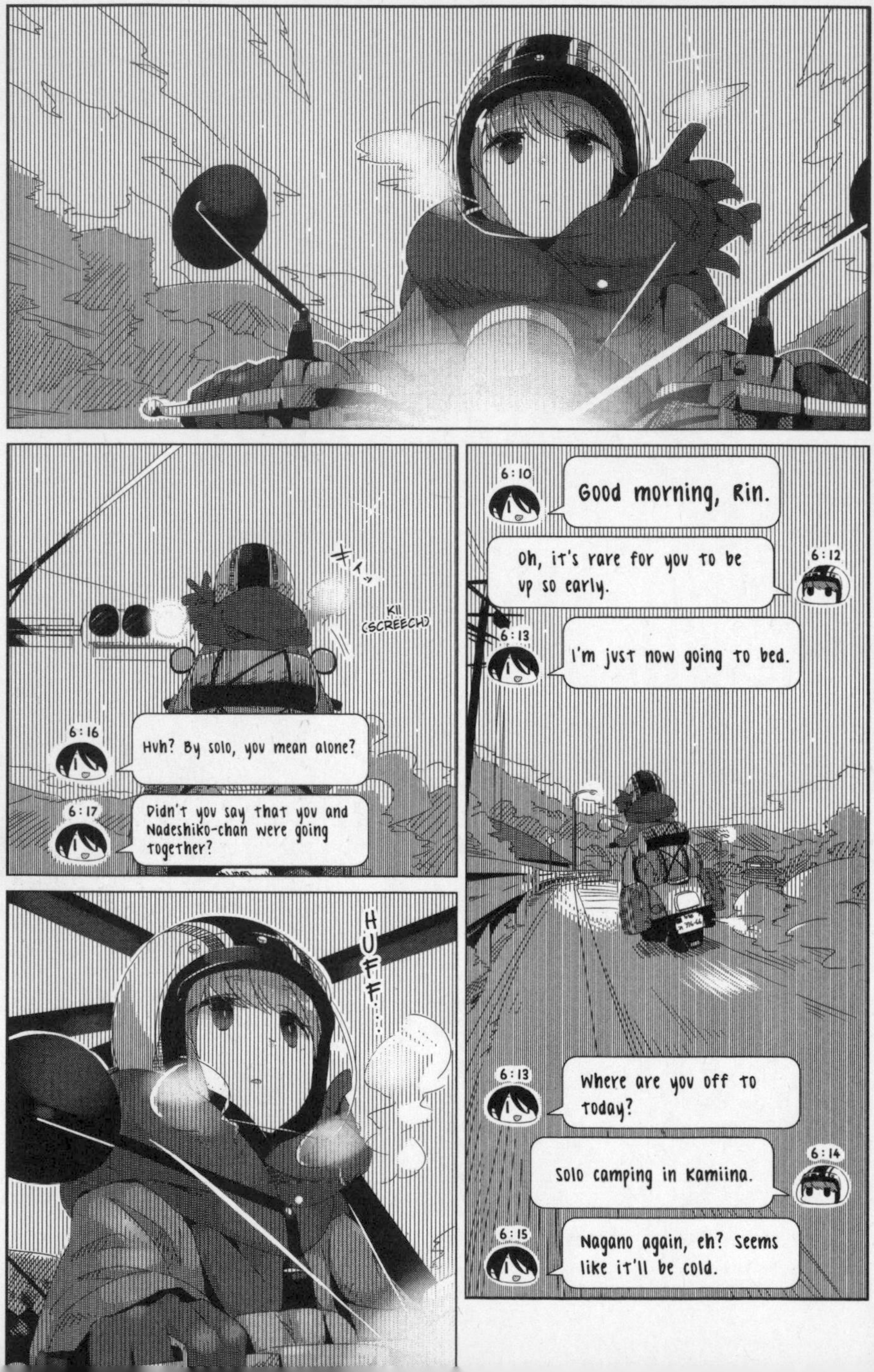
6:10
Good morning, Rin.
6:12
Oh, it's rare for you to be up so early.
6:13
I'm just now going to bed.
6:13
Where are you off to today?
6:14
Solo camping in Kamiina.
6:15
Nagano again, eh? Seems like it'll be cold.
キィッ
KII (SCREECH)
6:16
Huh? By solo, you mean alone?
6:17
Didn't you say that you and Nadeshiko-chan were going together?
HUFF...

Chapter 15
CATCHING A COLD AND THE SOLO JOURNEY

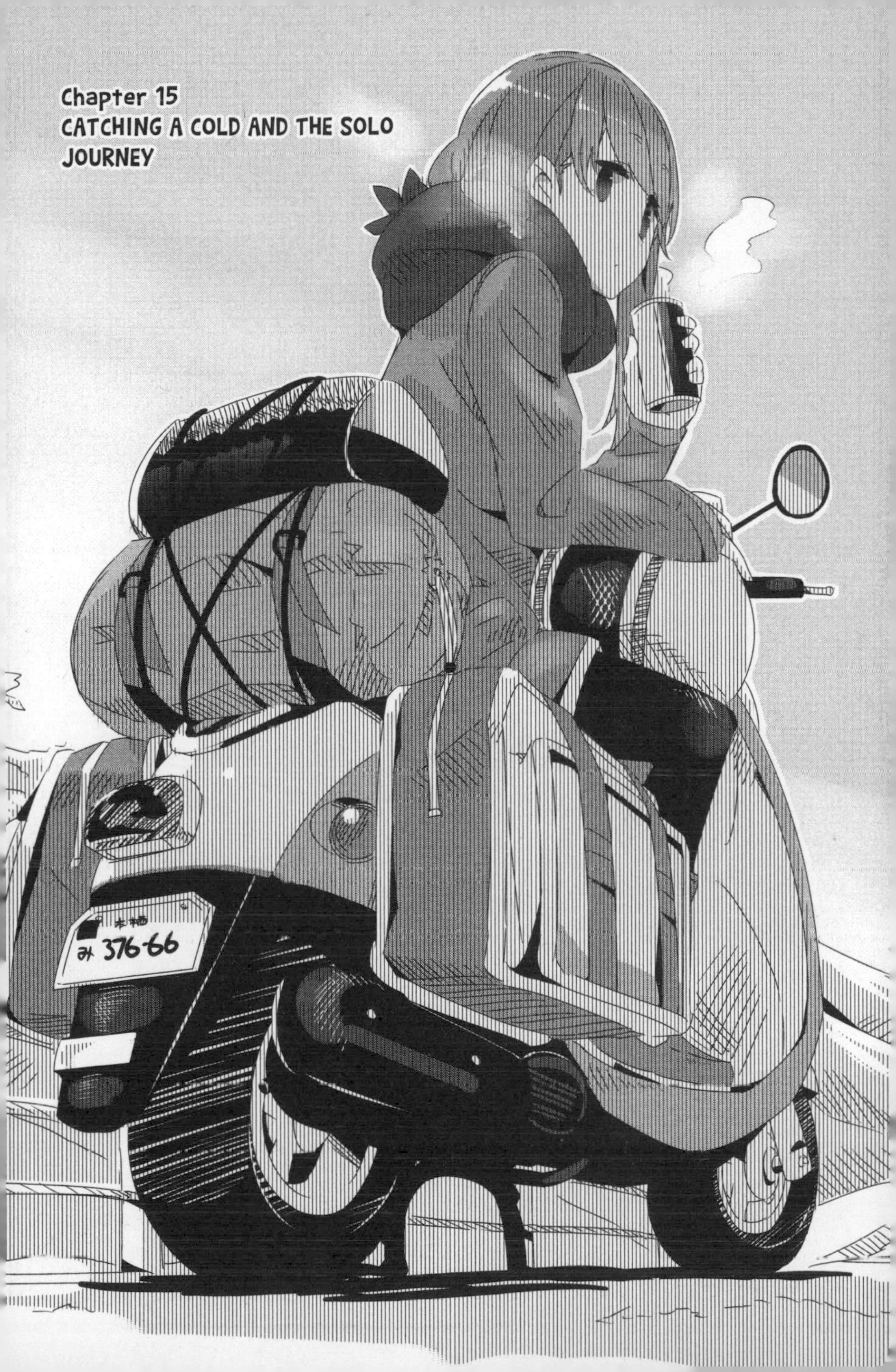
本栖
み 376-66

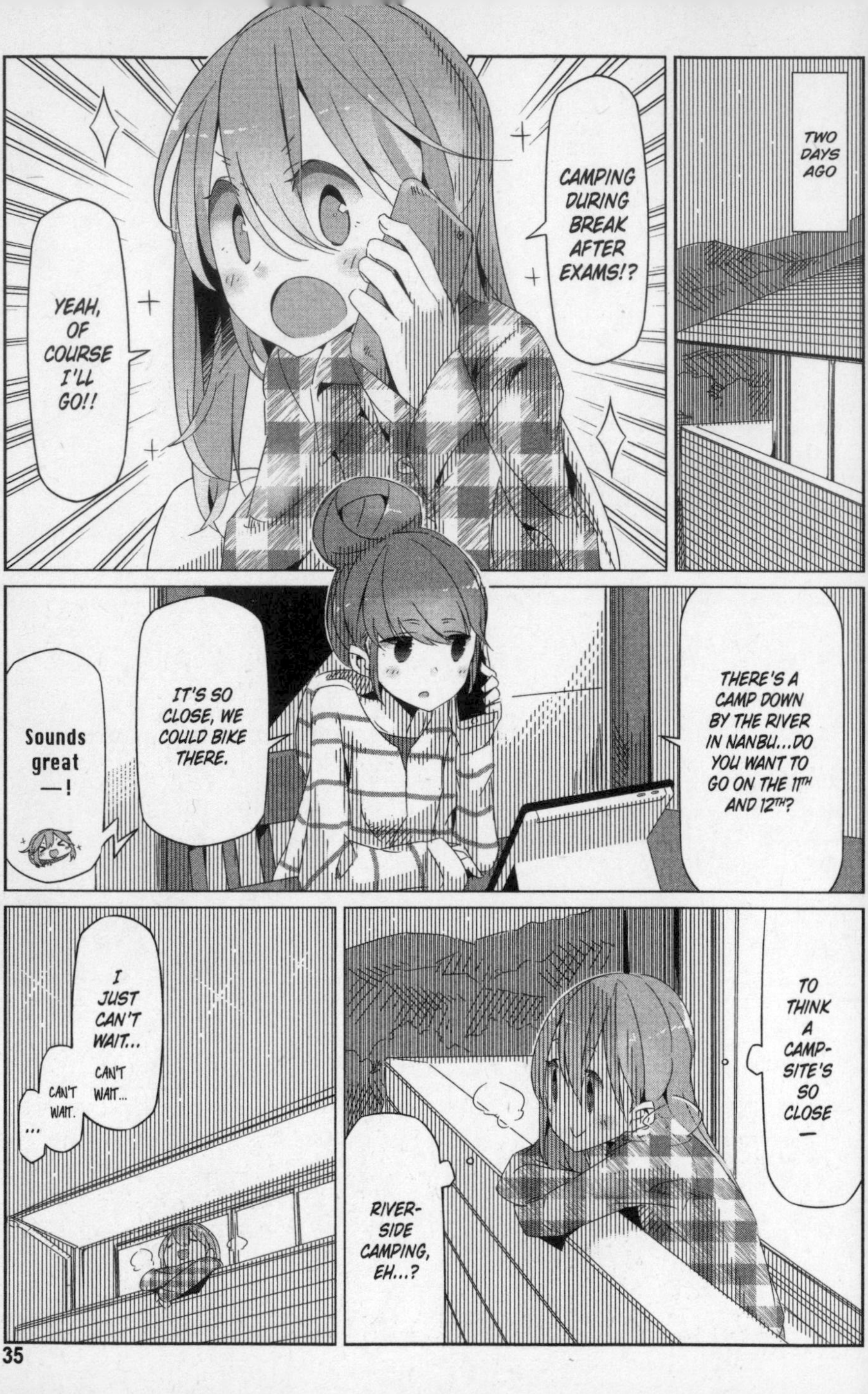
TWO DAYS AGO
CAMPING DURING BREAK AFTER EXAMS!?
YEAH, OF COURSE I'LL GO!!
THERE'S A CAMP DOWN BY THE RIVER IN NANBU...DO YOU WANT TO GO ON THE 11TH AND 12TH?
IT'S SO CLOSE, WE COULD BIKE THERE.
Sounds great—!
TO THINK A CAMPSITE'S SO CLOSE—
RIVERSIDE CAMPING, EH...?
I JUST CAN'T WAIT...
CAN'T WAIT...
CAN'T WAIT. ...

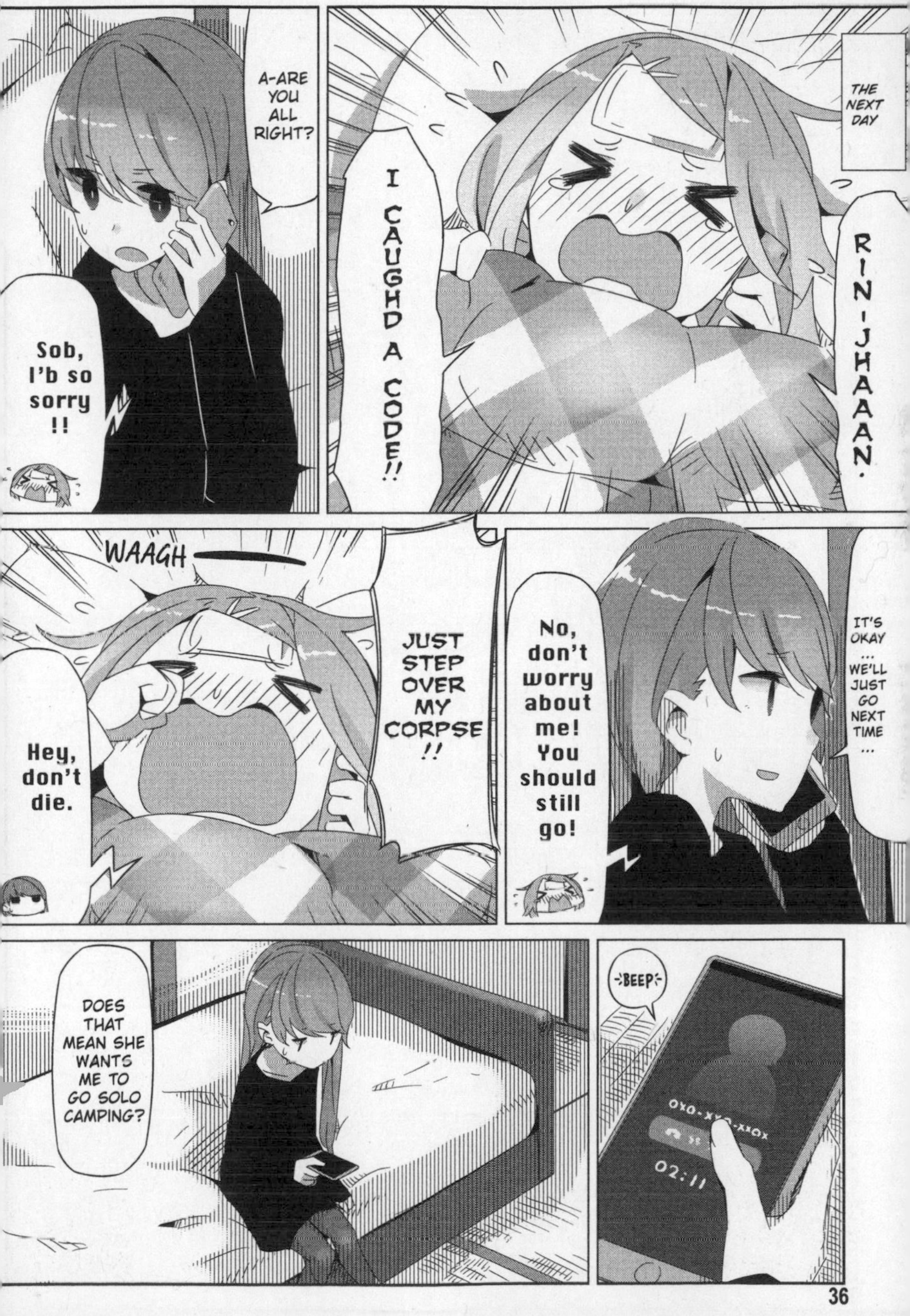
THE NEXT DAY
RIN-JHAAAN.
I CAUGHD A CODE!!
A-ARE YOU ALL RIGHT?
Sob, I'b so sorry !!
IT'S OKAY ... WE'LL JUST GO NEXT TIME ...
No, don't worry about me! You should still go!
JUST STEP OVER MY CORPSE!!
WAAGH
Hey, don't die.
BEEP
02:11
DOES THAT MEAN SHE WANTS ME TO GO SOLO CAMPING?

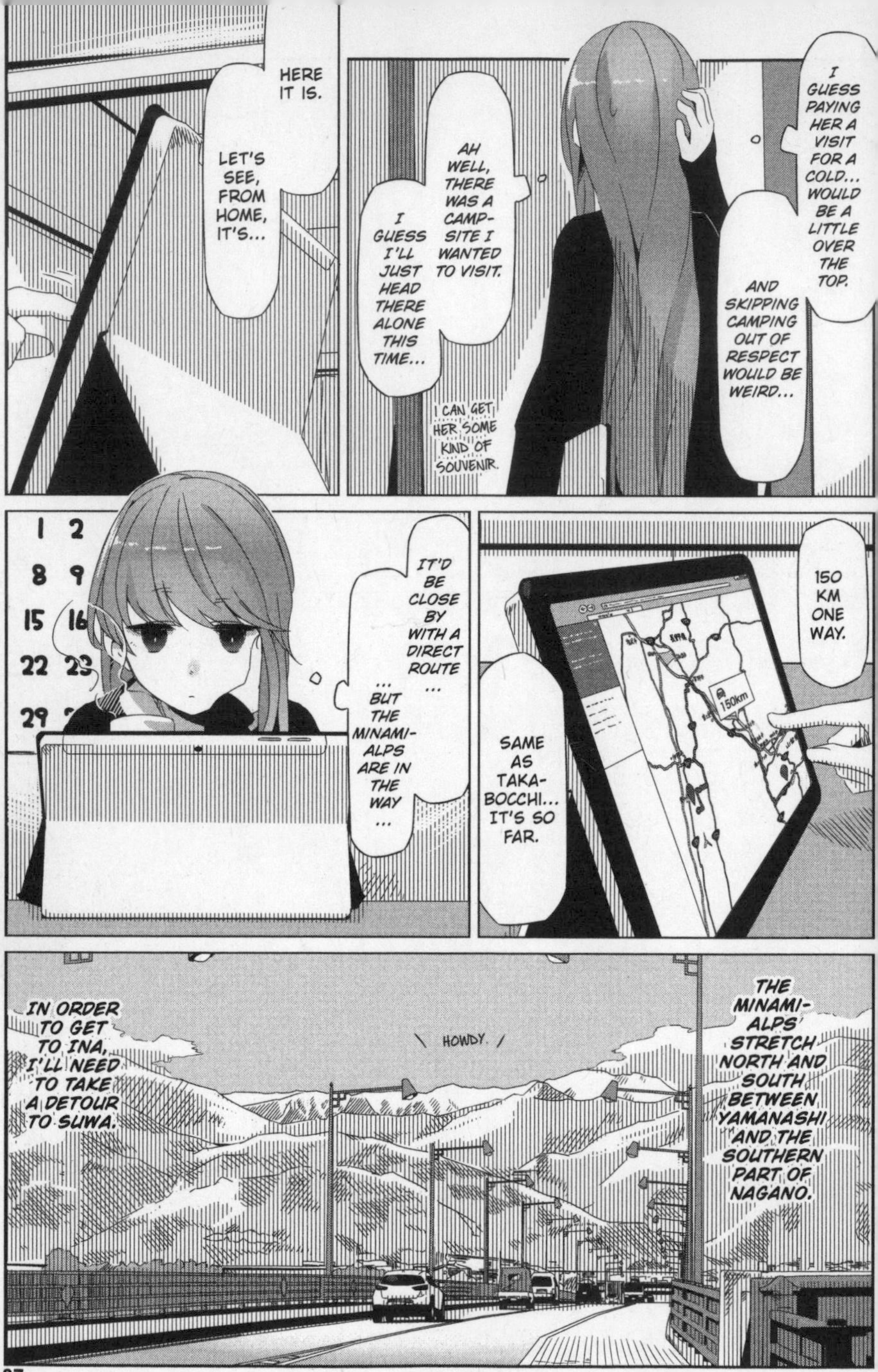
I GUESS PAYING HER A VISIT FOR A COLD... WOULD BE A LITTLE OVER THE TOP.
AND SKIPPING CAMPING OUT OF RESPECT WOULD BE WEIRD...
AH WELL, THERE WAS A CAMP-SITE I WANTED TO VISIT.
I GUESS I'LL JUST HEAD THERE ALONE THIS TIME...
I CAN GET HER SOME KIND OF SOUVENIR.
HERE IT IS.
LET'S SEE, FROM HOME, IT'S...
150 KM ONE WAY.
150km
SAME AS TAKA-BOCCHI... IT'S SO FAR.
IT'D BE CLOSE BY WITH A DIRECT ROUTE ...
... BUT THE MINAMI-ALPS ARE IN THE WAY ...
THE MINAMI-ALPS' STRETCH NORTH AND SOUTH BETWEEN YAMANASHI AND THE SOUTHERN PART OF NAGANO.
HOWDY.
IN ORDER TO GET TO INA, I'LL NEED TO TAKE A DETOUR TO SUWA.

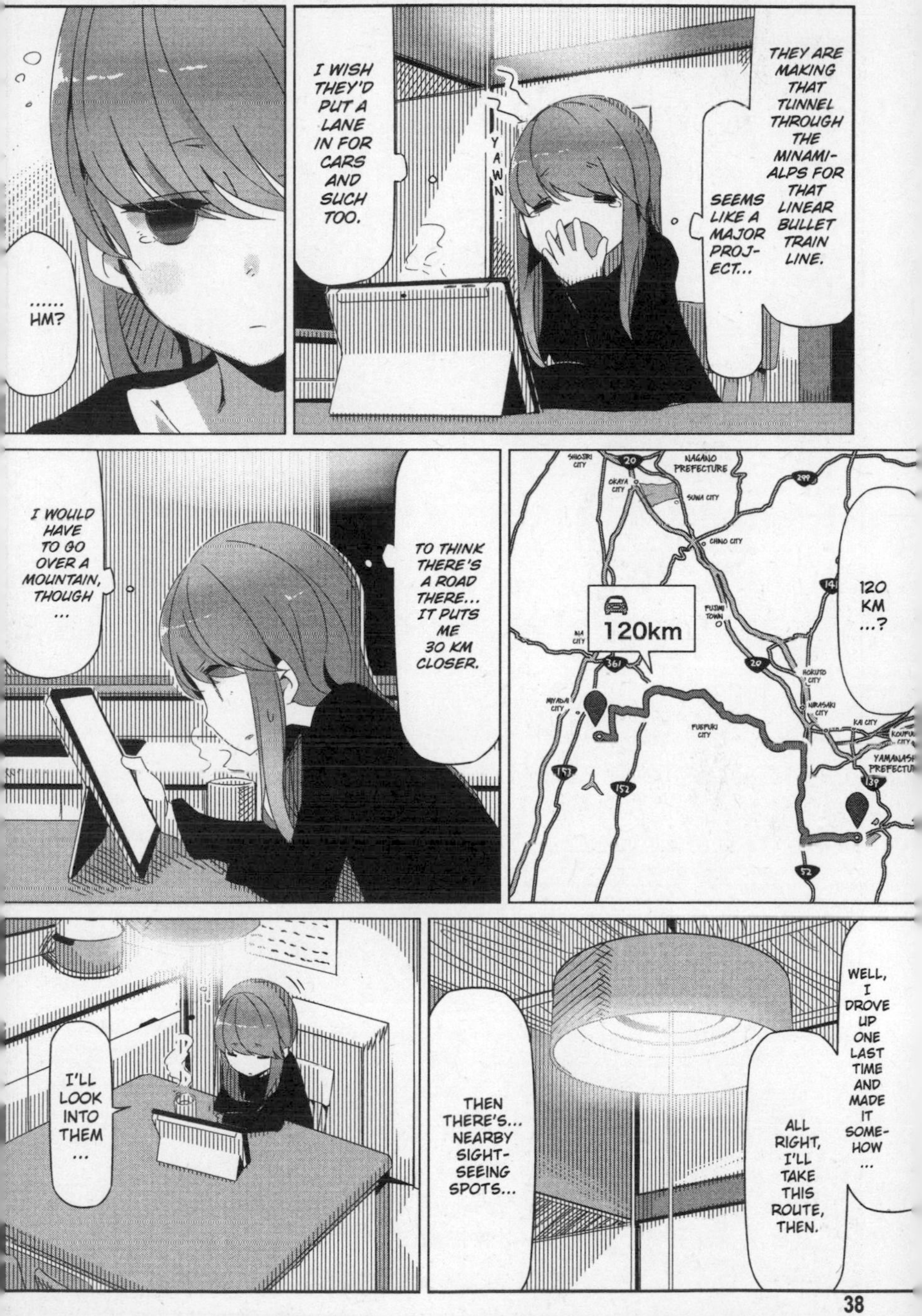

THEY ARE MAKING THAT TUNNEL THROUGH THE MINAMI-ALPS FOR THAT LINEAR BULLET TRAIN LINE.
SEEMS LIKE A MAJOR PROJ-ECT...
YAWN...
I WISH THEY'D PUT A LANE IN FOR CARS AND SUCH TOO.
...... HM?
NAGANO PREFECTURE
SUWA CITY
CHINO CITY
120km
HOKUTO CITY
NIRASAKI CITY
KAI CITY
FUEFUKI CITY
120 KM ...?
TO THINK THERE'S A ROAD THERE... IT PUTS ME 30 KM CLOSER.
I WOULD HAVE TO GO OVER A MOUNTAIN, THOUGH ...
WELL, I DROVE UP ONE LAST TIME AND MADE IT SOME-HOW ...
ALL RIGHT, I'LL TAKE THIS ROUTE, THEN.
THEN THERE'S... NEARBY SIGHT-SEEING SPOTS...
I'LL LOOK INTO THEM ...

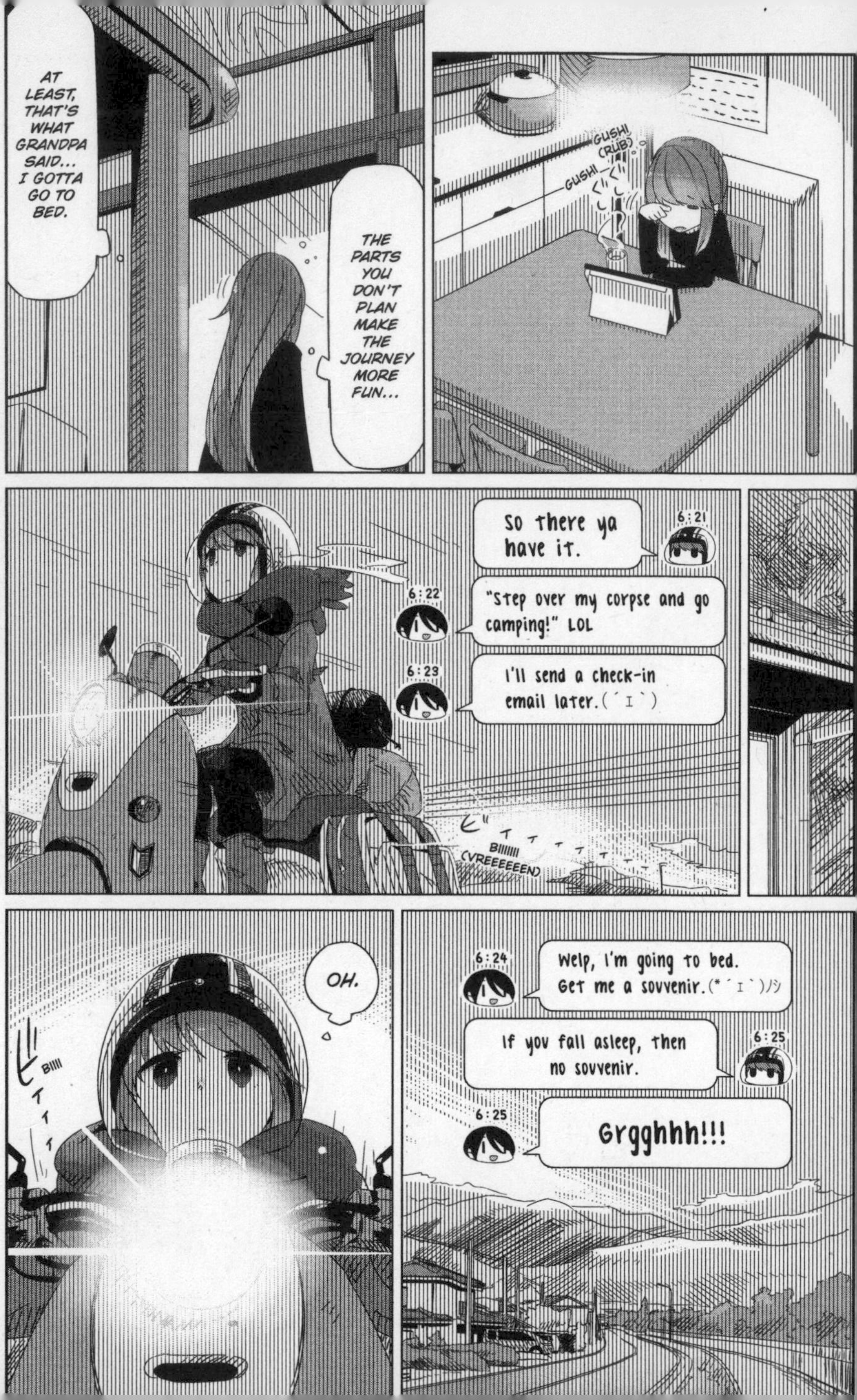
GUSHI GUSHI (RUB)
THE PARTS YOU DON'T PLAN MAKE THE JOURNEY MORE FUN...
AT LEAST, THAT'S WHAT GRANDPA SAID... I GOTTA GO TO BED.
6:21
So there ya have it.
6:22
"Step over my corpse and go camping!" LOL
6:23
I'll send a check-in email later.(´ｴ`)
BIIIIII (VREEEEEEN)
6:24
Welp, I'm going to bed. Get me a souvenir.(*´ｴ`)ﾉｼ
6:25
If you fall asleep, then no souvenir.
6:25
Grgghhh!!!
OH.
BIIII

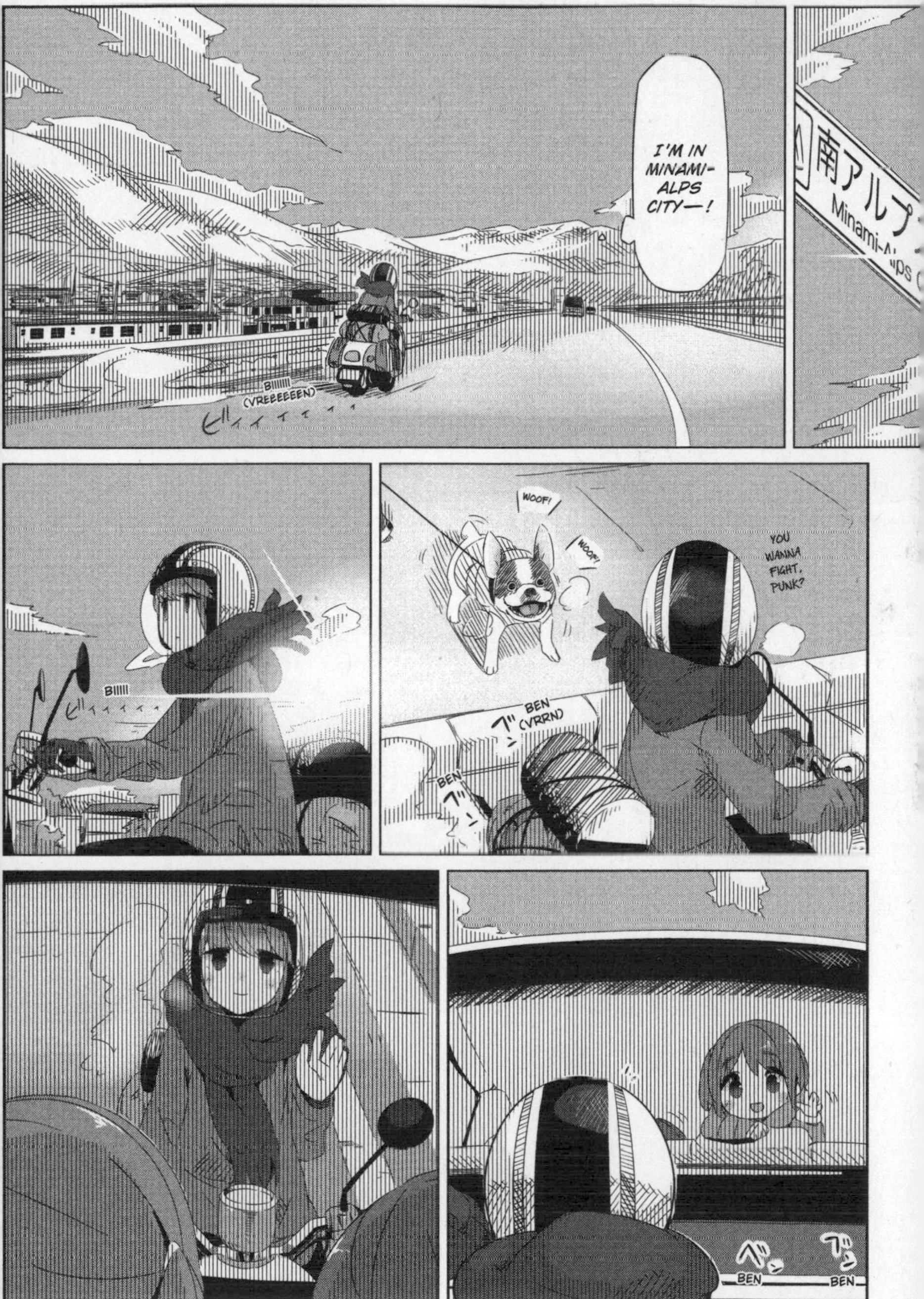

南アルプ
Minami-Alps
I'M IN MINAMI-ALPS CITY—!
BIIIIII (VREEEEEEN)
ビィイイィィィ
YOU WANNA FIGHT, PUNK?
WOOF!
WOOF!
BEN (VRRN)
ブン
BEN
ブン
BIIIII
ビィイイイィ
BEN
ブン
BEN
べン

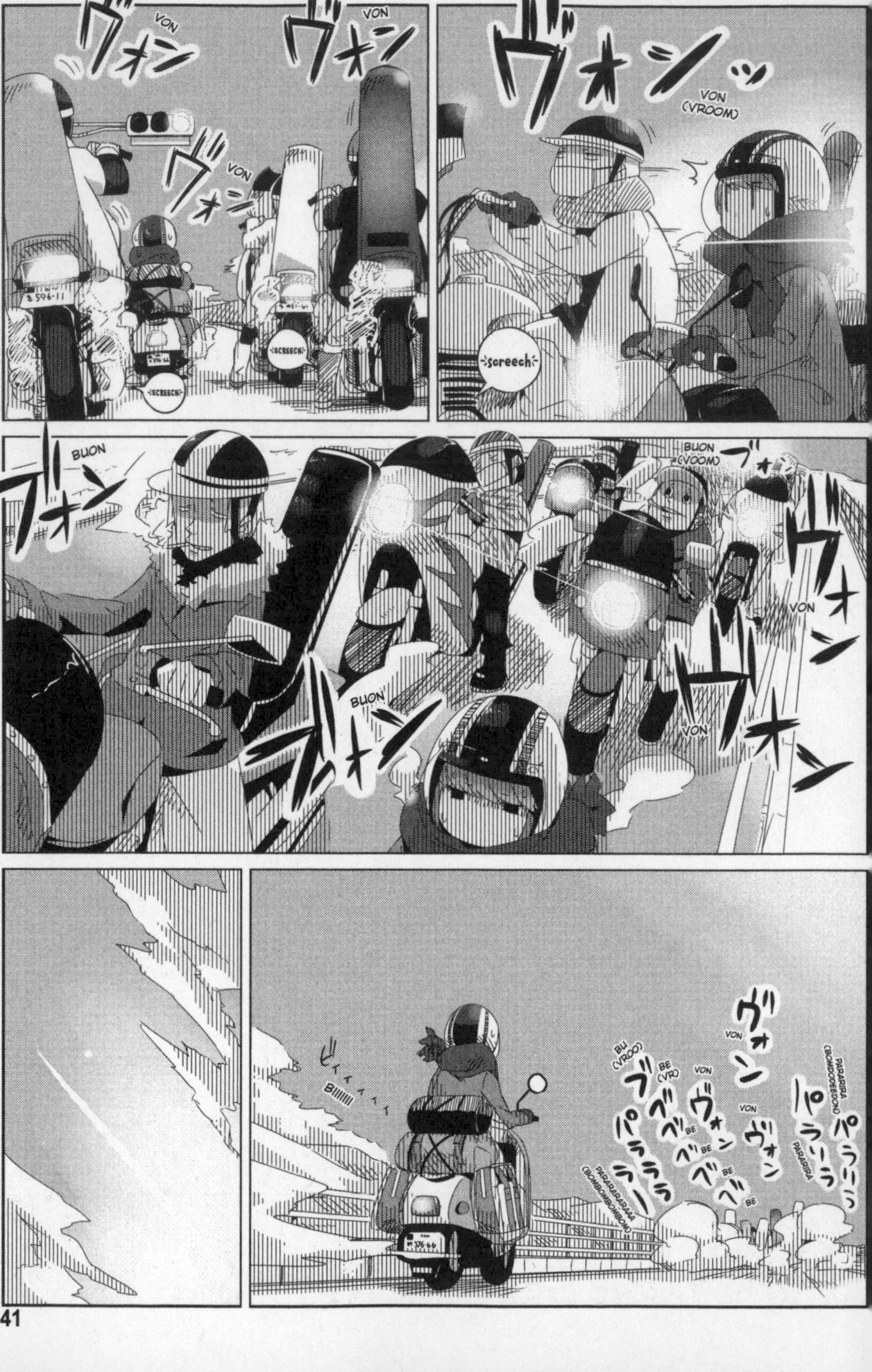
VON (VROOM)
-screech-
VON
VON
VON
-SCREECH-
-SCREECH-
BUON (VOOM)
VON
VON
BUON
BUON
PARARIRA (BOMDOEEDON)
PARARIRA
VON
VON
BE
BE
BE
BE
BE (VR)
BU (VROO)
PARARARARAAA (BOMBOMBOMBOM)
BIIIIIII

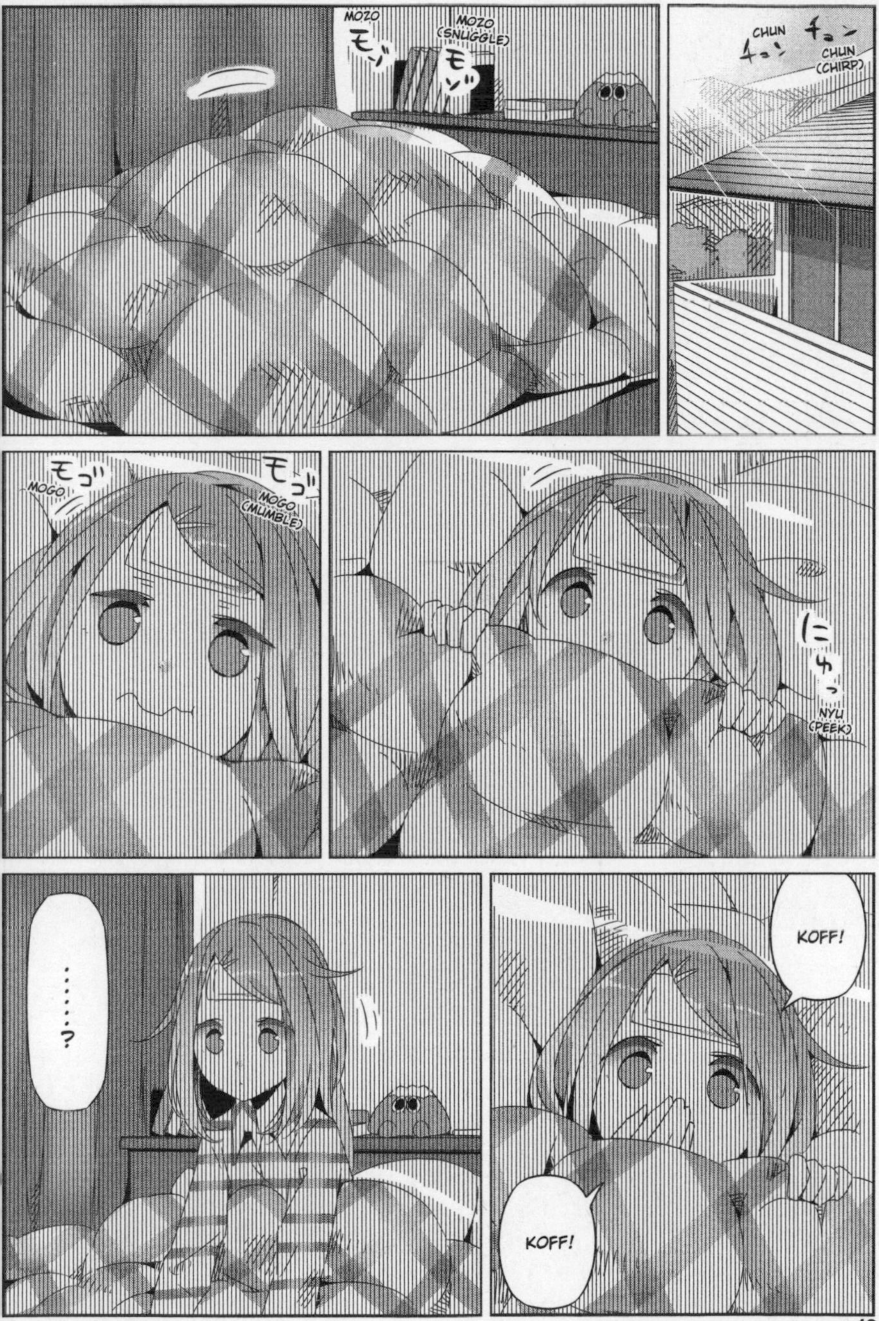

チュン
CHUN
チュン
CHUN (CHIRP)
MOZO
モゾ
MOZO (SNUGGLE)
モゾ
にゅっ
NYU (PEEK)
モゴ
MOGO
モゴ
MOGO (MUMBLE)
KOFF!
KOFF!
......?

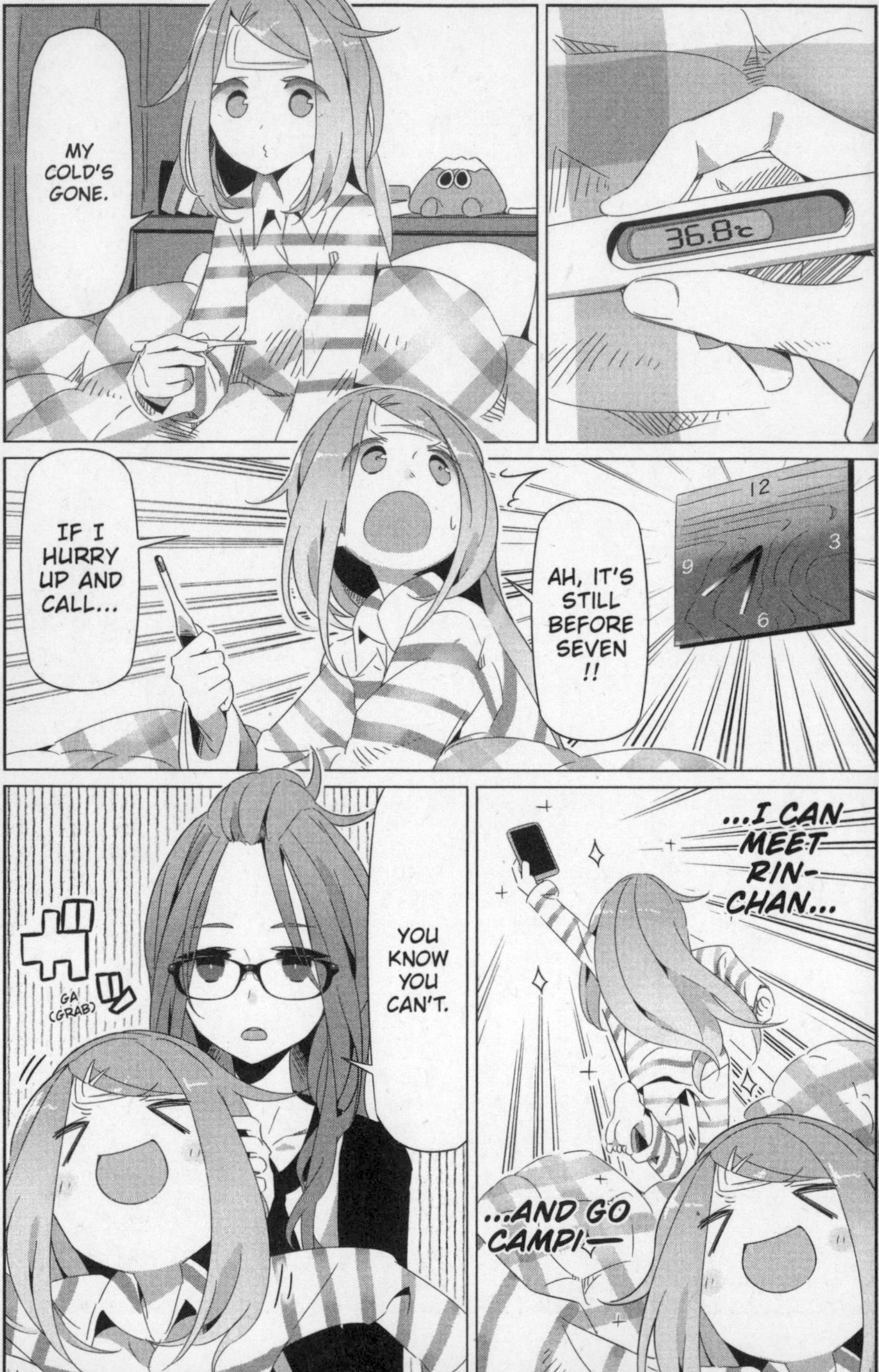
36.8℃
MY COLD'S GONE.
12
3
9
6
AH, IT'S STILL BEFORE SEVEN !!
IF I HURRY UP AND CALL...
...I CAN MEET RIN-CHAN...
...AND GO CAMPI—
YOU KNOW YOU CAN'T.
GA (GRAB)

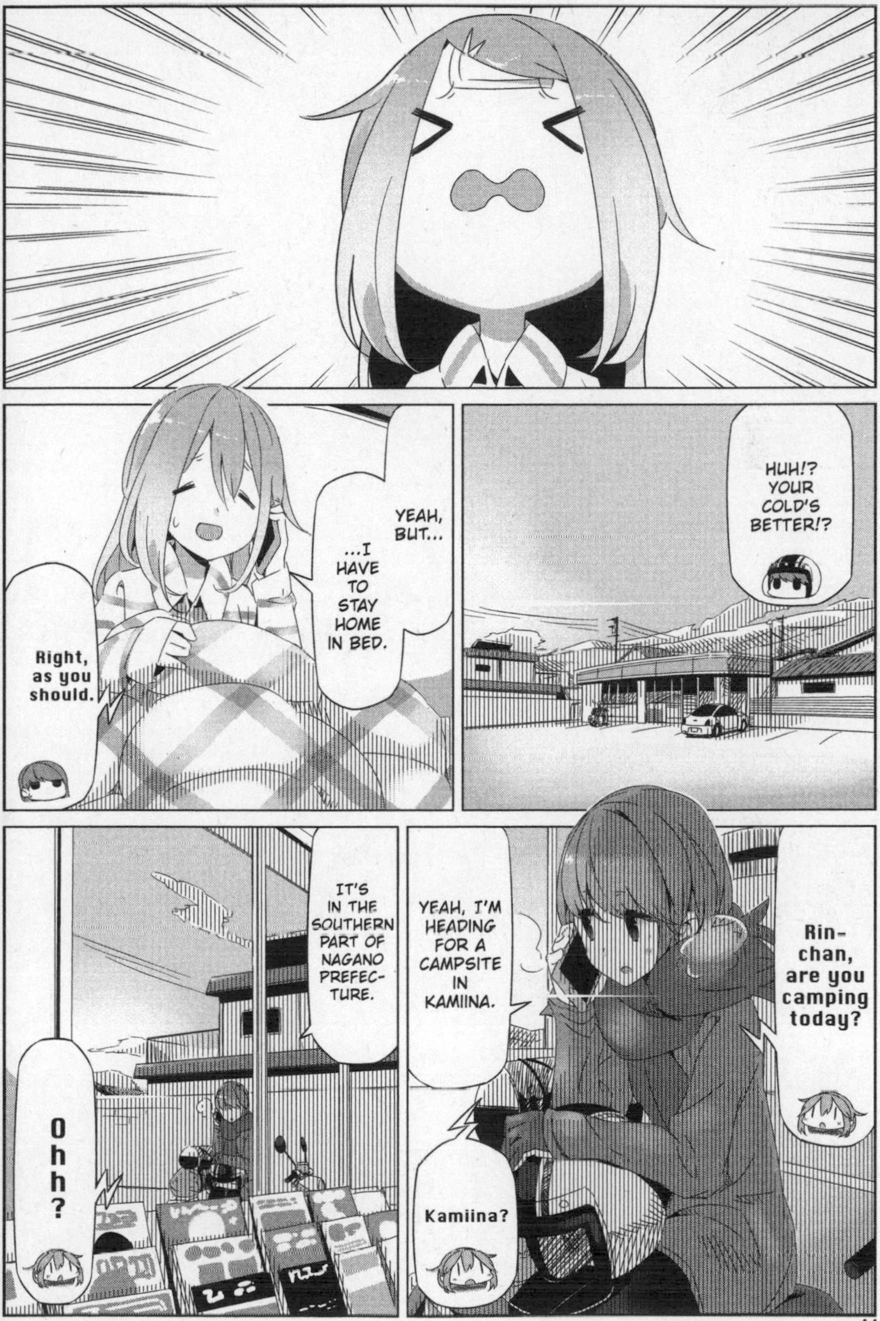
HUH!? YOUR COLD'S BETTER!?
YEAH, BUT...
...I HAVE TO STAY HOME IN BED.
Right, as you should.
Rin-chan, are you camping today?
YEAH, I'M HEADING FOR A CAMPSITE IN KAMIINA.
Kamiina?
IT'S IN THE SOUTHERN PART OF NAGANO PREFEC-TURE.
Ohh?

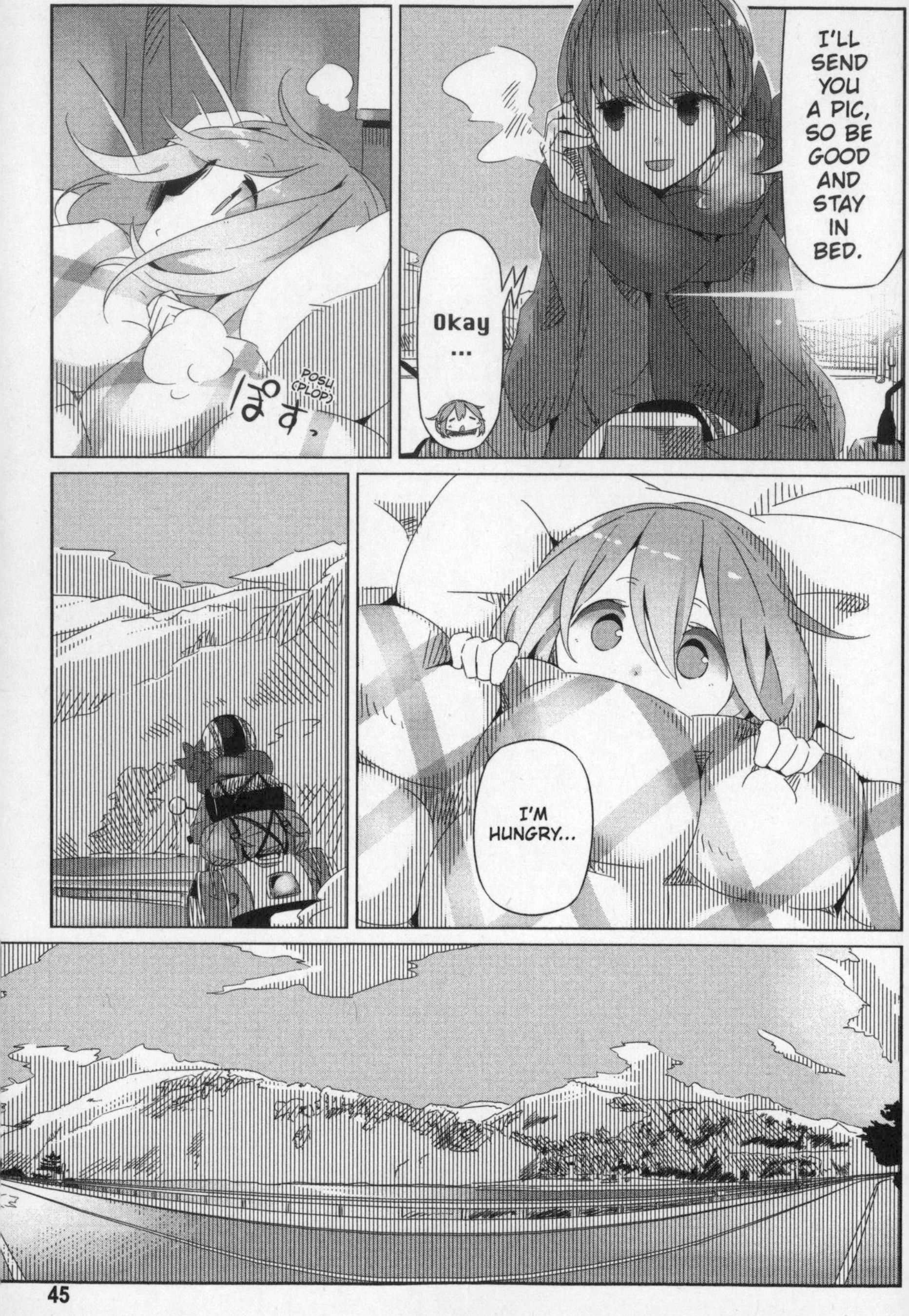
I'LL SEND YOU A PIC, SO BE GOOD AND STAY IN BED.
Okay ...
ぽす
POSU (PLOP)
I'M HUNGRY...

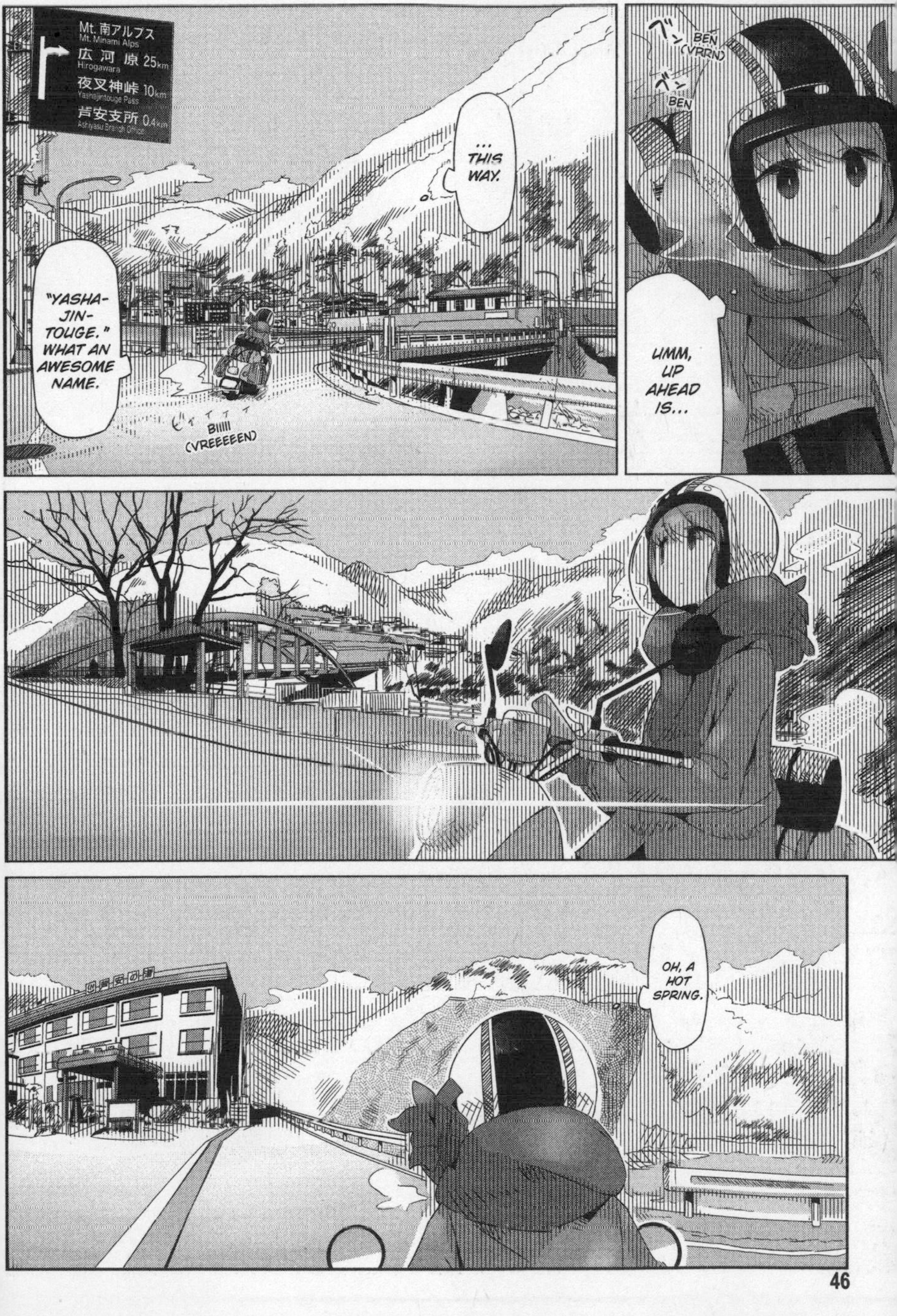
ベン
BEN (VRRN)
ベン
BEN
UMM, UP AHEAD IS...
Mt. 南アルプス
Mt. Minami Alps
広河原 25km
Hirogawara
夜叉神峠 10km
Yashajintouge Pass
芦安支所 0.4km
Ashiyasu Branch Office
... THIS WAY.
"YASHA-JIN-TOUGE." WHAT AN AWESOME NAME.
ビィィィィ
BIIIII (VREEEEEN)
OH, A HOT SPRING.

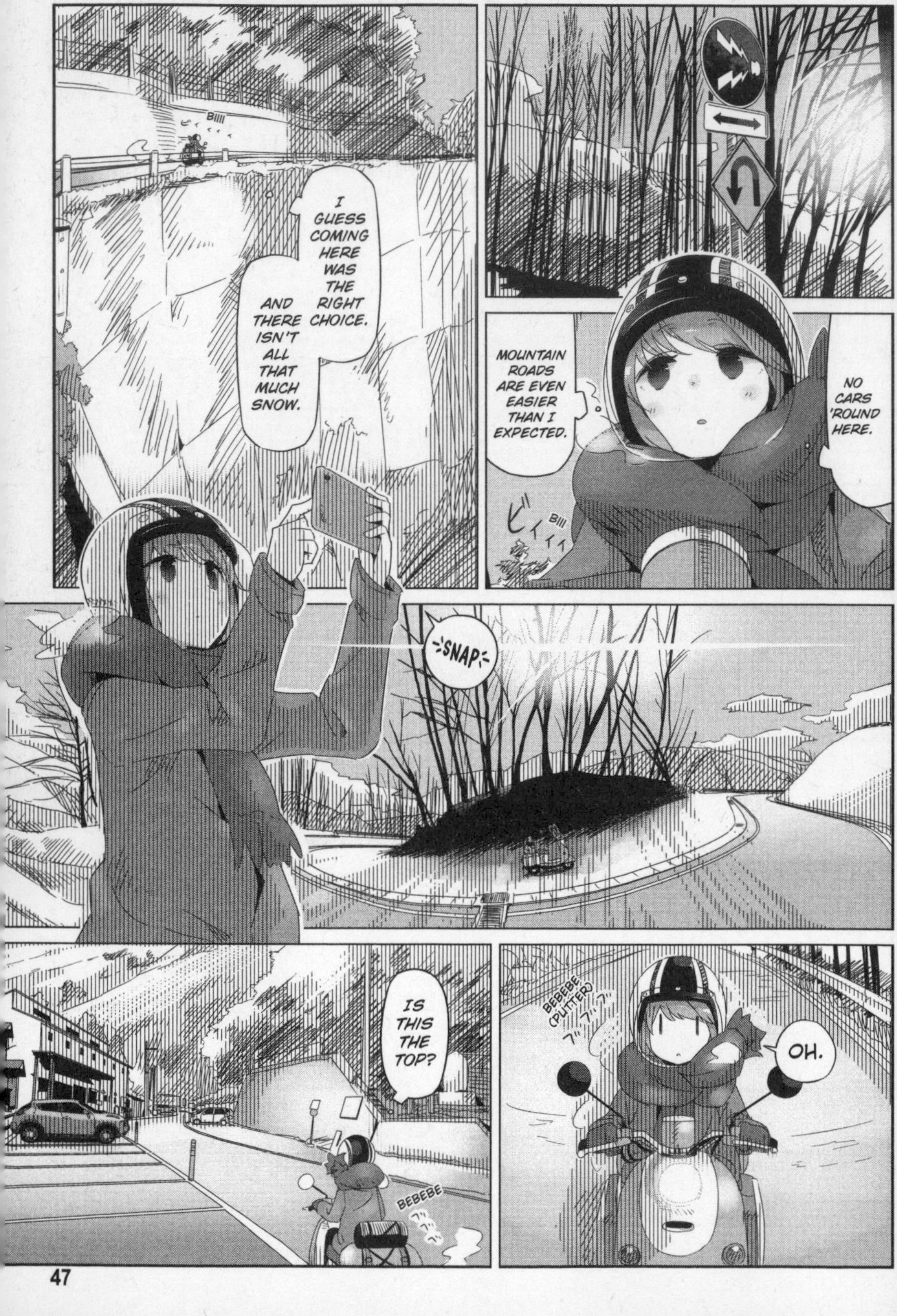
NO CARS 'ROUND HERE.
MOUNTAIN ROADS ARE EVEN EASIER THAN I EXPECTED.
BIII
BIIII
I GUESS COMING HERE WAS THE RIGHT CHOICE.
AND THERE ISN'T ALL THAT MUCH SNOW.
SNAP
BEBEBE (PUTTER)
OH.
IS THIS THE TOP?
BEBEBE

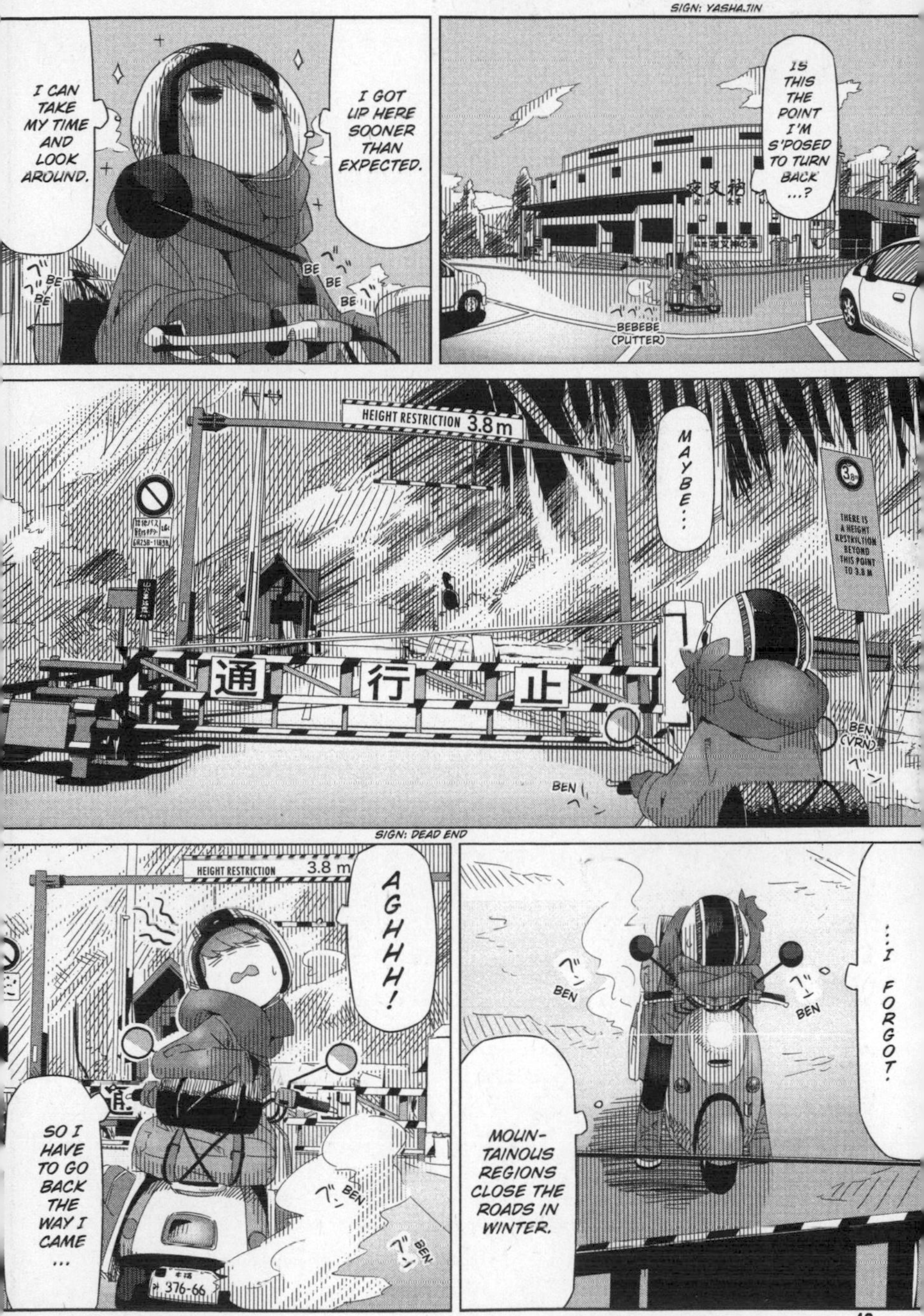
SIGN: YASHAJIN
IS THIS THE POINT I'M S'POSED TO TURN BACK ...?
BEBEBE (PUTTER)
I GOT UP HERE SOONER THAN EXPECTED.
I CAN TAKE MY TIME AND LOOK AROUND.
BE BE BE
BE BE BE
HEIGHT RESTRICTION 3.8 m
MAYBE...
THERE IS A HEIGHT RESTRICTION BEYOND THIS POINT TO 3.8 M
通行止
BEN (VRN)
BEN
...I FORGOT.
MOUNTAINOUS REGIONS CLOSE THE ROADS IN WINTER.
BEN
BEN
SIGN: DEAD END
HEIGHT RESTRICTION 3.8 m
AGHHH!
SO I HAVE TO GO BACK THE WAY I CAME...
BEN
BEN

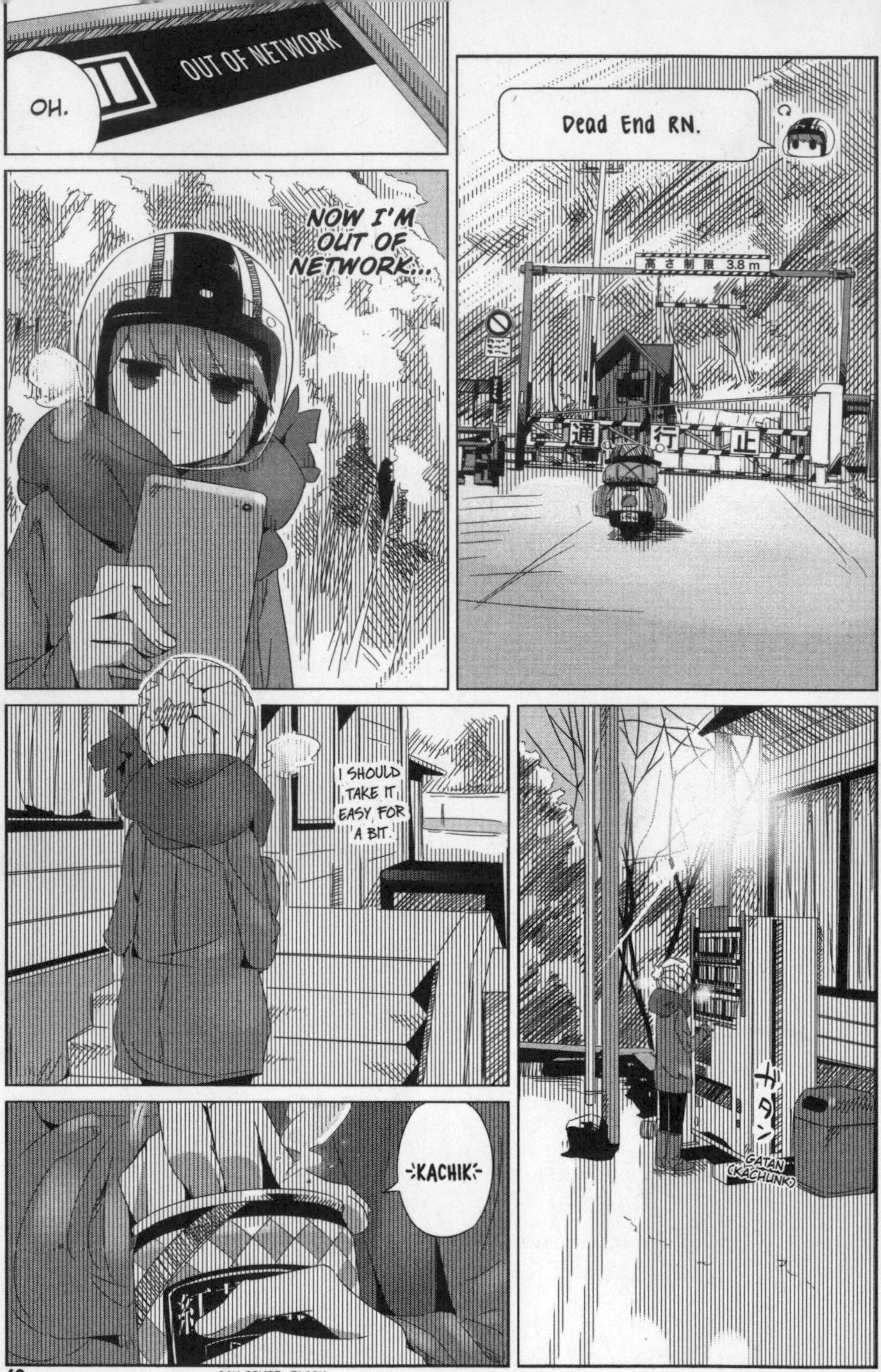
Dead End RN.
高さ制限 3.8 m
通行止
OUT OF NETWORK
OH.
NOW I'M OUT OF NETWORK...
ガタン
GATAN (KACHUNK)
I SHOULD TAKE IT EASY, FOR A BIT.
-KACHIK-

 CAN COVER: BLACK

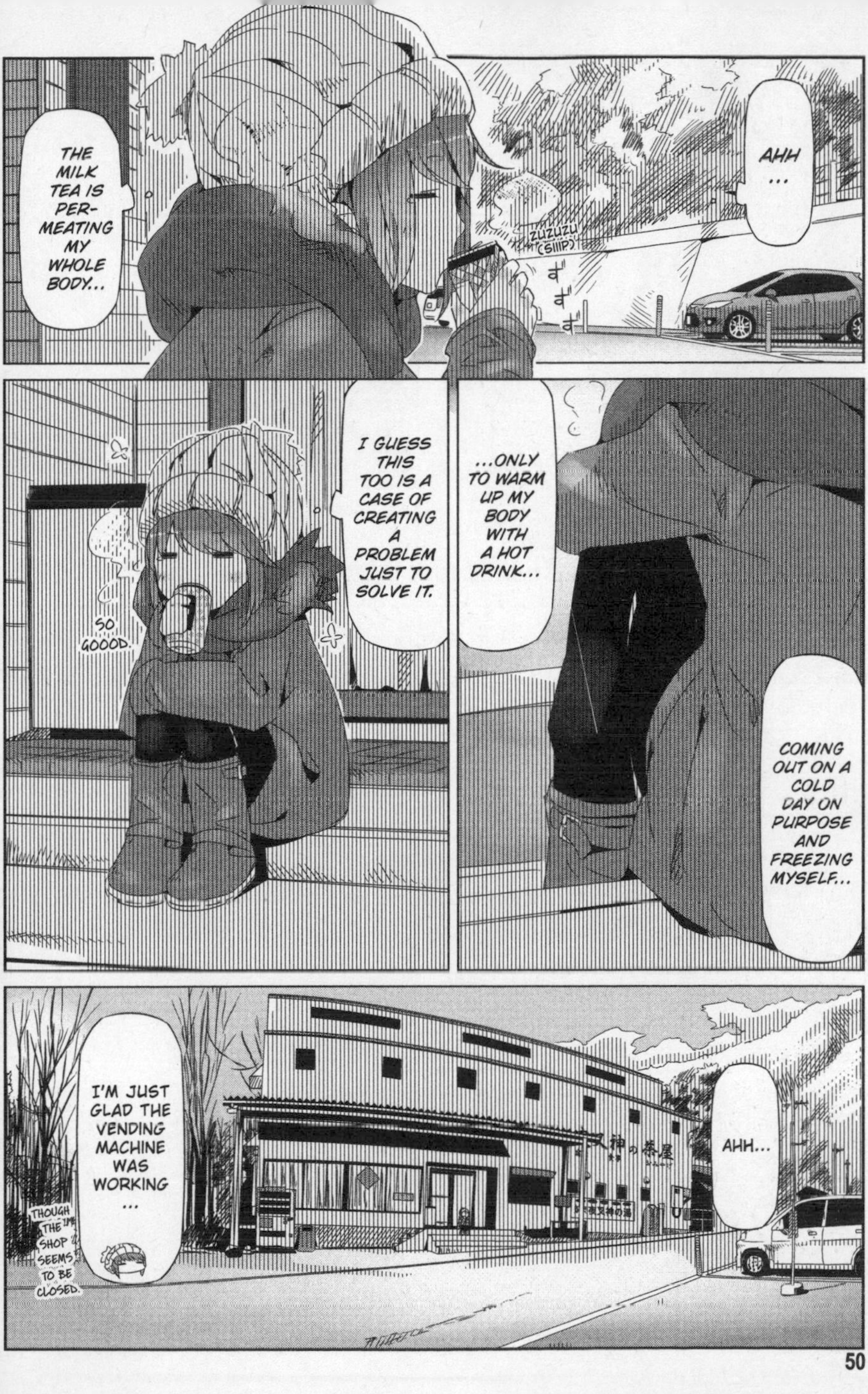
AHH ...
ZUZUZU (SIIIP)
ずずず
THE MILK TEA IS PER-MEATING MY WHOLE BODY...
COMING OUT ON A COLD DAY ON PURPOSE AND FREEZING MYSELF...
...ONLY TO WARM UP MY BODY WITH A HOT DRINK...
I GUESS THIS TOO IS A CASE OF CREATING A PROBLEM JUST TO SOLVE IT.
SO GOOOD.
AHH...
神の茶屋
I'M JUST GLAD THE VENDING MACHINE WAS WORKING ...
THOUGH THE SHOP SEEMS TO BE CLOSED.

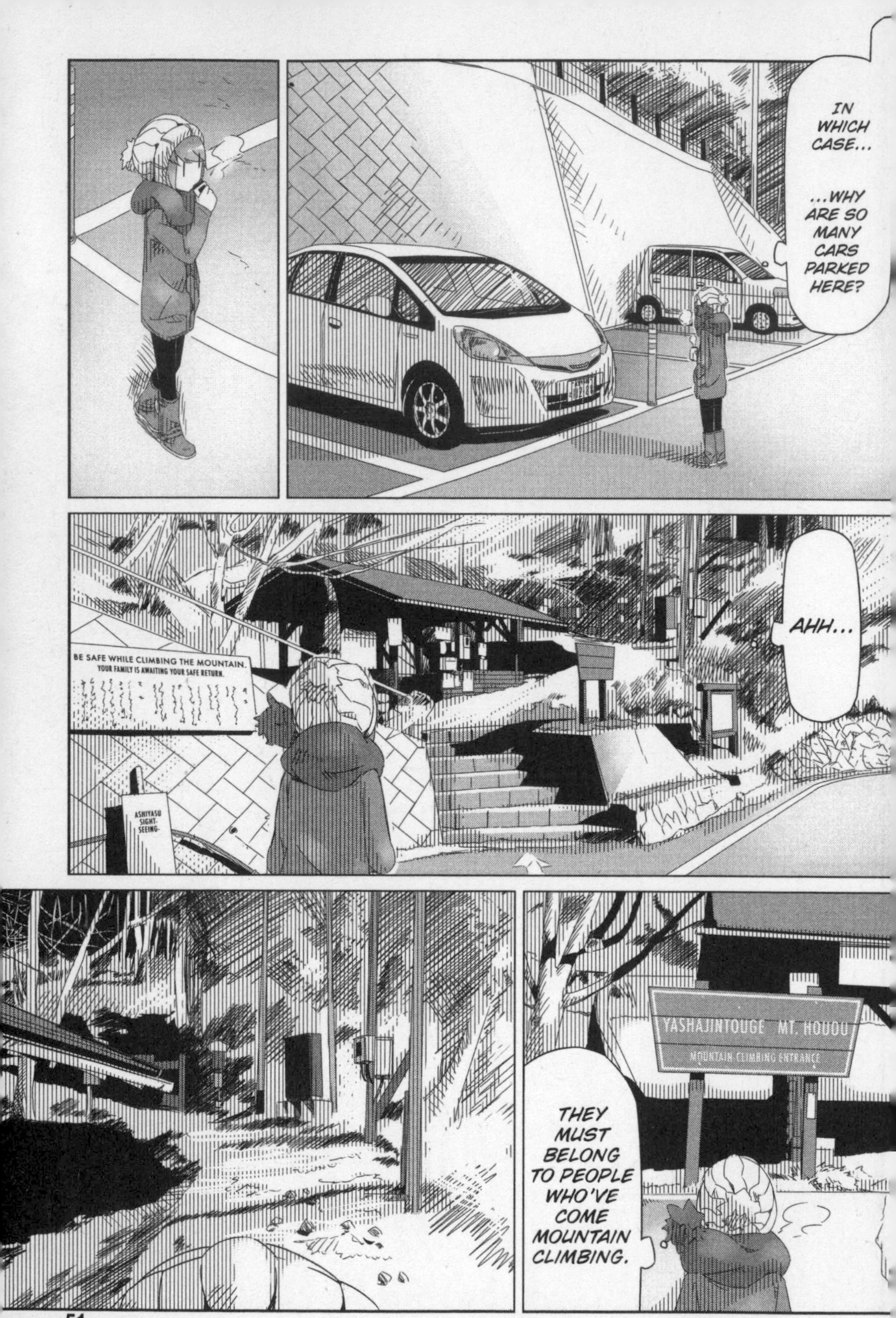
IN WHICH CASE...
...WHY ARE SO MANY CARS PARKED HERE?
AHH...
BE SAFE WHILE CLIMBING THE MOUNTAIN.
YOUR FAMILY IS AWAITING YOUR SAFE RETURN.
ASHIYASU SIGHT-SEEING-
YASHAJINTOUGE MT. HOUOU
MOUNTAIN CLIMBING ENTRANCE
THEY MUST BELONG TO PEOPLE WHO'VE COME MOUNTAIN CLIMBING.

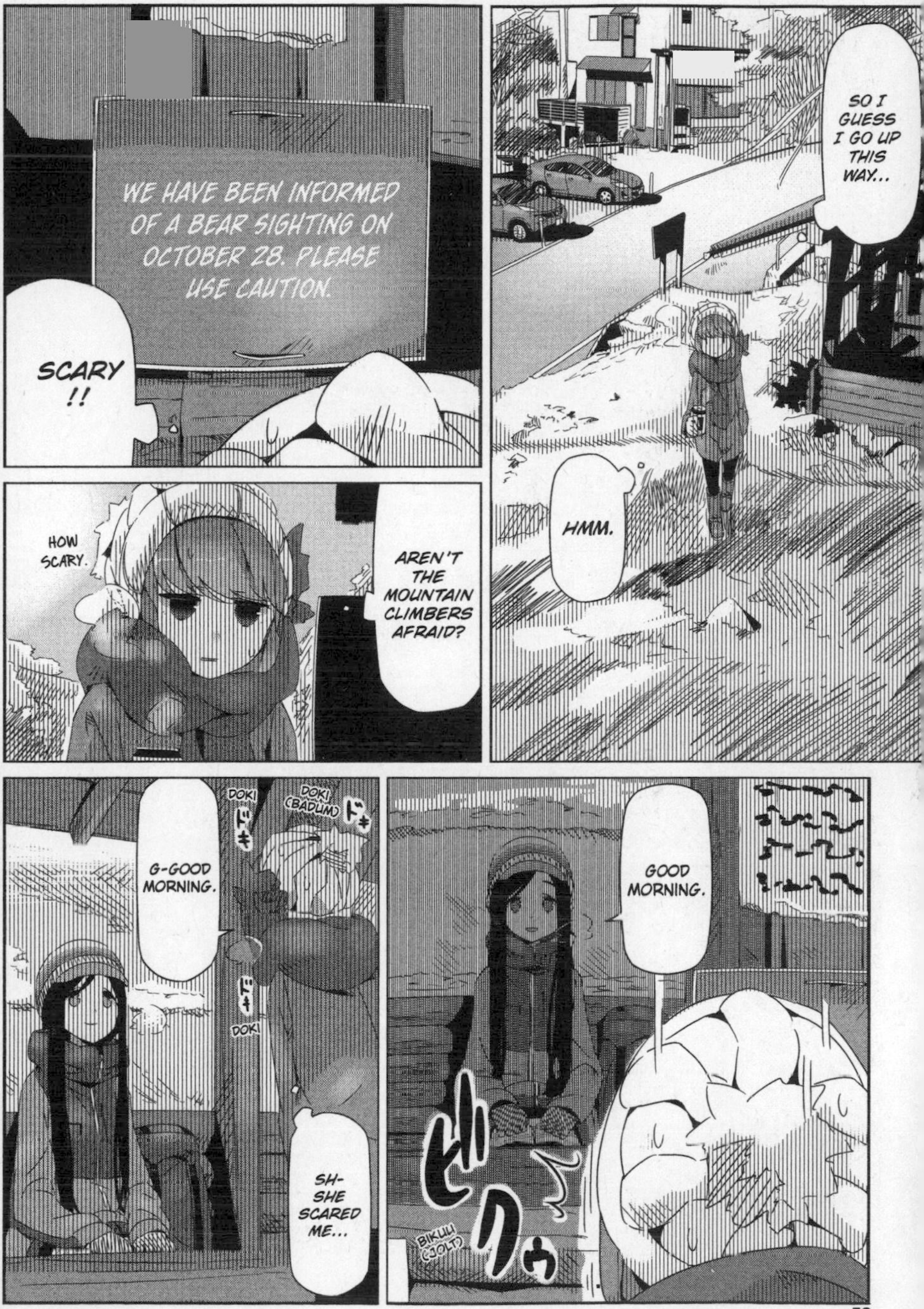
SO I GUESS I GO UP THIS WAY...
HMM.
WE HAVE BEEN INFORMED OF A BEAR SIGHTING ON OCTOBER 28. PLEASE USE CAUTION.
SCARY !!
AREN'T THE MOUNTAIN CLIMBERS AFRAID?
HOW SCARY.
GOOD MORNING.
BIKUU (JOLT)
DOKI (BADUM)
DOKI
G-GOOD MORNING.
DOKI
SH-SHE SCARED ME...

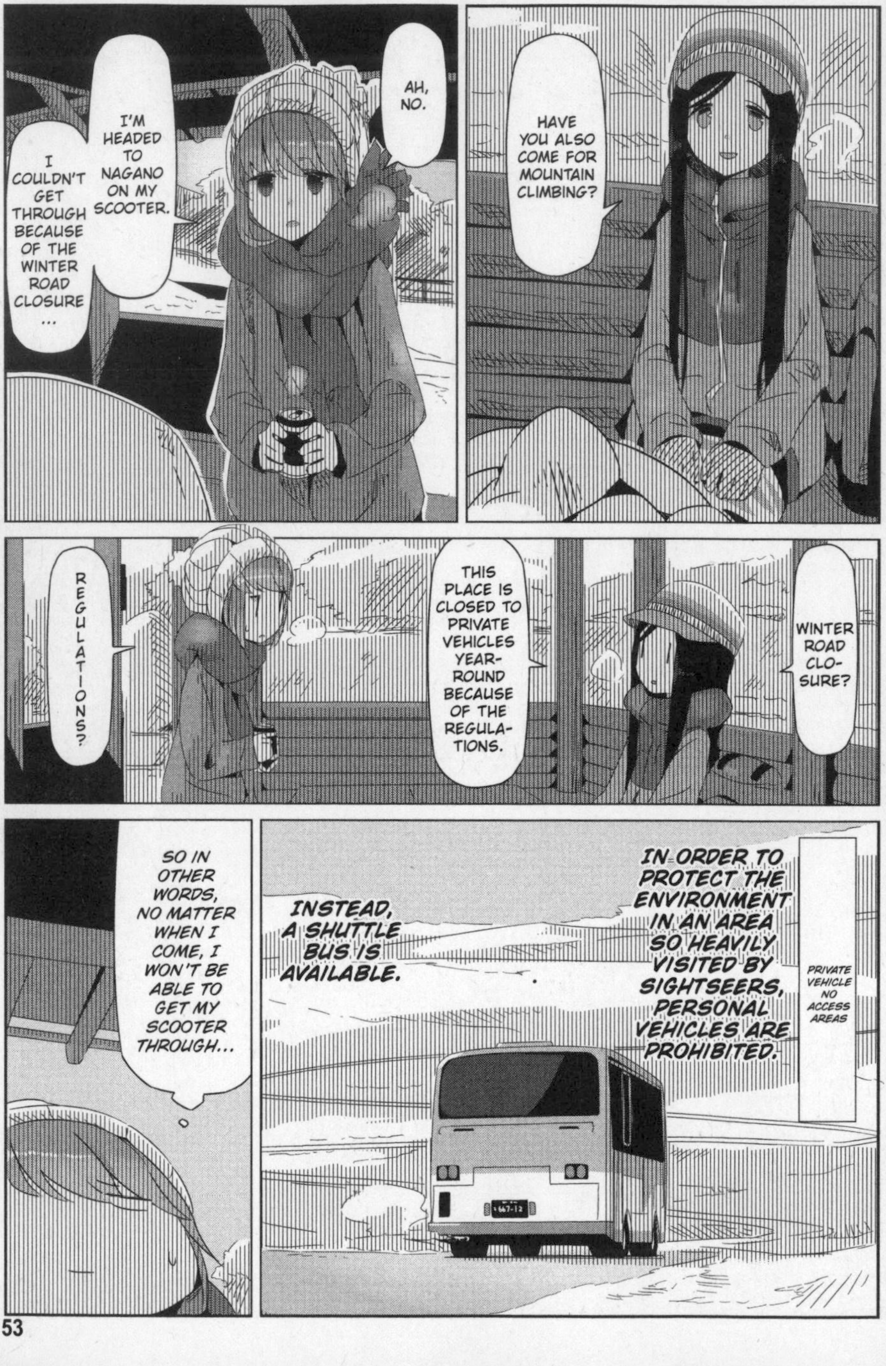
HAVE YOU ALSO COME FOR MOUNTAIN CLIMBING?
AH, NO.
I'M HEADED TO NAGANO ON MY SCOOTER.
I COULDN'T GET THROUGH BECAUSE OF THE WINTER ROAD CLOSURE...
WINTER ROAD CLO-SURE?
THIS PLACE IS CLOSED TO PRIVATE VEHICLES YEAR-ROUND BECAUSE OF THE REGULA-TIONS.
REGULATIONS?
PRIVATE VEHICLE NO ACCESS AREAS
IN ORDER TO PROTECT THE ENVIRONMENT IN AN AREA SO HEAVILY VISITED BY SIGHTSEERS, PERSONAL VEHICLES ARE PROHIBITED.
INSTEAD, A SHUTTLE BUS IS AVAILABLE.
SO IN OTHER WORDS, NO MATTER WHEN I COME, I WON'T BE ABLE TO GET MY SCOOTER THROUGH...

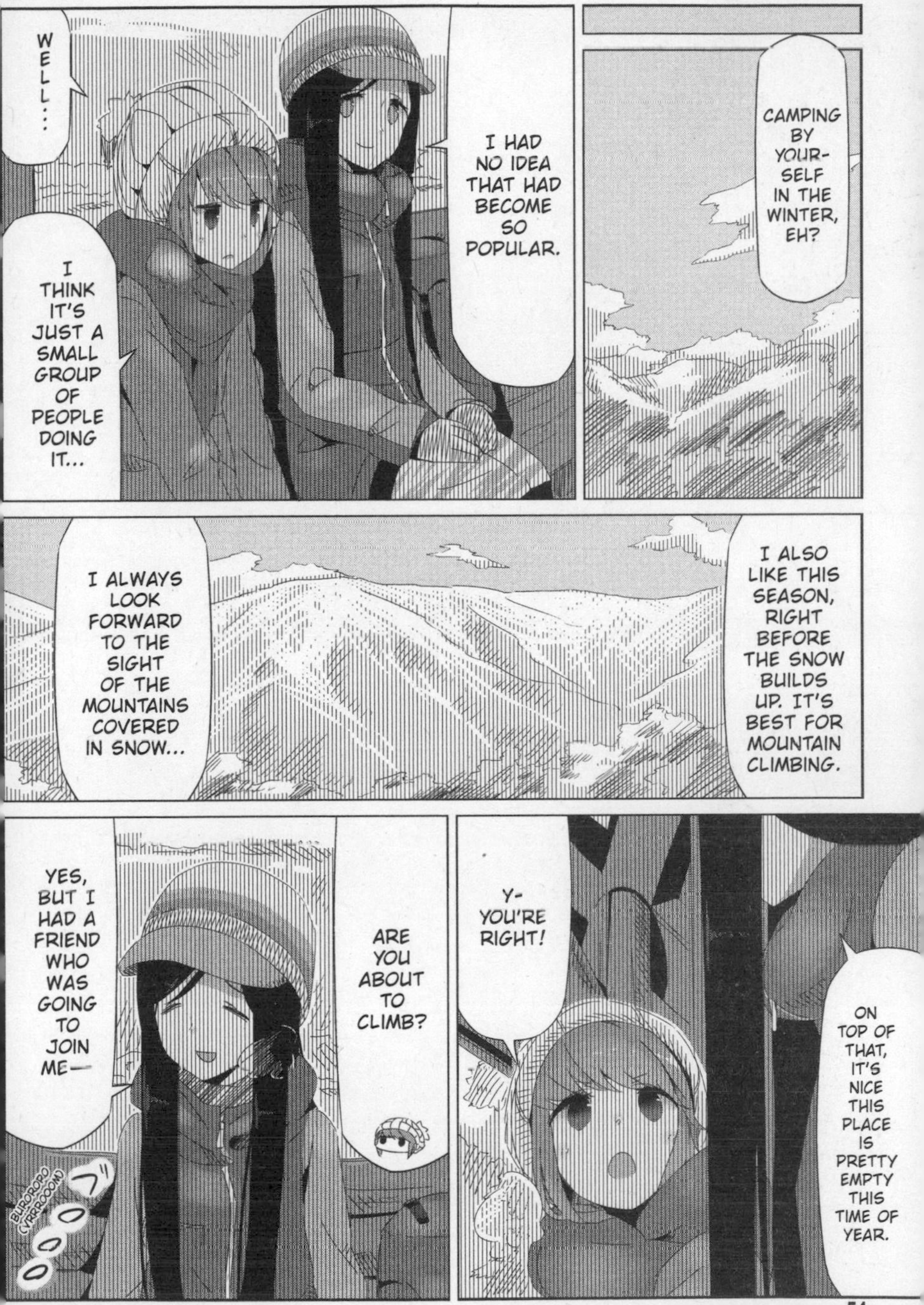
CAMPING BY YOURSELF IN THE WINTER, EH?
I HAD NO IDEA THAT HAD BECOME SO POPULAR.
WELL...
I THINK IT'S JUST A SMALL GROUP OF PEOPLE DOING IT...
I ALSO LIKE THIS SEASON, RIGHT BEFORE THE SNOW BUILDS UP. IT'S BEST FOR MOUNTAIN CLIMBING.
I ALWAYS LOOK FORWARD TO THE SIGHT OF THE MOUNTAINS COVERED IN SNOW...
ON TOP OF THAT, IT'S NICE THIS PLACE IS PRETTY EMPTY THIS TIME OF YEAR.
Y-YOU'RE RIGHT!
ARE YOU ABOUT TO CLIMB?
YES, BUT I HAD A FRIEND WHO WAS GOING TO JOIN ME—
BURORORO (VRRROOOM)

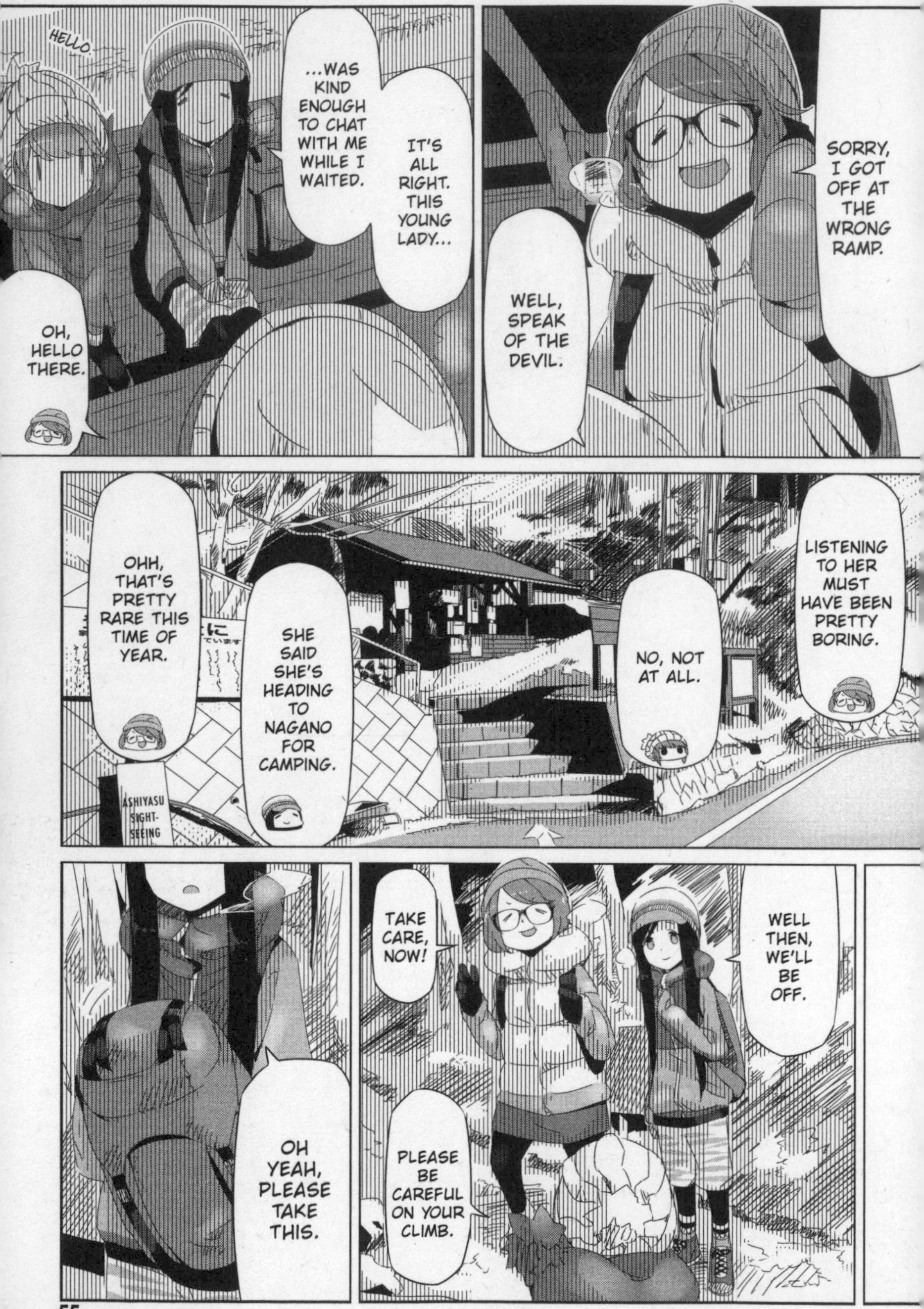
SORRY, I GOT OFF AT THE WRONG RAMP.
WELL, SPEAK OF THE DEVIL.
IT'S ALL RIGHT. THIS YOUNG LADY...
...WAS KIND ENOUGH TO CHAT WITH ME WHILE I WAITED.
HELLO.
OH, HELLO THERE.
LISTENING TO HER MUST HAVE BEEN PRETTY BORING.
NO, NOT AT ALL.
SHE SAID SHE'S HEADING TO NAGANO FOR CAMPING.
OHH, THAT'S PRETTY RARE THIS TIME OF YEAR.
ASHIYASU SIGHT-SEEING
WELL THEN, WE'LL BE OFF.
TAKE CARE, NOW!
PLEASE BE CAREFUL ON YOUR CLIMB.
OH YEAH, PLEASE TAKE THIS.

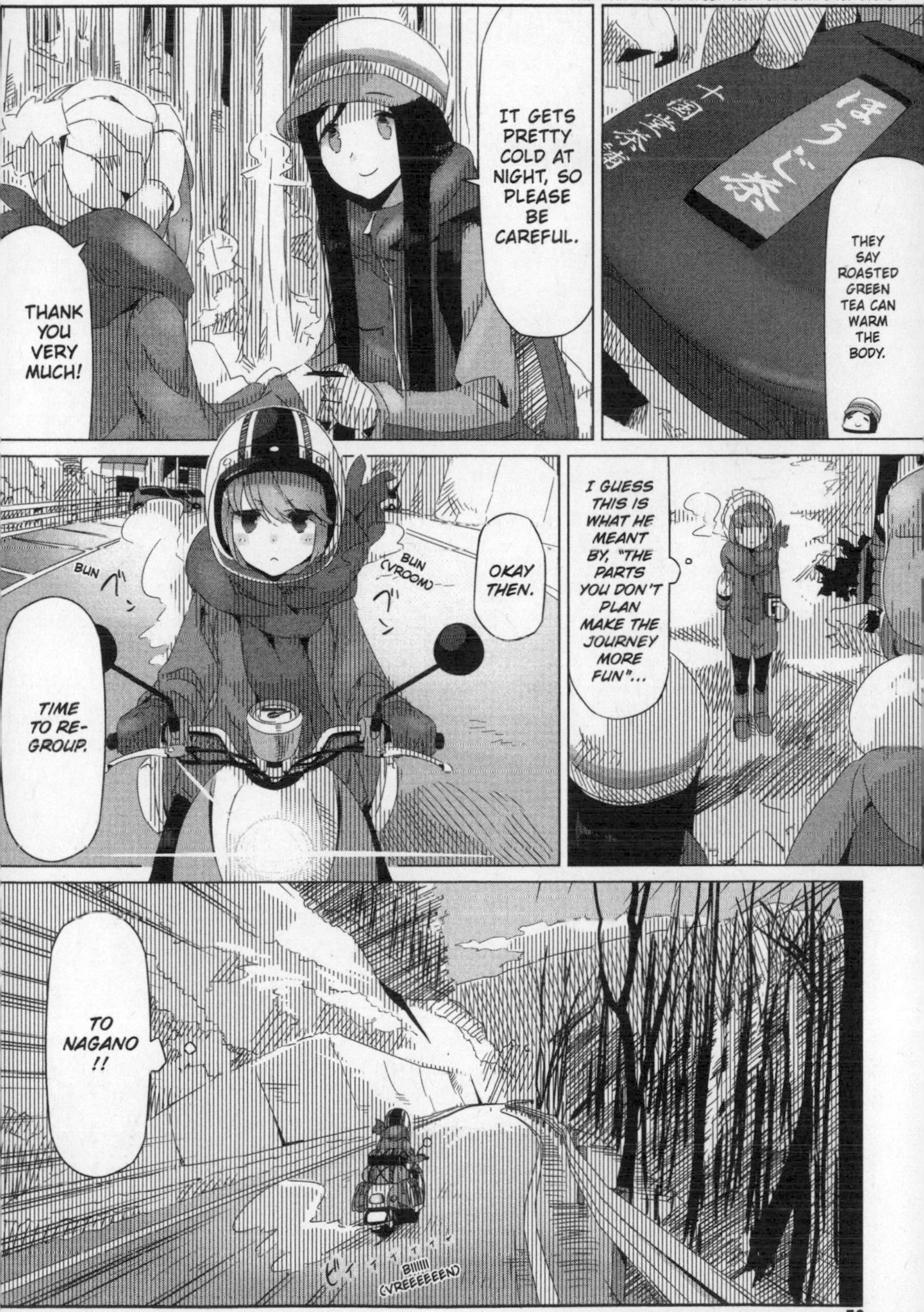
ほうじ茶
THEY SAY ROASTED GREEN TEA CAN WARM THE BODY.
IT GETS PRETTY COLD AT NIGHT, SO PLEASE BE CAREFUL.
THANK YOU VERY MUCH!
I GUESS THIS IS WHAT HE MEANT BY, "THE PARTS YOU DON'T PLAN MAKE THE JOURNEY MORE FUN"...
OKAY THEN.
BUN (VROOM)
BUN
TIME TO RE-GROUP.
TO NAGANO !!
BIIIIII (VREEEEEEN)

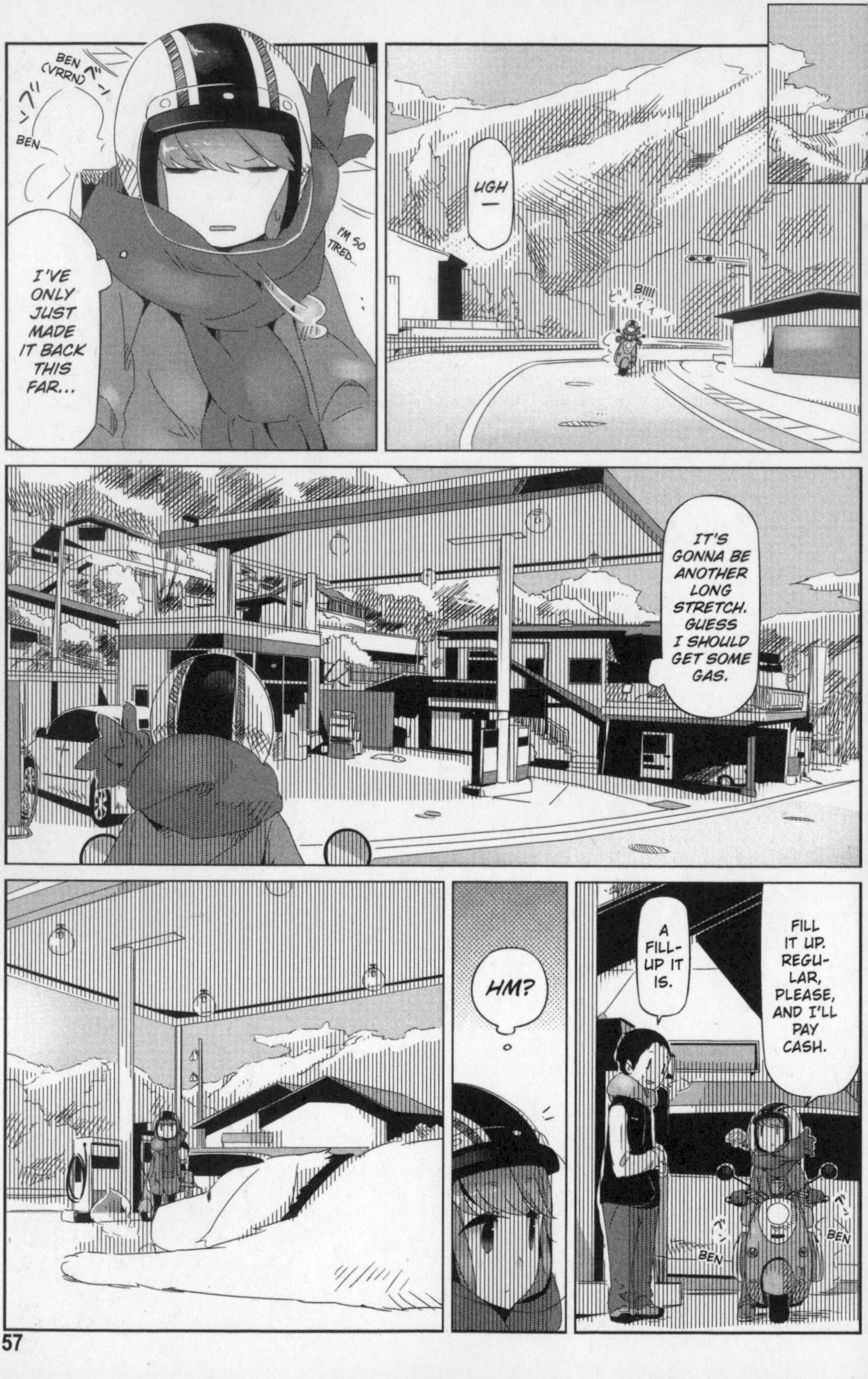
UGH—
BIIII
BEN (VRRN)
BEN
I'M SO TIRED...
I'VE ONLY JUST MADE IT BACK THIS FAR...
IT'S GONNA BE ANOTHER LONG STRETCH. GUESS I SHOULD GET SOME GAS.
FILL IT UP. REGU-LAR, PLEASE, AND I'LL PAY CASH.
A FILL-UP IT IS.
BEN
BEN
HM?

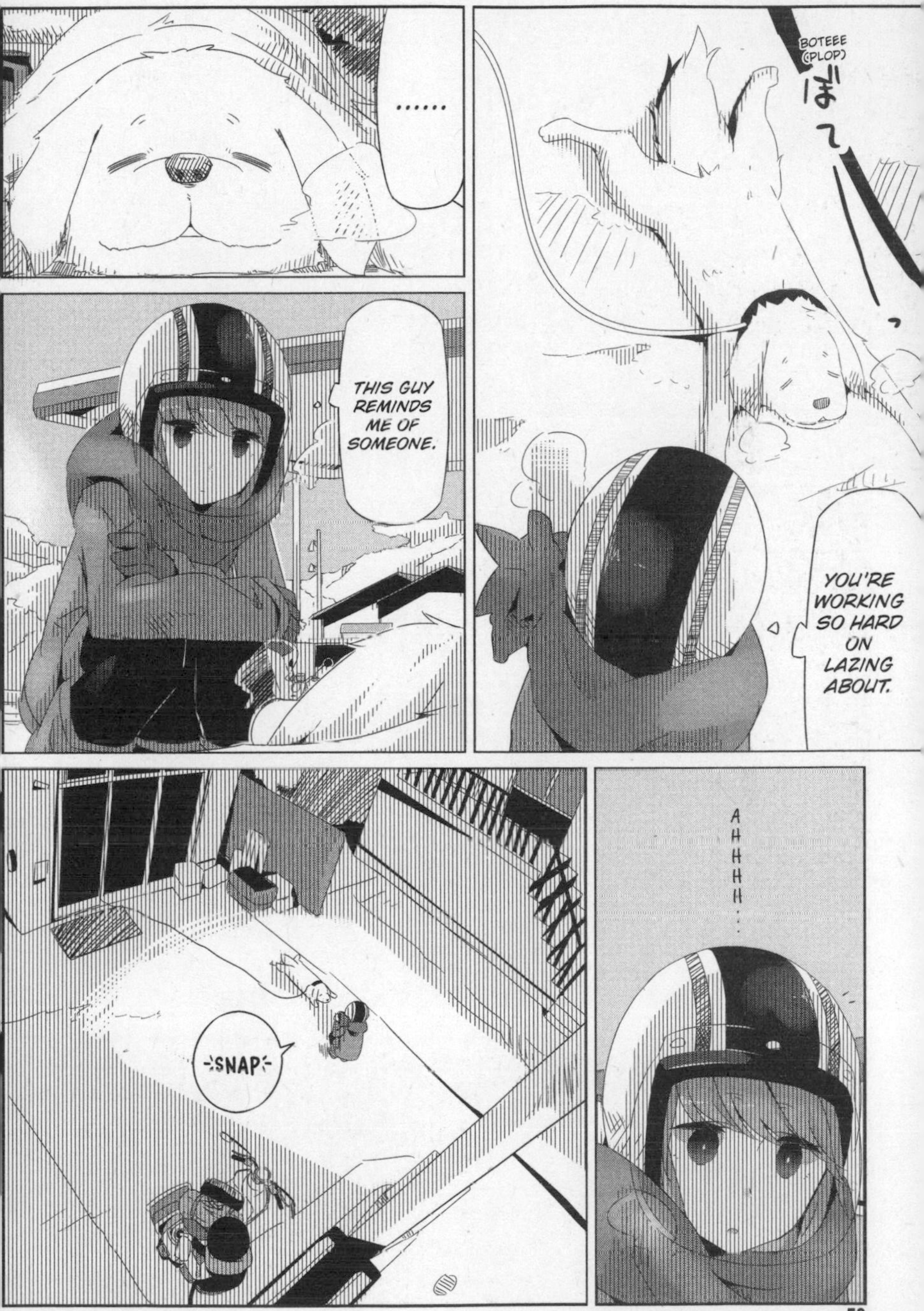
BOTEEE (PLOP)
ぼて
YOU'RE WORKING SO HARD ON LAZING ABOUT.
......
THIS GUY REMINDS ME OF SOMEONE.
AHHHH...
-SNAP-

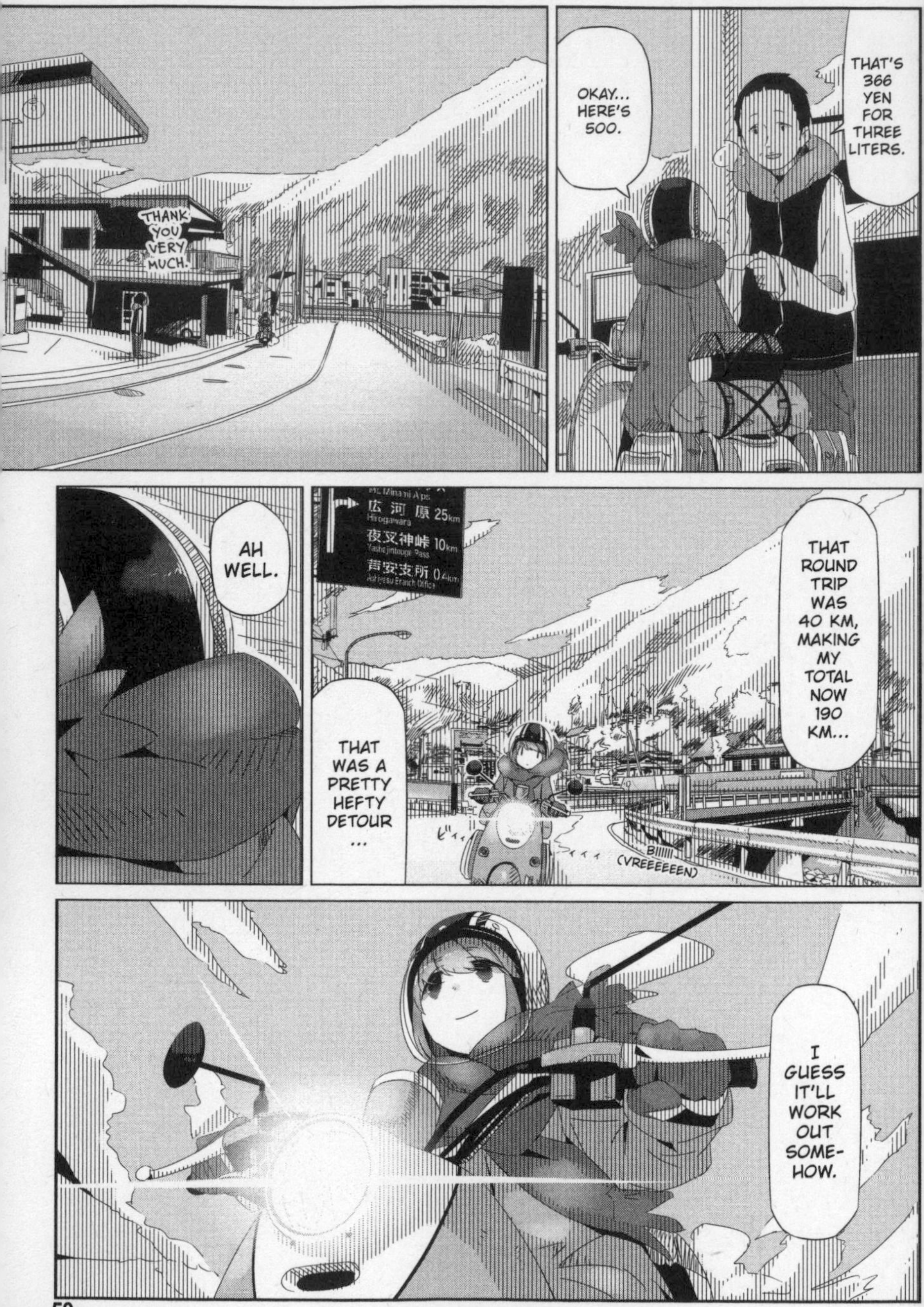

THAT'S 366 YEN FOR THREE LITERS.
OKAY... HERE'S 500.
THANK YOU VERY MUCH.
広河原 25km
Hirogawara
夜叉神峠 10km
Yashajintoge Pass
芦安支所 0.4km
THAT ROUND TRIP WAS 40 KM, MAKING MY TOTAL NOW 190 KM...
THAT WAS A PRETTY HEFTY DETOUR...
ビィィ
ィィィ
BIIIIII (VREEEEEEN)
AH WELL.
I GUESS IT'LL WORK OUT SOME-HOW.

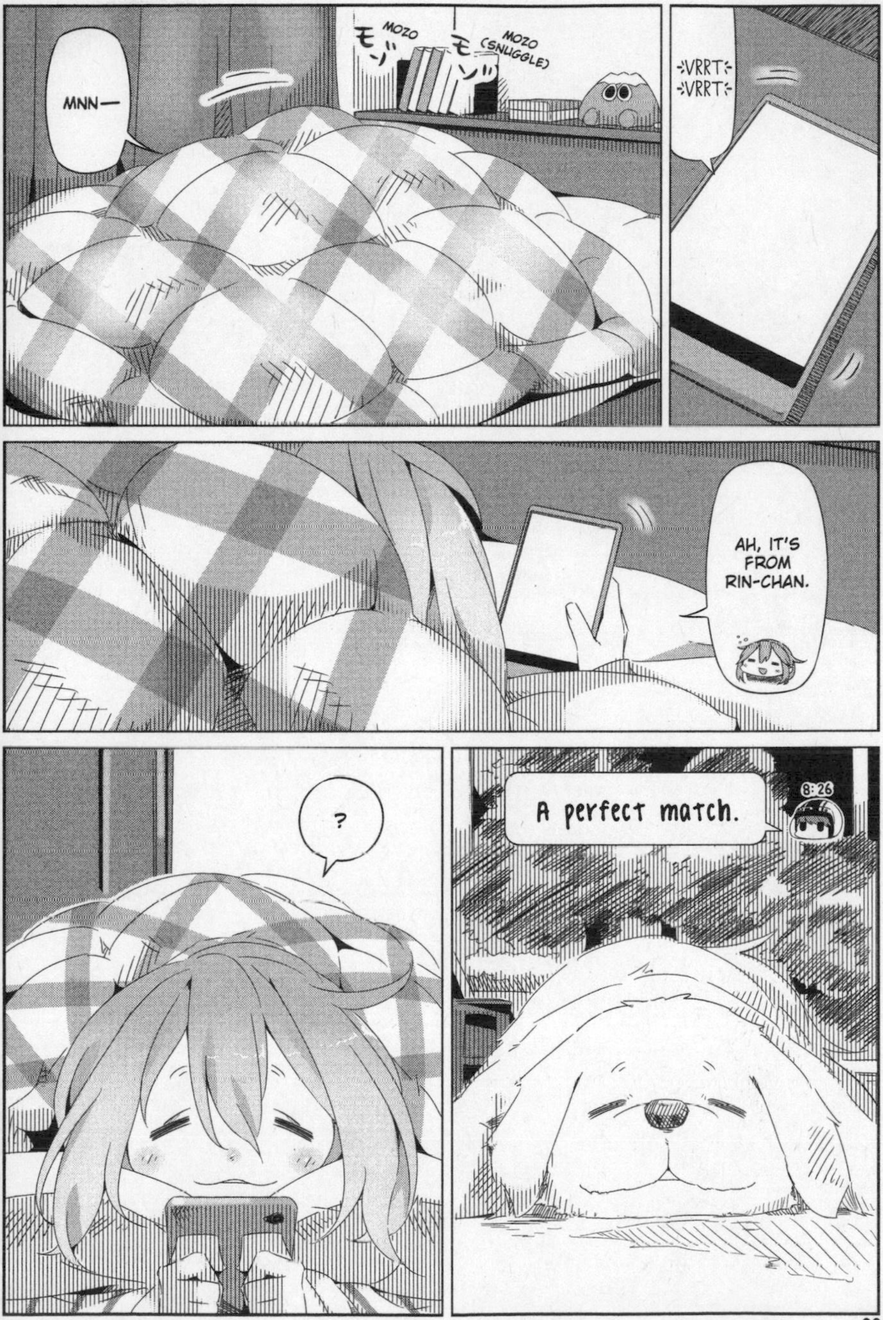
-VRRT-
-VRRT-
MOZO
モゾ
MOZO (SNUGGLE)
モゾ
MNN—
AH, IT'S FROM RIN-CHAN.
8:26
A perfect match.
?

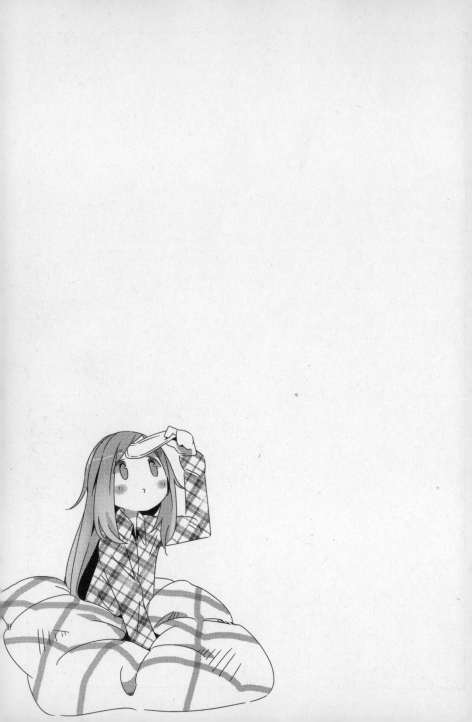

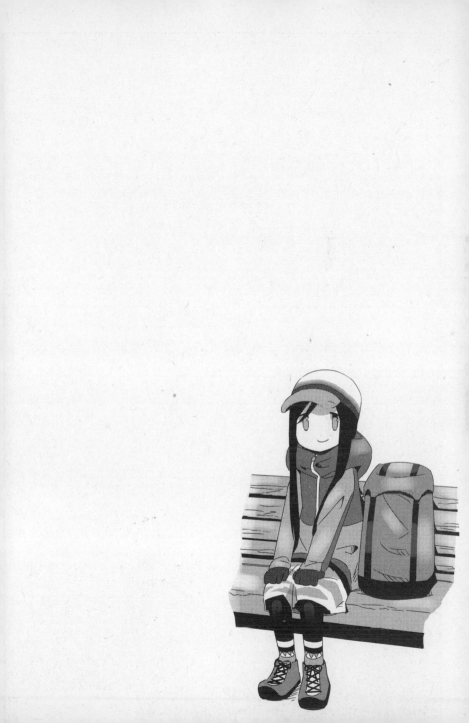

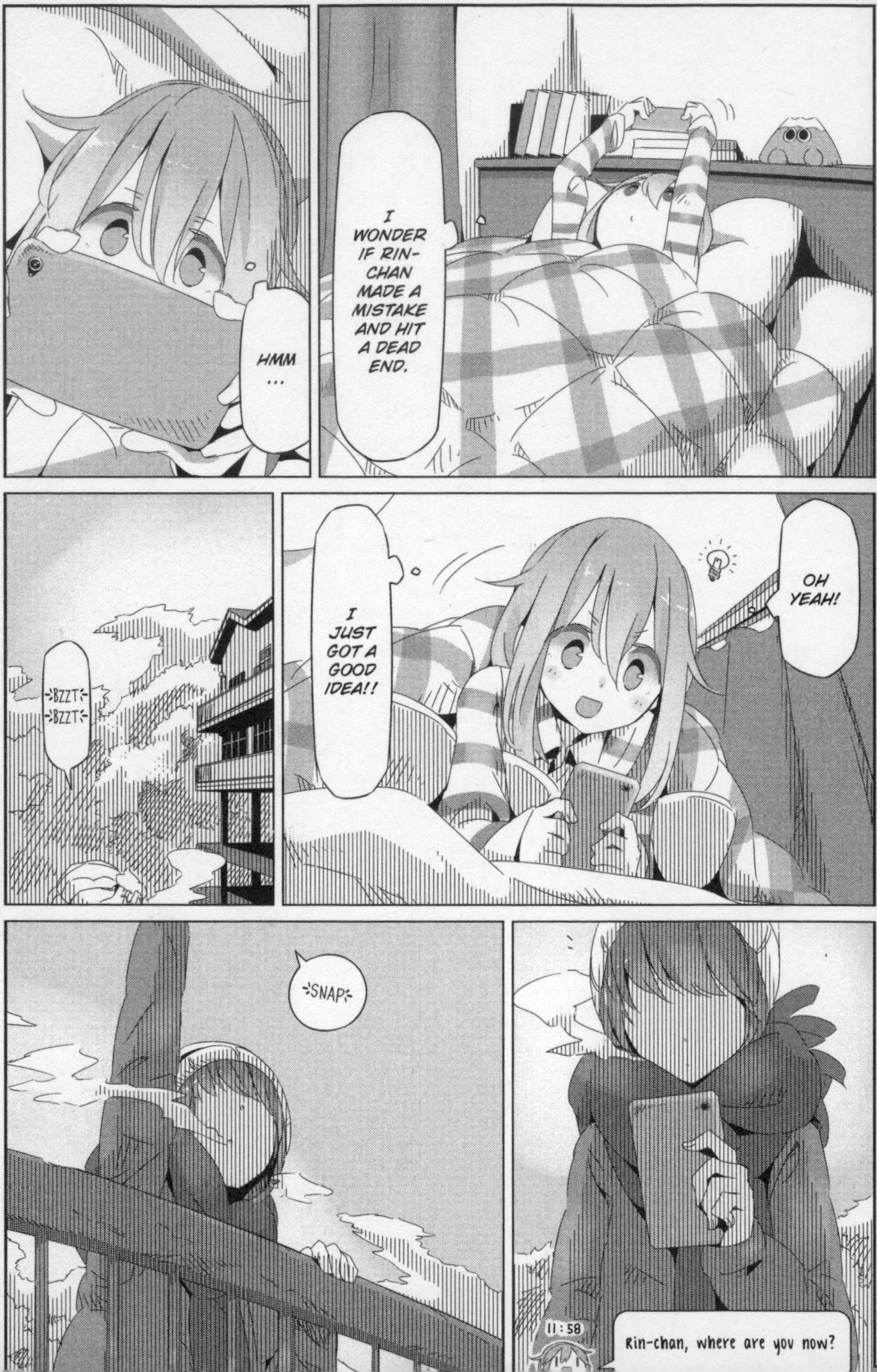
I WONDER IF RIN-CHAN MADE A MISTAKE AND HIT A DEAD END.
HMM...
OH YEAH!
I JUST GOT A GOOD IDEA!!
BZZT BZZT
11:58
Rin-chan, where are you now?
SNAP

CHAPTER 16 NADESHIKO-NAVI RECOMMENDS!

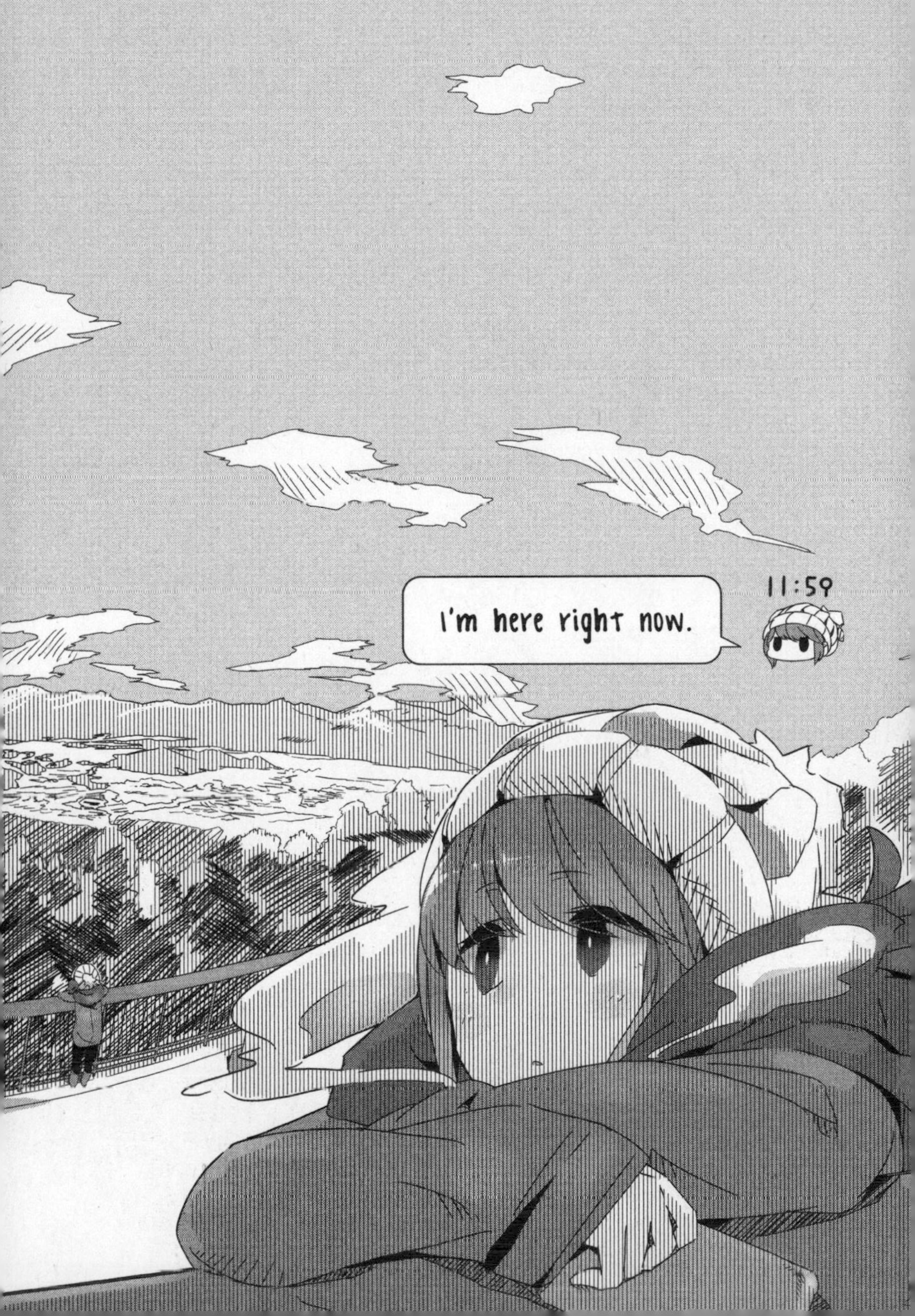
11:59
I'm here right now.

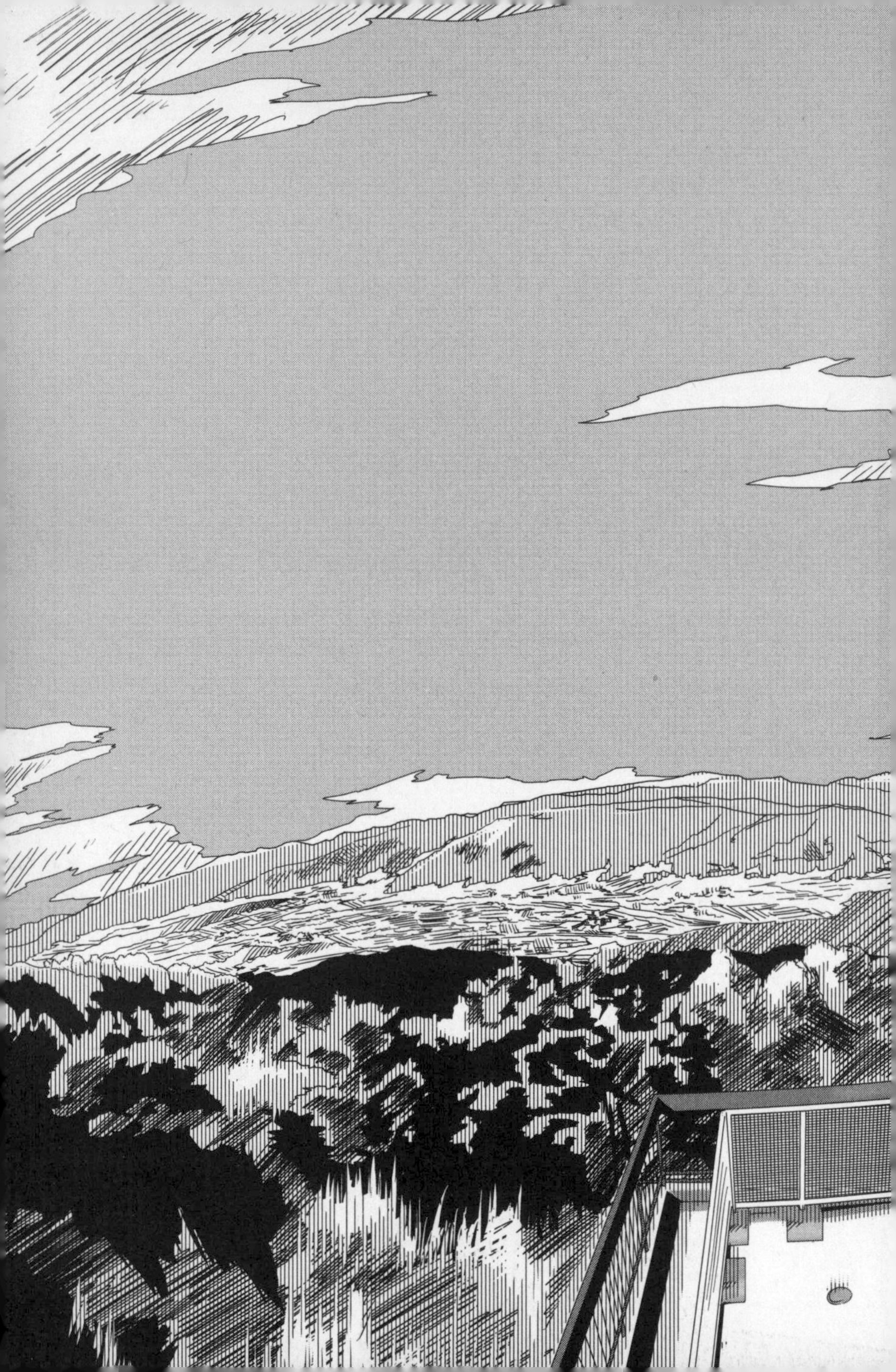

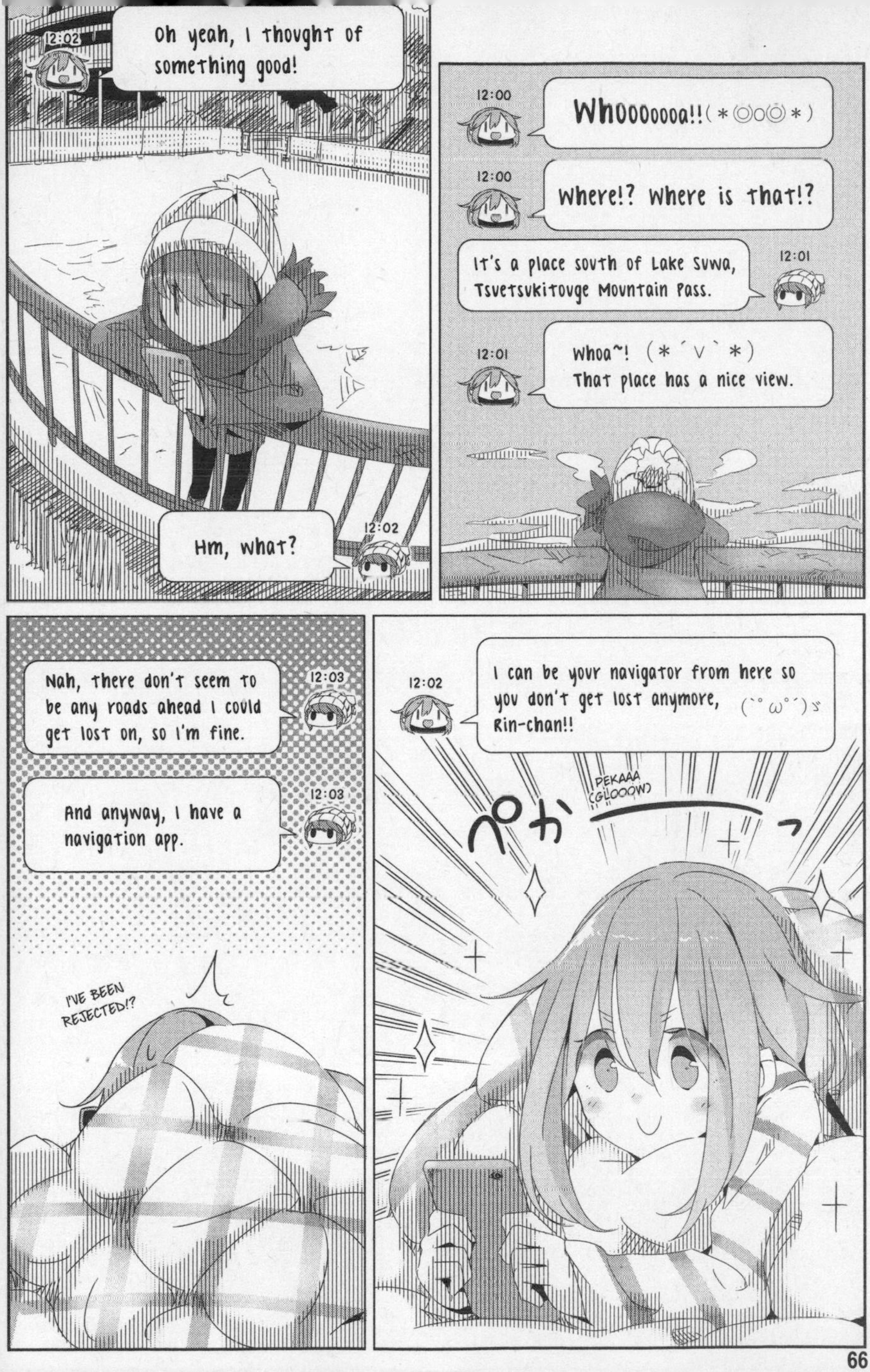
12:00
Whoooooooa!!(*◎o◎*)
12:00
Where!? Where is that!?
12:01
It's a place south of Lake Suwa, Tsuetsukitouge Mountain Pass.
12:01
Whoa~! (*´v`*) That place has a nice view.
12:02
Oh yeah, I thought of something good!
12:02
Hm, what?
12:02
I can be your navigator from here so you don't get lost anymore, Rin-chan!! (゜ω゜)ゞ
ぺかーっ
PEKAAA (GLOOOW)
12:03
Nah, there don't seem to be any roads ahead I could get lost on, so I'm fine.
12:03
And anyway, I have a navigation app.
I'VE BEEN REJECTED!?

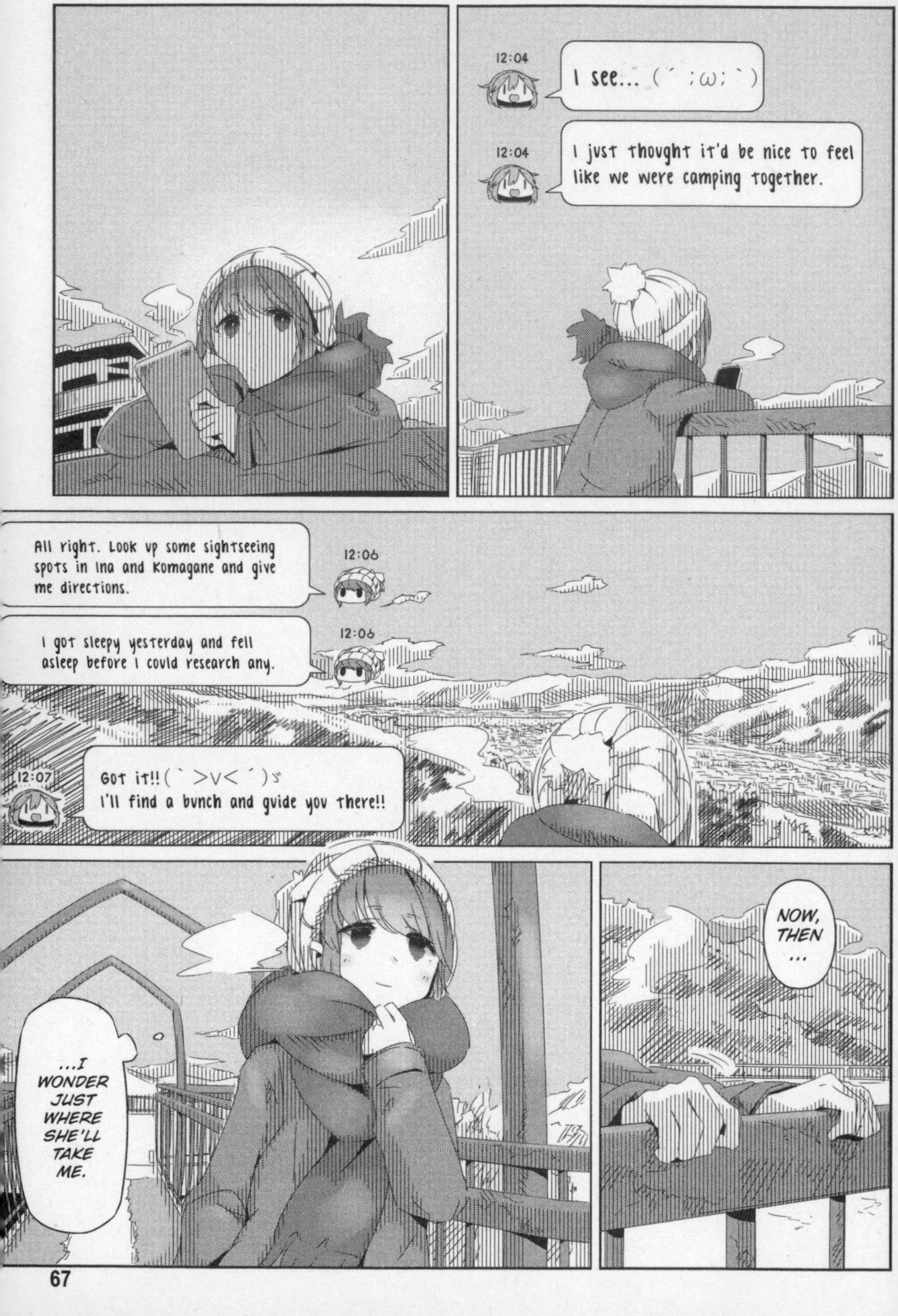
12:04
I see... (´ ;ω; `)
12:04
I just thought it'd be nice to feel like we were camping together.
All right. Look up some sightseeing spots in Ina and Komagane and give me directions.
12:06
I got sleepy yesterday and fell asleep before I could research any.
12:06
12:07
Got it!! (` >v< ´)ゞ
I'll find a bunch and guide you there!!
NOW, THEN ...
...I WONDER JUST WHERE SHE'LL TAKE ME.

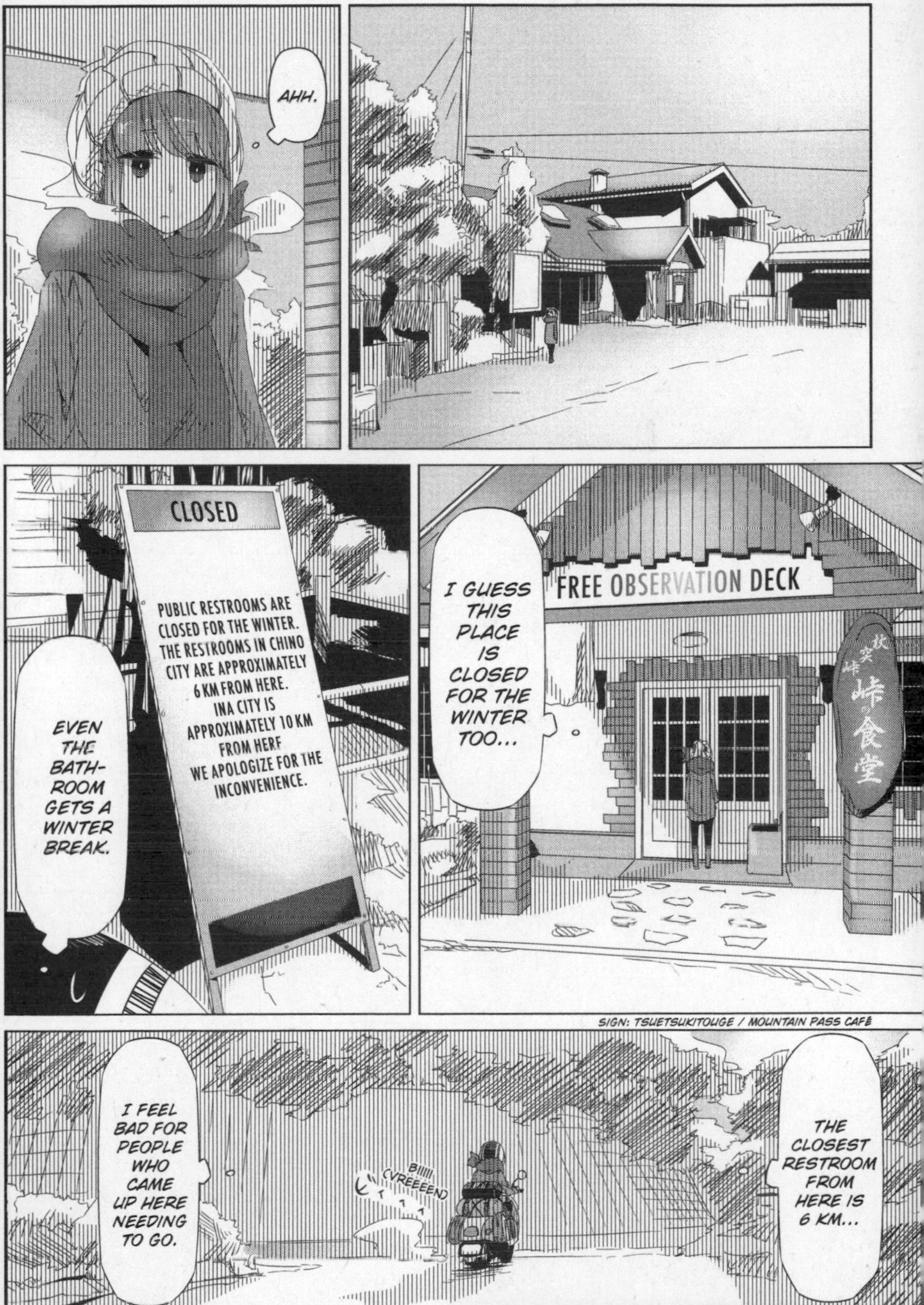
AHH.
I GUESS THIS PLACE IS CLOSED FOR THE WINTER TOO...
FREE OBSERVATION DECK
杖突峠
峠の食堂
CLOSED
PUBLIC RESTROOMS ARE CLOSED FOR THE WINTER. THE RESTROOMS IN CHINO CITY ARE APPROXIMATELY 6 KM FROM HERE. INA CITY IS APPROXIMATELY 10 KM FROM HERE. WE APOLOGIZE FOR THE INCONVENIENCE.
EVEN THE BATHROOM GETS A WINTER BREAK.
SIGN: TSUETSUKITOUGE / MOUNTAIN PASS CAFÉ
THE CLOSEST RESTROOM FROM HERE IS 6 KM...
BIIIII (VREEEEEN)
I FEEL BAD FOR PEOPLE WHO CAME UP HERE NEEDING TO GO.

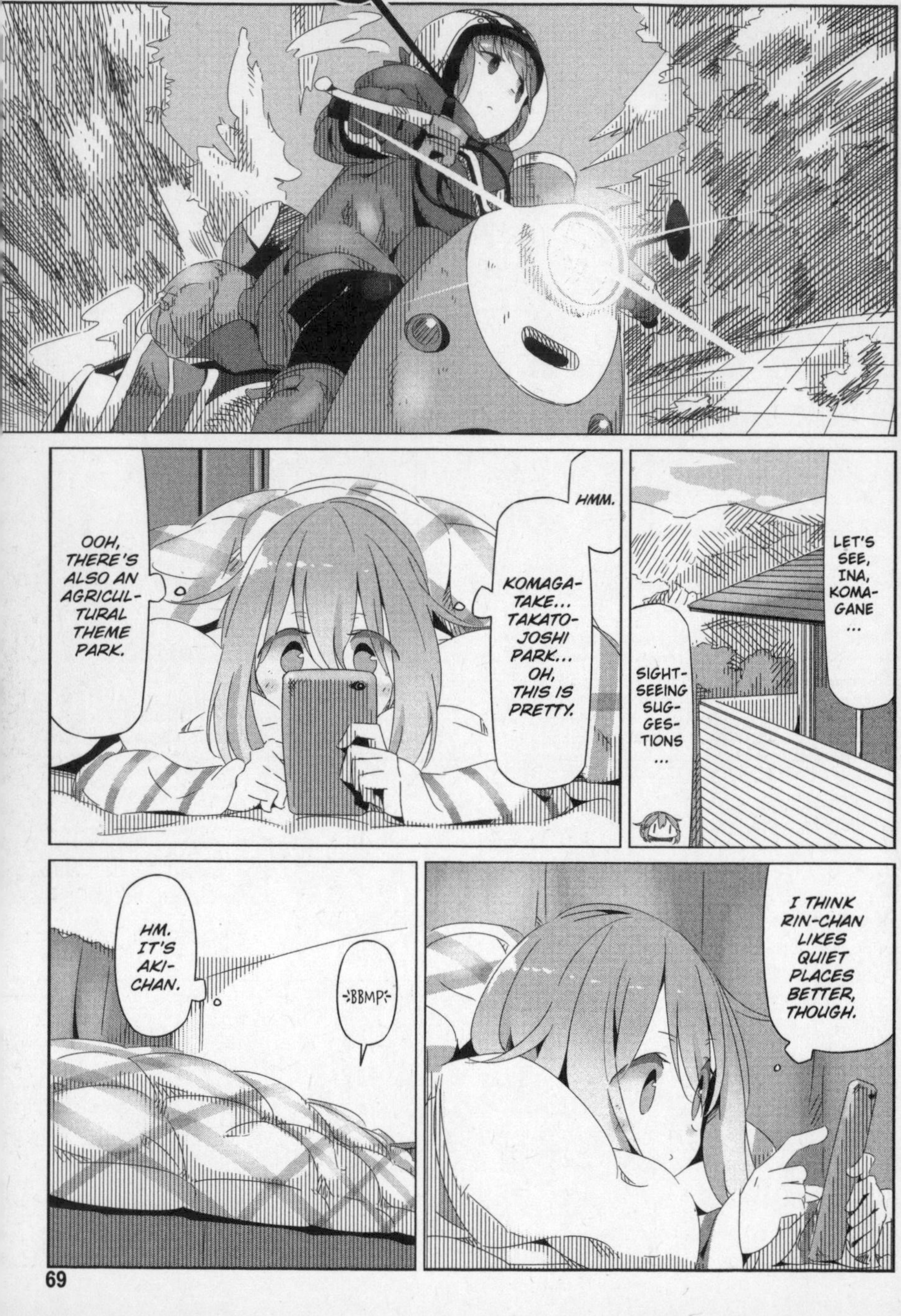

LET'S SEE, INA, KOMAGANE...
SIGHTSEEING SUGGESTIONS...
HMM.
KOMAGATAKE... TAKATOJOSHI PARK... OH, THIS IS PRETTY.
OOH, THERE'S ALSO AN AGRICULTURAL THEME PARK.
I THINK RIN-CHAN LIKES QUIET PLACES BETTER, THOUGH.
-BBMP-
HM. IT'S AKI-CHAN.

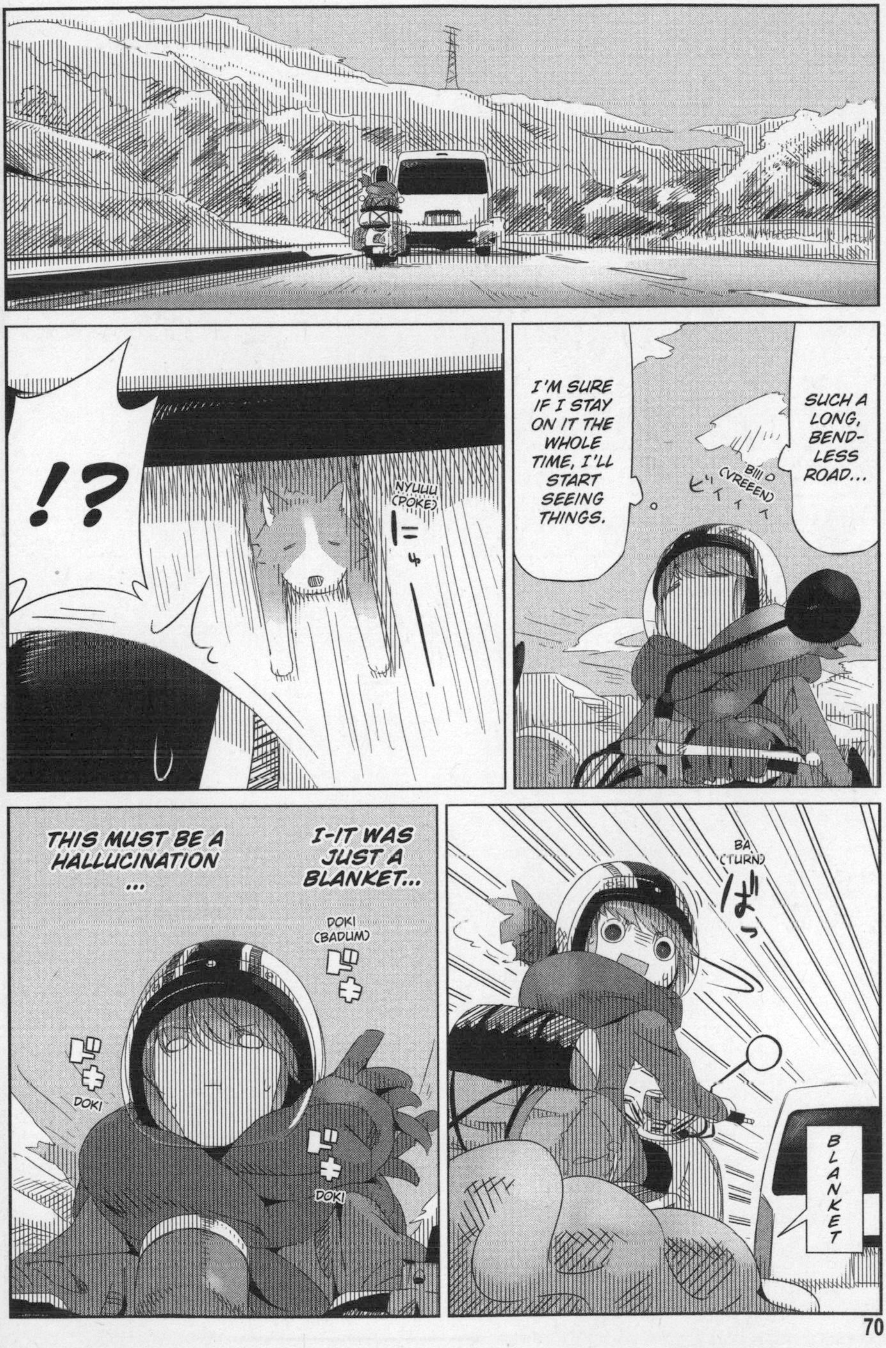
SUCH A LONG, BENDLESS ROAD...
I'M SURE IF I STAY ON IT THE WHOLE TIME, I'LL START SEEING THINGS.
BIII (VREEEN)
ビィイイ
NYUUU (POKE)
にゅ
!?
BA (TURN)
ばっ
BLANKET
I-IT WAS JUST A BLANKET...
THIS MUST BE A HALLUCINATION ...
DOKI (BADUM)
ドキ
ドキ
DOKI
ドキ
DOKI

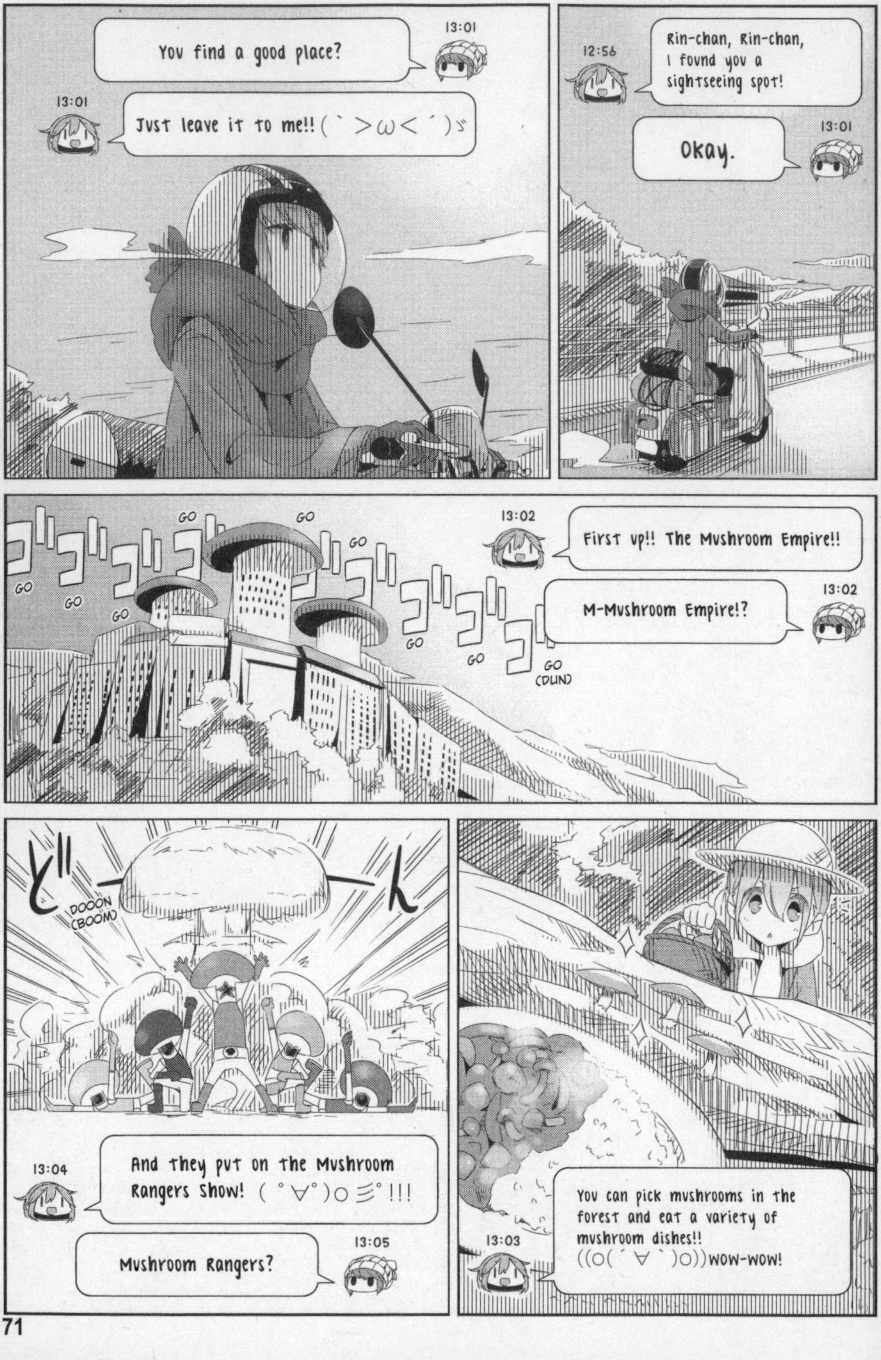
12:56
Rin-chan, Rin-chan, I found you a sightseeing spot!
13:01
Okay.
13:01
You find a good place?
13:01
Just leave it to me!! (｀>ω<´)ゞ
13:02
First up!! The Mushroom Empire!!
13:02
M-Mushroom Empire!?
GO GO GO GO GO GO GO GO GO
(DUN)
13:03
You can pick mushrooms in the forest and eat a variety of mushroom dishes!! ((o(´∀`)o))Wow-wow!
DOOON (BOOM)
13:04
And they put on the Mushroom Rangers Show! (ﾟ∀ﾟ)o彡ﾟ!!!
13:05
Mushroom Rangers?

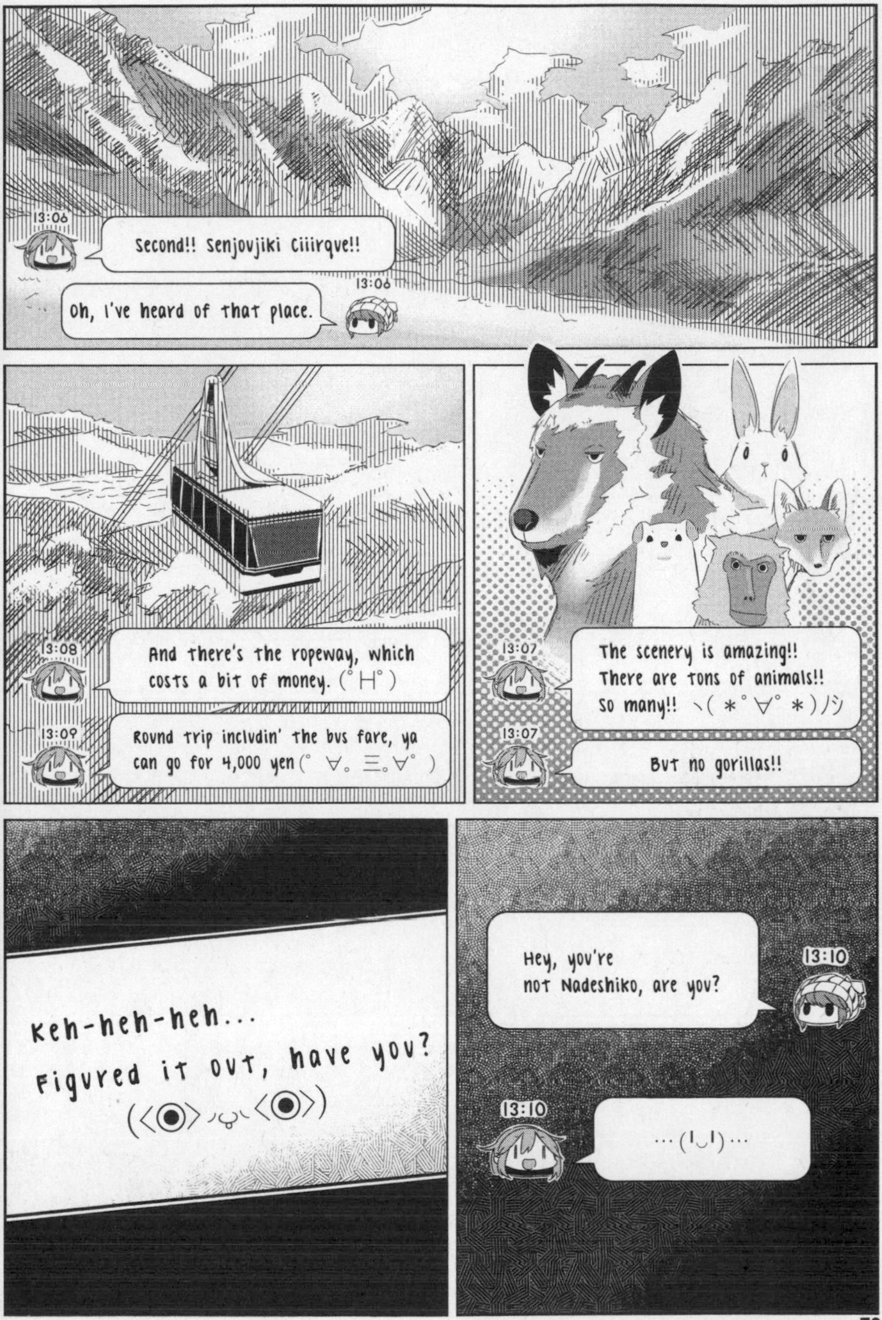
13:06
Second!! Senjoujiki Ciiirque!!
13:06
Oh, I've heard of that place.
13:07
The scenery is amazing!! There are tons of animals!! So many!! ヽ(*°∀°*)ノシ
13:07
But no gorillas!!
13:08
And there's the ropeway, which costs a bit of money. (°H°)
13:09
Round trip includin' the bus fare, ya can go for 4,000 yen (° ∀。三。∀°)
13:10
Hey, you're not Nadeshiko, are you?
13:10
...(I◡I)...
Keh-heh-heh...
Figured it out, have you?
(<◉>ںڡں<◉>)

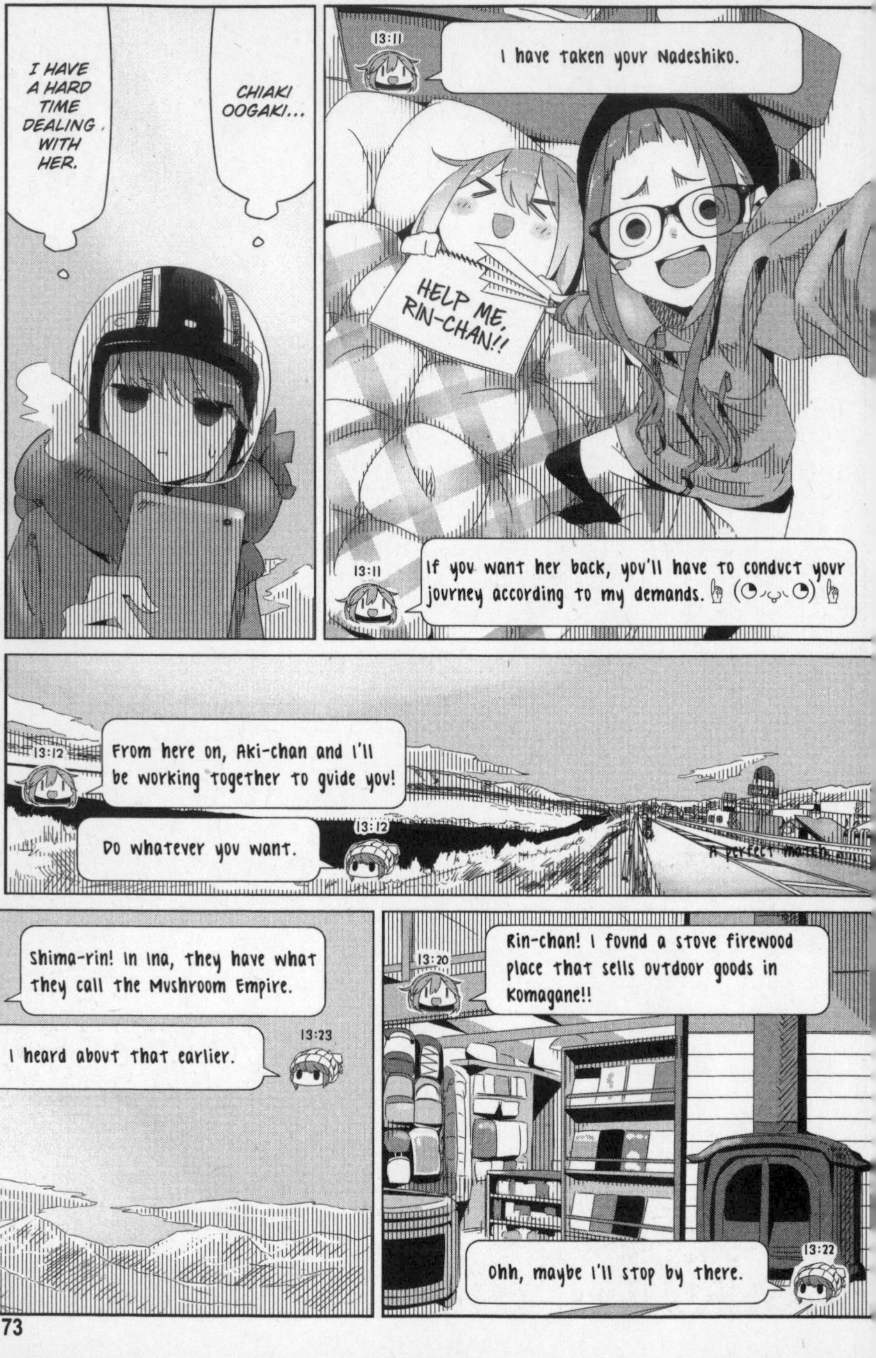
13:11
I have taken your Nadeshiko.
HELP ME, RIN-CHAN!!
13:11
If you want her back, you'll have to conduct your journey according to my demands.
CHIAKI OOGAKI...
I HAVE A HARD TIME DEALING WITH HER.
13:12
From here on, Aki-chan and I'll be working together to guide you!
13:12
Do whatever you want.
A perfect match.
13:20
Rin-chan! I found a stove firewood place that sells outdoor goods in Komagane!!
13:22
Ohh, maybe I'll stop by there.
13:23
Shima-rin! In Ina, they have what they call the Mushroom Empire.
13:23
I heard about that earlier.

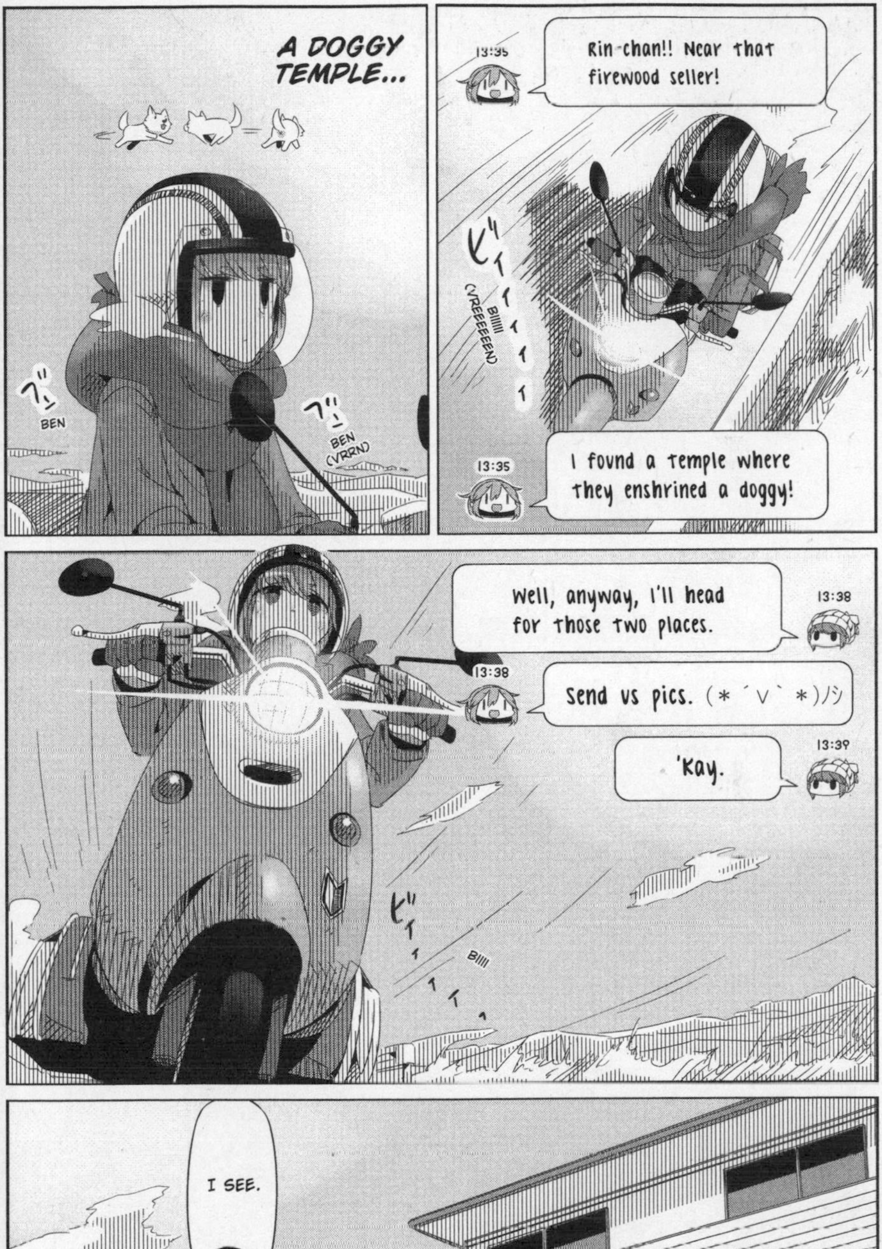
13:35
Rin-chan!! Near that firewood seller!
BIIIII (VREEEEEEN)
13:35
I found a temple where they enshrined a doggy!
A DOGGY TEMPLE...
BEN
BEN (VRRN)
13:38
Well, anyway, I'll head for those two places.
13:38
Send us pics. (*´∨`*)ノシ
13:39
'Kay.
BIIII
I SEE.

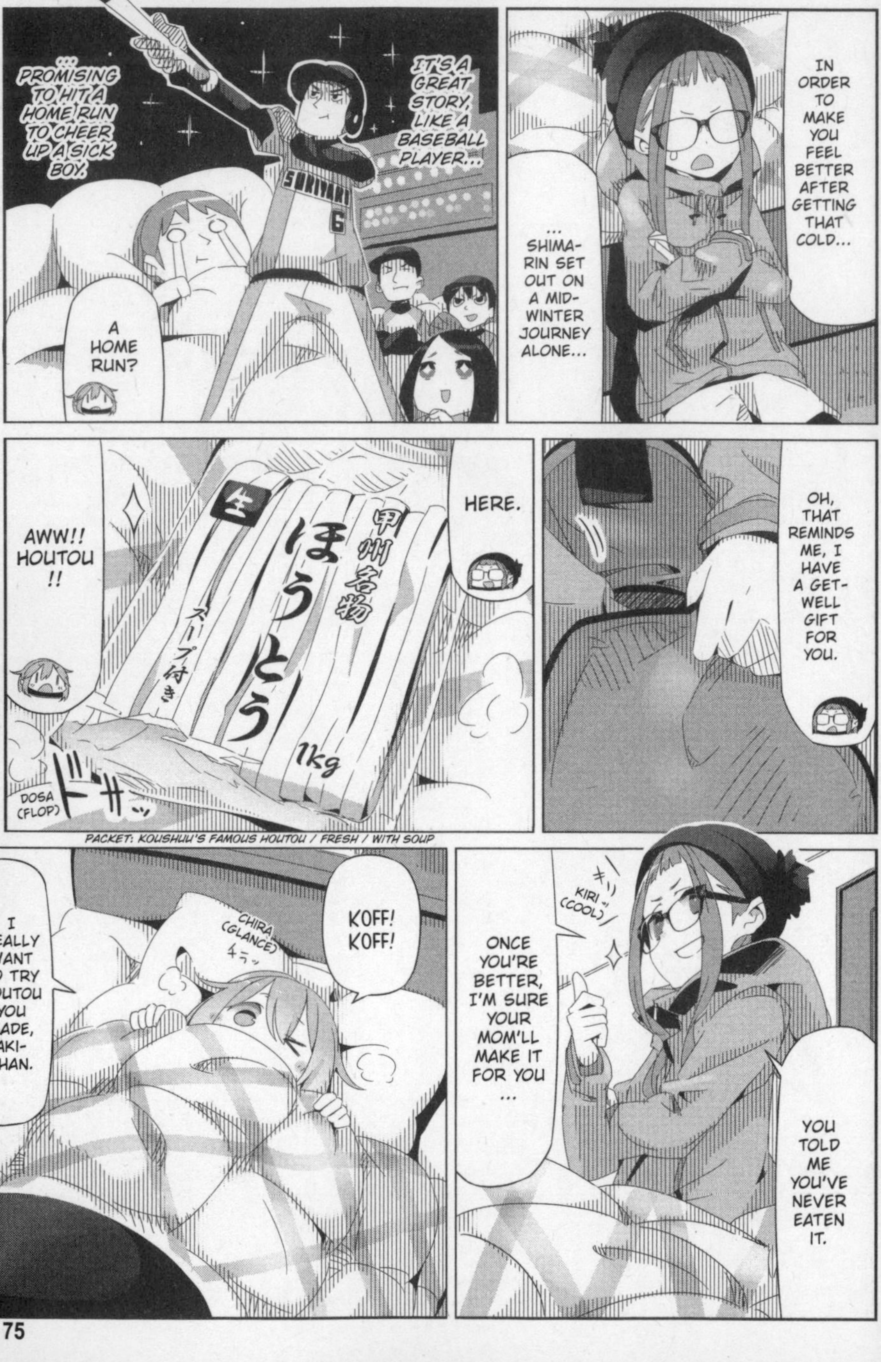
IN ORDER TO MAKE YOU FEEL BETTER AFTER GETTING THAT COLD...
...SHIMA-RIN SET OUT ON A MID-WINTER JOURNEY ALONE...
IT'S A GREAT STORY, LIKE A BASEBALL PLAYER...
...PROMISING TO HIT A HOME RUN TO CHEER UP A SICK BOY.
A HOME RUN?
OH, THAT REMINDS ME, I HAVE A GET-WELL GIFT FOR YOU.
HERE.
AWW!! HOUTOU!!
甲州名物
生
ほうとう
スープ付き
1kg
DOSA (FLOP)
ドサッ
PACKET: KOUSHUU'S FAMOUS HOUTOU / FRESH / WITH SOUP
KIRI (COOL)
キリッ
ONCE YOU'RE BETTER, I'M SURE YOUR MOM'LL MAKE IT FOR YOU...
YOU TOLD ME YOU'VE NEVER EATEN IT.
KOFF! KOFF!
CHIRA (GLANCE)
チラッ
I REALLY WANT TO TRY HOUTOU YOU MADE, AKI-CHAN.

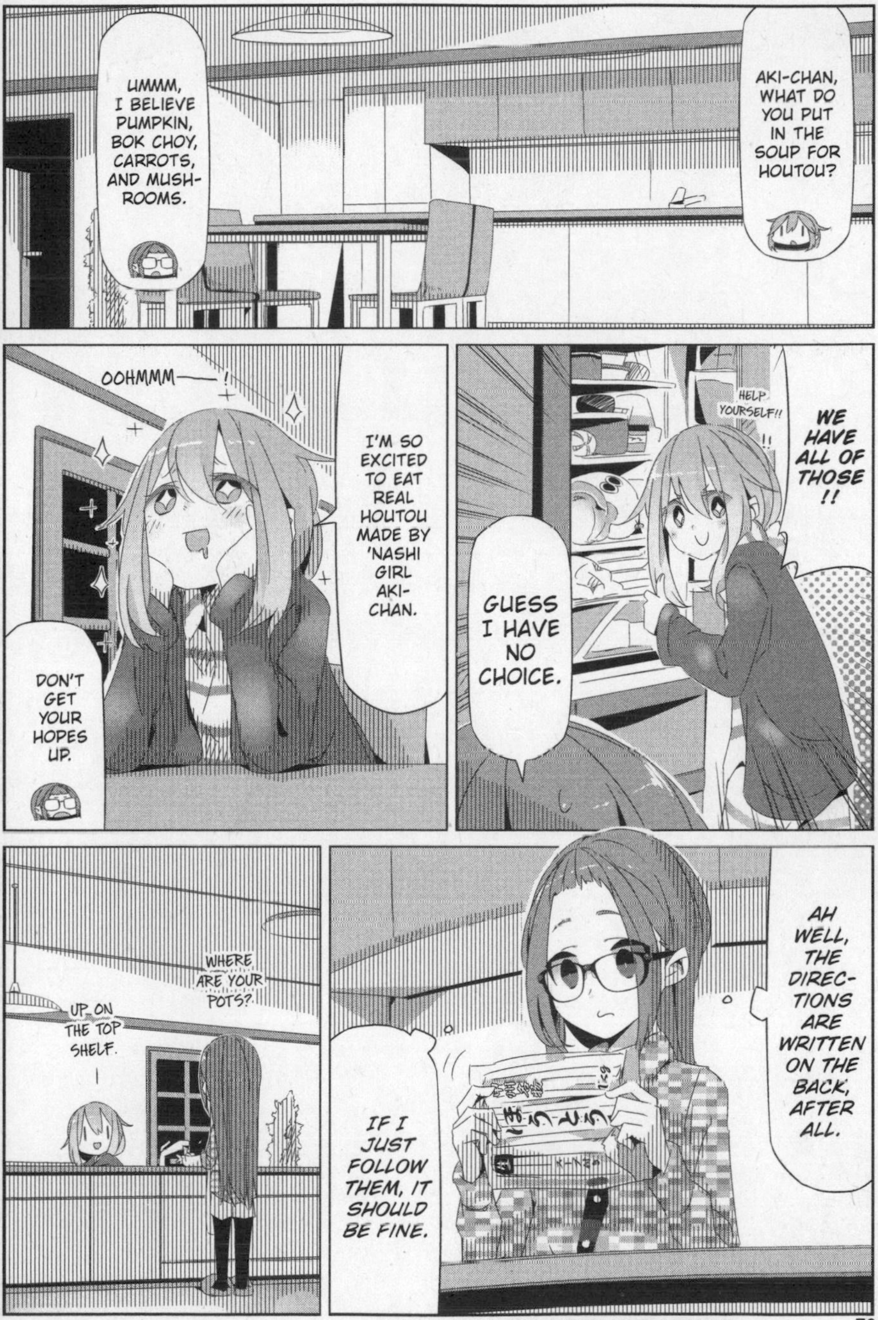
AKI-CHAN, WHAT DO YOU PUT IN THE SOUP FOR HOUTOU?
UMMM, I BELIEVE PUMPKIN, BOK CHOY, CARROTS, AND MUSH-ROOMS.
WE HAVE ALL OF THOSE!!
HELP YOURSELF!!
!!
GUESS I HAVE NO CHOICE.
OOHMMM—!
I'M SO EXCITED TO EAT REAL HOUTOU MADE BY 'NASHI GIRL AKI-CHAN.
DON'T GET YOUR HOPES UP.
AH WELL, THE DIRECTIONS ARE WRITTEN ON THE BACK, AFTER ALL.
IF I JUST FOLLOW THEM, IT SHOULD BE FINE.
WHERE ARE YOUR POTS?
UP ON THE TOP SHELF.
!

PACKET: KOUSHUU'S FAMOUS HOUTOU / FRESH / WITH SOUP

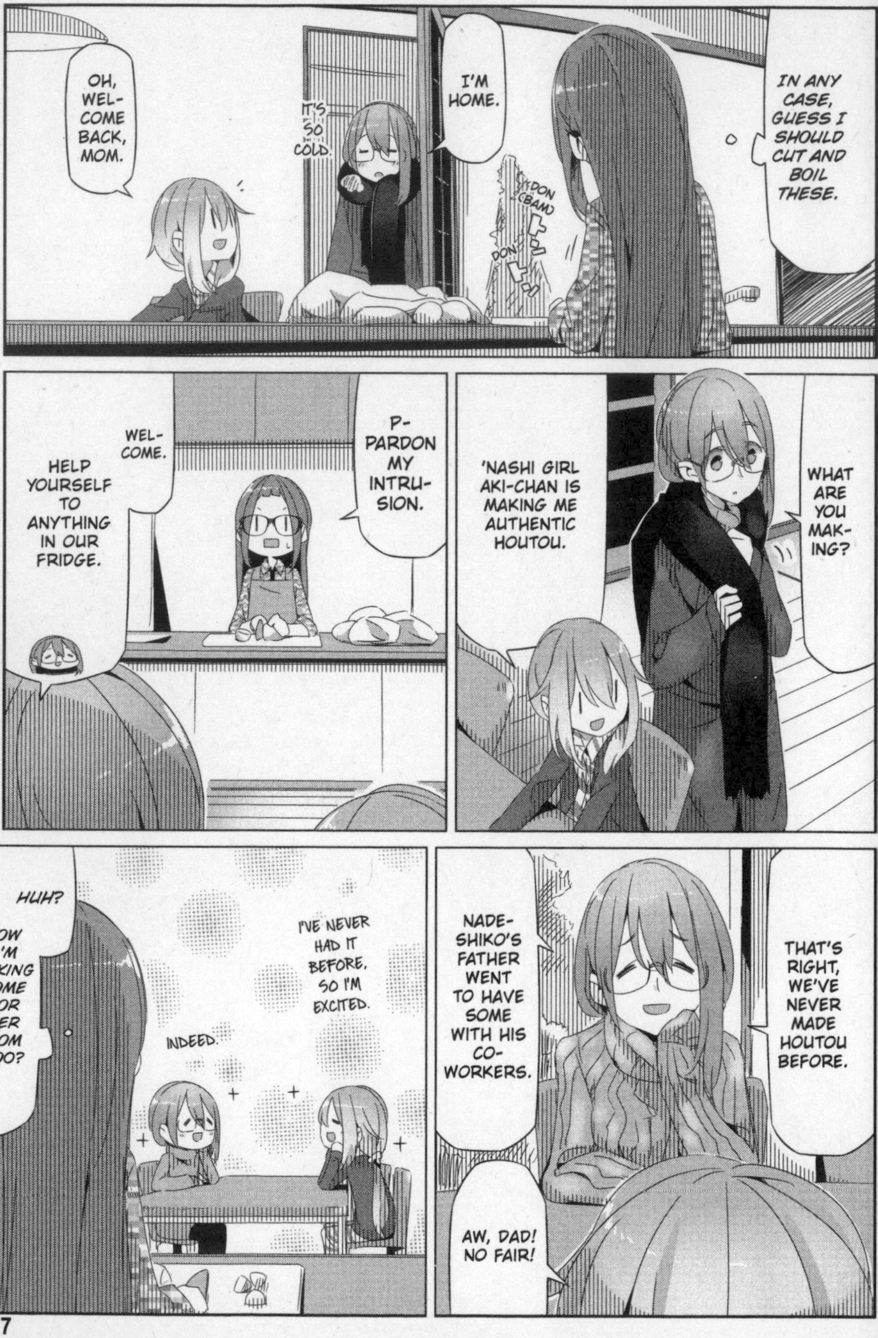
IN ANY CASE, GUESS I SHOULD CUT AND BOIL THESE.
DON (BAM)
DON
I'M HOME.
IT'S SO COLD.
OH, WEL-COME BACK, MOM.
WHAT ARE YOU MAK-ING?
'NASHI GIRL AKI-CHAN IS MAKING ME AUTHENTIC HOUTOU.
P-PARDON MY INTRU-SION.
WEL-COME.
HELP YOURSELF TO ANYTHING IN OUR FRIDGE.
THAT'S RIGHT, WE'VE NEVER MADE HOUTOU BEFORE.
NADE-SHIKO'S FATHER WENT TO HAVE SOME WITH HIS CO-WORKERS.
AW, DAD! NO FAIR!
I'VE NEVER HAD IT BEFORE, SO I'M EXCITED.
INDEED.
HUH?
NOW I'M MAKING SOME FOR HER MOM TOO?

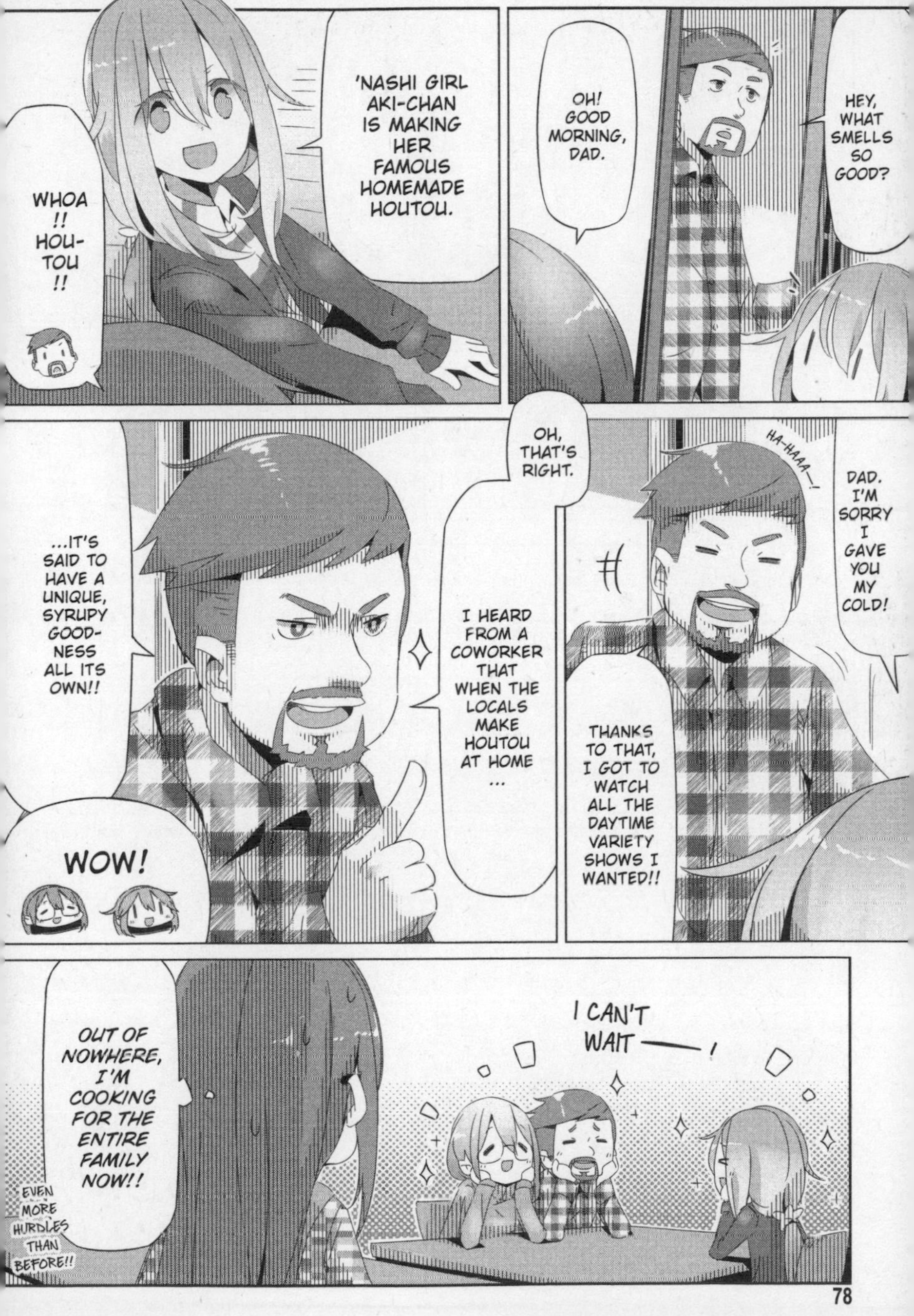
HEY, WHAT SMELLS SO GOOD?
OH! GOOD MORNING, DAD.
'NASHI GIRL AKI-CHAN IS MAKING HER FAMOUS HOMEMADE HOUTOU.
WHOA!! HOU-TOU!!
HA-HAAA—!
DAD. I'M SORRY I GAVE YOU MY COLD!
THANKS TO THAT, I GOT TO WATCH ALL THE DAYTIME VARIETY SHOWS I WANTED!!
OH, THAT'S RIGHT.
I HEARD FROM A COWORKER THAT WHEN THE LOCALS MAKE HOUTOU AT HOME...
...IT'S SAID TO HAVE A UNIQUE, SYRUPY GOODNESS ALL ITS OWN!!
WOW!
I CAN'T WAIT—!
OUT OF NOWHERE, I'M COOKING FOR THE ENTIRE FAMILY NOW!!
EVEN MORE HURDLES THAN BEFORE!!

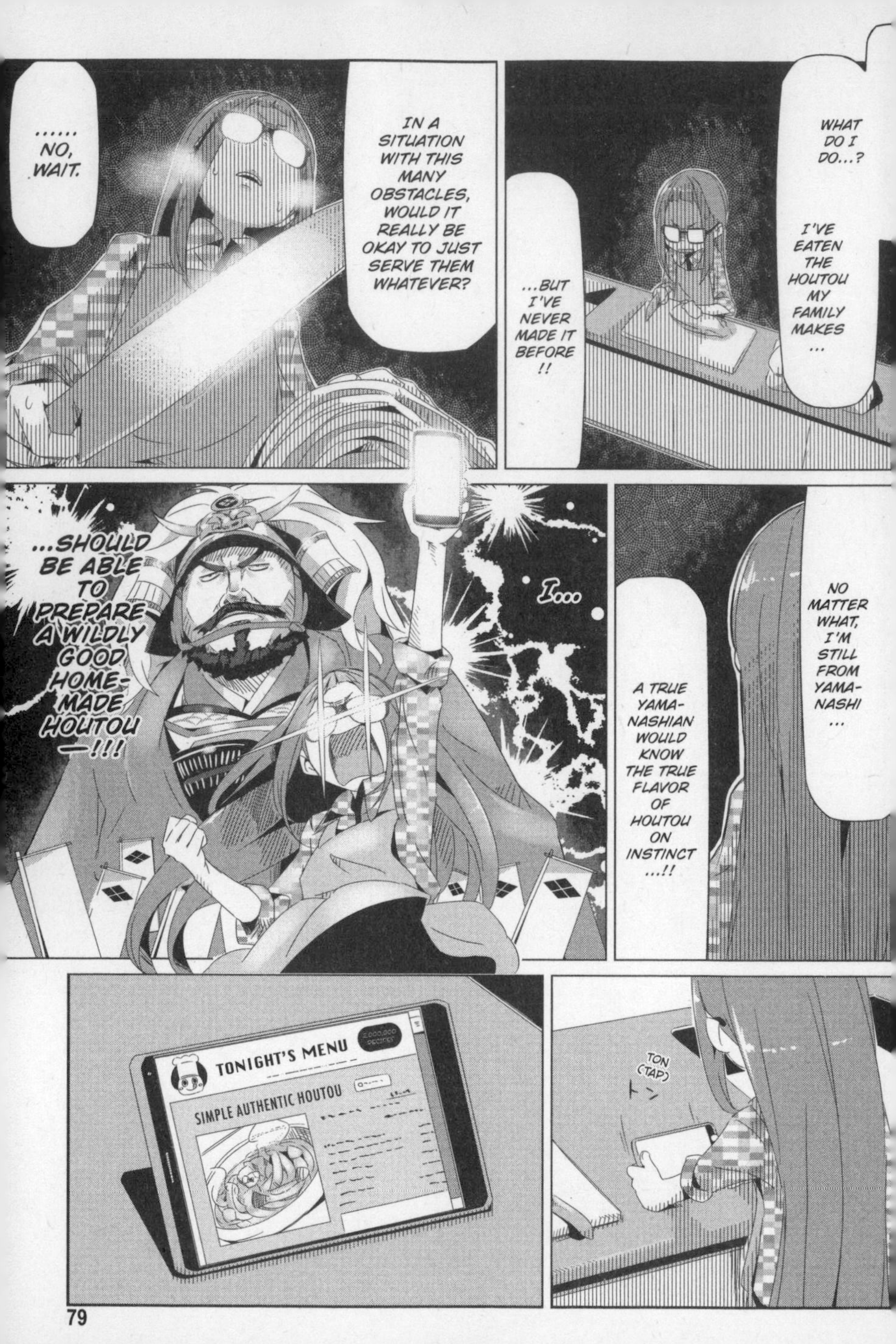
WHAT DO I DO...?
I'VE EATEN THE HOUTOU MY FAMILY MAKES...
...BUT I'VE NEVER MADE IT BEFORE!!
IN A SITUATION WITH THIS MANY OBSTACLES, WOULD IT REALLY BE OKAY TO JUST SERVE THEM WHATEVER?
......NO, WAIT.
NO MATTER WHAT, I'M STILL FROM YAMA-NASHI...
A TRUE YAMA-NASHIAN WOULD KNOW THE TRUE FLAVOR OF HOUTOU ON INSTINCT...!!
I...
...SHOULD BE ABLE TO PREPARE A WILDLY GOOD HOME-MADE HOUTOU—!!!
TON (TAP)
TONIGHT'S MENU
SIMPLE AUTHENTIC HOUTOU

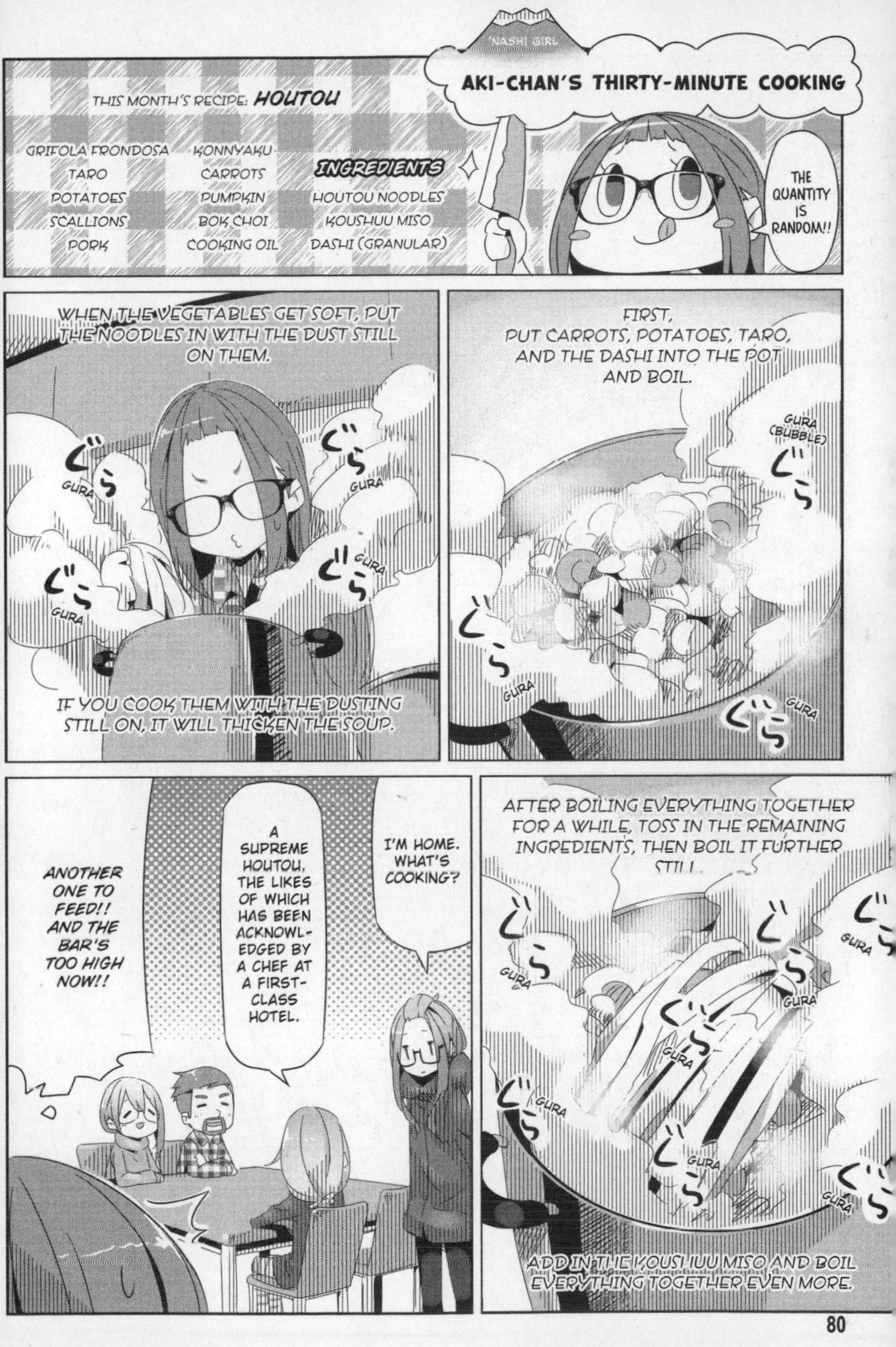
'NASHI GIRL
AKI-CHAN'S THIRTY-MINUTE COOKING
THE QUANTITY IS RANDOM!!
THIS MONTH'S RECIPE: HOUTOU
INGREDIENTS
HOUTOU NOODLES
KOUSHUU MISO
DASHI (GRANULAR)
KONNYAKU
CARROTS
PUMPKIN
BOK CHOI
COOKING OIL
GRIFOLA FRONDOSA
TARO
POTATOES
SCALLIONS
PORK
FIRST, PUT CARROTS, POTATOES, TARO, AND THE DASHI INTO THE POT AND BOIL.
GURA (BUBBLE)
GURA
GURA
WHEN THE VEGETABLES GET SOFT, PUT THE NOODLES IN WITH THE DUST STILL ON THEM.
GURA
GURA
GURA
GURA
IF YOU COOK THEM WITH THE DUSTING STILL ON, IT WILL THICKEN THE SOUP.
AFTER BOILING EVERYTHING TOGETHER FOR A WHILE, TOSS IN THE REMAINING INGREDIENTS, THEN BOIL IT FURTHER STILL.
GURA
GURA
GURA
GURA
GURA
GURA
GURA
ADD IN THE KOUSHUU MISO AND BOIL EVERYTHING TOGETHER EVEN MORE.
I'M HOME. WHAT'S COOKING?
A SUPREME HOUTOU, THE LIKES OF WHICH HAS BEEN ACKNOWLEDGED BY A CHEF AT A FIRST-CLASS HOTEL.
ANOTHER ONE TO FEED!! AND THE BAR'S TOO HIGH NOW!!

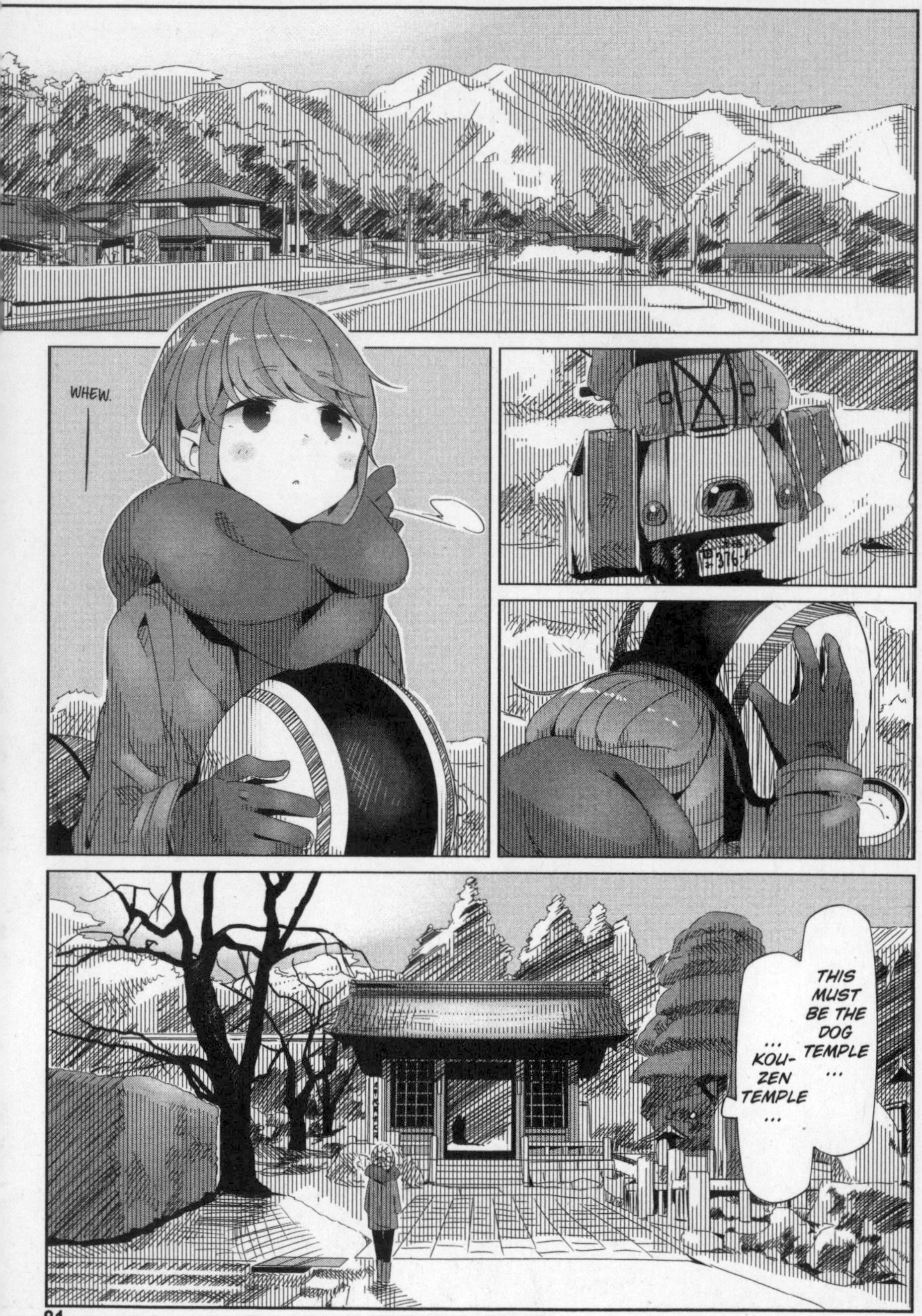
WHEW.
THIS MUST BE THE DOG TEMPLE ...
... KOU-ZEN TEMPLE ...

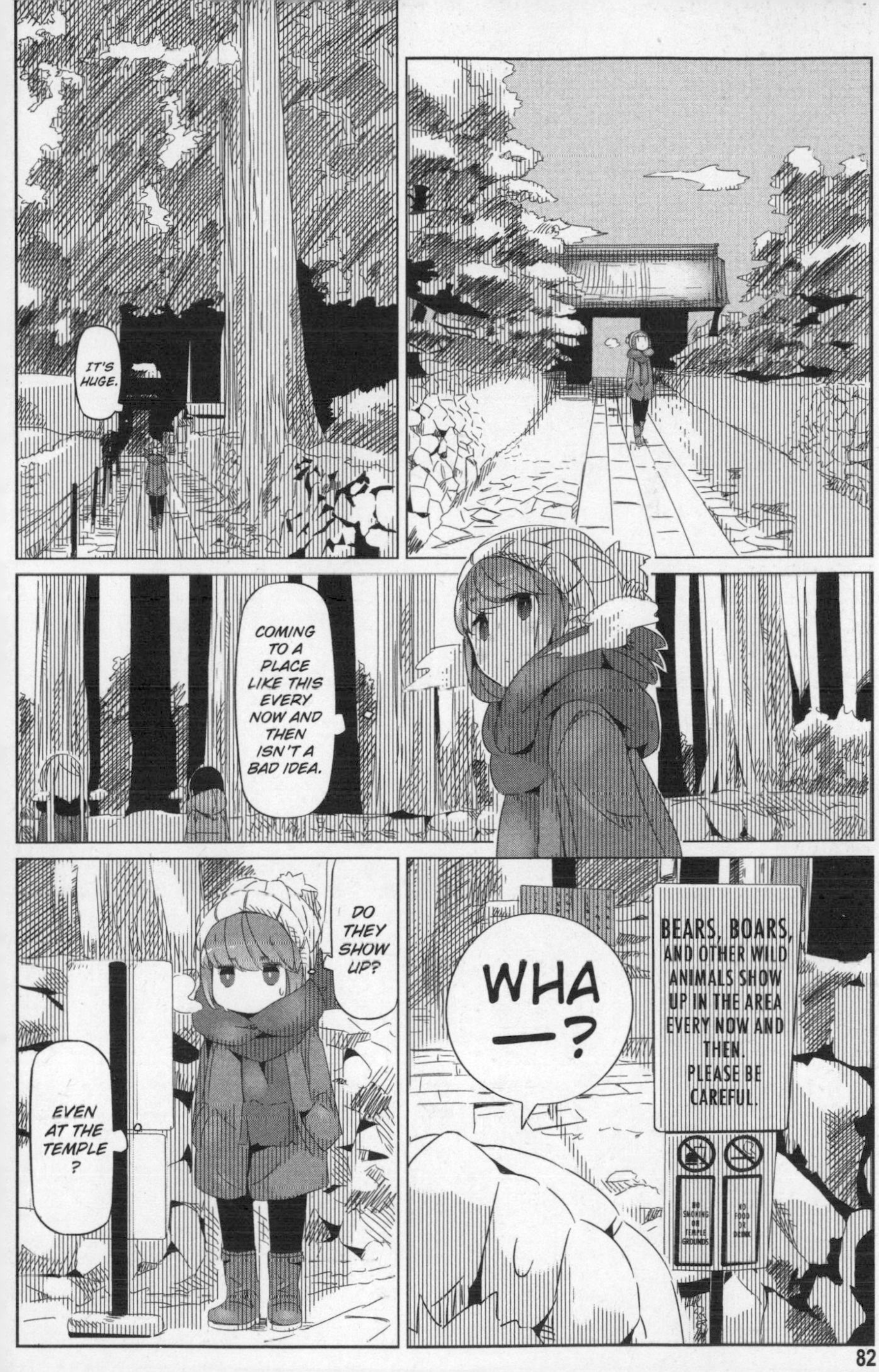
IT'S HUGE.
COMING TO A PLACE LIKE THIS EVERY NOW AND THEN ISN'T A BAD IDEA.
BEARS, BOARS, AND OTHER WILD ANIMALS SHOW UP IN THE AREA EVERY NOW AND THEN. PLEASE BE CAREFUL.
NO SMOKING ON TEMPLE GROUNDS
NO FOOD OR DRINK
WHA —?
DO THEY SHOW UP?
EVEN AT THE TEMPLE ?

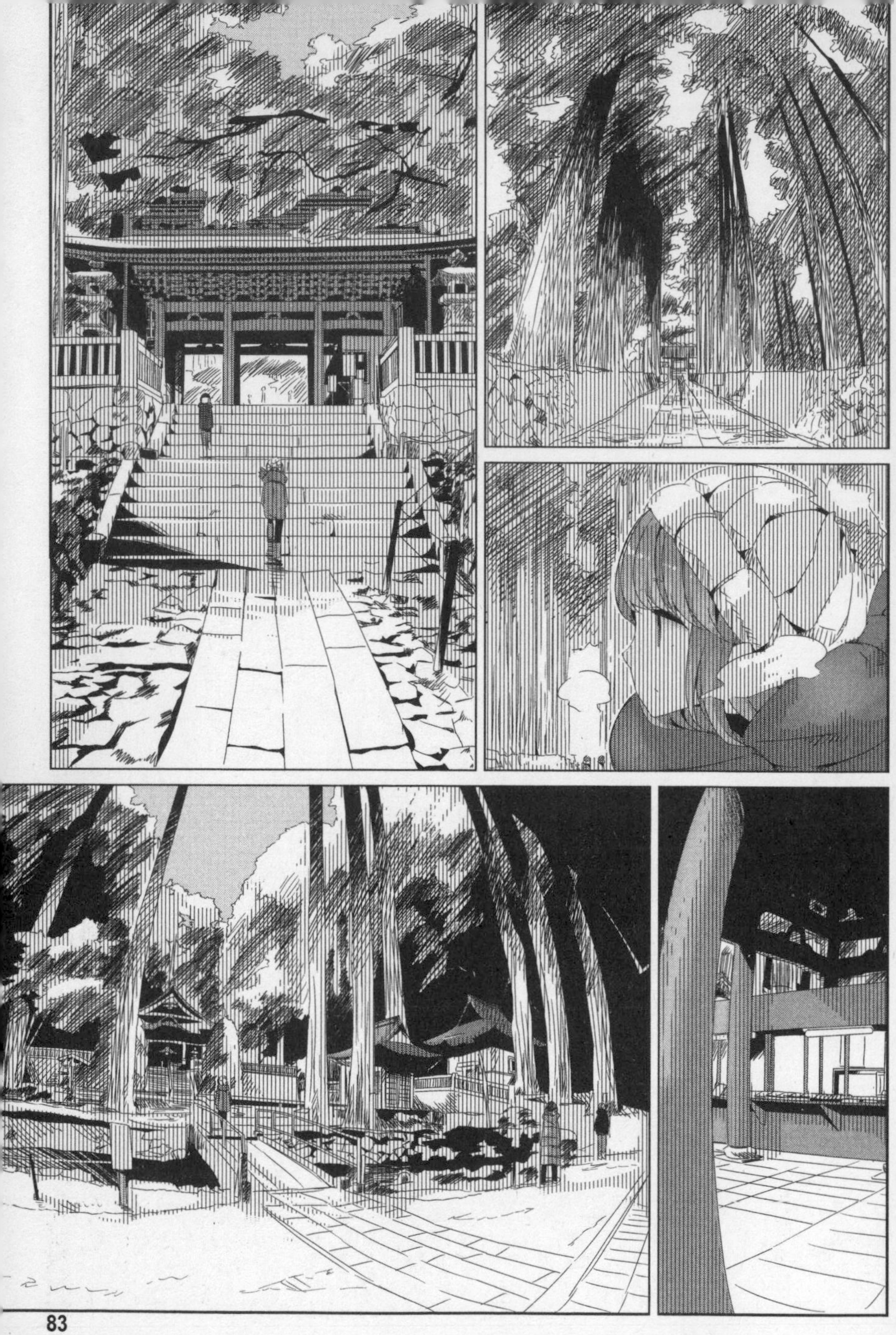

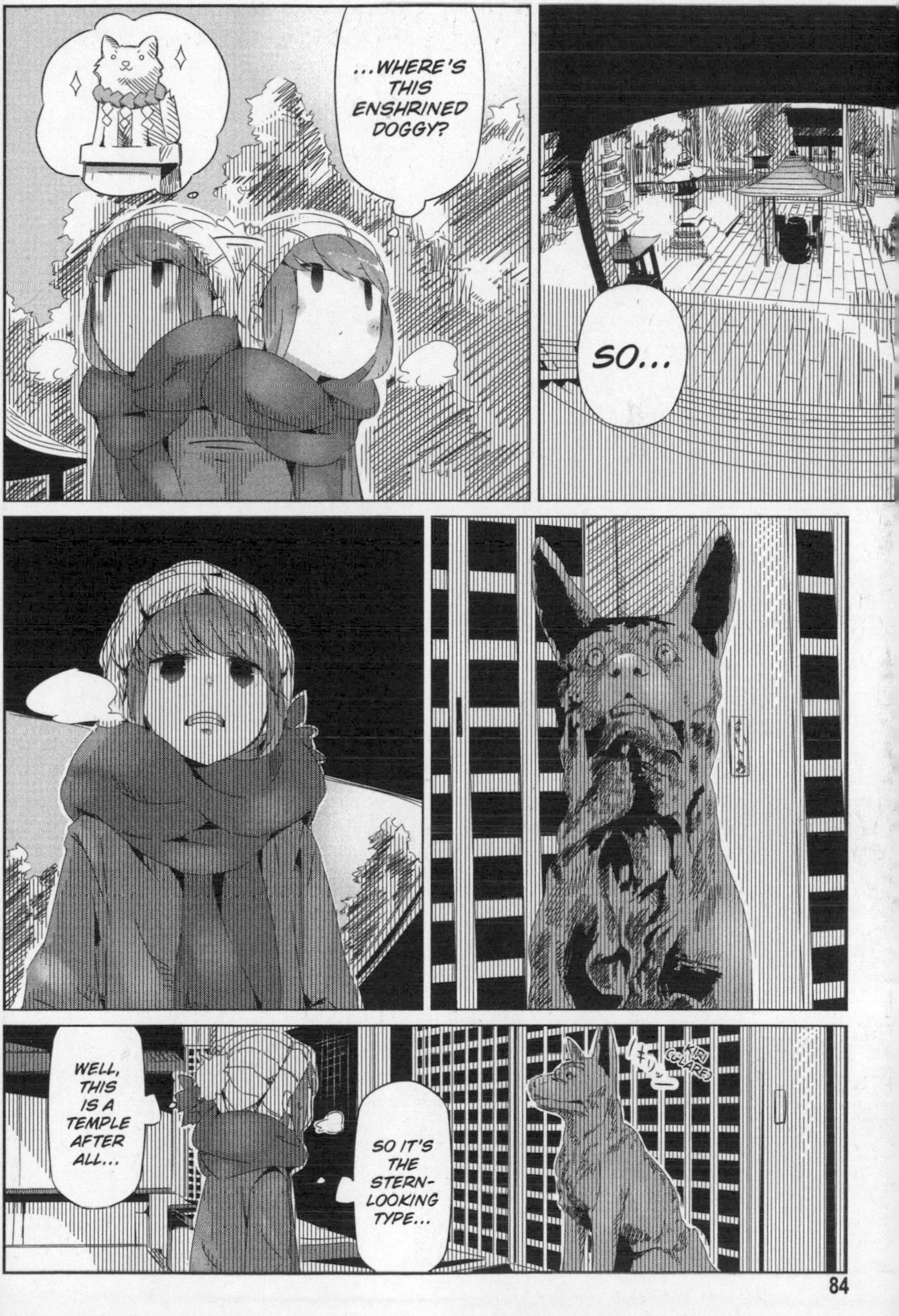
SO...
...WHERE'S THIS ENSHRINED DOGGY?
KIRI (GLARE)
WELL, THIS IS A TEMPLE AFTER ALL...
SO IT'S THE STERN-LOOKING TYPE...

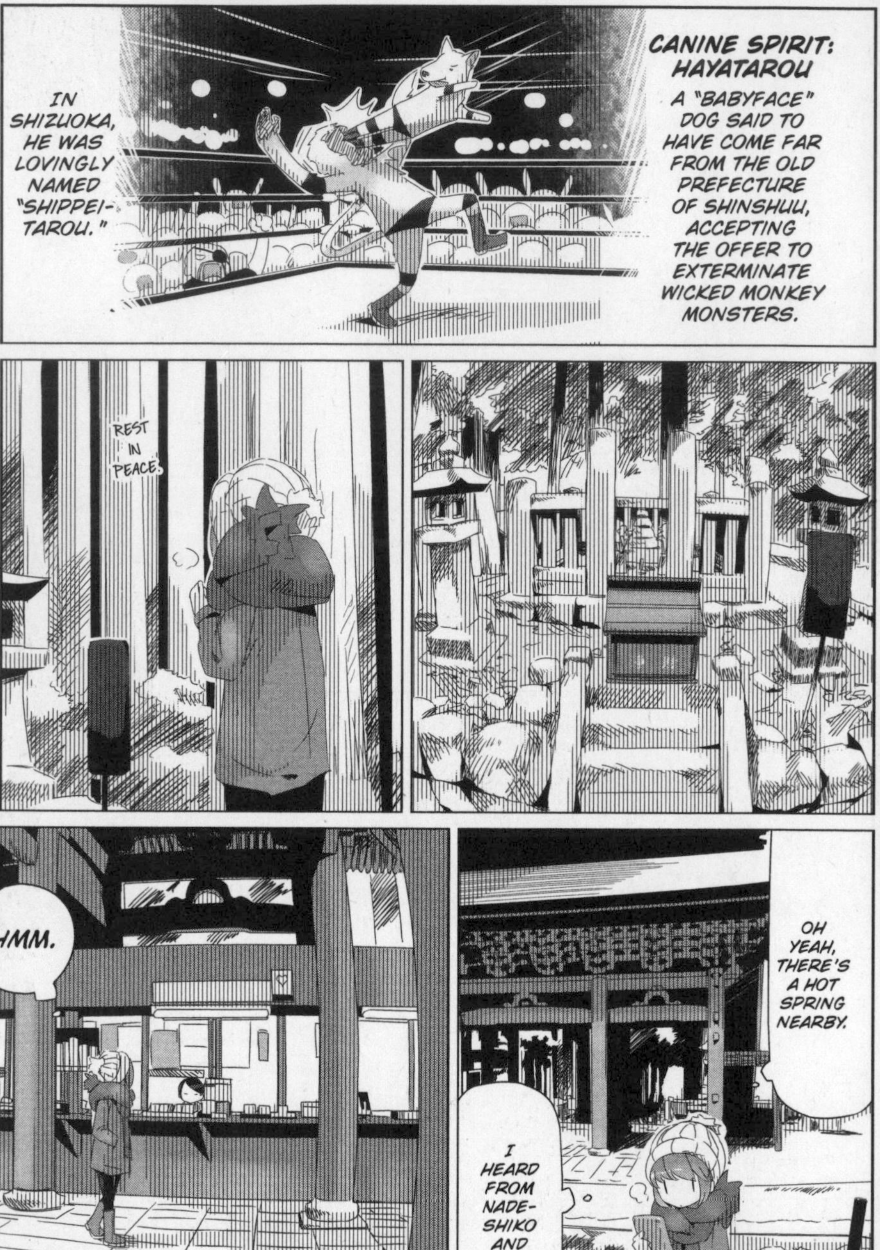
CANINE SPIRIT: HAYATAROU
A "BABYFACE" DOG SAID TO HAVE COME FAR FROM THE OLD PREFECTURE OF SHINSHUU, ACCEPTING THE OFFER TO EXTERMINATE WICKED MONKEY MONSTERS.
IN SHIZUOKA, HE WAS LOVINGLY NAMED "SHIPPEI-TAROU."
REST IN PEACE.
OH YEAH, THERE'S A HOT SPRING NEARBY.
I HEARD FROM NADE-SHIKO AND CHIAKI.
HMM.

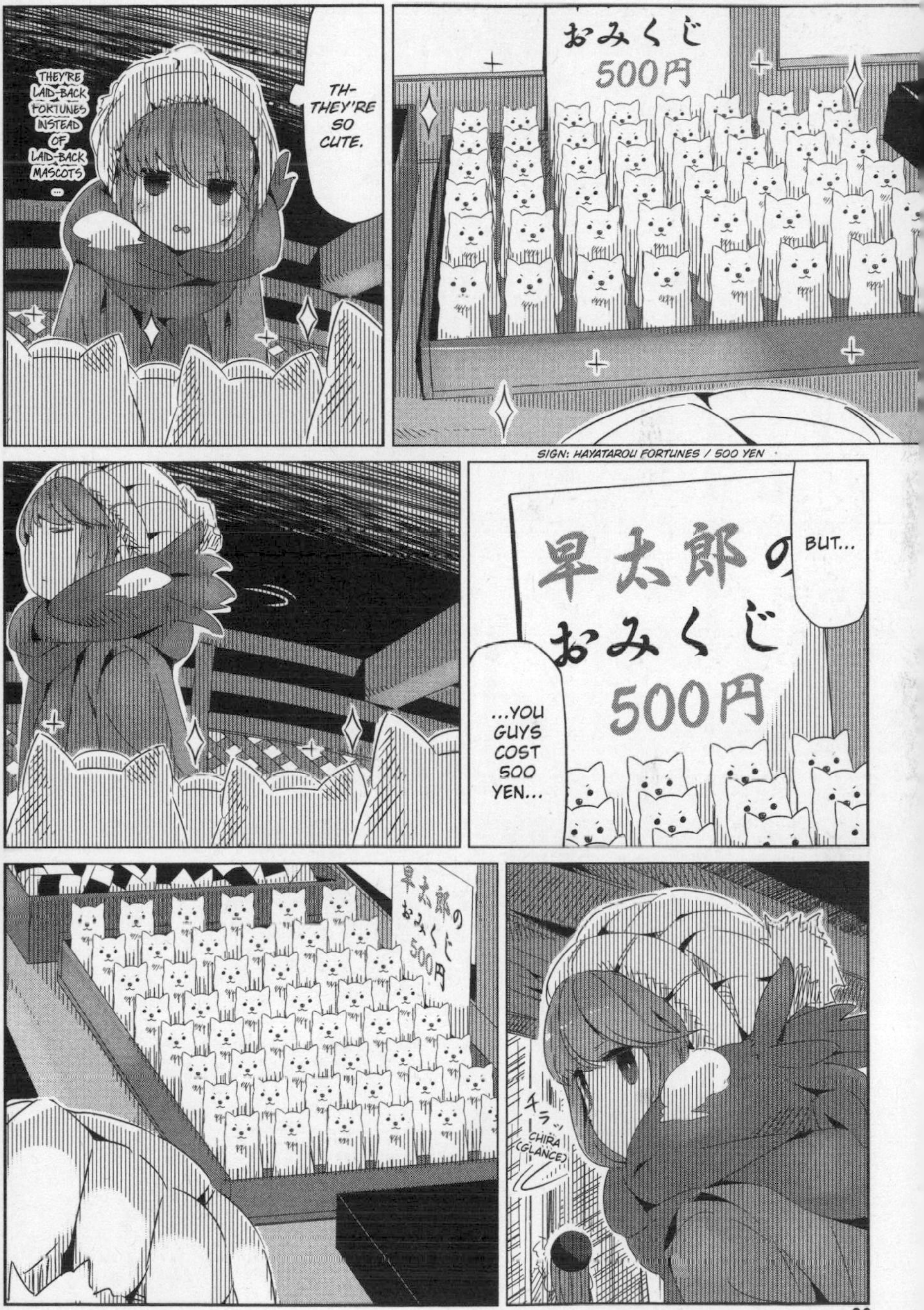
おみくじ
500円
TH-THEY'RE SO CUTE.
THEY'RE LAID-BACK FORTUNES INSTEAD OF LAID-BACK MASCOTS...
SIGN: HAYATAROU FORTUNES / 500 YEN
早太郎の
おみくじ
500円
BUT...
...YOU GUYS COST 500 YEN...
チラッ
CHIRA (GLANCE)
早太郎の
おみくじ
500円

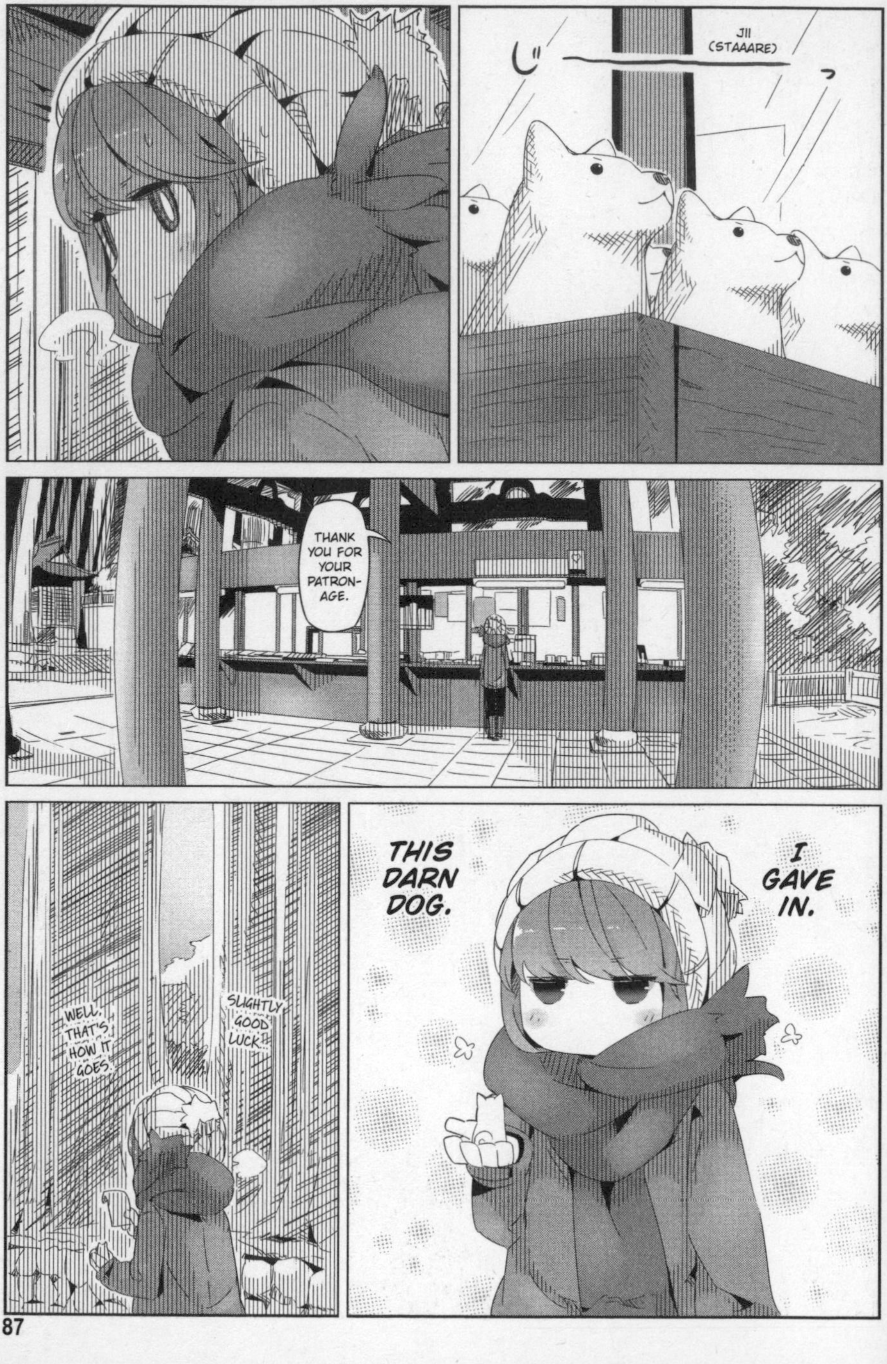
じーーっ
JII (STAAARE)
THANK YOU FOR YOUR PATRON-AGE.
I GAVE IN.
THIS DARN DOG.
SLIGHTLY GOOD LUCK...
WELL, THAT'S HOW IT GOES.

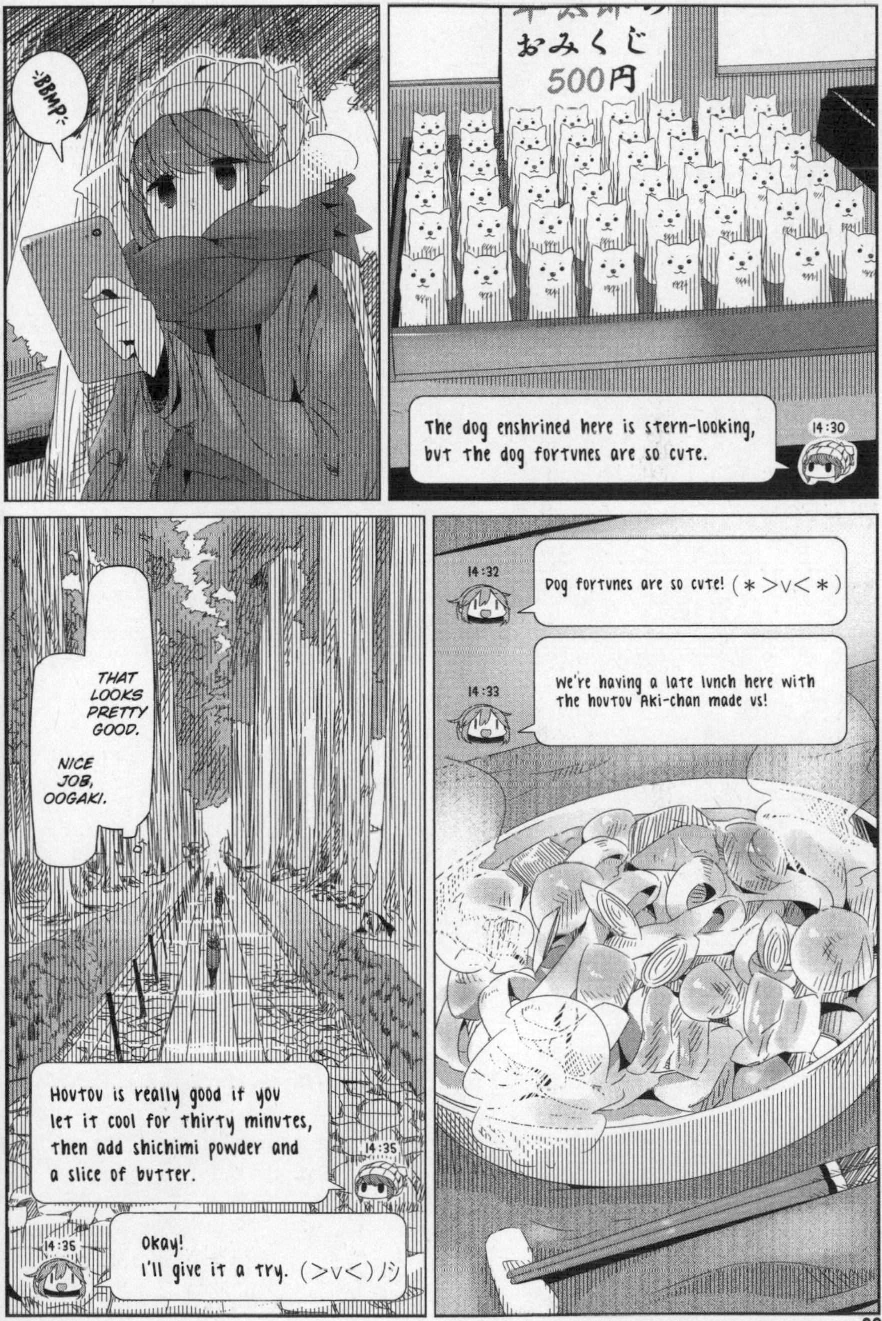
おみくじ
500円
The dog enshrined here is stern-looking, but the dog fortunes are so cute.
14:30
BBMP
14:32
Dog fortunes are so cute! (＊>v<＊)
14:33
We're having a late lunch here with the houtou Aki-chan made us!
THAT LOOKS PRETTY GOOD.
NICE JOB, OOGAKI.
Houtou is really good if you let it cool for thirty minutes, then add shichimi powder and a slice of butter.
14:35
14:35
Okay!
I'll give it a try. (>v<)ノシ

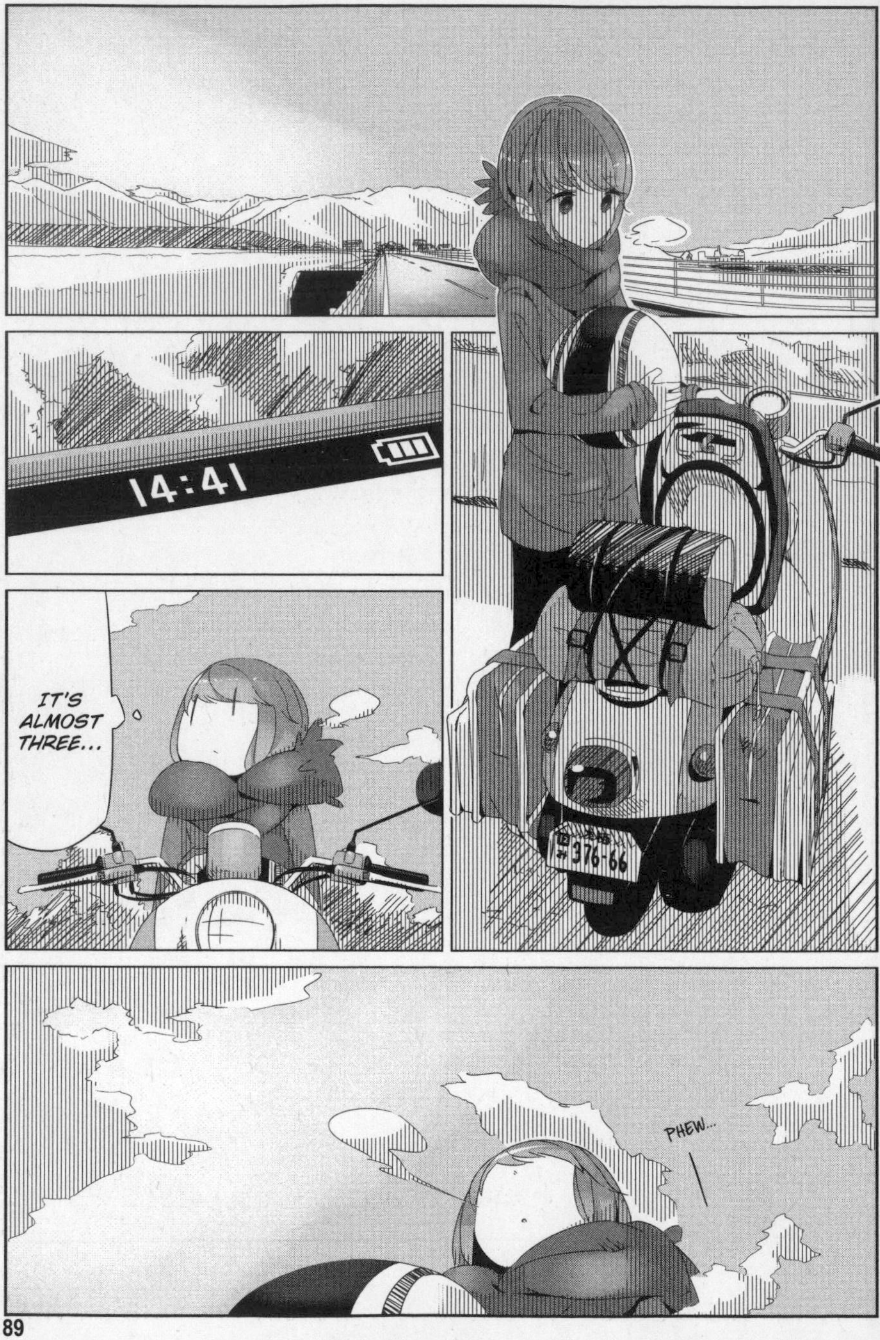
376-66
14:41
IT'S ALMOST THREE...
PHEW...

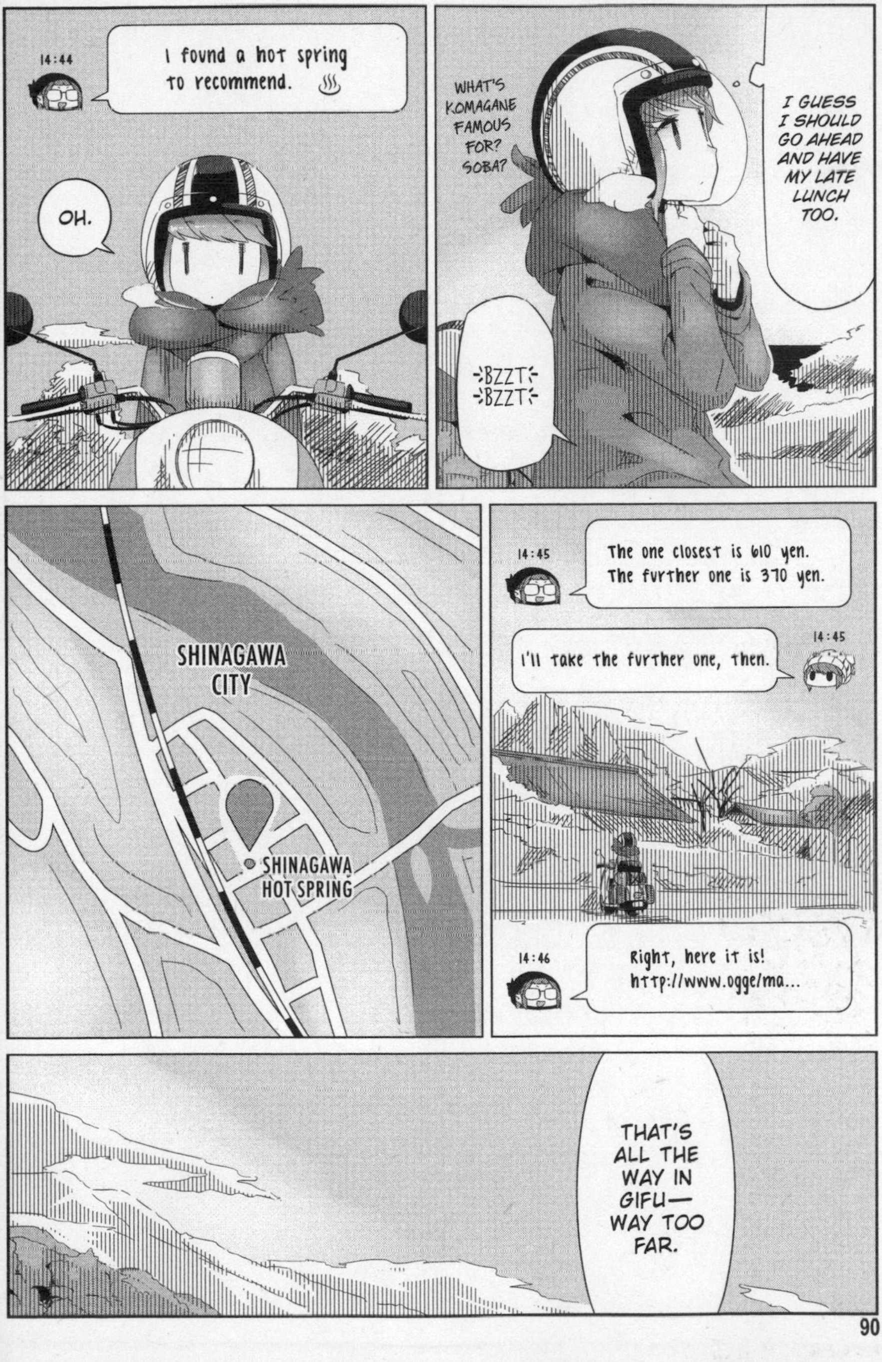
I GUESS I SHOULD GO AHEAD AND HAVE MY LATE LUNCH TOO.
WHAT'S KOMAGANE FAMOUS FOR? SOBA?
-BZZT- -BZZT-
14:44
I found a hot spring to recommend. ♨
OH.
14:45
The one closest is 610 yen. The further one is 370 yen.
14:45
I'll take the further one, then.
14:46
Right, here it is! http://www.ogge/ma...
SHINAGAWA CITY
SHINAGAWA HOT SPRING
THAT'S ALL THE WAY IN GIFU— WAY TOO FAR.

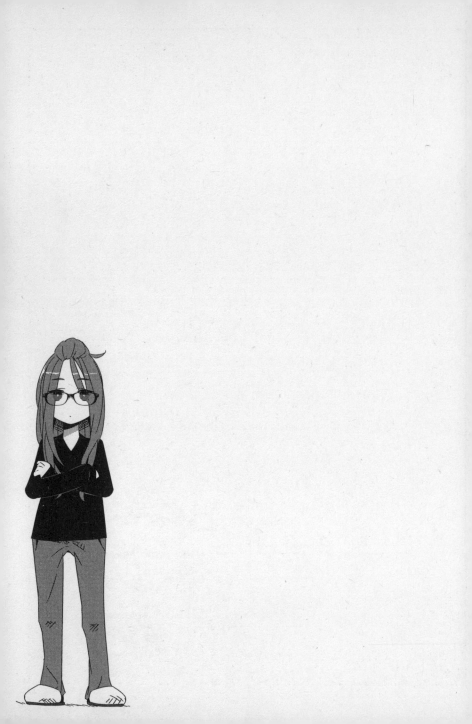

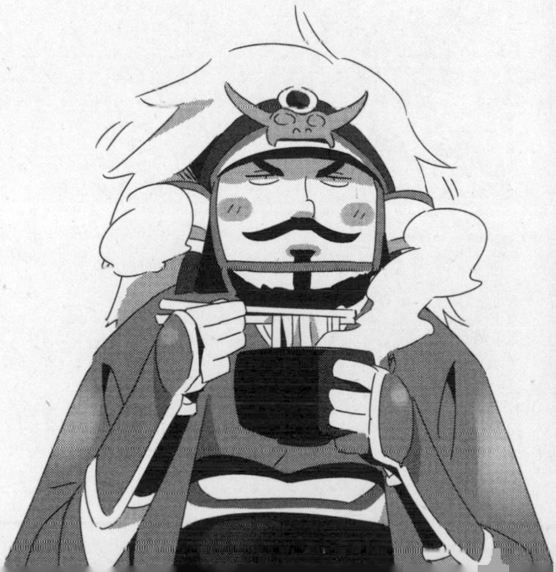

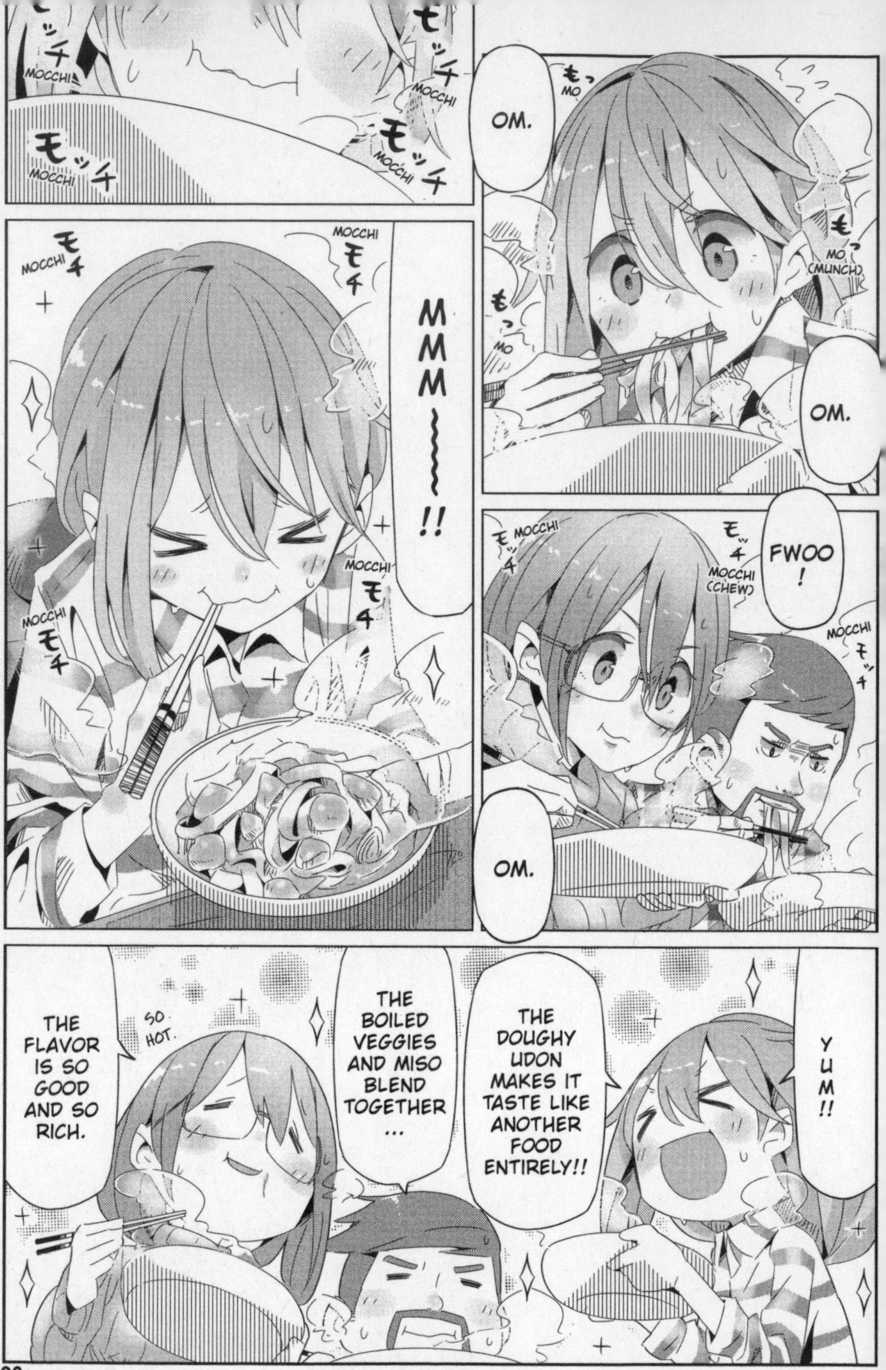

OM.
もっ MO
もっ MO (MUNCH)
もっ MO
OM.
モッチ MOCCHI
モッチ MOCCHI
モッチ MOCCHI
モッチ MOCCHI
FWOO!
モッチ MOCCHI (CHEW)
モッチ MOCCHI
モッチ MOCCHI
OM.
MOCCHI モチ
MOCCHI モチ
MMM~~!!
MOCCHI モチ
MOCCHI モチ
YUM!!
THE DOUGHY UDON MAKES IT TASTE LIKE ANOTHER FOOD ENTIRELY!!
THE BOILED VEGGIES AND MISO BLEND TOGETHER...
SO HOT.
THE FLAVOR IS SO GOOD AND SO RICH.

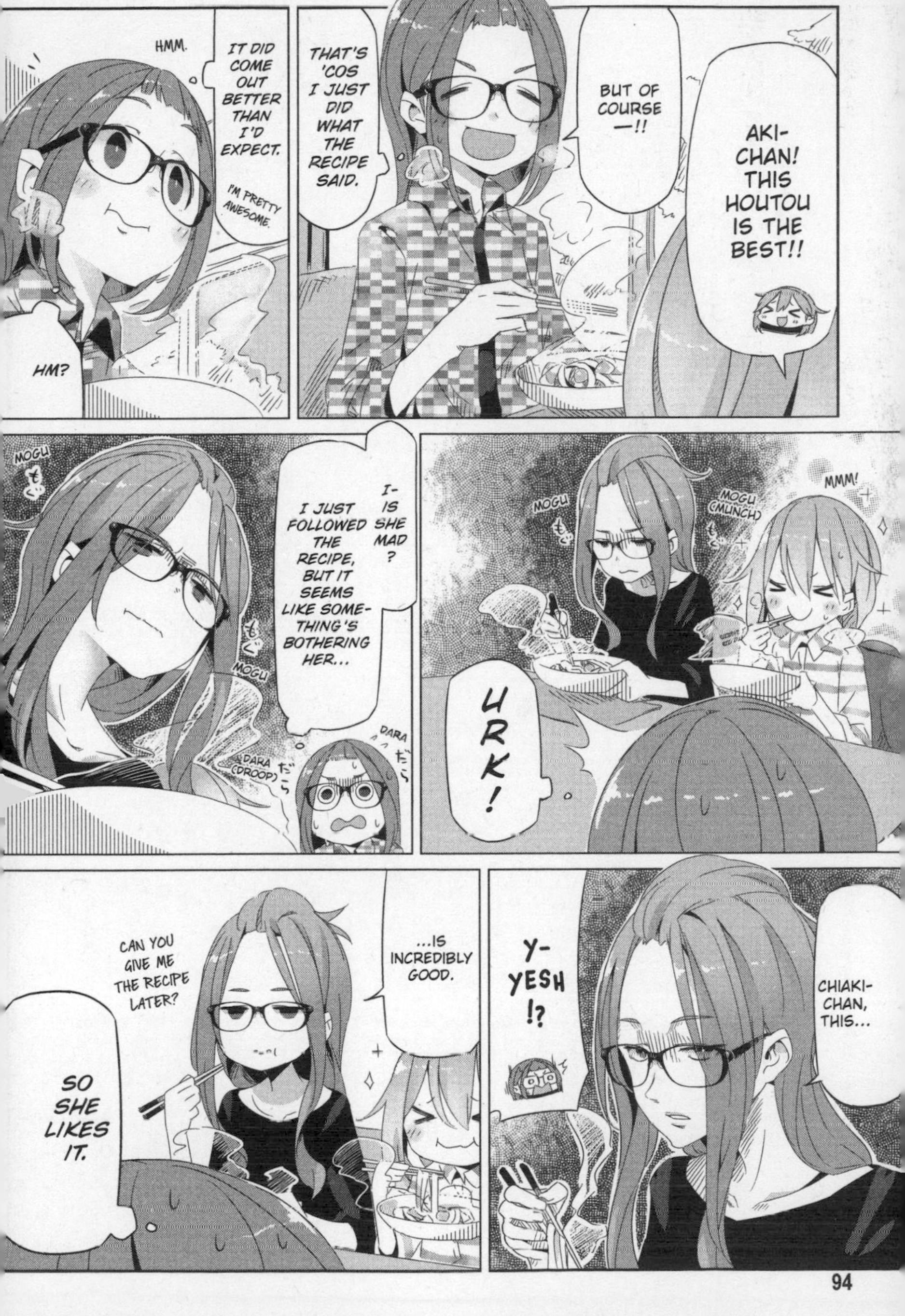
AKI-CHAN! THIS HOUTOU IS THE BEST!!
BUT OF COURSE—!!
THAT'S 'COS I JUST DID WHAT THE RECIPE SAID.
IT DID COME OUT BETTER THAN I'D EXPECT.
HMM.
I'M PRETTY AWESOME.
HM?
MMM!
MOGU (MUNCH)
MOGU
URK!
I- IS SHE MAD?
I JUST FOLLOWED THE RECIPE, BUT IT SEEMS LIKE SOME-THING'S BOTHERING HER...
MOGU
MOGU
DARA
DARA (DROOP)
CHIAKI-CHAN, THIS...
Y-YESH!?
...IS INCREDIBLY GOOD.
CAN YOU GIVE ME THE RECIPE LATER?
SO SHE LIKES IT.

SIGN: KOMAGANE BATHS

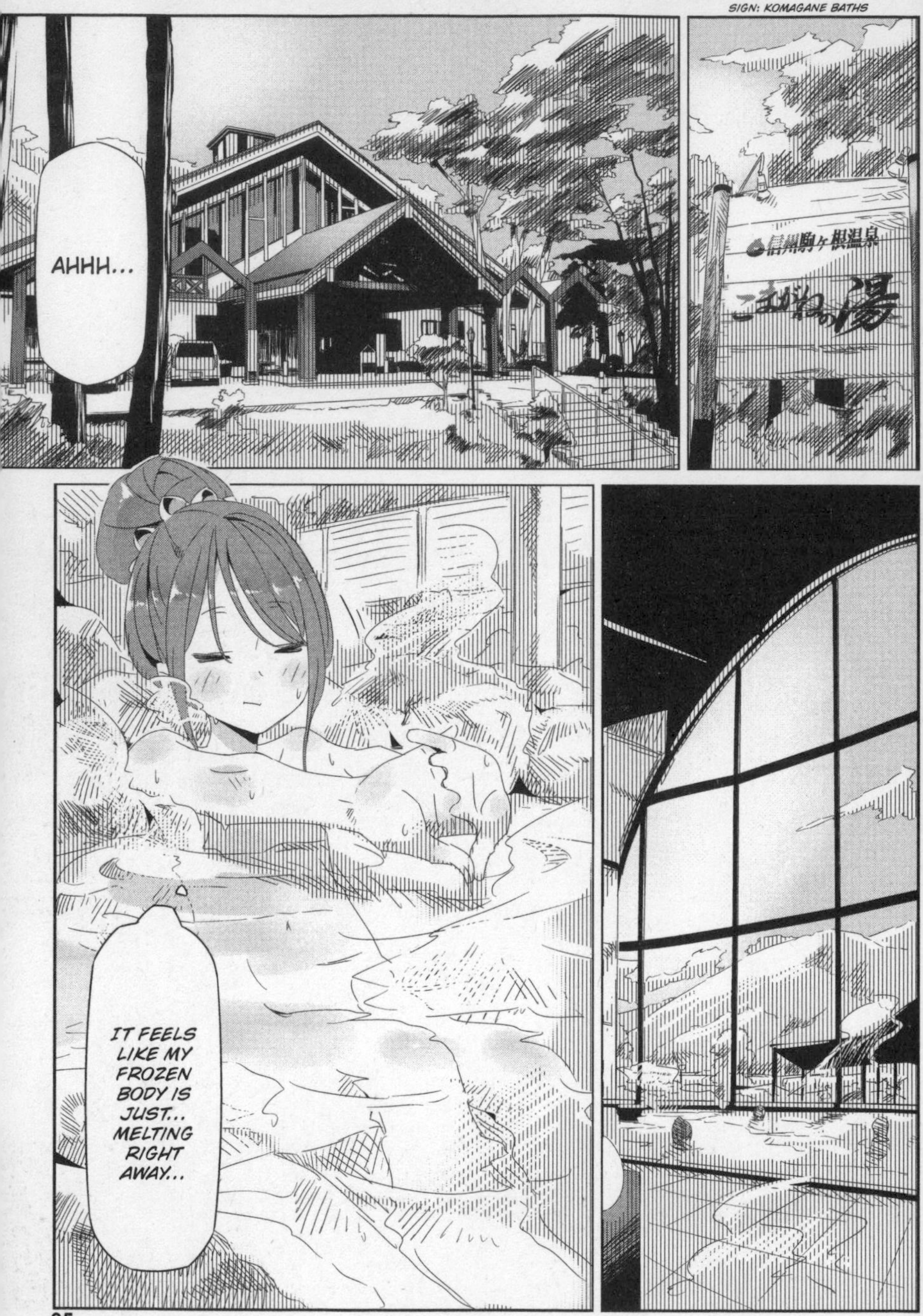

信州駒ヶ根温泉
こまがねの湯
AHHH...
IT FEELS LIKE MY FROZEN BODY IS JUST... MELTING RIGHT AWAY...

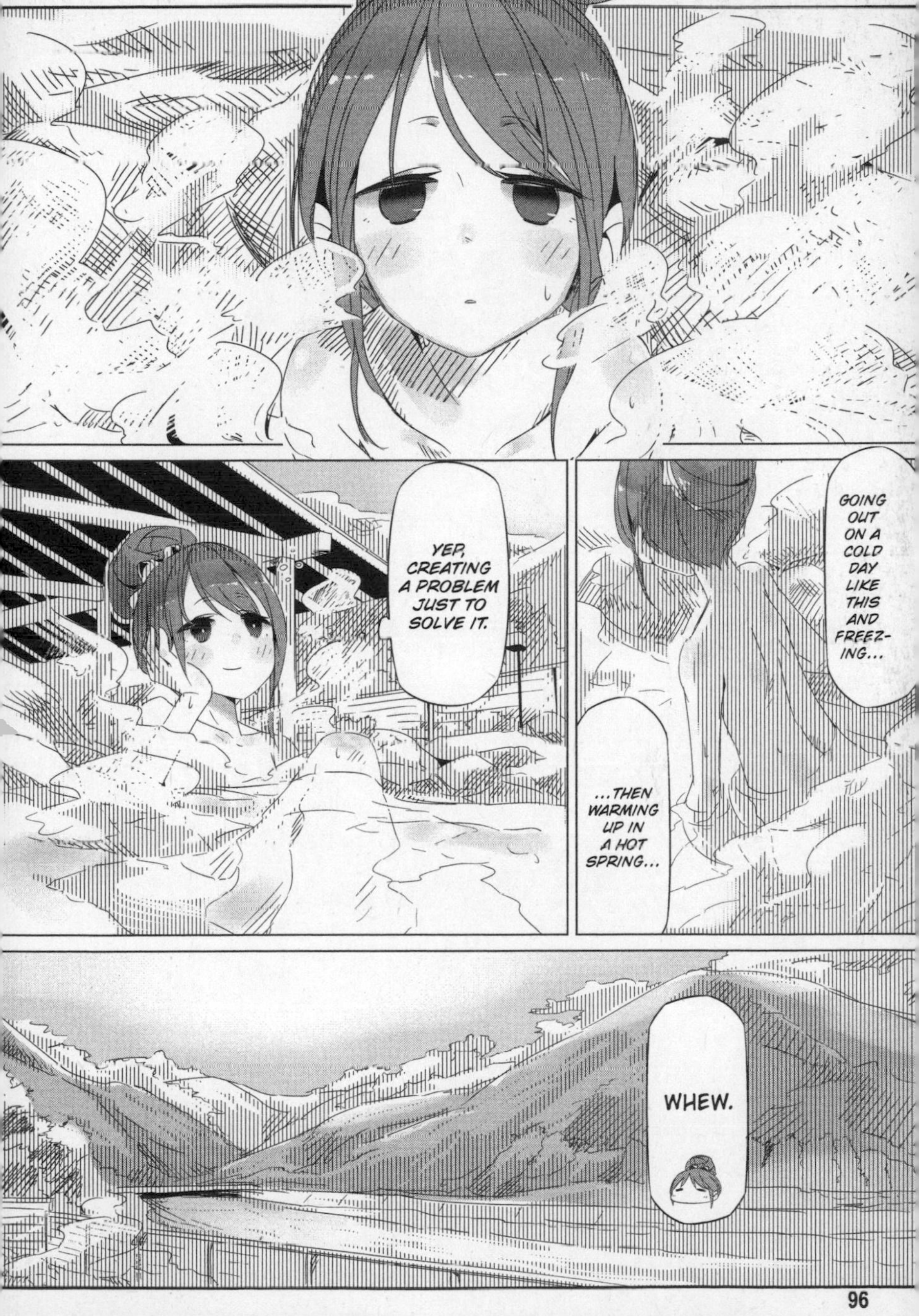
GOING OUT ON A COLD DAY LIKE THIS AND FREEZING...
...THEN WARMING UP IN A HOT SPRING...
YEP, CREATING A PROBLEM JUST TO SOLVE IT.
WHEW.

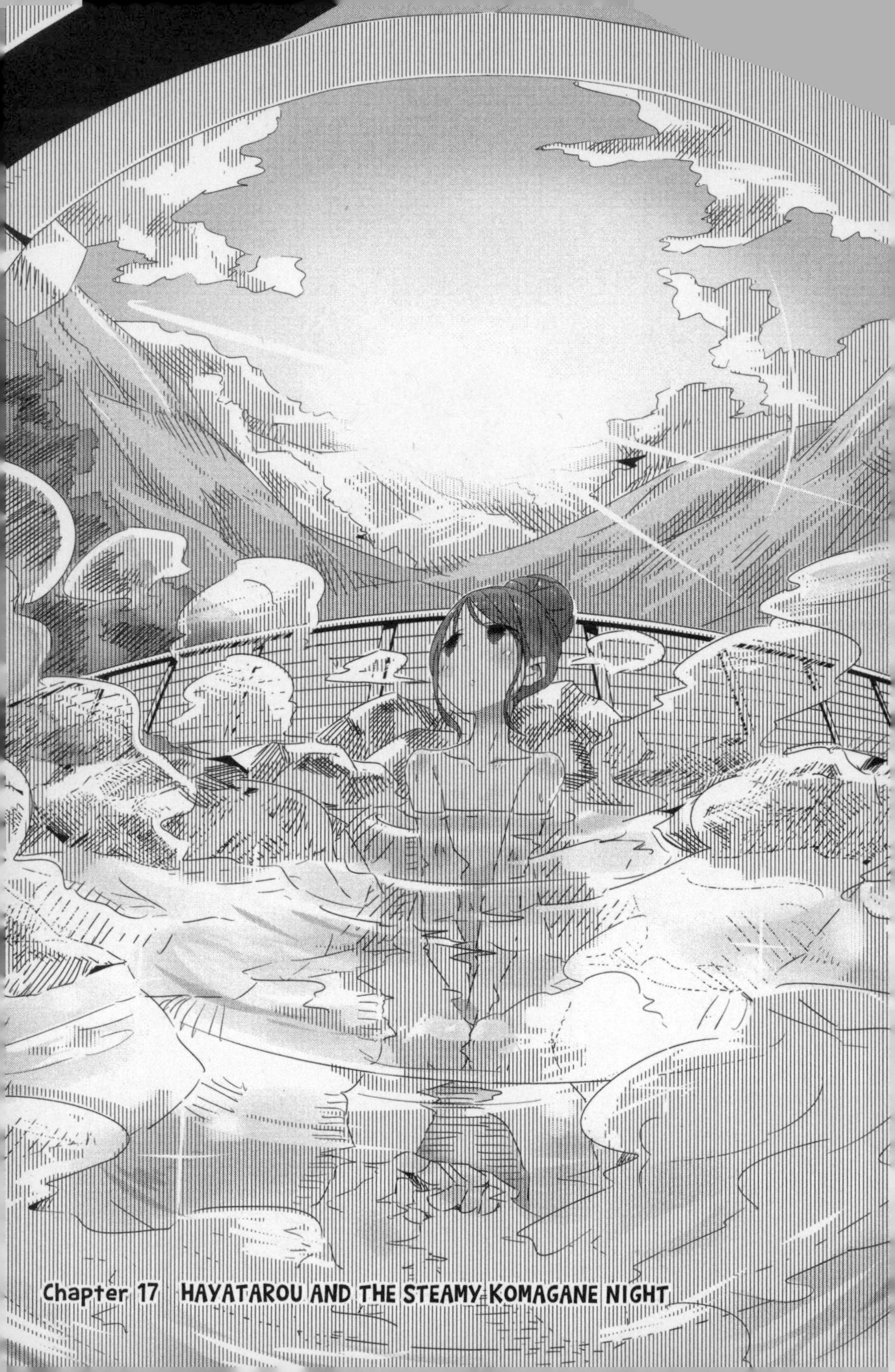

Chapter 17 HAYATAROU AND THE STEAMY KOMAGANE NIGHT

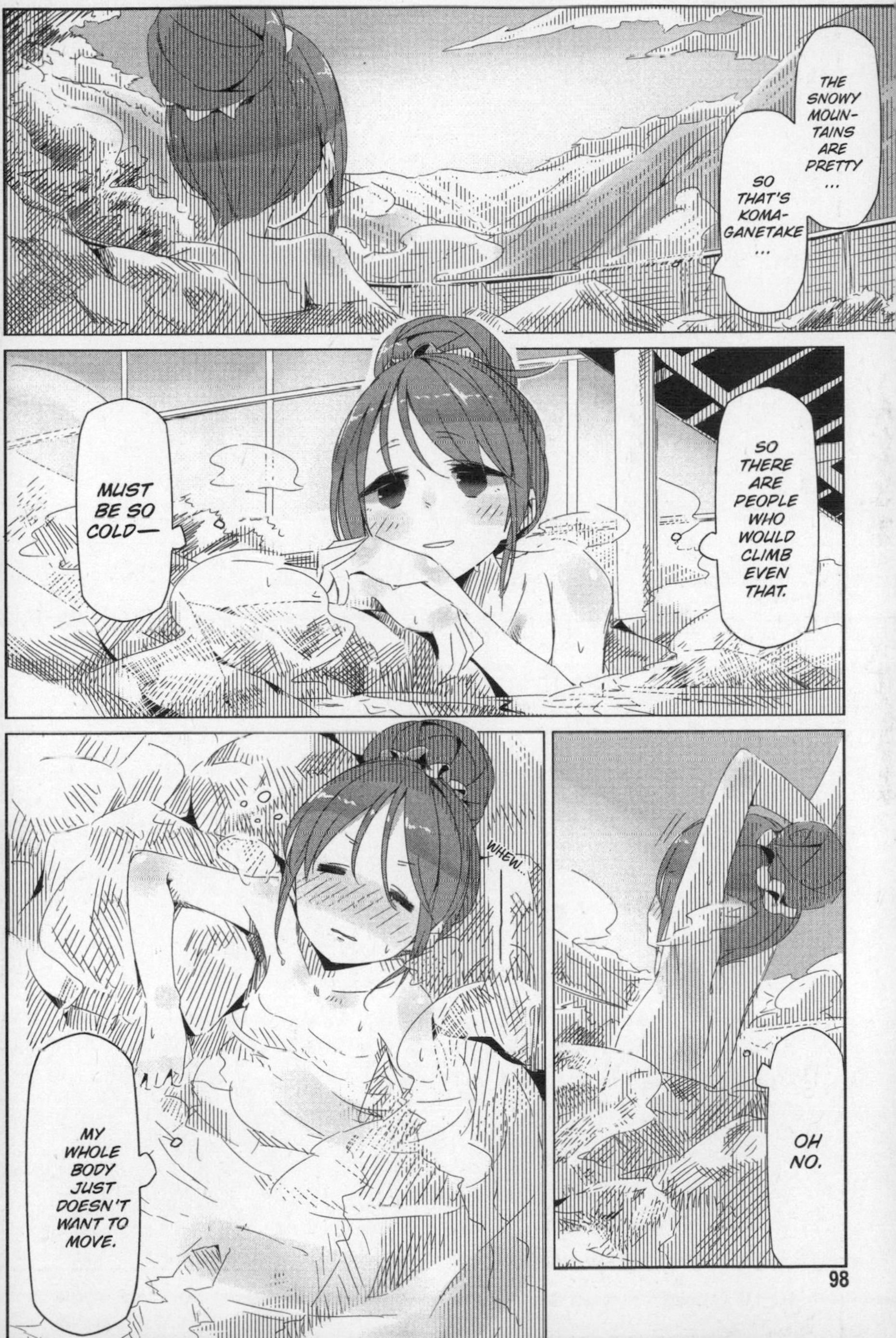
THE SNOWY MOUNTAINS ARE PRETTY...
SO THAT'S KOMAGANETAKE...
SO THERE ARE PEOPLE WHO WOULD CLIMB EVEN THAT.
MUST BE SO COLD—
OH NO.
WHEW...
MY WHOLE BODY JUST DOESN'T WANT TO MOVE.

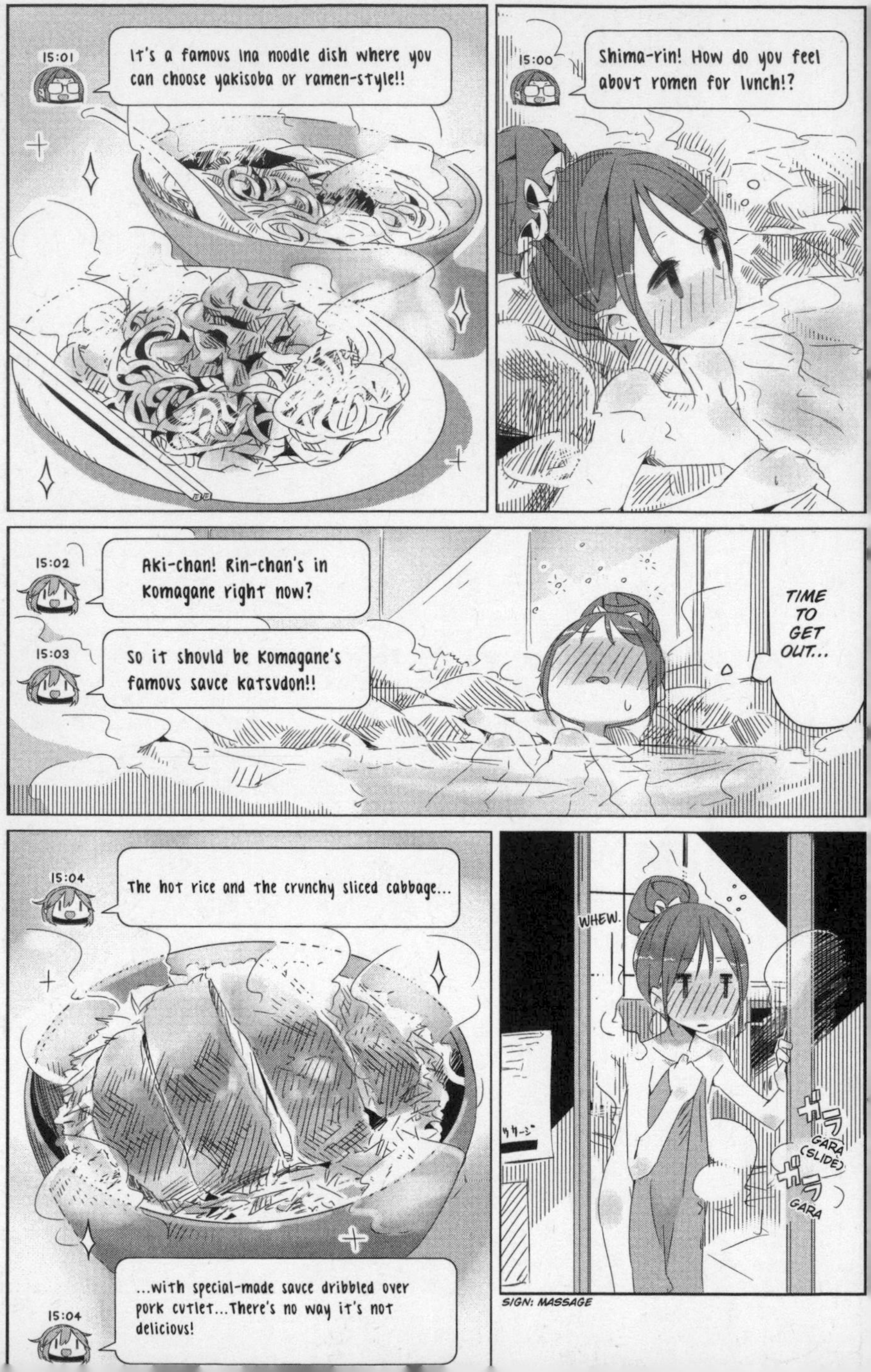
15:00
Shima-rin! How do you feel about romen for lunch!?
15:01
It's a famous Ina noodle dish where you can choose yakisoba or ramen-style!!
TIME TO GET OUT...
15:02
Aki-chan! Rin-chan's in Komagane right now?
15:03
So it should be Komagane's famous sauce katsudon!!
WHEW.
ガラ GARA (SLIDE)
ガラ GARA
SIGN: MASSAGE
15:04
The hot rice and the crunchy sliced cabbage...
15:04
...with special-made sauce dribbled over pork cutlet...There's no way it's not delicious!

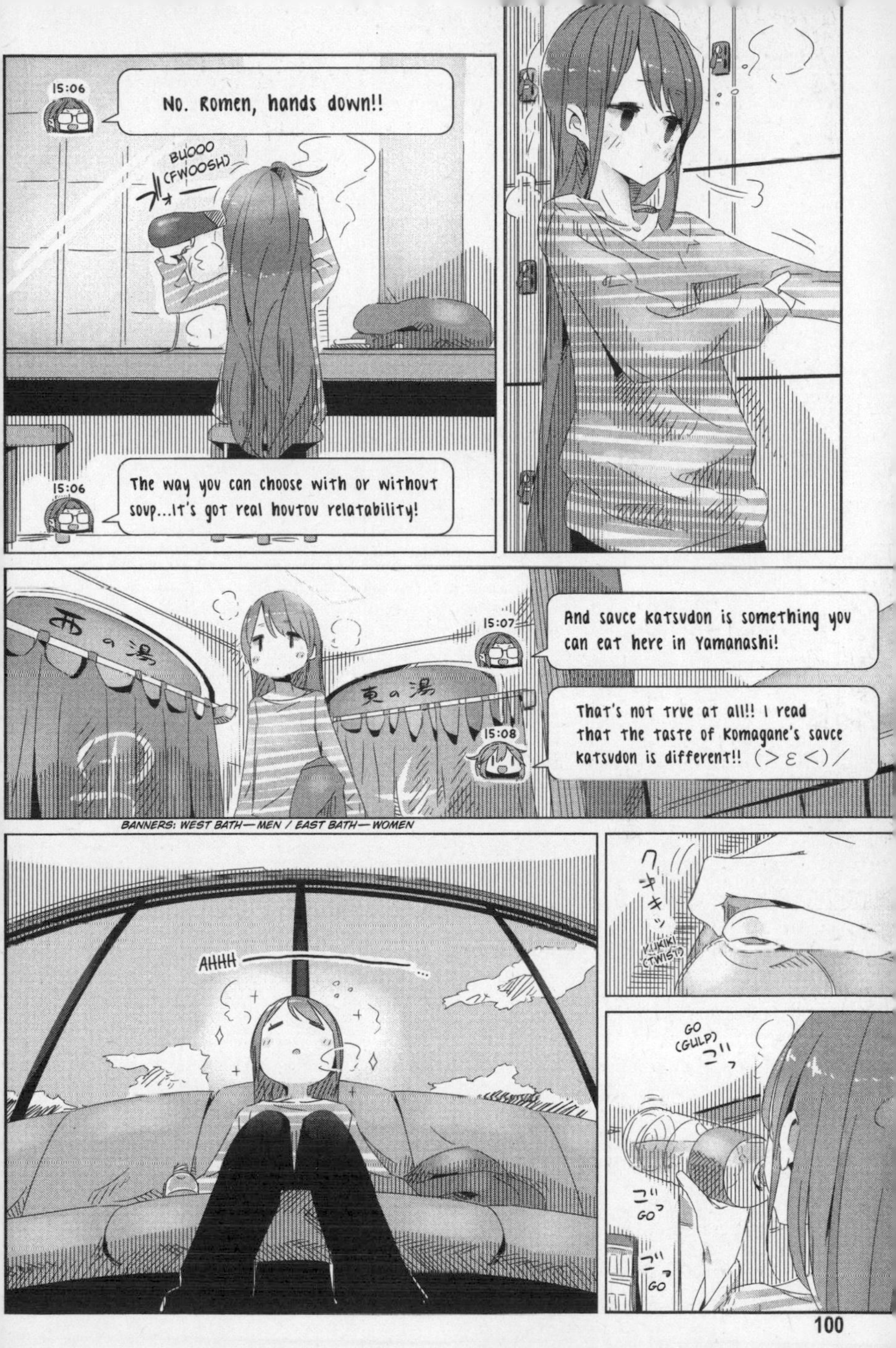
15:06
No. Romen, hands down!!
BUOOO (FWOOSH)
15:06
The way you can choose with or without soup...it's got real houtou relatability!
15:07
And sauce katsudon is something you can eat here in Yamanashi!
15:08
That's not true at all!! I read that the taste of Komagane's sauce katsudon is different!! (>ε<)/
BANNERS: WEST BATH—MEN / EAST BATH—WOMEN
KUKIKI (TWIST)
GO (GULP)
GO
GO
AHHH——...

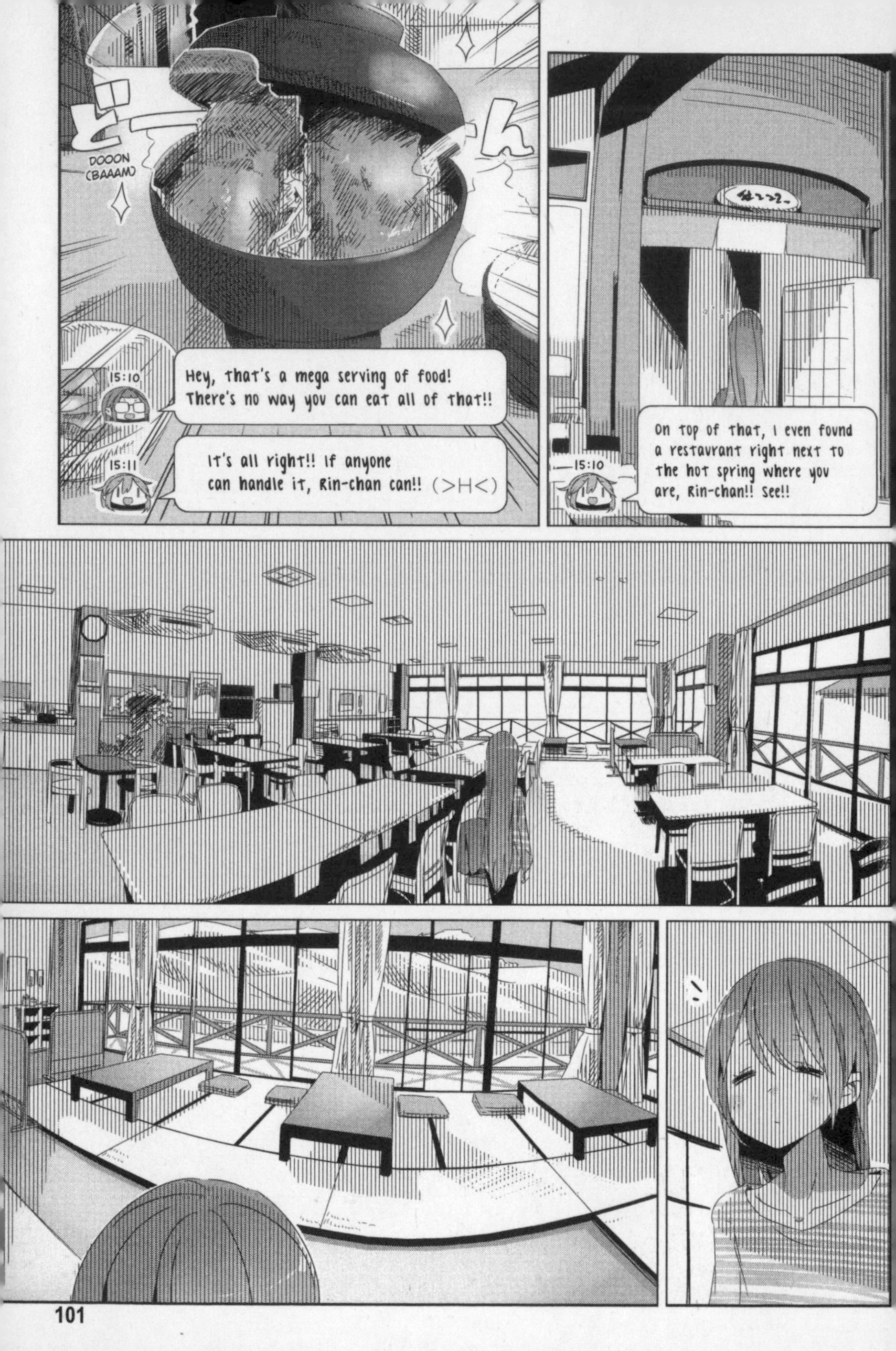
15:10
On top of that, I even found a restaurant right next to the hot spring where you are, Rin-chan!! See!!
どーん
DOOON (BAAAM)
15:10
Hey, that's a mega serving of food! There's no way you can eat all of that!!
15:11
It's all right!! If anyone can handle it, Rin-chan can!! (>H<)

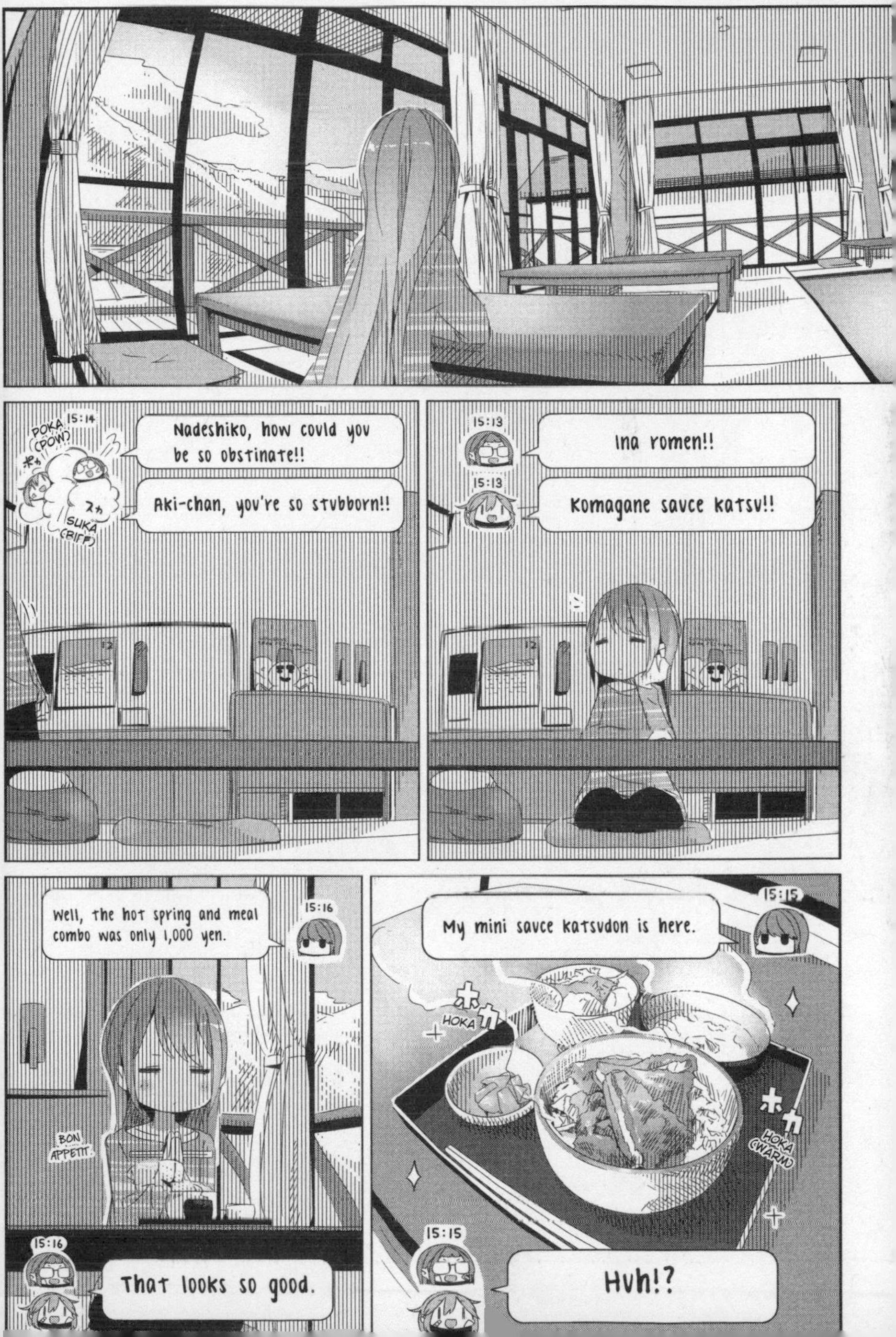
15:13
Ina romen!!
15:13
Komagane sauce katsu!!
15:14
POKA (POW)
ポカ
スカ
SUKA (BIFF)
Nadeshiko, how could you be so obstinate!!
Aki-chan, you're so stubborn!!
15:15
My mini sauce katsudon is here.
ホカ
HOKA
ホカ
HOKA (WARM)
15:15
Huh!?
15:16
Well, the hot spring and meal combo was only 1,000 yen.
BON APPETIT.
15:16
That looks so good.

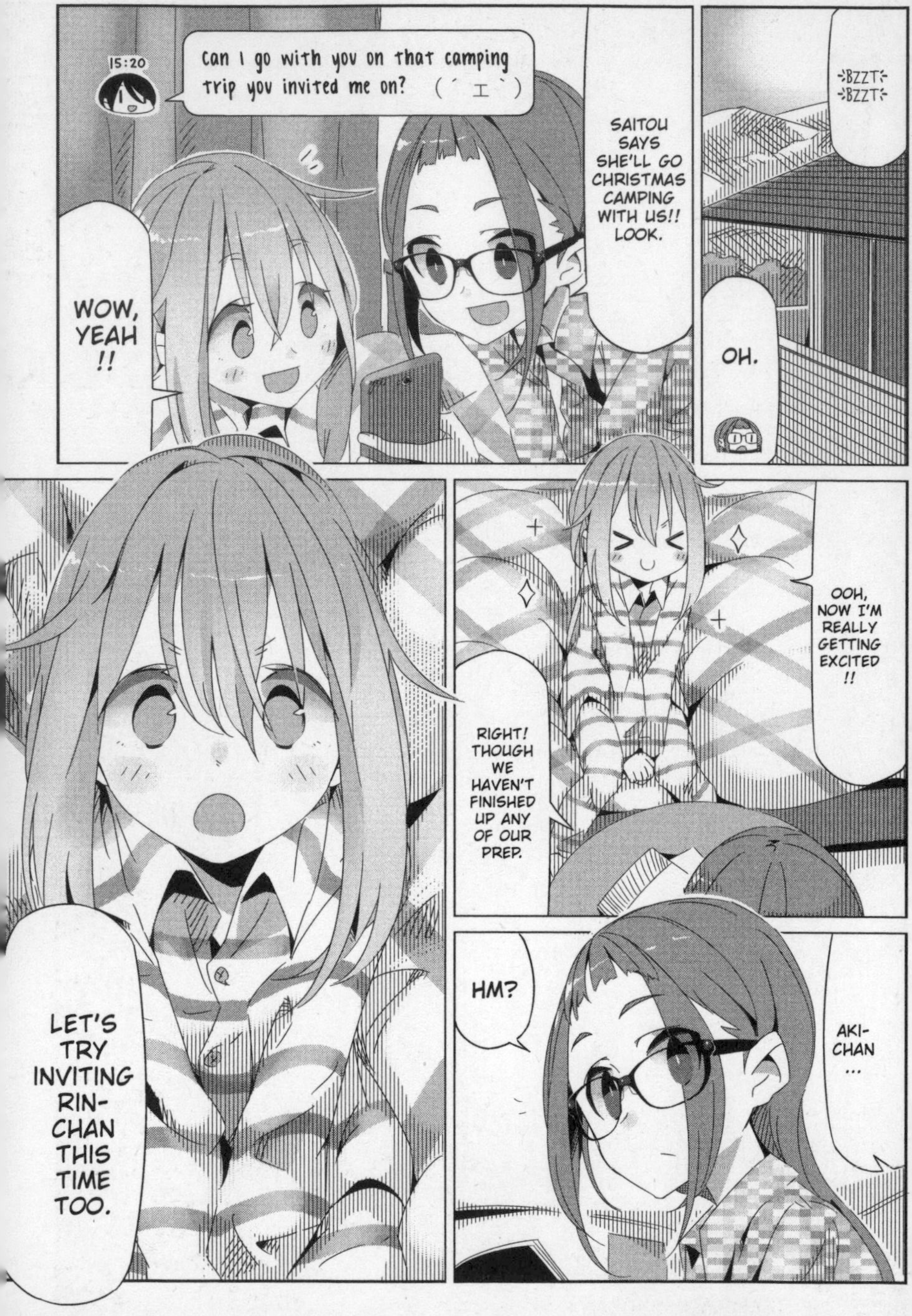

BZZT BZZT
OH.
15:20
Can I go with you on that camping trip you invited me on? (´エ`)
SAITOU SAYS SHE'LL GO CHRISTMAS CAMPING WITH US!! LOOK.
WOW, YEAH!!
OOH, NOW I'M REALLY GETTING EXCITED!!
RIGHT! THOUGH WE HAVEN'T FINISHED UP ANY OF OUR PREP.
AKI-CHAN...
HM?
LET'S TRY INVITING RIN-CHAN THIS TIME TOO.

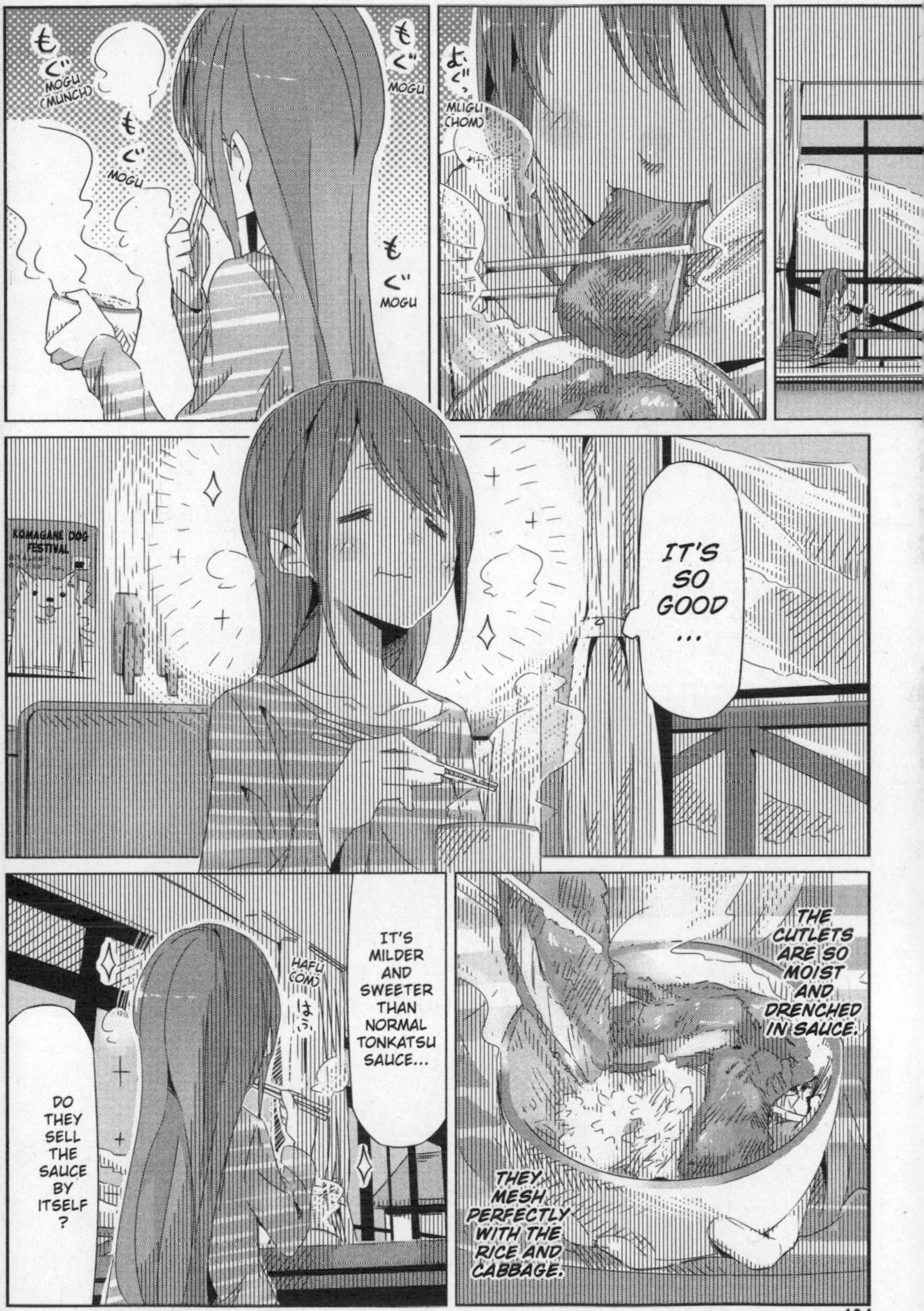
よぐっ
MUGU (CHOM)
もぐ
MOGU
もぐ
MOGU (MUNCH)
もぐ
MOGU
もぐ
MOGU
KOMAGANE DOG FESTIVAL
IT'S SO GOOD...
THE CUTLETS ARE SO MOIST AND DRENCHED IN SAUCE.
THEY MESH PERFECTLY WITH THE RICE AND CABBAGE.
IT'S MILDER AND SWEETER THAN NORMAL TONKATSU SAUCE...
はふっ
HAFU (OM)
DO THEY SELL THE SAUCE BY ITSELF?

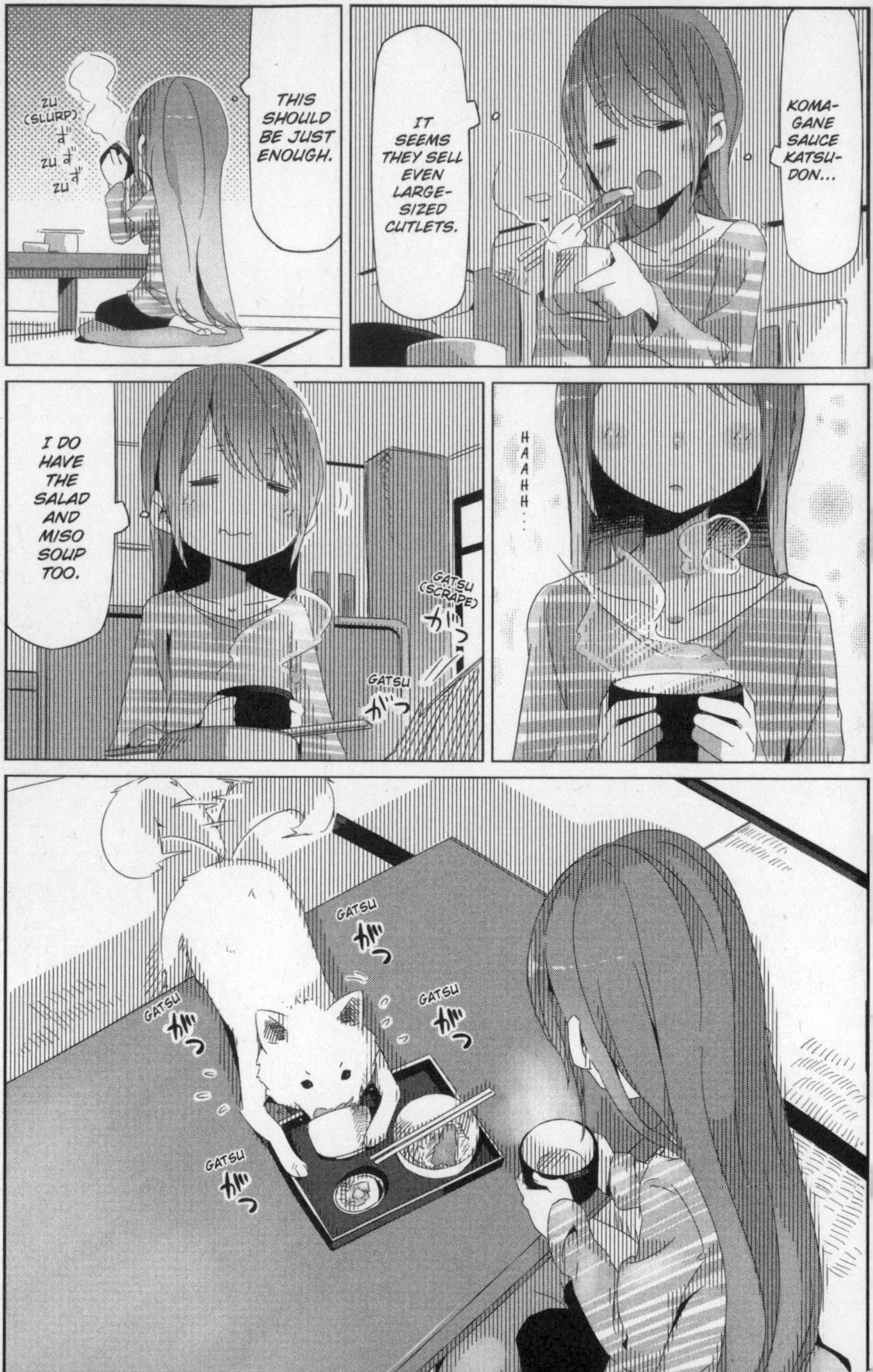
KOMA-GANE SAUCE KATSU-DON...
IT SEEMS THEY SELL EVEN LARGE-SIZED CUTLETS.
THIS SHOULD BE JUST ENOUGH.
ZU (SLURP) ず
ZU ず
ZU
HAAAHH...
I DO HAVE THE SALAD AND MISO SOUP TOO.
GATSU (SCRAPE) がつ
GATSU がつ
GATSU がつ
GATSU がつ
GATSU がつ
GATSU がつ

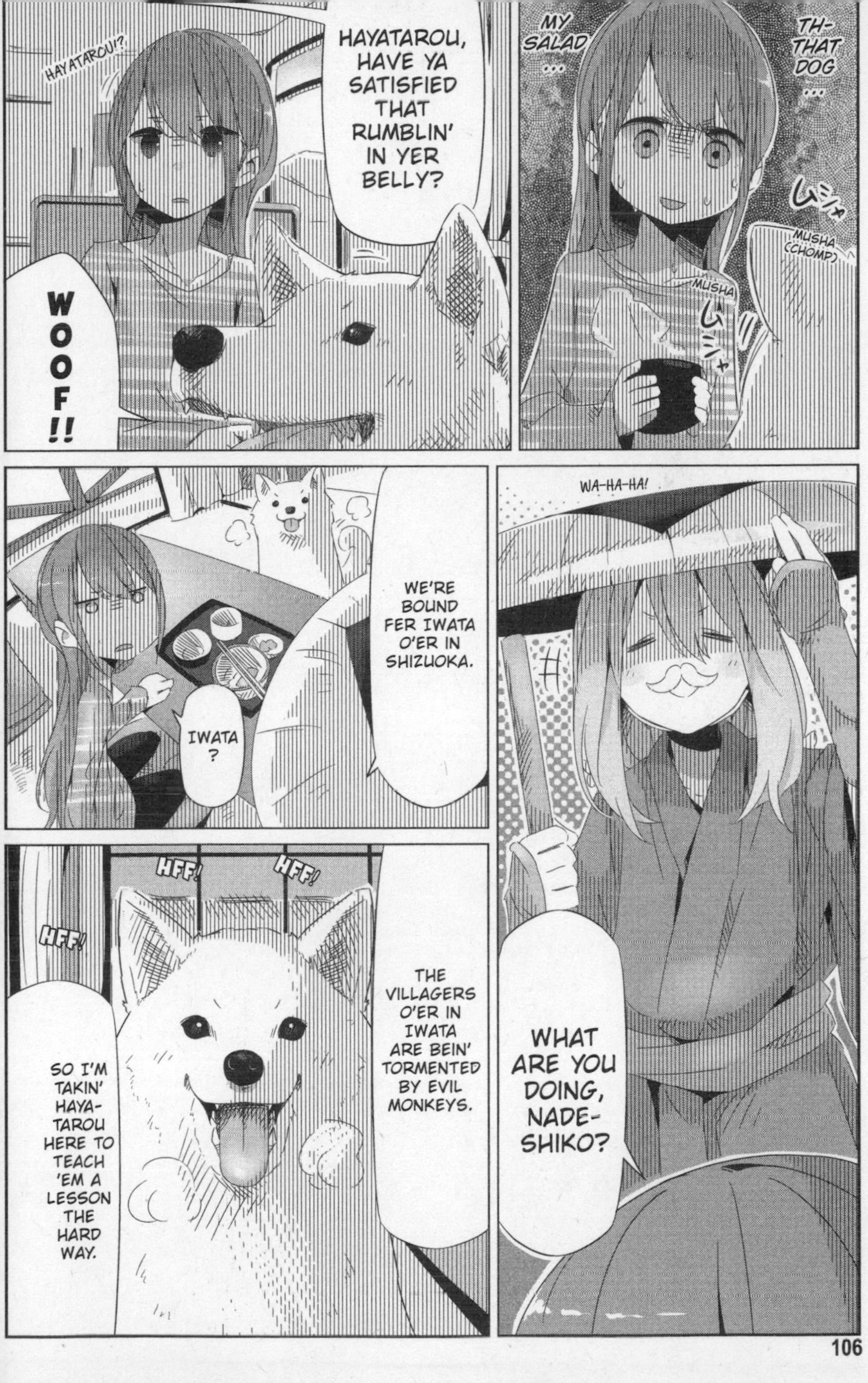
TH-THAT DOG ...
MY SALAD ...
ムシャ
MUSHA (CHOMP)
MUSHA
ムシャ
HAYATAROU, HAVE YA SATISFIED THAT RUMBLIN' IN YER BELLY?
HAYATAROU!?
WOOF!!
WA-HA-HA!
WHAT ARE YOU DOING, NADE-SHIKO?
WE'RE BOUND FER IWATA O'ER IN SHIZUOKA.
IWATA?
HFF!
HFF!
HFF!
THE VILLAGERS O'ER IN IWATA ARE BEIN' TORMENTED BY EVIL MONKEYS.
SO I'M TAKIN' HAYA-TAROU HERE TO TEACH 'EM A LESSON THE HARD WAY.

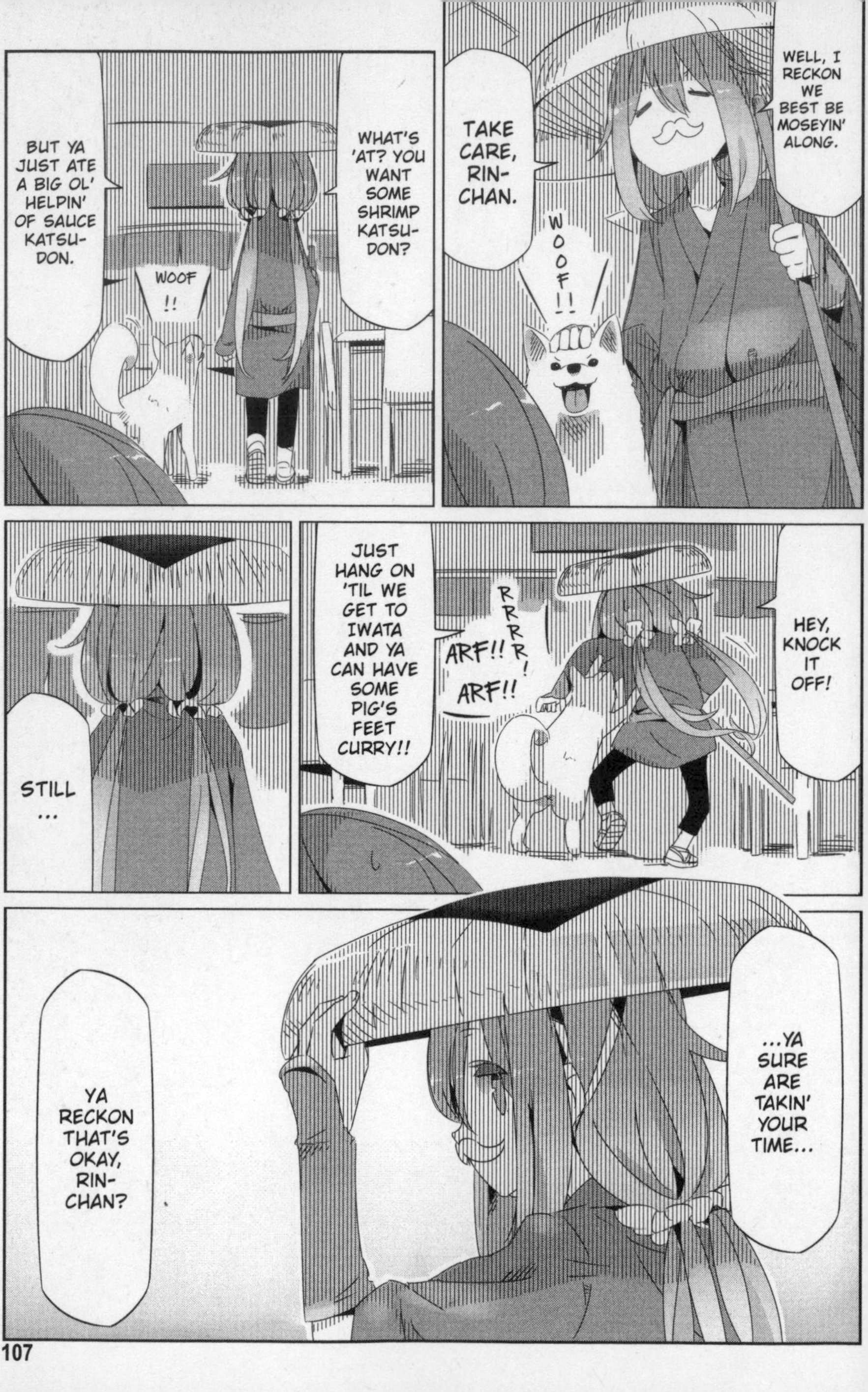
WELL, I RECKON WE BEST BE MOSEYIN' ALONG.
TAKE CARE, RIN-CHAN.
WOOF!!
WHAT'S 'AT? YOU WANT SOME SHRIMP KATSU-DON?
WOOF !!
BUT YA JUST ATE A BIG OL' HELPIN' OF SAUCE KATSU-DON.
HEY, KNOCK IT OFF!
RRRR!
ARF!!
ARF!!
JUST HANG ON 'TIL WE GET TO IWATA AND YA CAN HAVE SOME PIG'S FEET CURRY!!
STILL ...
...YA SURE ARE TAKIN' YOUR TIME...
YA RECKON THAT'S OKAY, RIN-CHAN?

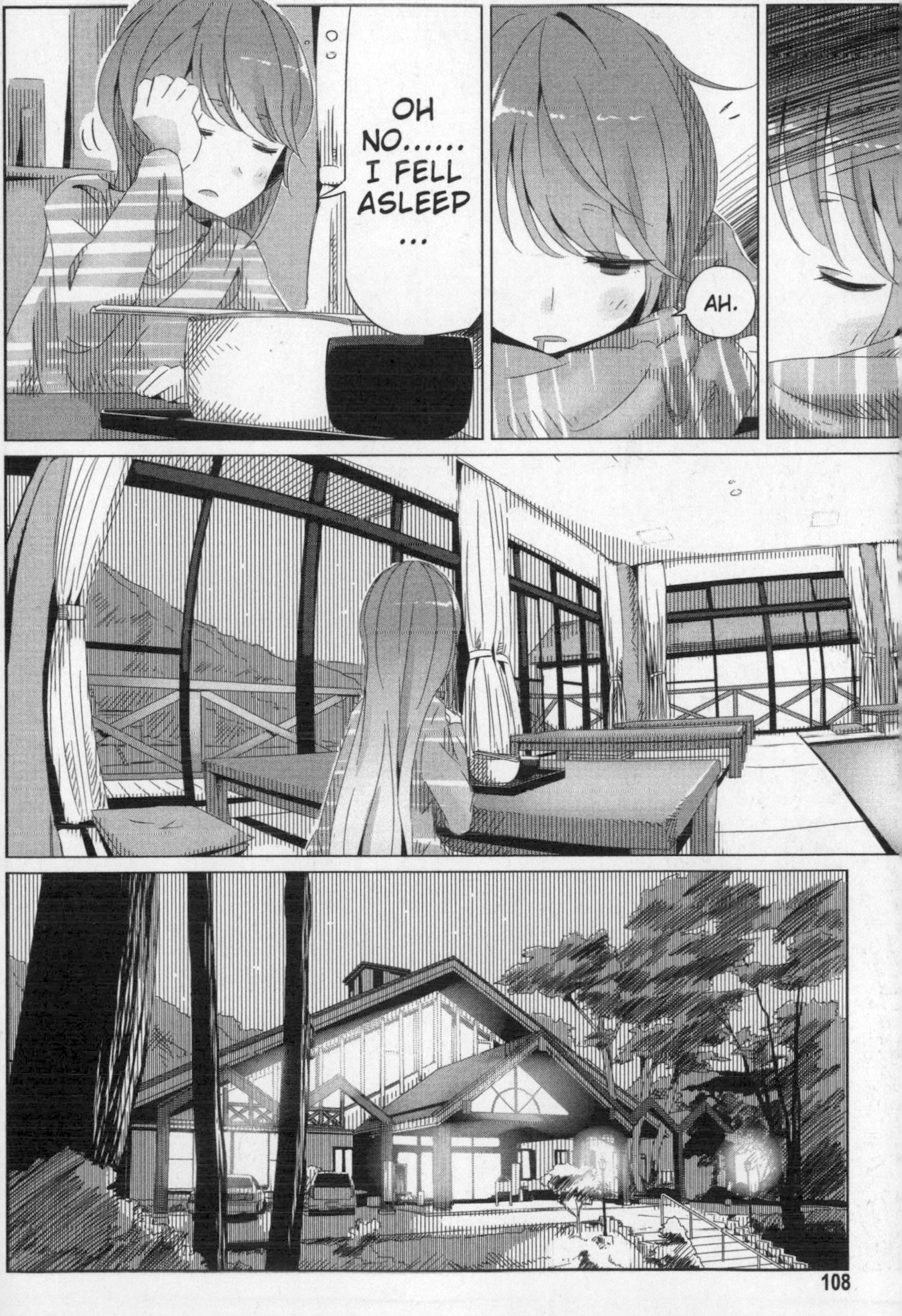
AH.
OH NO...... I FELL ASLEEP ...

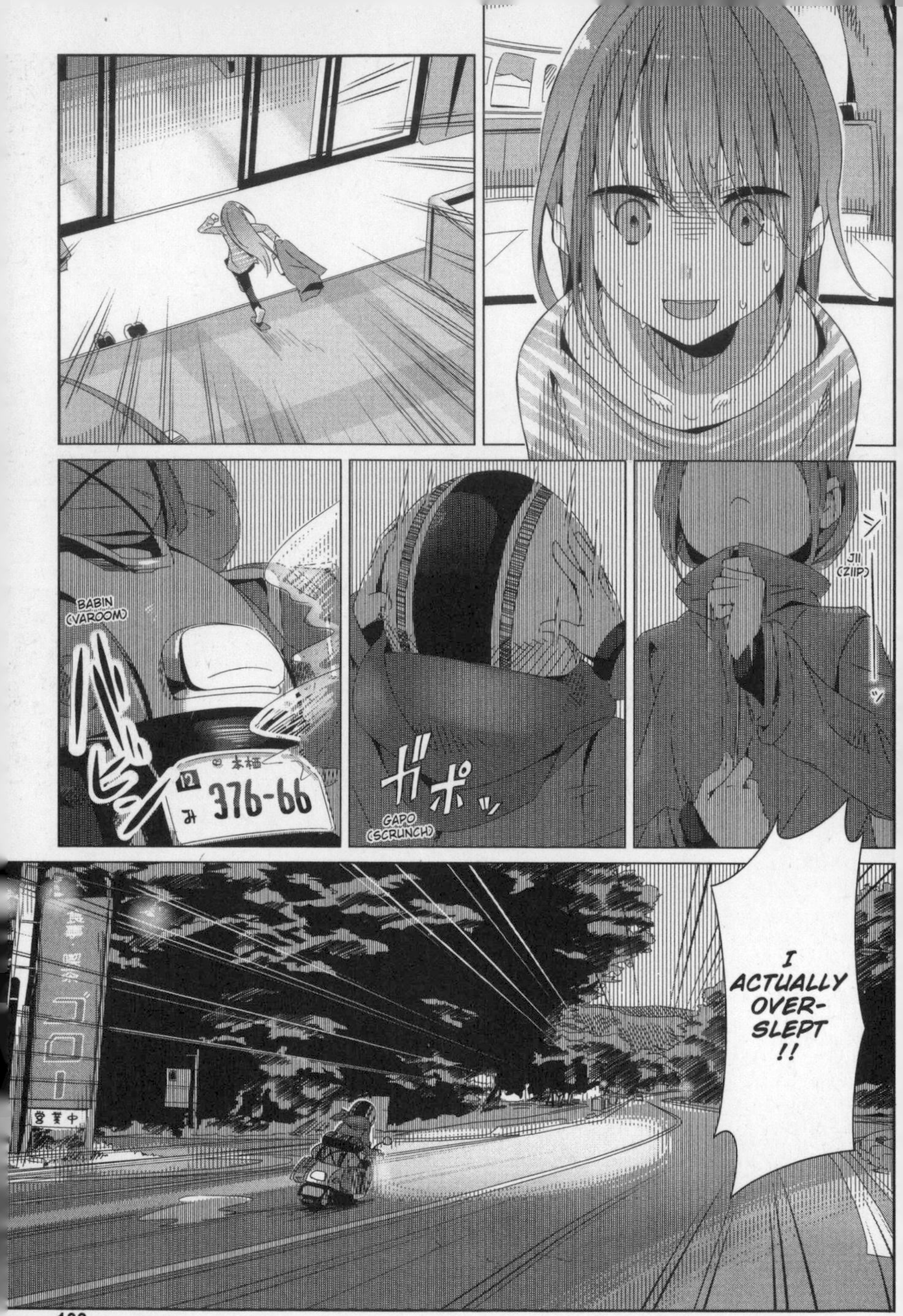
JII
(ZIIP)
ガポッ
GAPO
(SCRUNCH)
BABIN
(VAROOM)
本栖
376-66
み
I ACTUALLY OVER-SLEPT!!
営業中

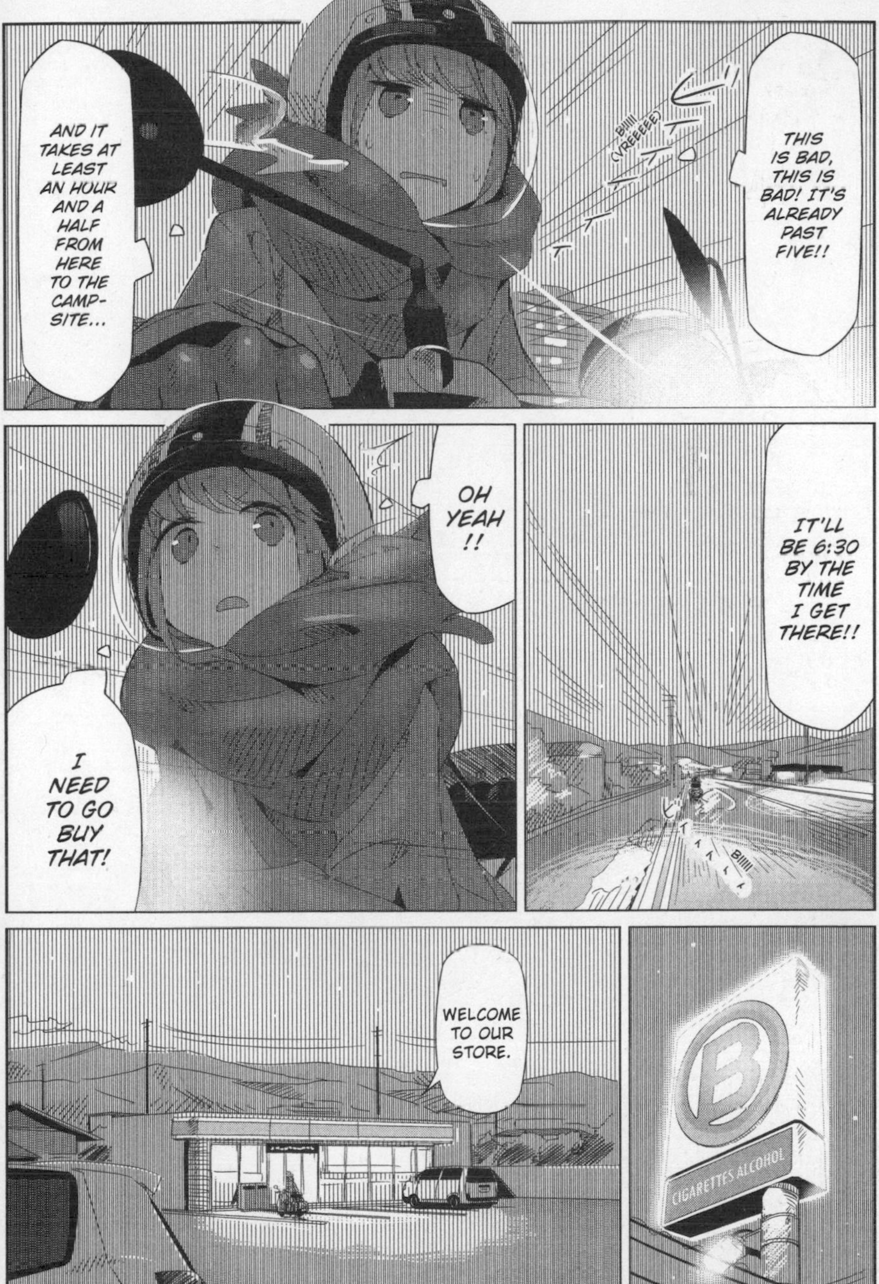
THIS IS BAD, THIS IS BAD! IT'S ALREADY PAST FIVE!!
BIIIII (VREEEEEE)
AND IT TAKES AT LEAST AN HOUR AND A HALF FROM HERE TO THE CAMP-SITE...
IT'LL BE 6:30 BY THE TIME I GET THERE!!
BIIIII
OH YEAH!!
I NEED TO GO BUY THAT!
B
CIGARETTES ALCOHOL
WELCOME TO OUR STORE.

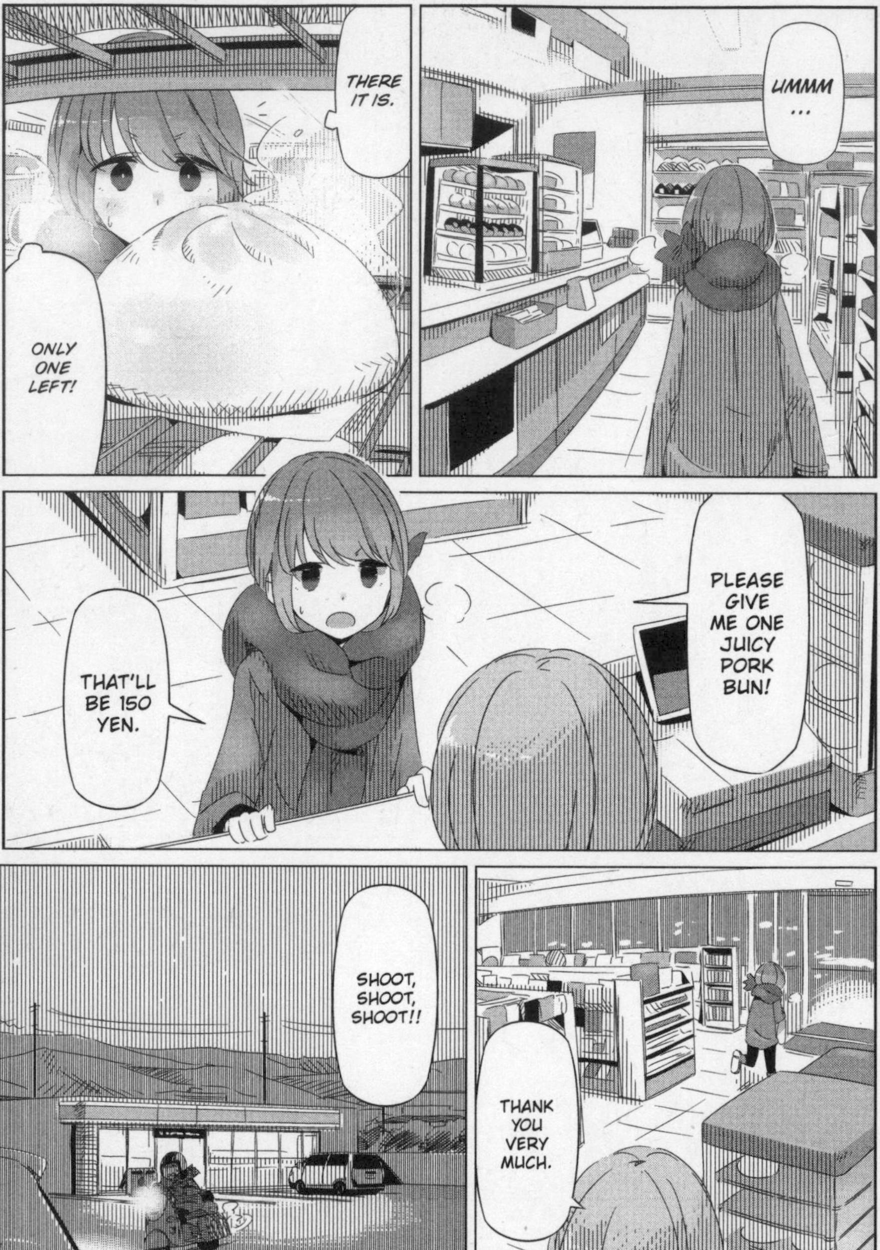
UMMM ...
THERE IT IS.
ONLY ONE LEFT!
PLEASE GIVE ME ONE JUICY PORK BUN!
THAT'LL BE 150 YEN.
THANK YOU VERY MUCH.
SHOOT, SHOOT, SHOOT!!

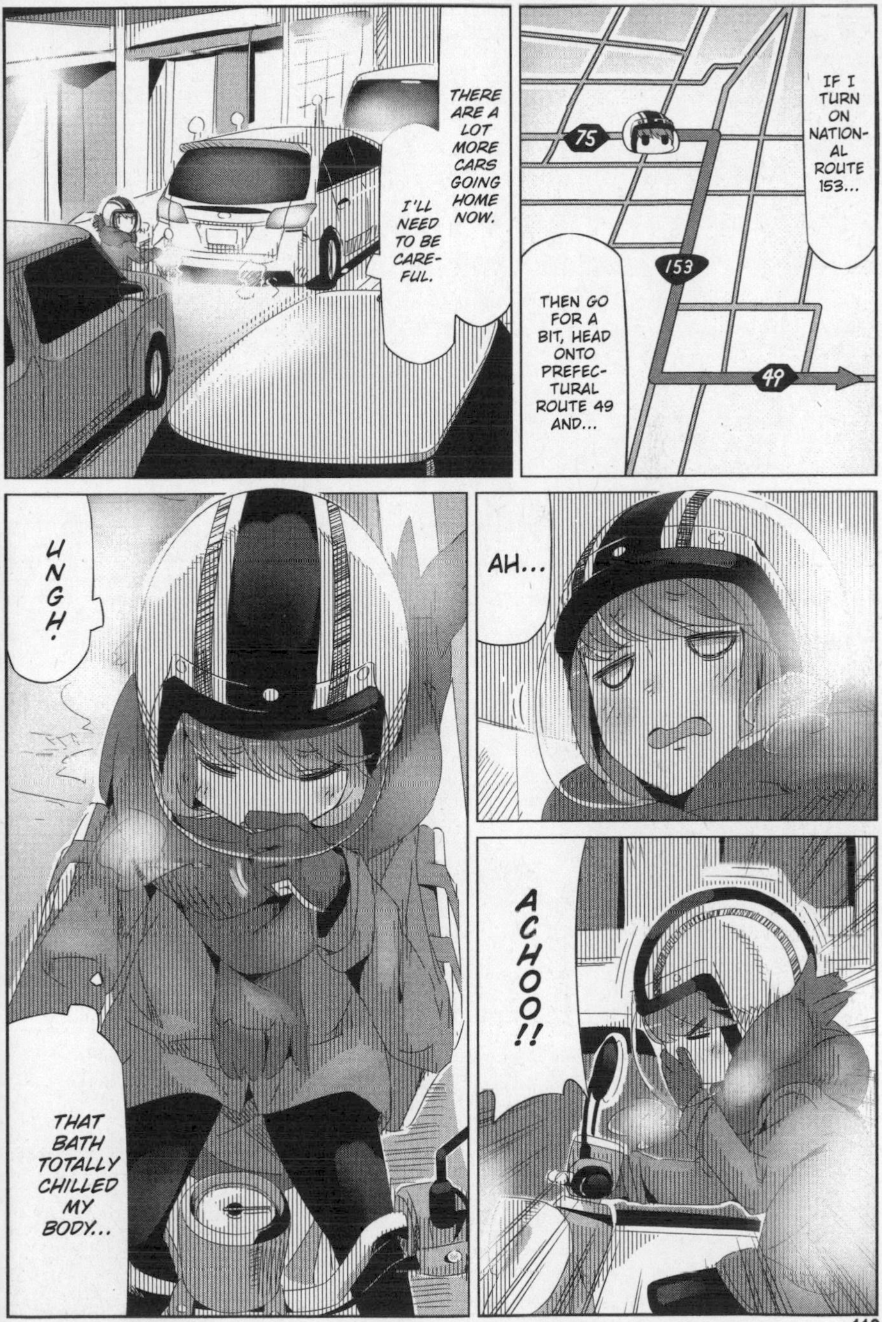
IF I TURN ON NATIONAL ROUTE 153...
75
153
49
THEN GO FOR A BIT, HEAD ONTO PREFECTURAL ROUTE 49 AND...
THERE ARE A LOT MORE CARS GOING HOME NOW.
I'LL NEED TO BE CAREFUL.
AH...
ACHOO!!
UNGH!
THAT BATH TOTALLY CHILLED MY BODY...

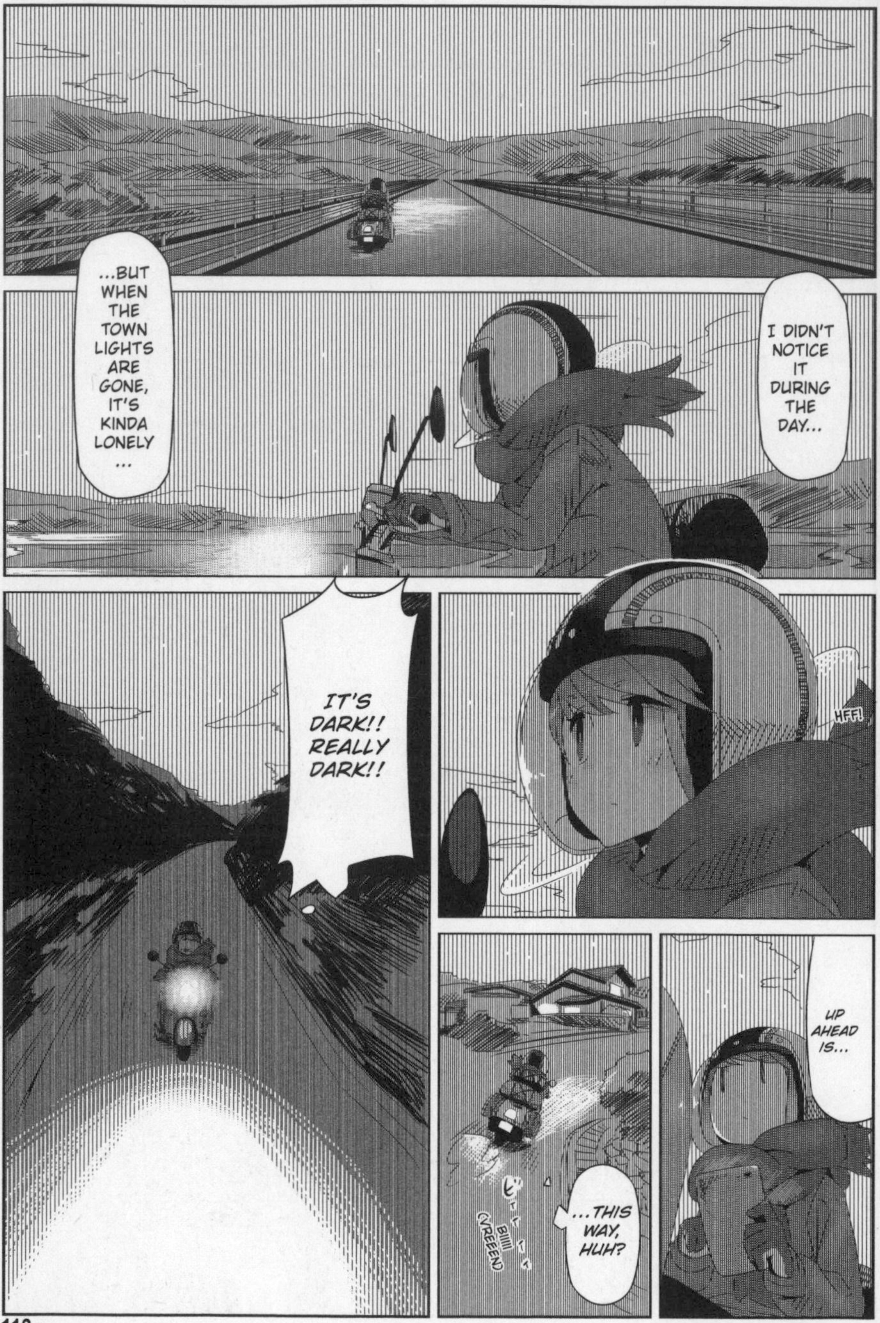
I DIDN'T NOTICE IT DURING THE DAY...
...BUT WHEN THE TOWN LIGHTS ARE GONE, IT'S KINDA LONELY...
HFF!
UP AHEAD IS...
...THIS WAY, HUH?
BIIIII (VREEEN)
IT'S DARK!! REALLY DARK!!

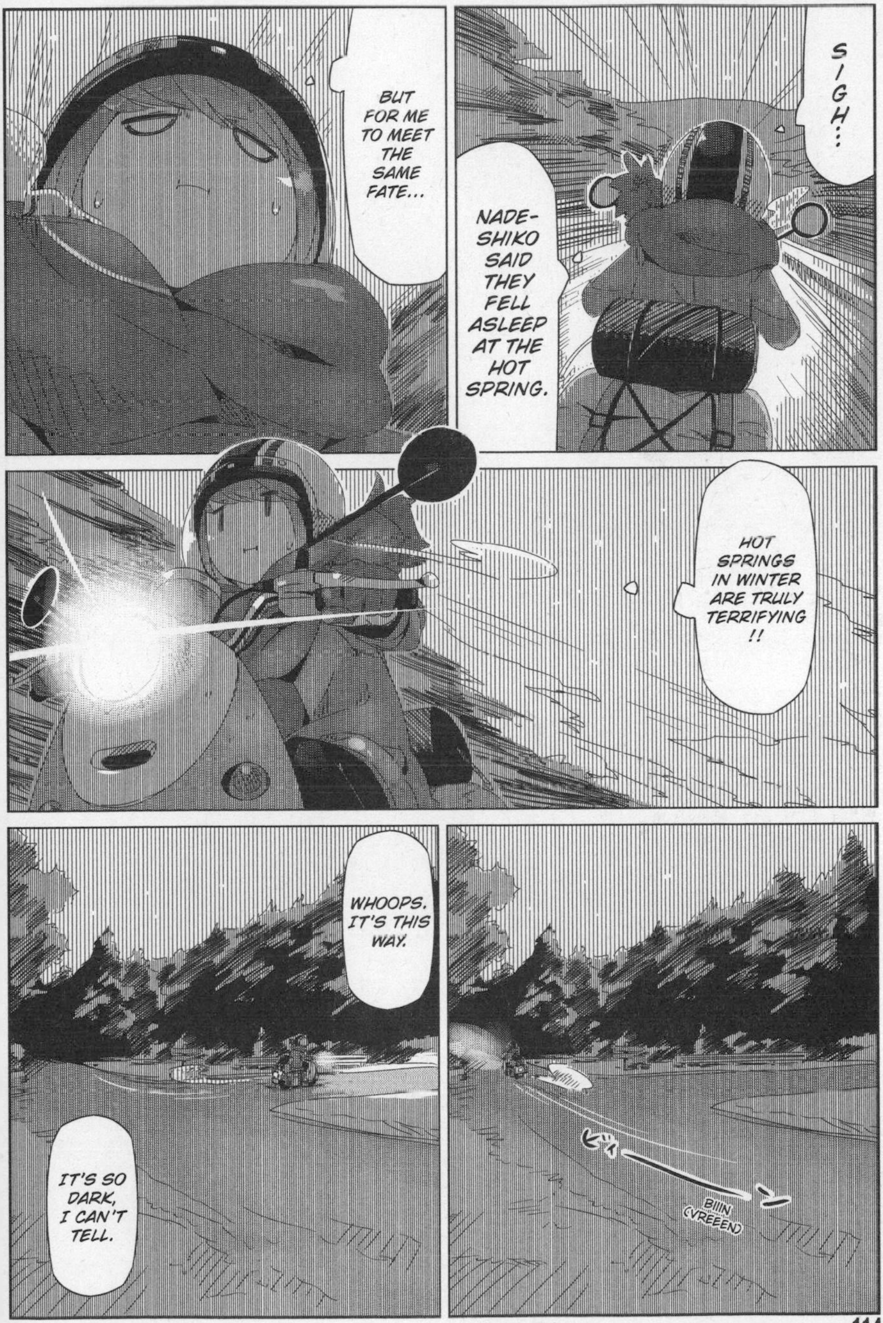
SIGH...
NADESHIKO SAID THEY FELL ASLEEP AT THE HOT SPRING.
BUT FOR ME TO MEET THE SAME FATE...
HOT SPRINGS IN WINTER ARE TRULY TERRIFYING!!
BIIN (VREEEN)
WHOOPS. IT'S THIS WAY.
IT'S SO DARK, I CAN'T TELL.

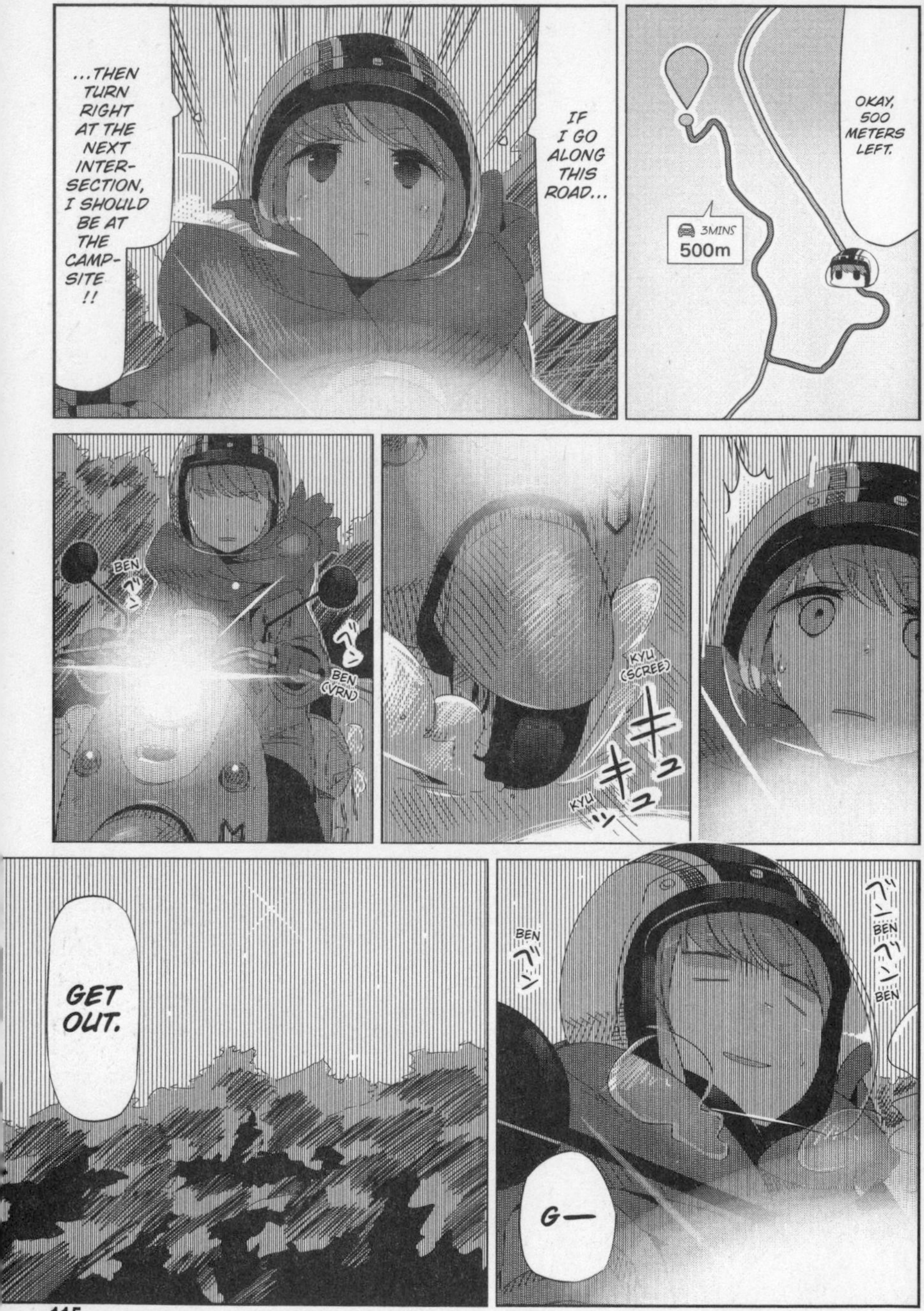

OKAY, 500 METERS LEFT.
3MINS
500m
IF I GO ALONG THIS ROAD...
...THEN TURN RIGHT AT THE NEXT INTER-SECTION, I SHOULD BE AT THE CAMP-SITE!!
KYU (SCREE)
キュ
キュ
KYU
BEN
BEN (VRN)
ベン
BEN
ベン
BEN
BEN
ベン
G—
GET OUT.

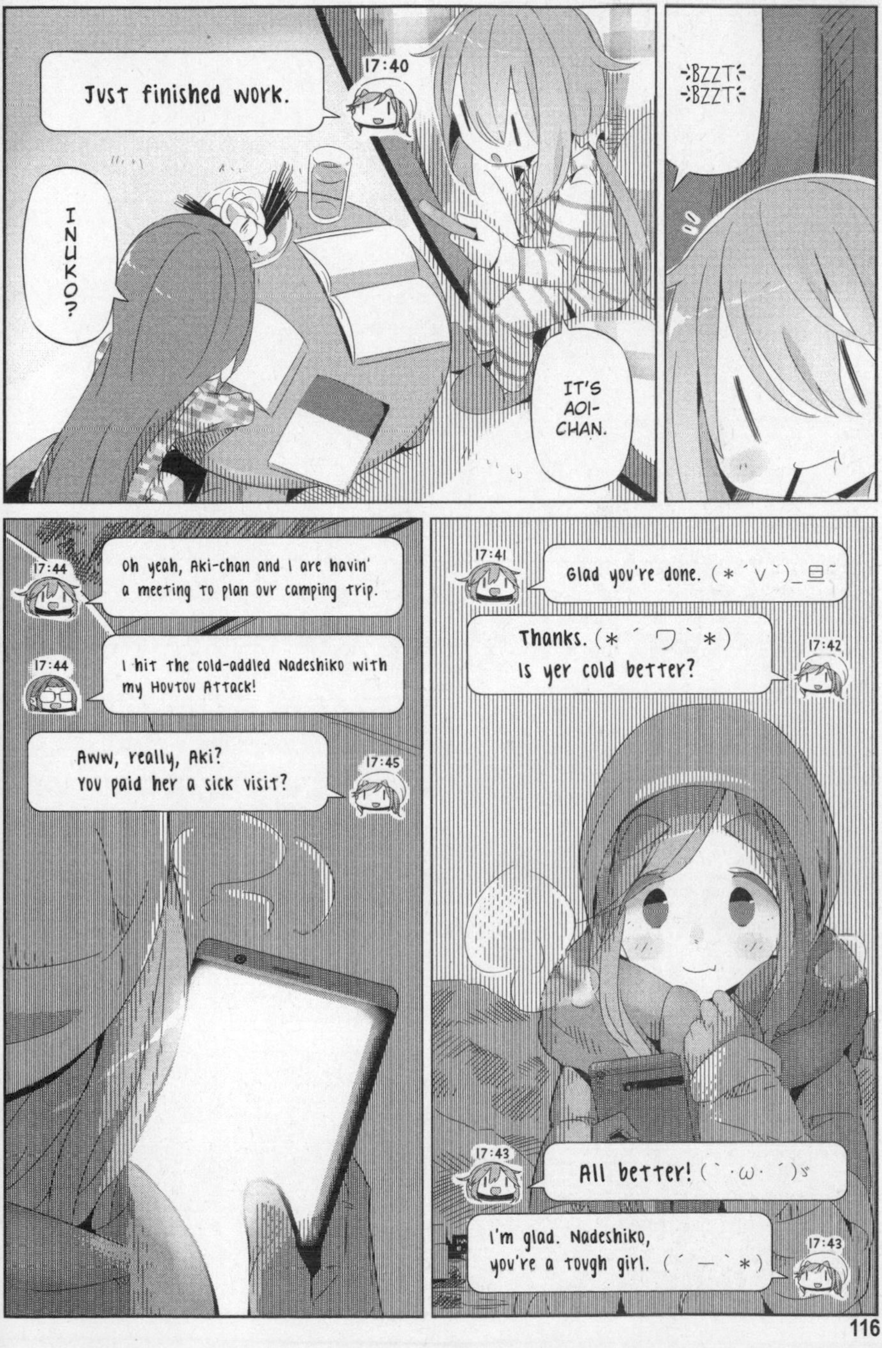

-BZZT-
-BZZT-
17:40
Just finished work.
INUKO?
IT'S AOI-CHAN.
17:41
Glad you're done. (*´∨`)_旦~
Thanks. (*´ワ`*)
Is yer cold better?
17:42
17:43
All better! (`・ω・´)ゞ
I'm glad. Nadeshiko,
you're a tough girl. (´ー`*)
17:43
17:44
Oh yeah, Aki-chan and I are havin' a meeting to plan our camping trip.
17:44
I hit the cold-addled Nadeshiko with my Houtou Attack!
Aww, really, Aki?
You paid her a sick visit?
17:45

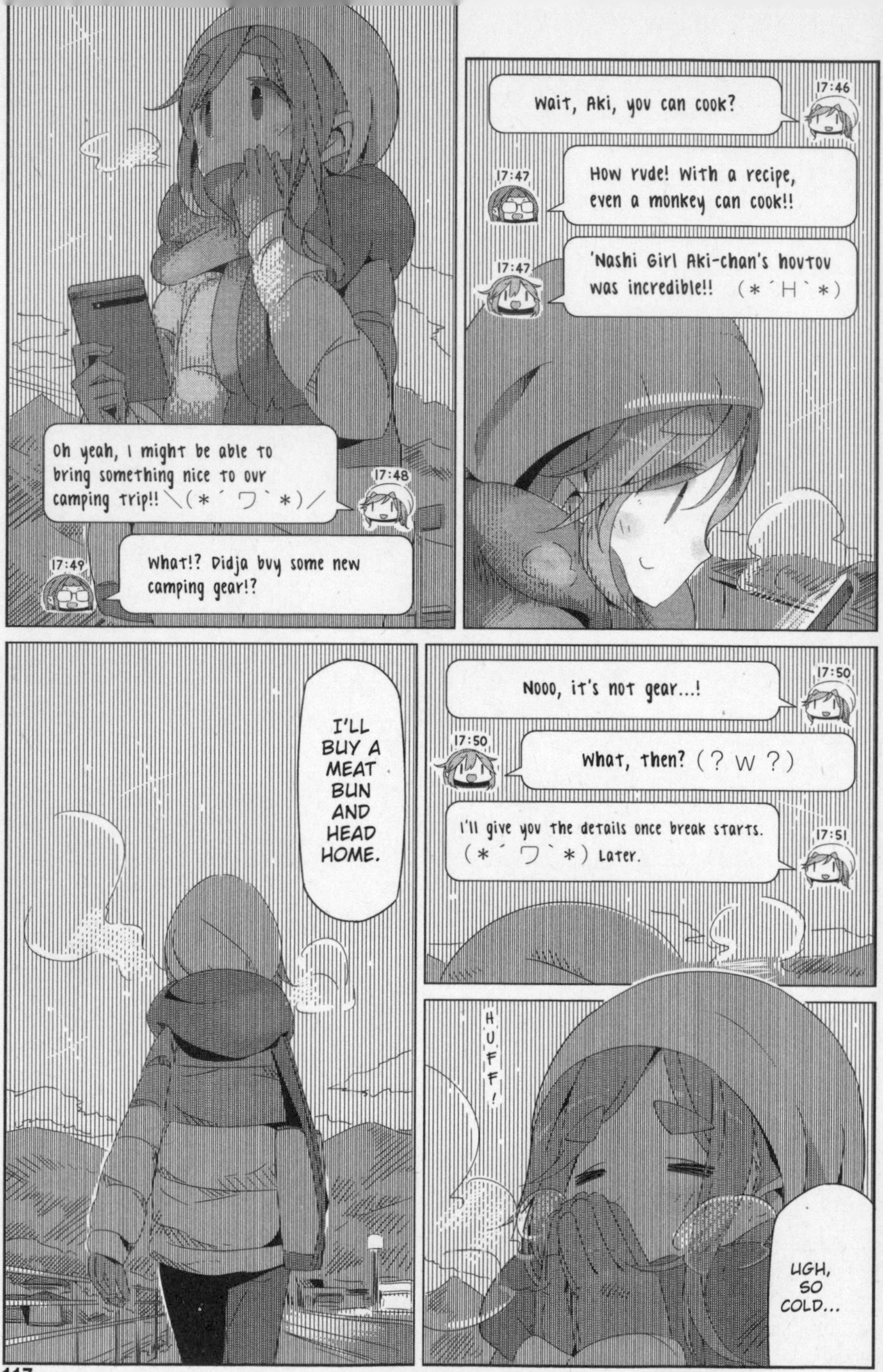

17:46
Wait, Aki, you can cook?
17:47
How rude! With a recipe, even a monkey can cook!!
17:47
'Nashi Girl Aki-chan's houtou was incredible!! (＊´H`＊)
Oh yeah, I might be able to bring something nice to our camping trip!! ＼(＊´ワ`＊)／
17:48
17:49
What!? Didja buy some new camping gear!?
17:50
Nooo, it's not gear...!
17:50
What, then? (？w？)
I'll give you the details once break starts. (＊´ワ`＊) Later.
17:51
HUFF!
UGH, SO COLD...
I'LL BUY A MEAT BUN AND HEAD HOME.

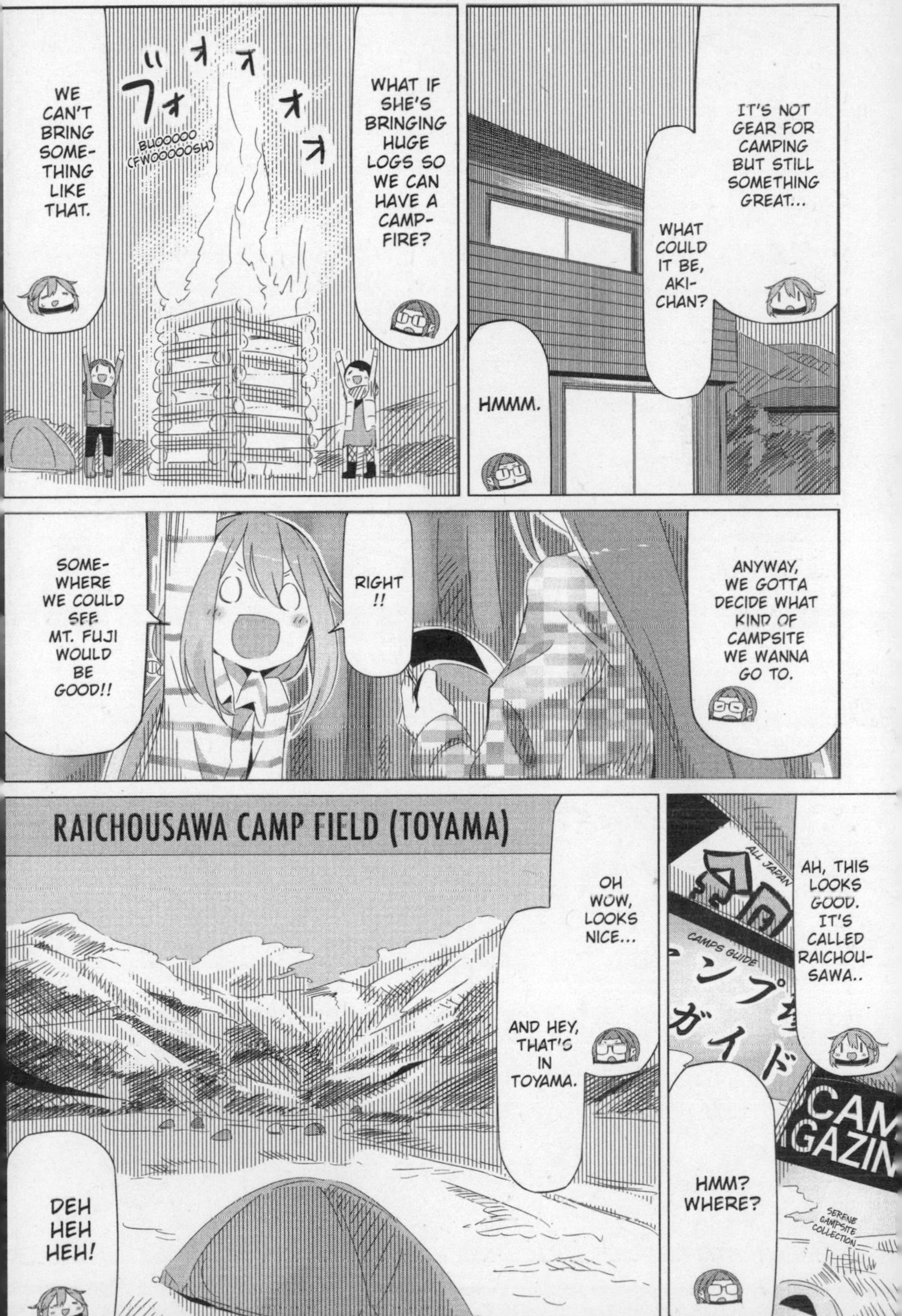
IT'S NOT GEAR FOR CAMPING BUT STILL SOMETHING GREAT...
WHAT COULD IT BE, AKI-CHAN?
HMMM.
WHAT IF SHE'S BRINGING HUGE LOGS SO WE CAN HAVE A CAMP-FIRE?
ブォォォォォ
BUOOOOO (FWOOOOOSH)
WE CAN'T BRING SOME-THING LIKE THAT.
ANYWAY, WE GOTTA DECIDE WHAT KIND OF CAMPSITE WE WANNA GO TO.
RIGHT!!
SOME-WHERE WE COULD SEE MT. FUJI WOULD BE GOOD!!
AH, THIS LOOKS GOOD. IT'S CALLED RAICHOU-SAWA..
ALL JAPAN
CAMPS GUIDE
ンプ場ガイド
CAM
GAZIN
SERENE CAMPSITE COLLECTION
HMM? WHERE?
RAICHOUSAWA CAMP FIELD (TOYAMA)
OH WOW, LOOKS NICE...
AND HEY, THAT'S IN TOYAMA.
DEH HEH HEH!

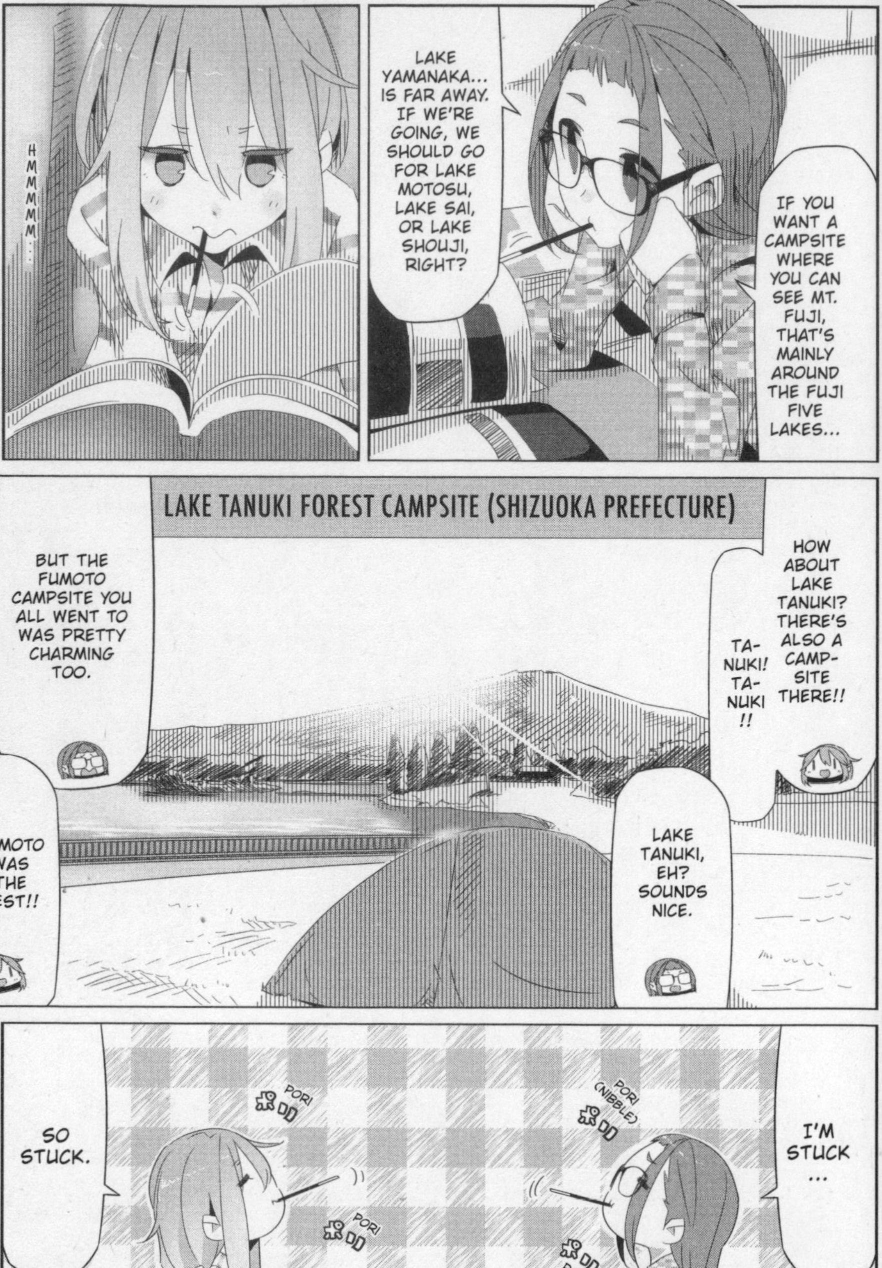
IF YOU WANT A CAMPSITE WHERE YOU CAN SEE MT. FUJI, THAT'S MAINLY AROUND THE FUJI FIVE LAKES...
LAKE YAMANAKA... IS FAR AWAY. IF WE'RE GOING, WE SHOULD GO FOR LAKE MOTOSU, LAKE SAI, OR LAKE SHOUJI, RIGHT?
HMMMMM...
LAKE TANUKI FOREST CAMPSITE (SHIZUOKA PREFECTURE)
HOW ABOUT LAKE TANUKI? THERE'S ALSO A CAMP-SITE THERE!!
TA-NUKI! TA-NUKI!!
LAKE TANUKI, EH? SOUNDS NICE.
BUT THE FUMOTO CAMPSITE YOU ALL WENT TO WAS PRETTY CHARMING TOO.
FUMOTO WAS THE BEST!!
I'M STUCK...
PORI (NIBBLE)
PORI
PORI
PORI
SO STUCK.

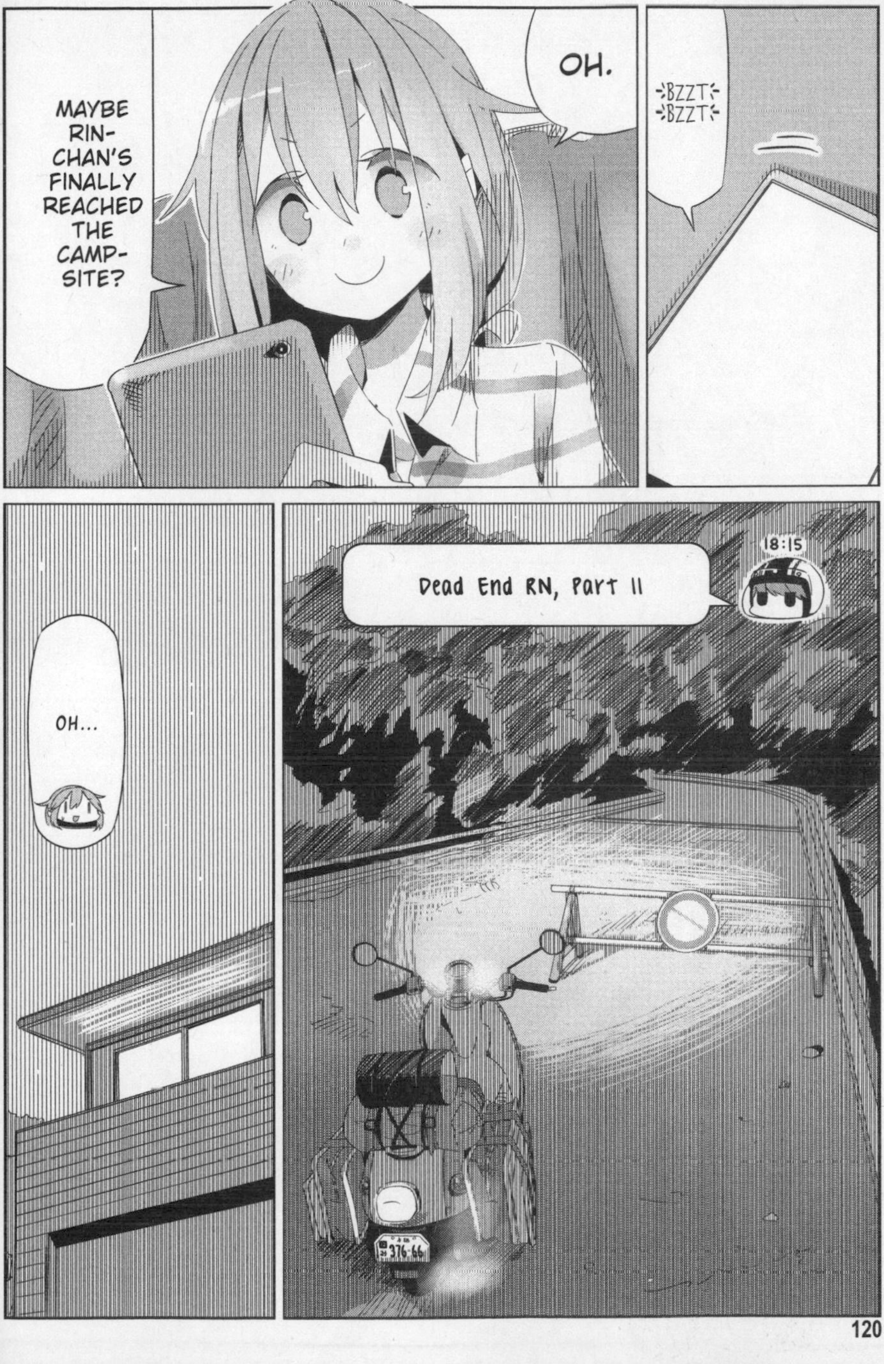
BZZT
BZZT
OH.
MAYBE RIN-CHAN'S FINALLY REACHED THE CAMP-SITE?
18:15
Dead End RN, Part II
OH...

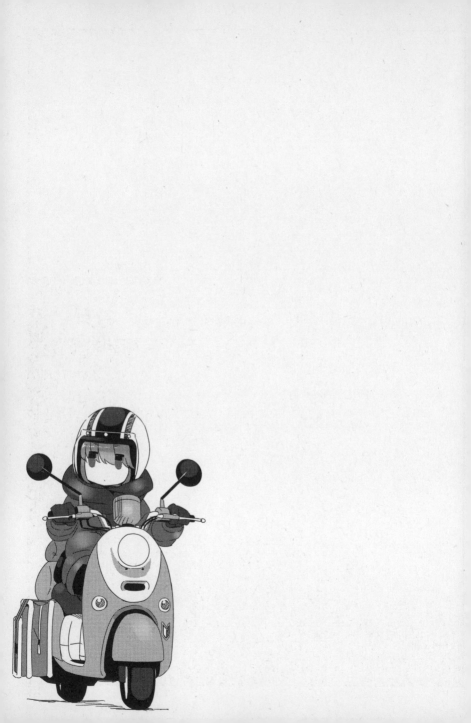

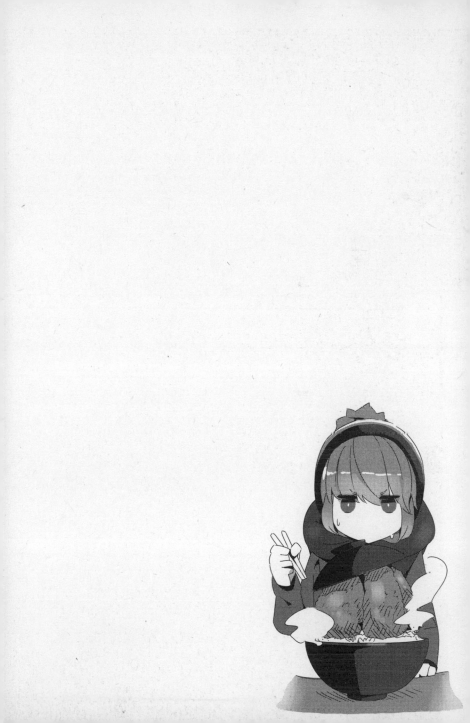

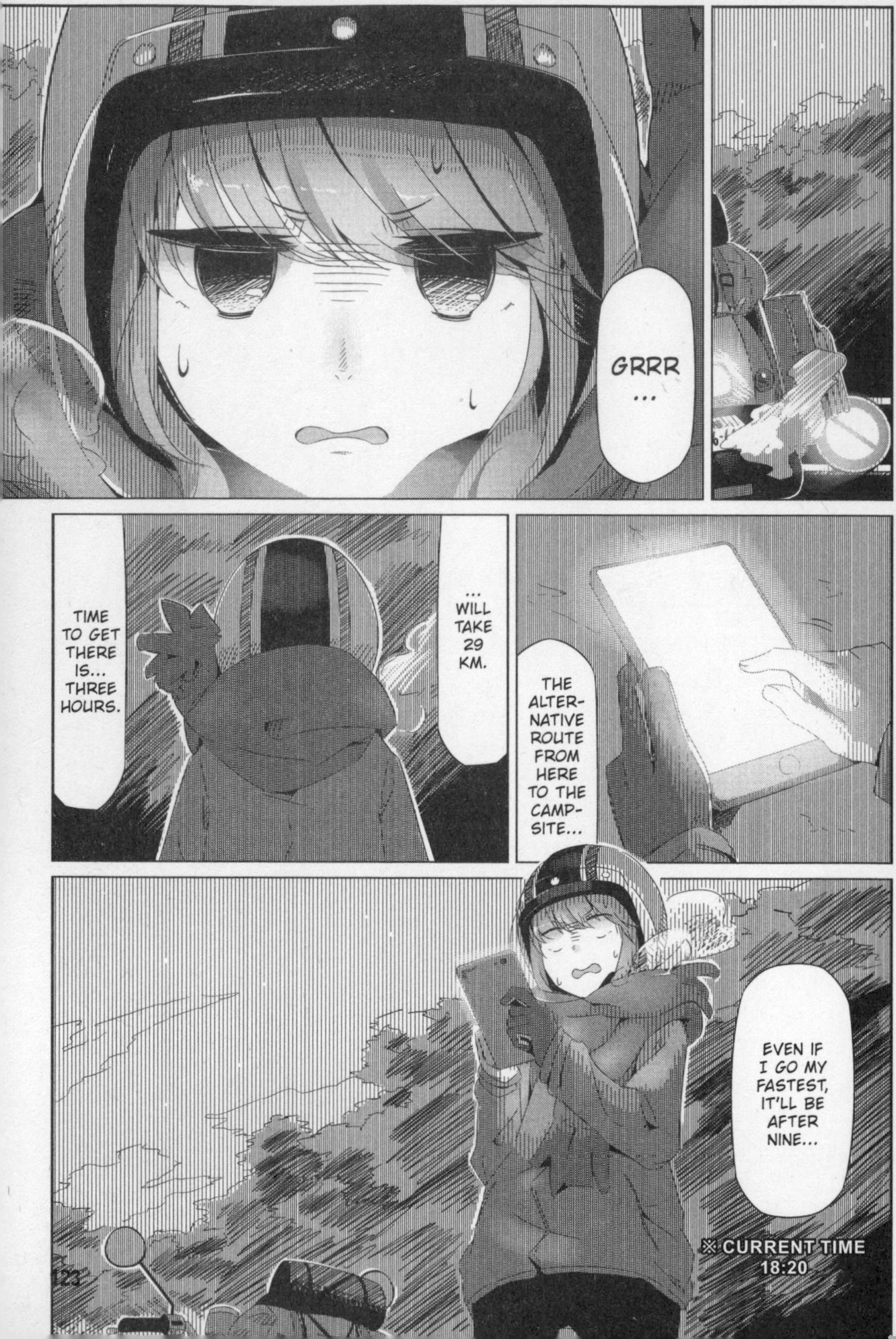
GRRR ...
THE ALTERNATIVE ROUTE FROM HERE TO THE CAMPSITE...
... WILL TAKE 29 KM.
TIME TO GET THERE IS... THREE HOURS.
EVEN IF I GO MY FASTEST, IT'LL BE AFTER NINE...
※ CURRENT TIME 18:20

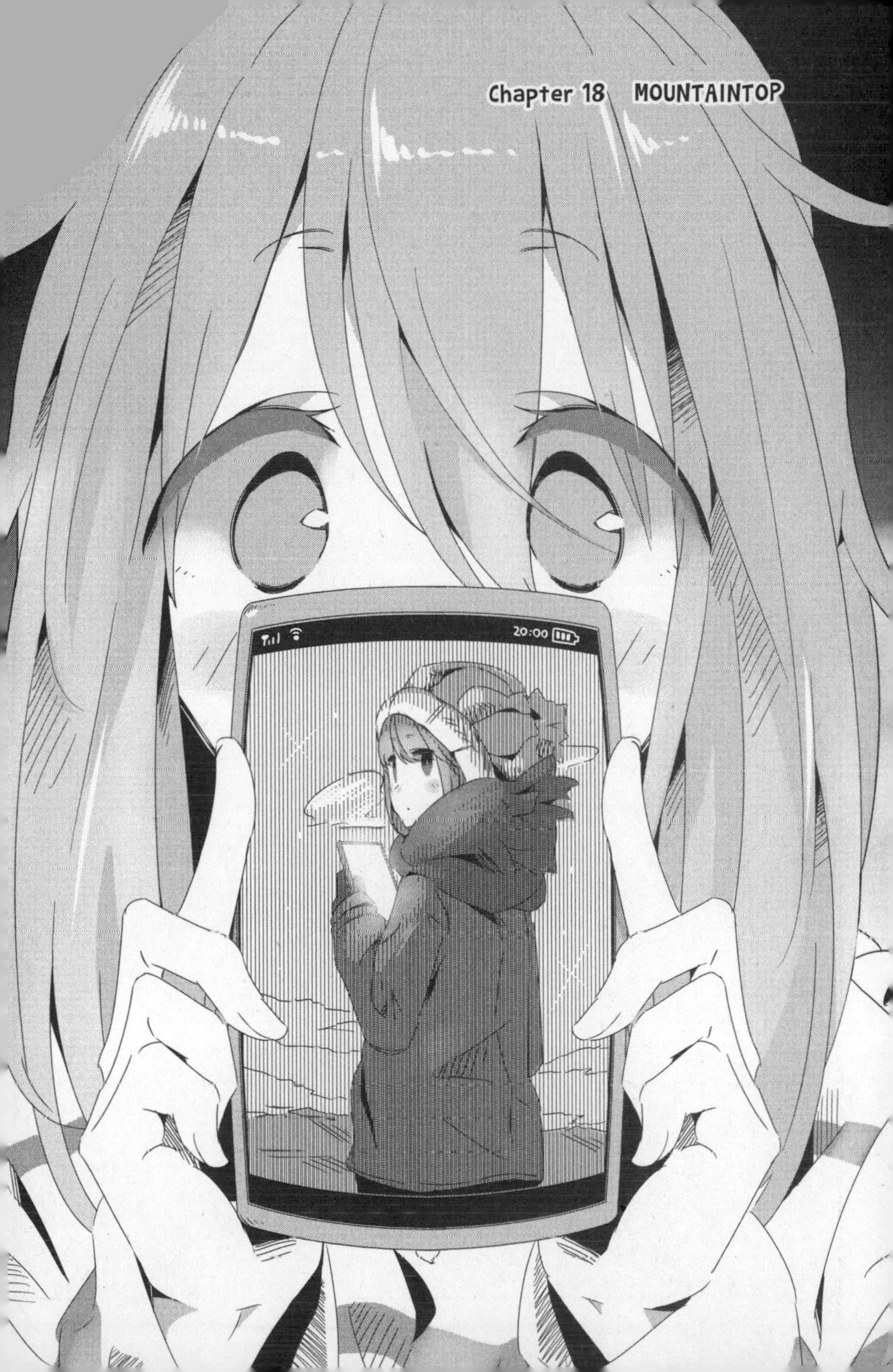
Chapter 18 MOUNTAINTOP
20:00

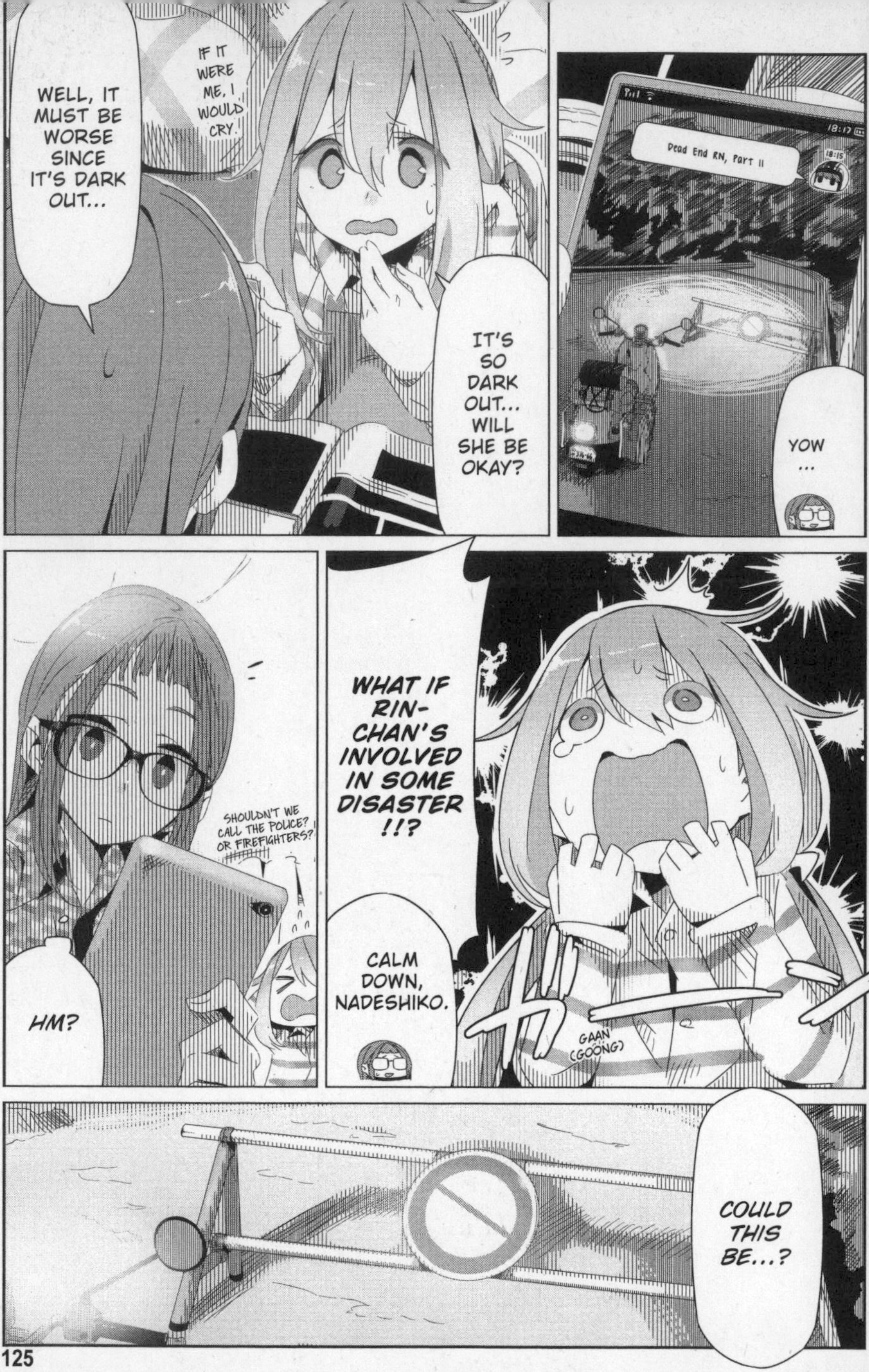
18:17
Dead End RN, Part II
18:15
YOW ...
IT'S SO DARK OUT... WILL SHE BE OKAY?
IF IT WERE ME, I WOULD CRY.
WELL, IT MUST BE WORSE SINCE IT'S DARK OUT...
WHAT IF RIN-CHAN'S INVOLVED IN SOME DISASTER!!?
GAAN (GOONG)
CALM DOWN, NADESHIKO.
SHOULDN'T WE CALL THE POLICE? OR FIREFIGHTERS?
HM?
COULD THIS BE...?

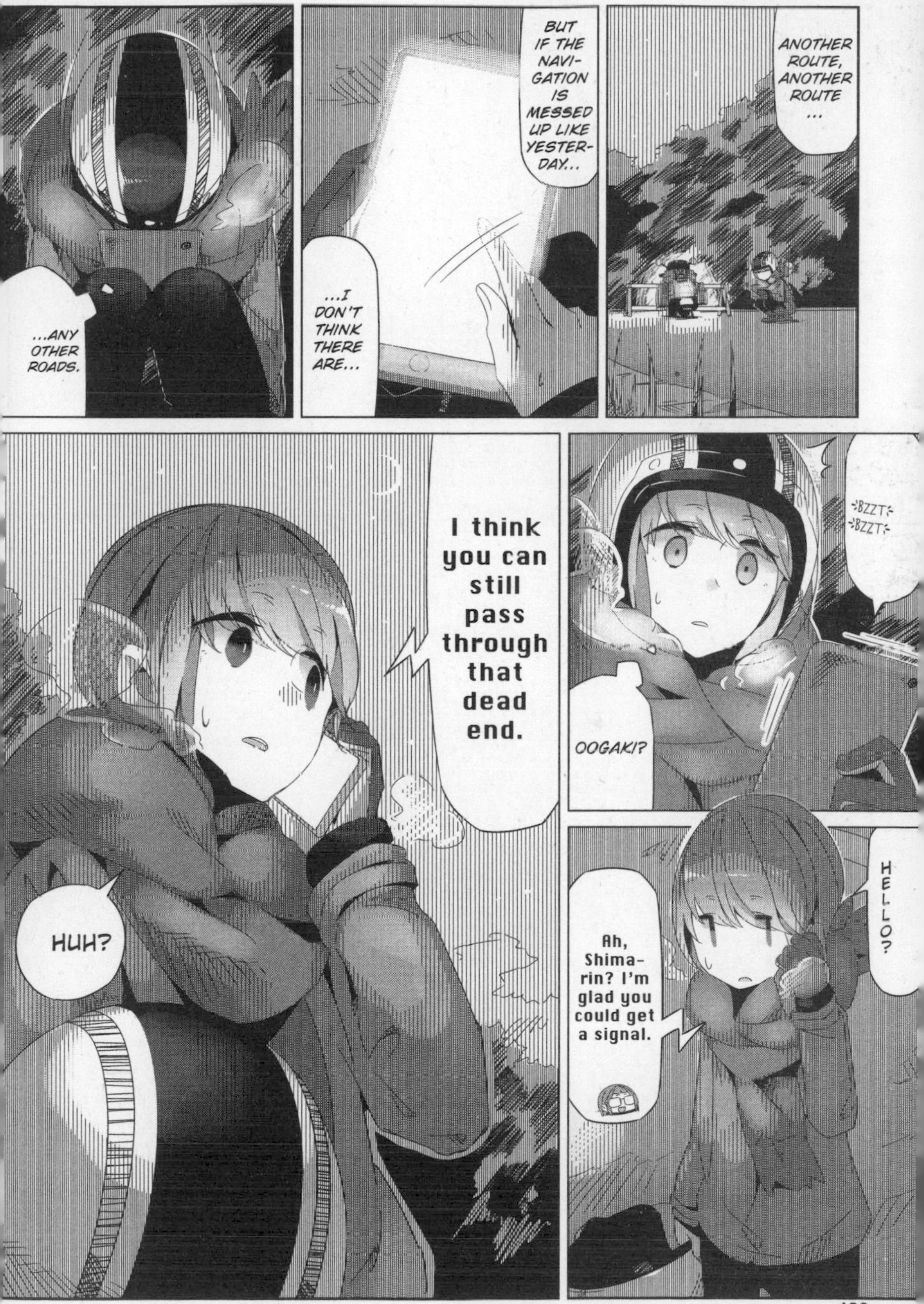
ANOTHER ROUTE, ANOTHER ROUTE ...
BUT IF THE NAVIGATION IS MESSED UP LIKE YESTERDAY...
...I DON'T THINK THERE ARE...
...ANY OTHER ROADS.
BZZT BZZT
OOGAKI?
HELLO?
Ah, Shimarin? I'm glad you could get a signal.
I think you can still pass through that dead end.
HUH?

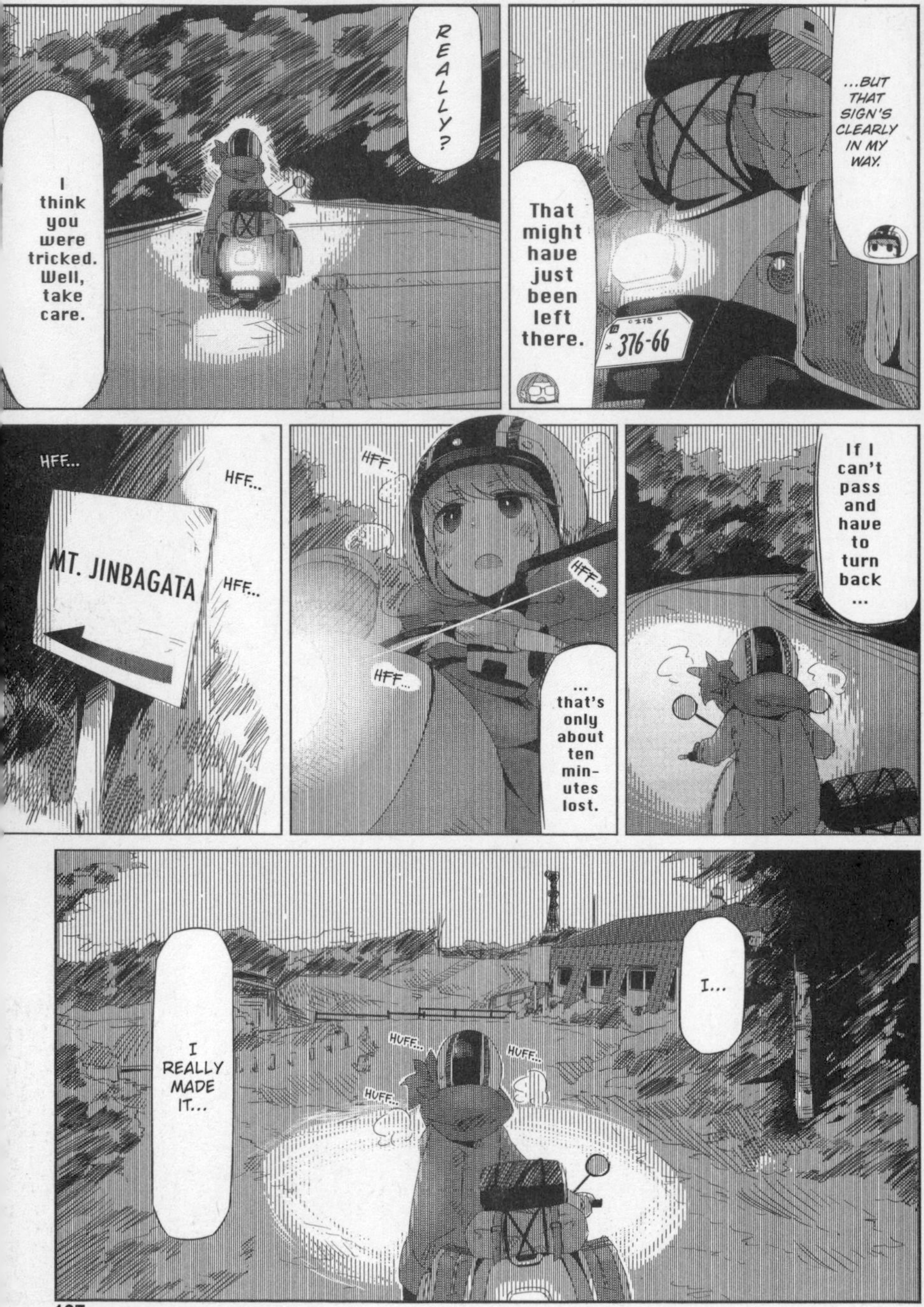
...BUT THAT SIGN'S CLEARLY IN MY WAY.
That might have just been left there.
376-66
REALLY?
I think you were tricked. Well, take care.
If I can't pass and have to turn back ...
HFF...
HFF...
HFF...
... that's only about ten minutes lost.
HFF...
HFF...
HFF...
MT. JINBAGATA
I...
HUFF...
HUFF...
HUFF...
I REALLY MADE IT...

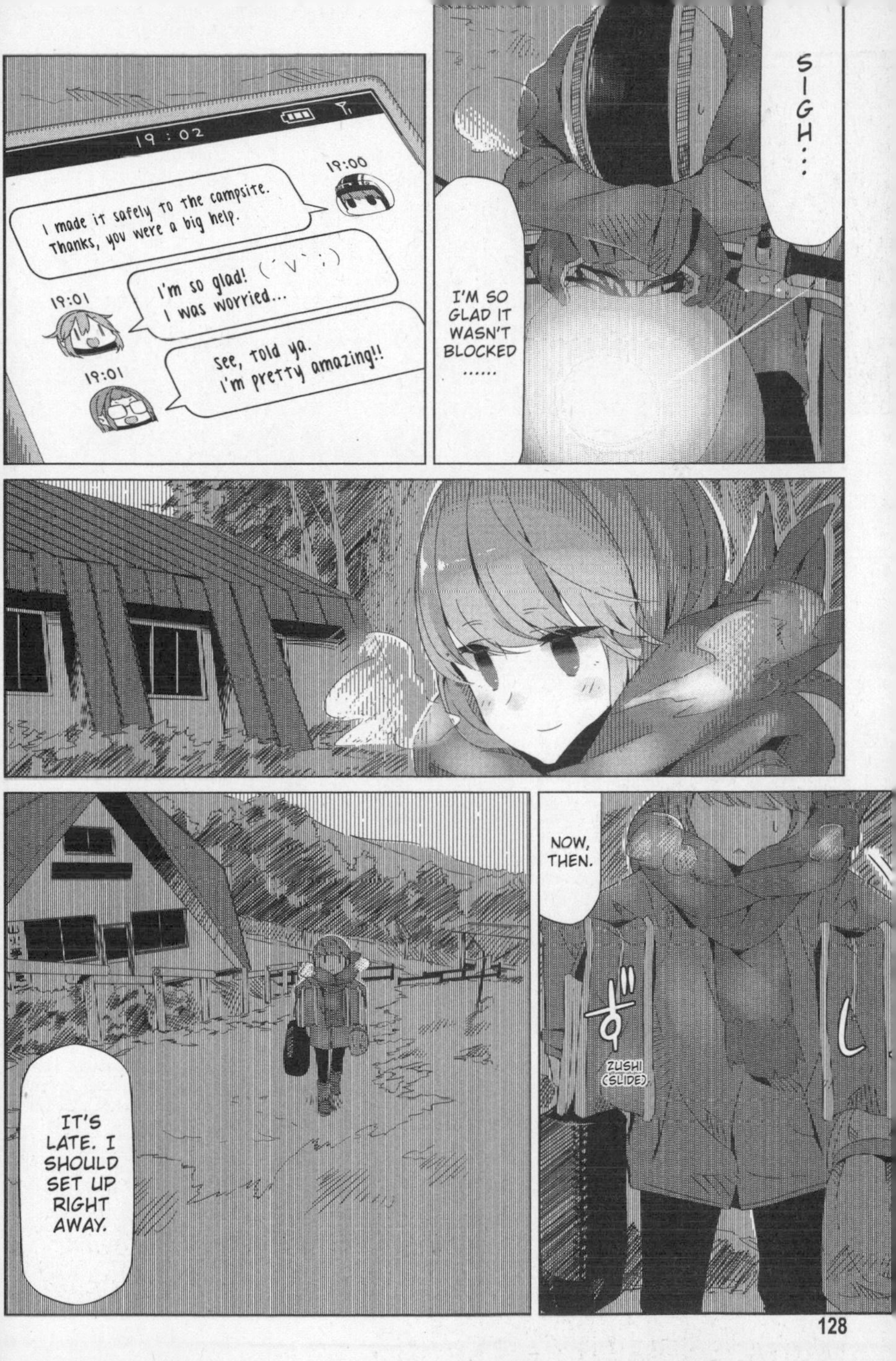
SIGH...
I'M SO GLAD IT WASN'T BLOCKED......
19:02
19:00
I made it safely to the campsite. Thanks, you were a big help.
19:01
I'm so glad! (´∨`;) I was worried...
19:01
See, told ya. I'm pretty amazing!!
NOW, THEN.
ずし
ZUSHI (SLIDE)
IT'S LATE. I SHOULD SET UP RIGHT AWAY.

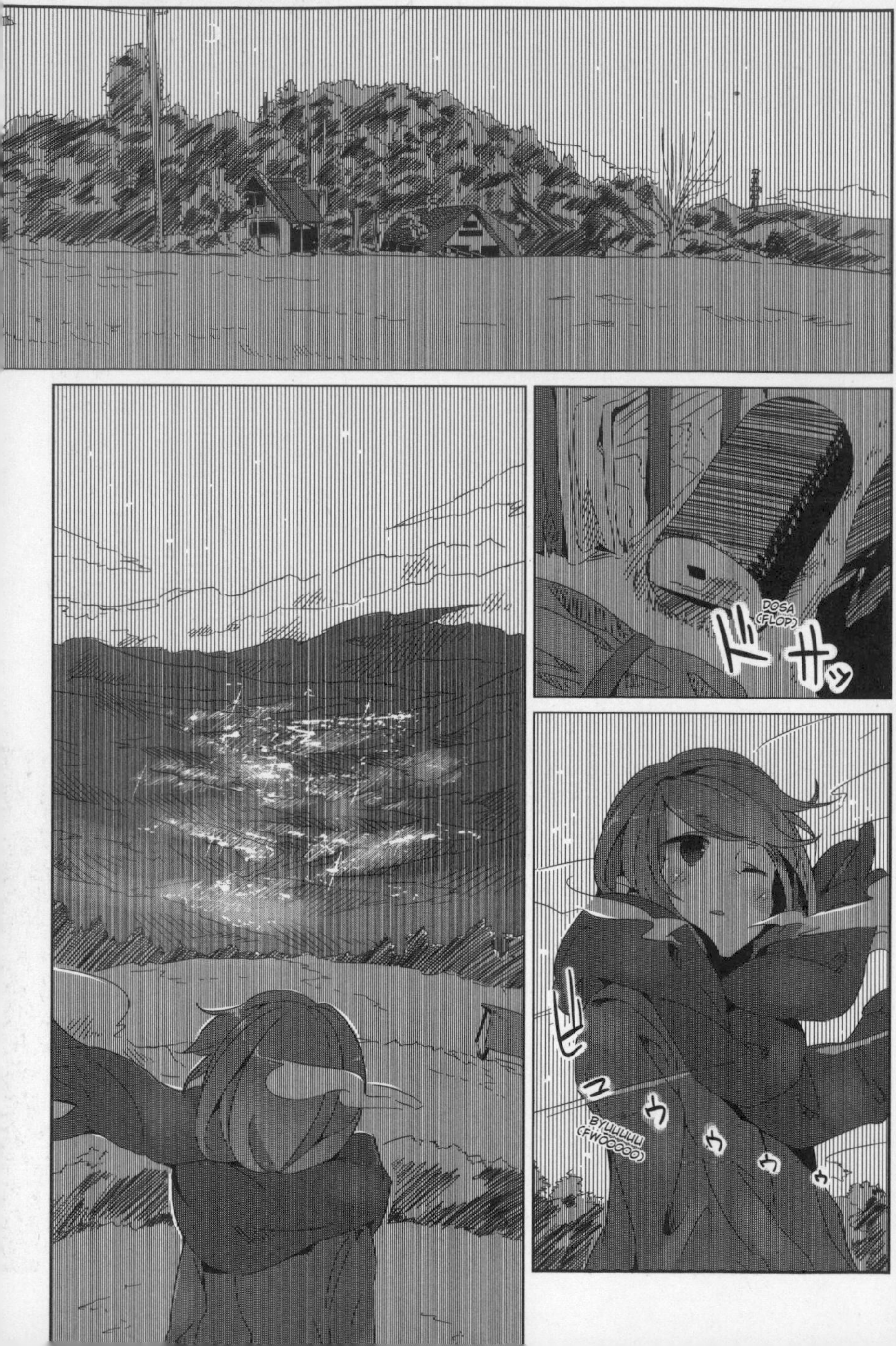
DOSA (FLOP)
BYUUUUU (FWOOOOO)

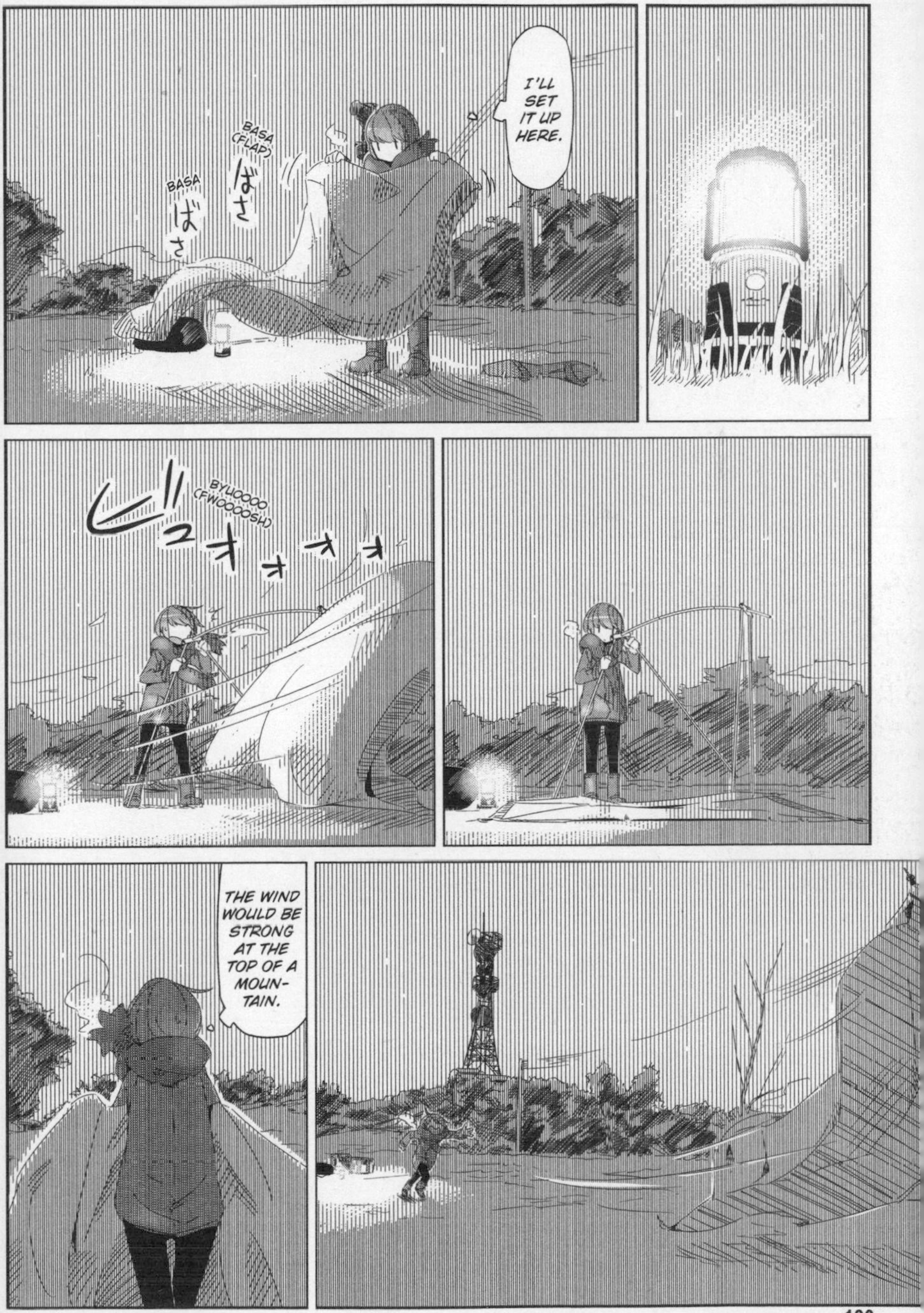
I'LL SET IT UP HERE.
BASA (FLAP)
ばさ
BASA
ばさ
BYUOOOO (FWOOOOSH)
ビュオオオオ
THE WIND WOULD BE STRONG AT THE TOP OF A MOUN-TAIN.

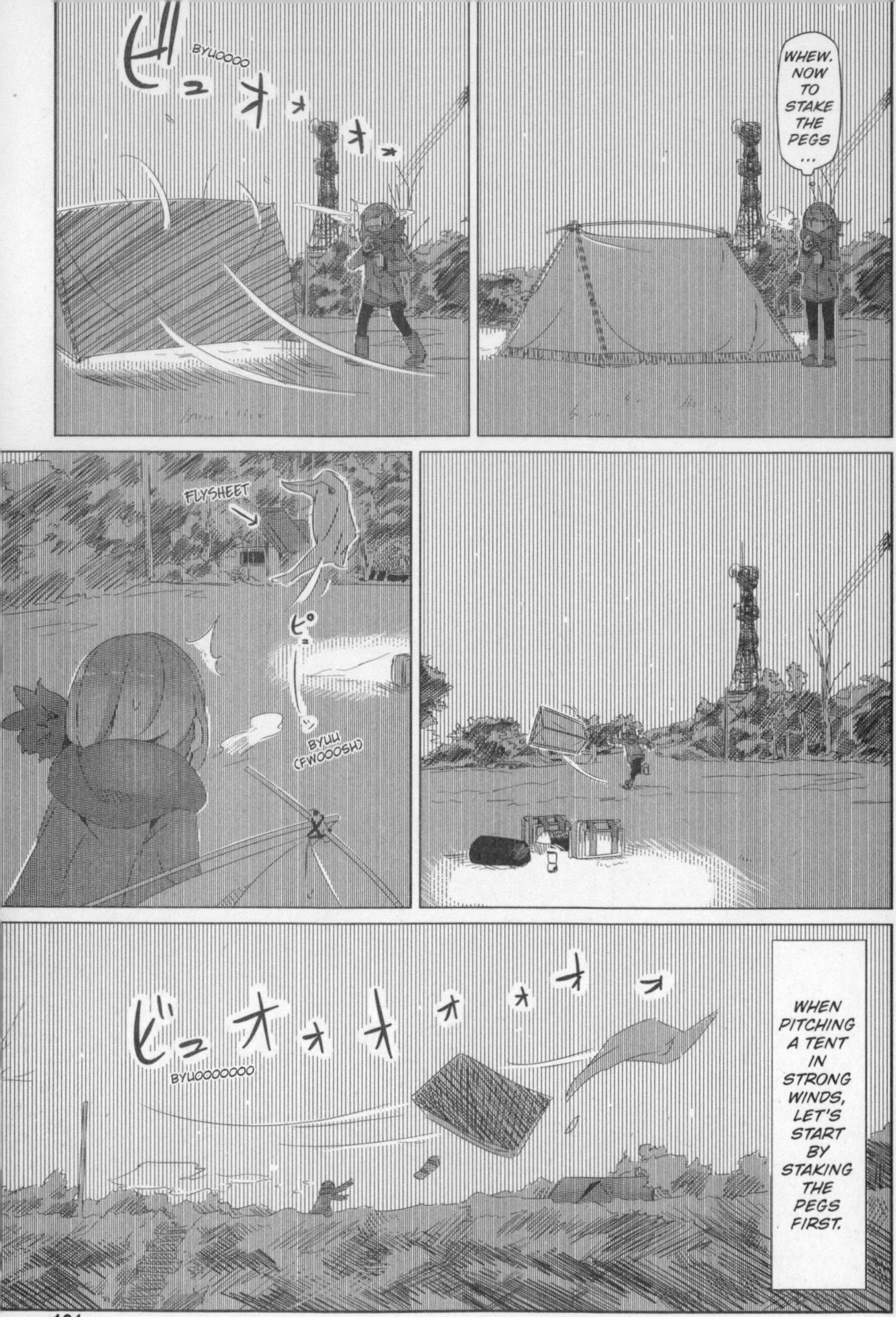

WHEW. NOW TO STAKE THE PEGS...
ビュオォオォ
BYUOOOO
FLYSHEET
ピューッ
BYUU (FWOOOSH)
WHEN PITCHING A TENT IN STRONG WINDS, LET'S START BY STAKING THE PEGS FIRST.
ビュオォオォオォ
BYUOOOOOOO

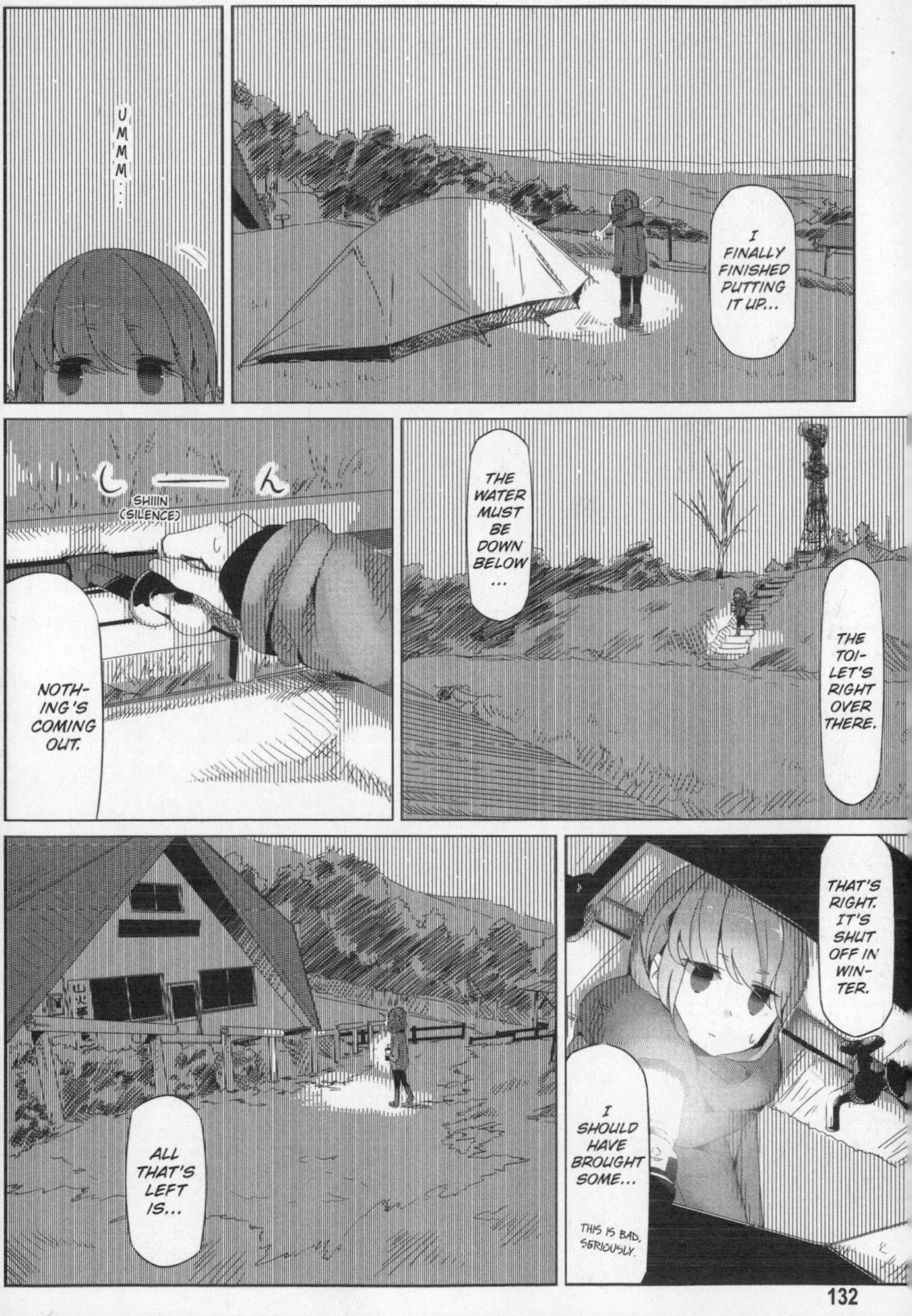
I FINALLY FINISHED PUTTING IT UP...
UMMM...
THE TOI-LET'S RIGHT OVER THERE.
THE WATER MUST BE DOWN BELOW...
しーーん
SHIIN (SILENCE)
NOTH-ING'S COMING OUT.
THAT'S RIGHT. IT'S SHUT OFF IN WIN-TER.
I SHOULD HAVE BROUGHT SOME...
THIS IS BAD, SERIOUSLY.
ALL THAT'S LEFT IS...

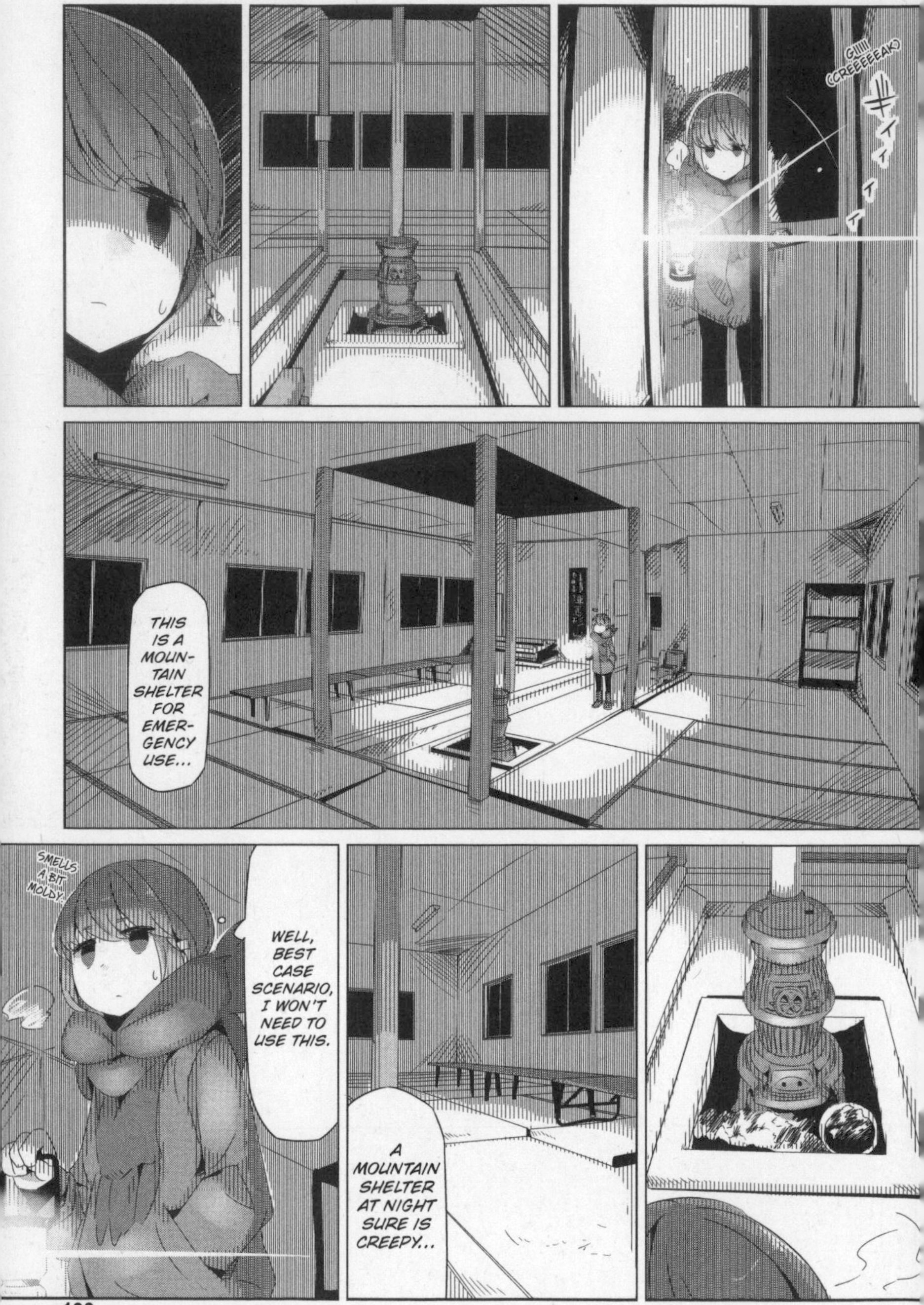
ギイイイイ
GIIIII
(CREEEEEAK)
THIS IS A MOUNTAIN SHELTER FOR EMERGENCY USE...
A MOUNTAIN SHELTER AT NIGHT SURE IS CREEPY...
WELL, BEST CASE SCENARIO, I WON'T NEED TO USE THIS.
SMELLS A BIT MOLDY.

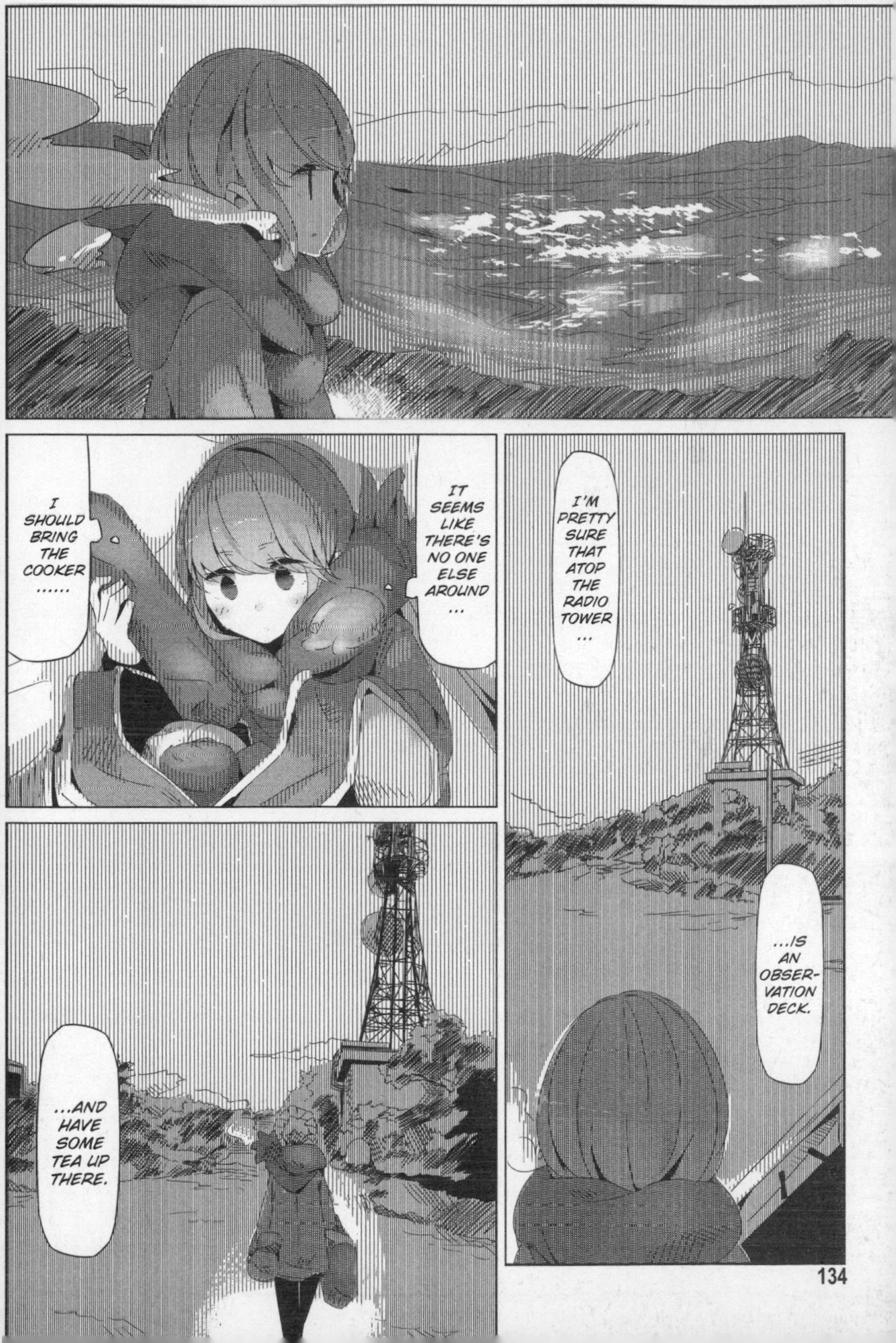
I'M PRETTY SURE THAT ATOP THE RADIO TOWER ...
...IS AN OBSER-VATION DECK.
IT SEEMS LIKE THERE'S NO ONE ELSE AROUND ...
I SHOULD BRING THE COOKER ......
...AND HAVE SOME TEA UP THERE.

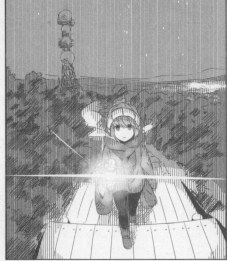

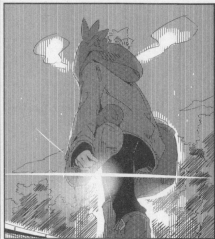

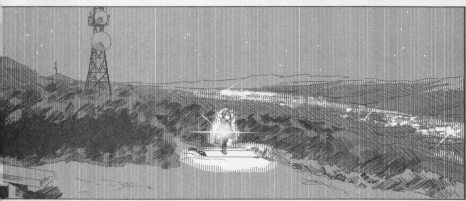

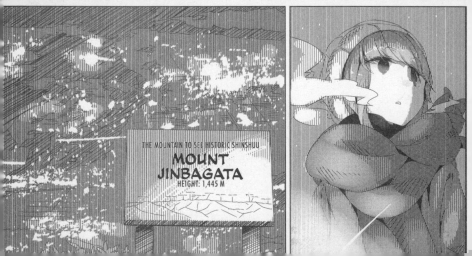

THE MOUNTAIN TO SEE HISTORIC SHINSHUU

MOUNT
JINBAGATA
HEIGHT: 1,445 M

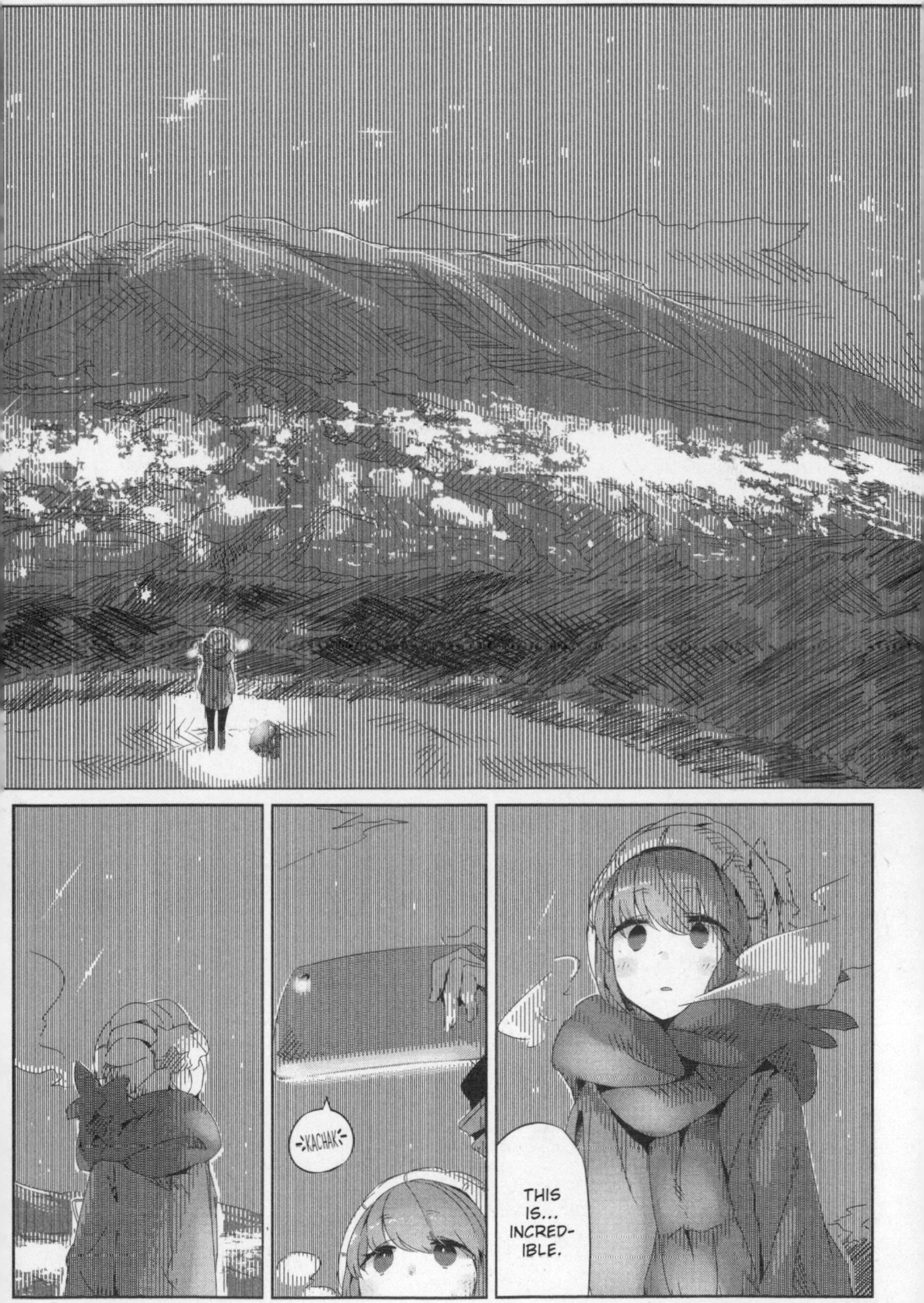
THIS IS... INCREDIBLE.
KACHAK

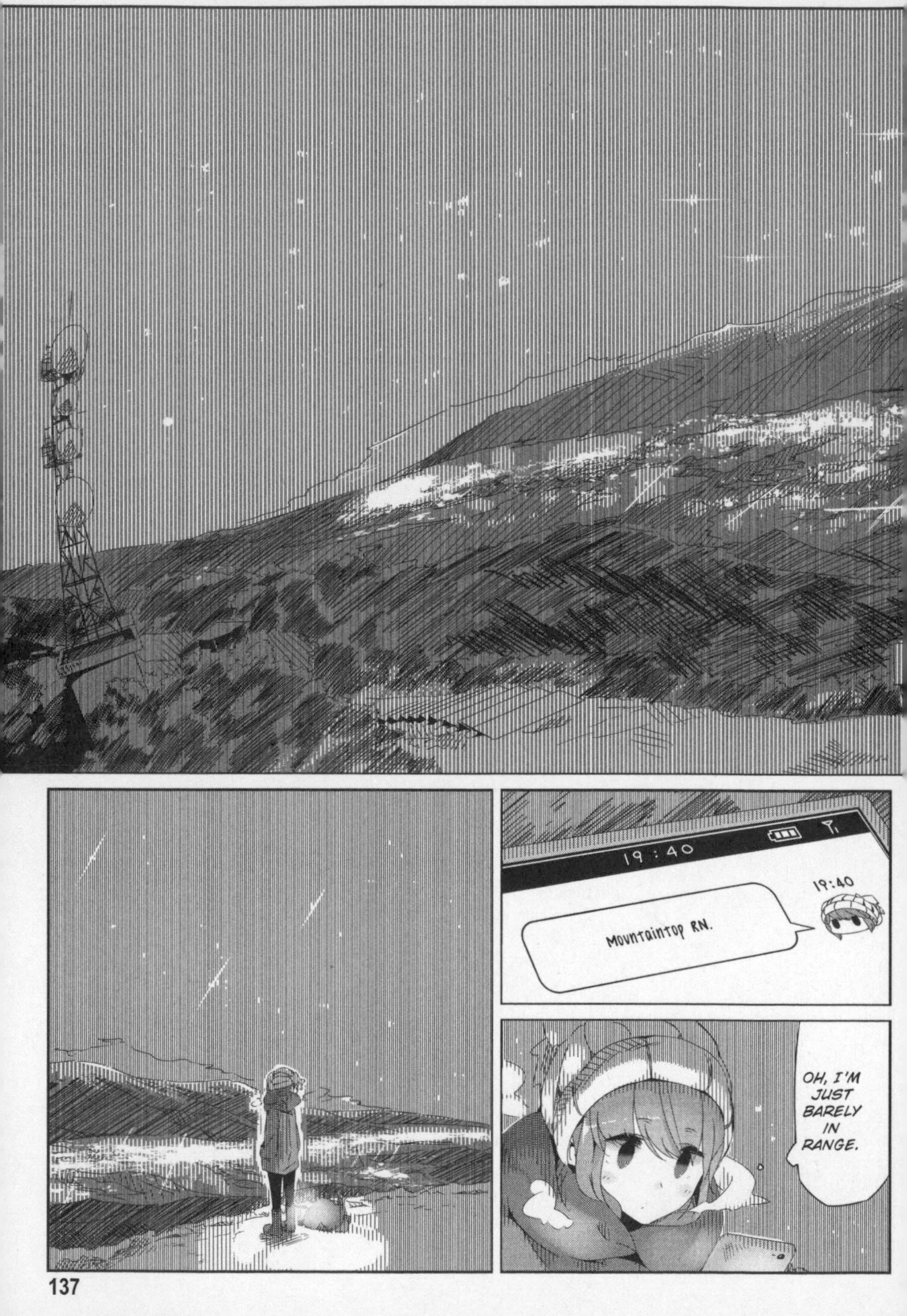
19:40
19:40
Mountaintop RN.
OH, I'M JUST BARELY IN RANGE.

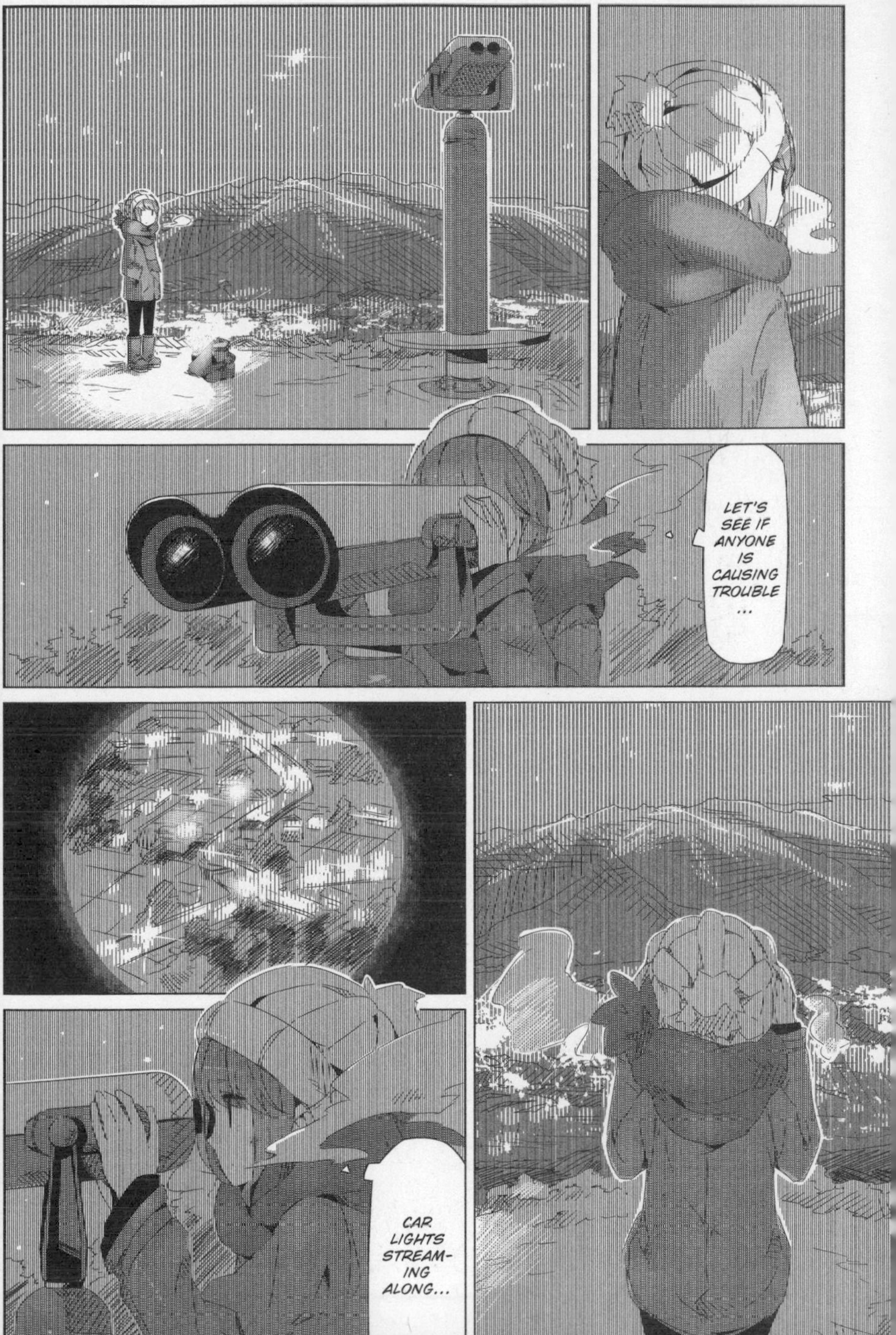
LET'S SEE IF ANYONE IS CAUSING TROUBLE ...
CAR LIGHTS STREAM-ING ALONG...

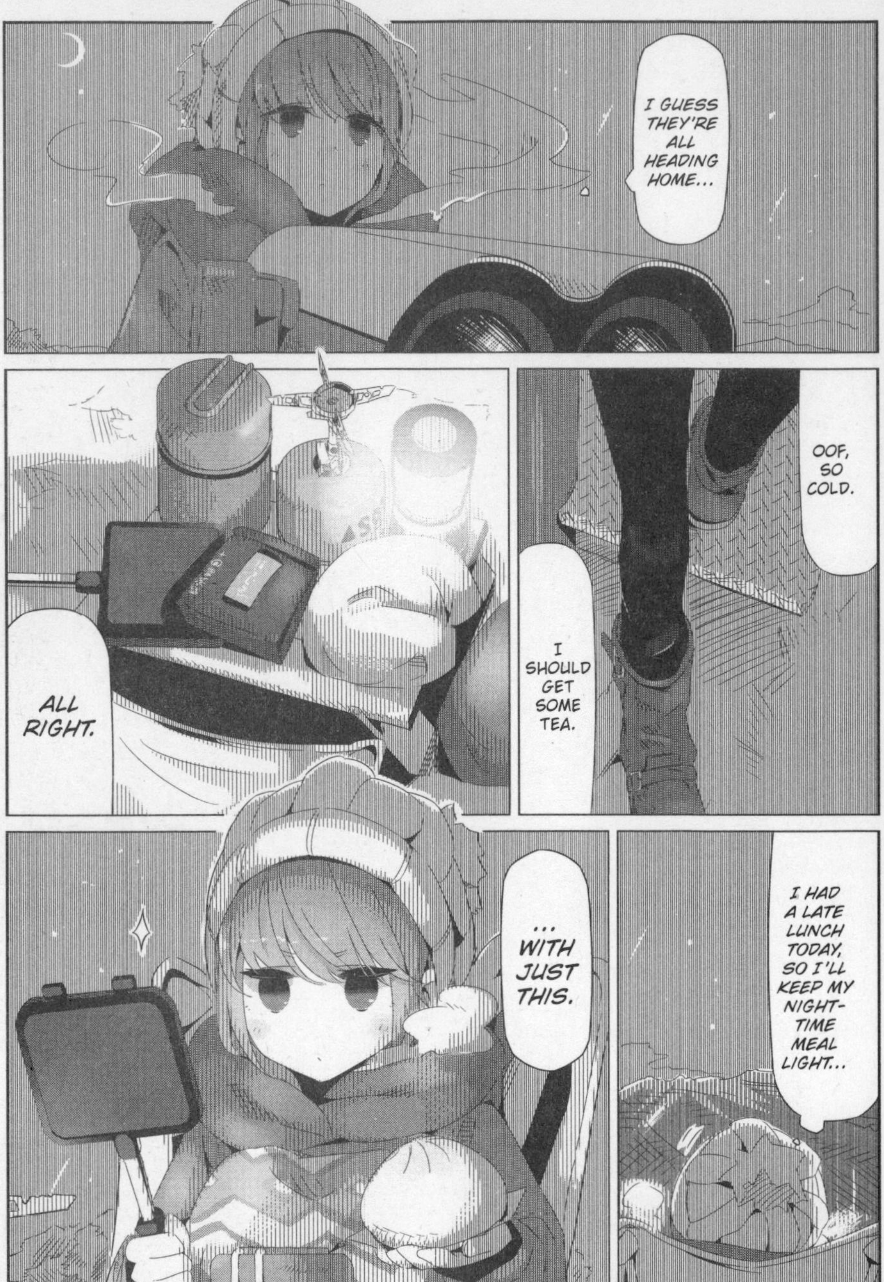
I GUESS THEY'RE ALL HEADING HOME...
OOF, SO COLD.
I SHOULD GET SOME TEA.
ALL RIGHT.
I HAD A LATE LUNCH TODAY, SO I'LL KEEP MY NIGHT-TIME MEAL LIGHT...
...WITH JUST THIS.

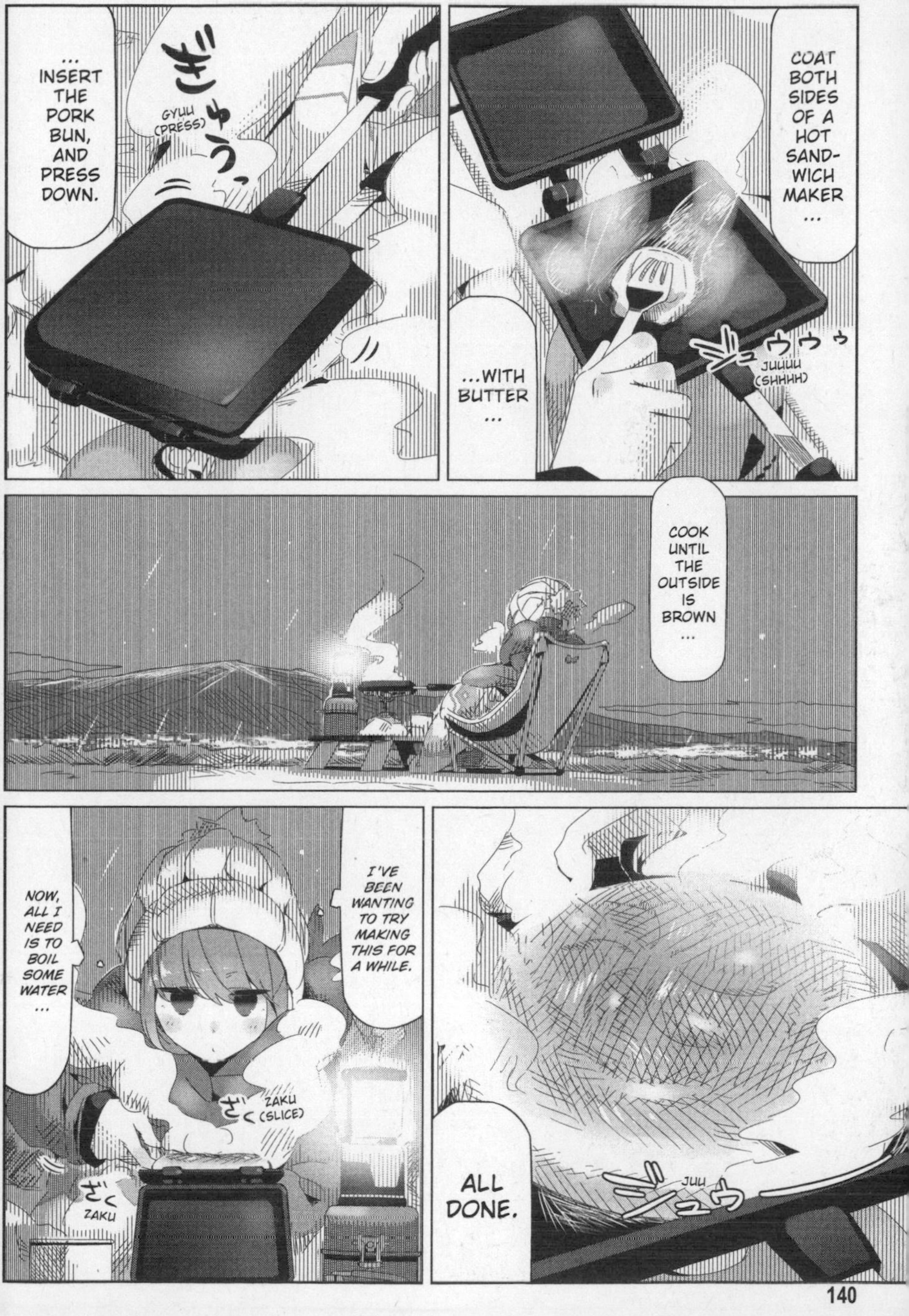

COAT BOTH SIDES OF A HOT SANDWICH MAKER...
...WITH BUTTER...
ジュウウゥ
JUUUU (SHHHH)
...INSERT THE PORK BUN, AND PRESS DOWN.
ぎゅうっ
GYUU (PRESS)
COOK UNTIL THE OUTSIDE IS BROWN...
ALL DONE.
ジュウー
JUU
I'VE BEEN WANTING TO TRY MAKING THIS FOR A WHILE.
NOW, ALL I NEED IS TO BOIL SOME WATER...
ざく
ZAKU (SLICE)
ざく
ZAKU

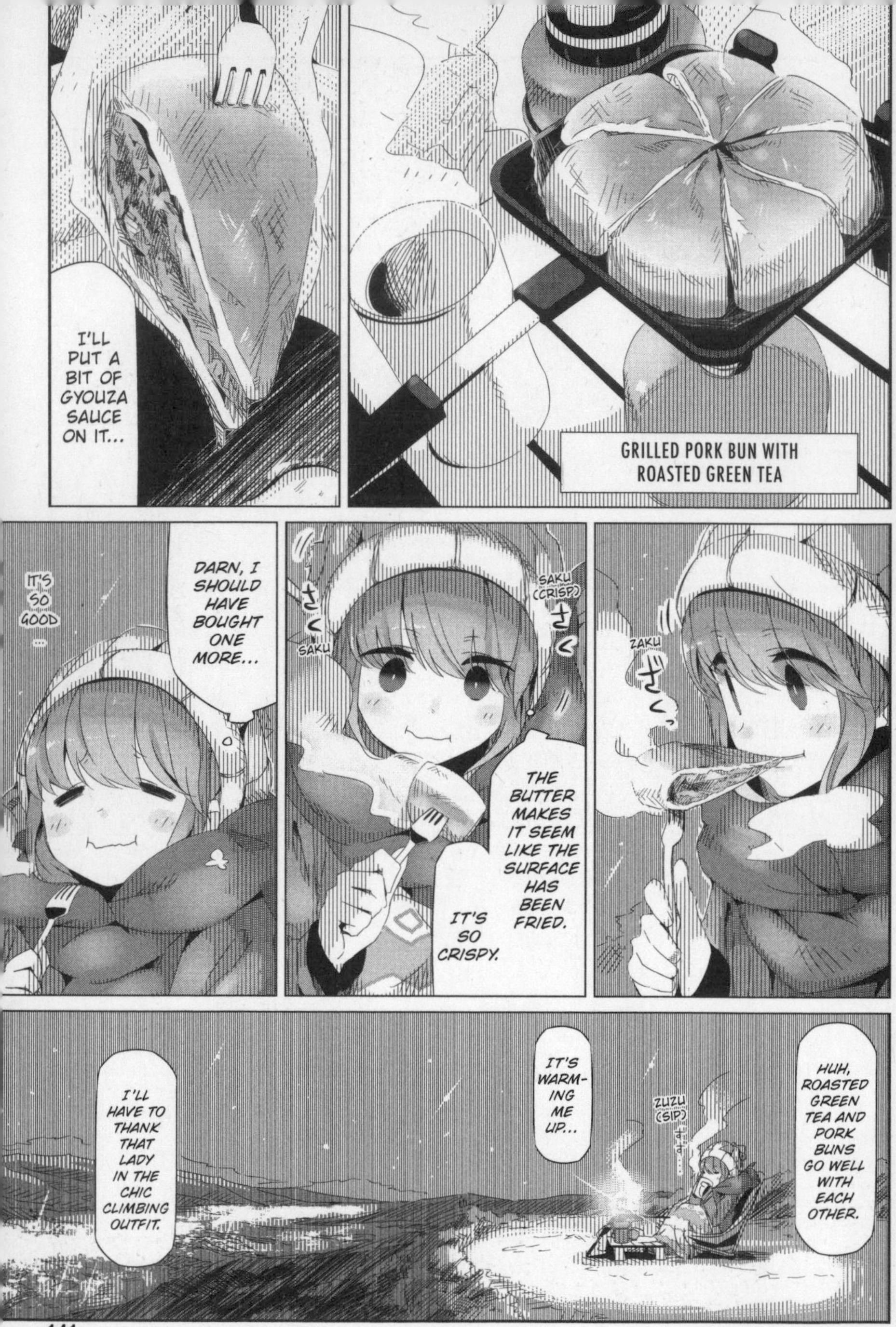
GRILLED PORK BUN WITH ROASTED GREEN TEA
I'LL PUT A BIT OF GYOUZA SAUCE ON IT...
ZAKU
ざくっ
SAKU (CRISP)
さく
SAKU
さく
THE BUTTER MAKES IT SEEM LIKE THE SURFACE HAS BEEN FRIED.
IT'S SO CRISPY.
DARN, I SHOULD HAVE BOUGHT ONE MORE...
IT'S SO GOOD...
HUH, ROASTED GREEN TEA AND PORK BUNS GO WELL WITH EACH OTHER.
ZUZU (SIP)
ずず…
IT'S WARMING ME UP...
I'LL HAVE TO THANK THAT LADY IN THE CHIC CLIMBING OUTFIT.

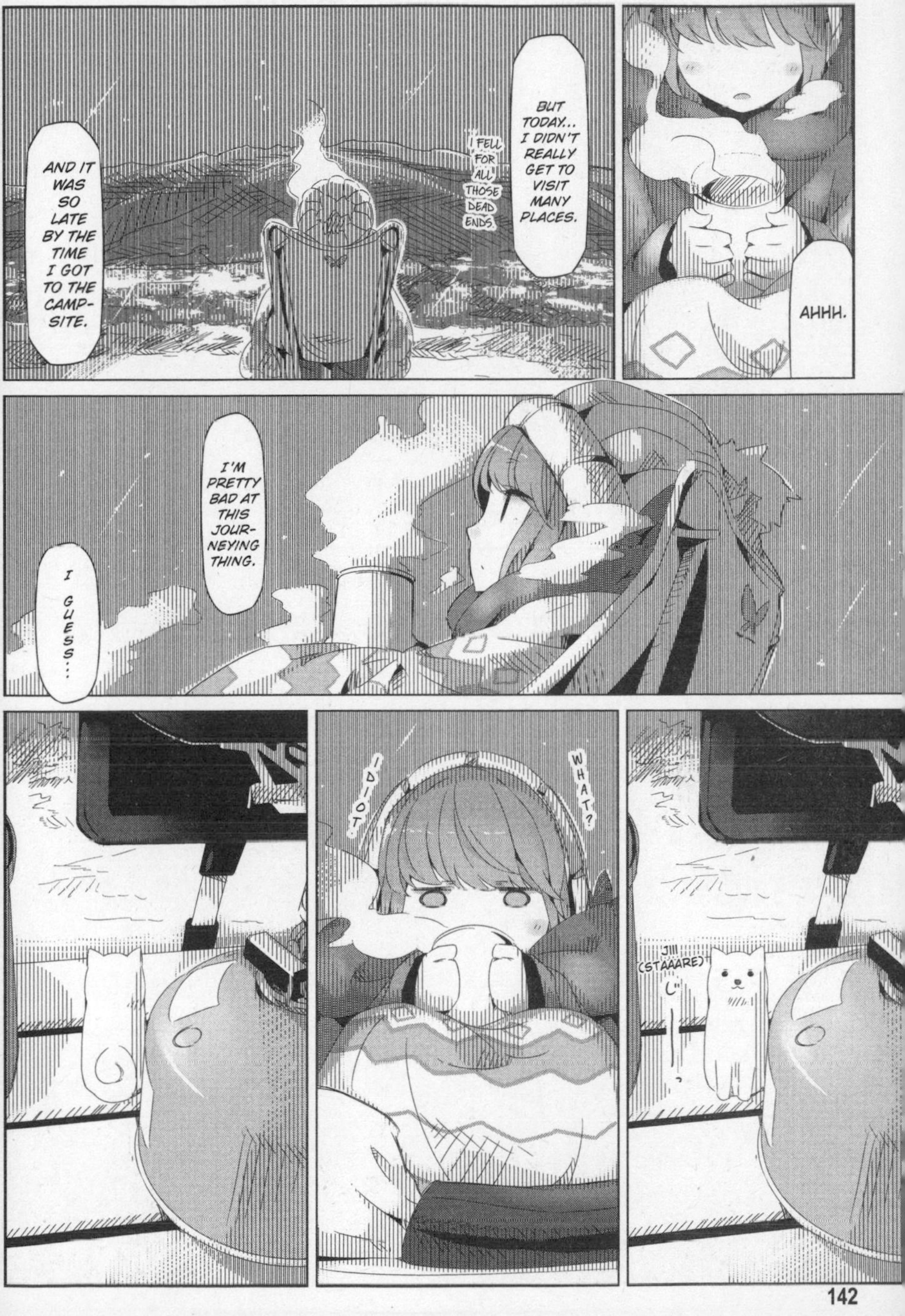
AHHH.
BUT TODAY... I DIDN'T REALLY GET TO VISIT MANY PLACES.
I FELL FOR ALL THOSE DEAD ENDS.
AND IT WAS SO LATE BY THE TIME I GOT TO THE CAMP-SITE.
I'M PRETTY BAD AT THIS JOUR-NEYING THING.
I GUESS...
JIII (STAAARE)
WHAT?
IDIOT.

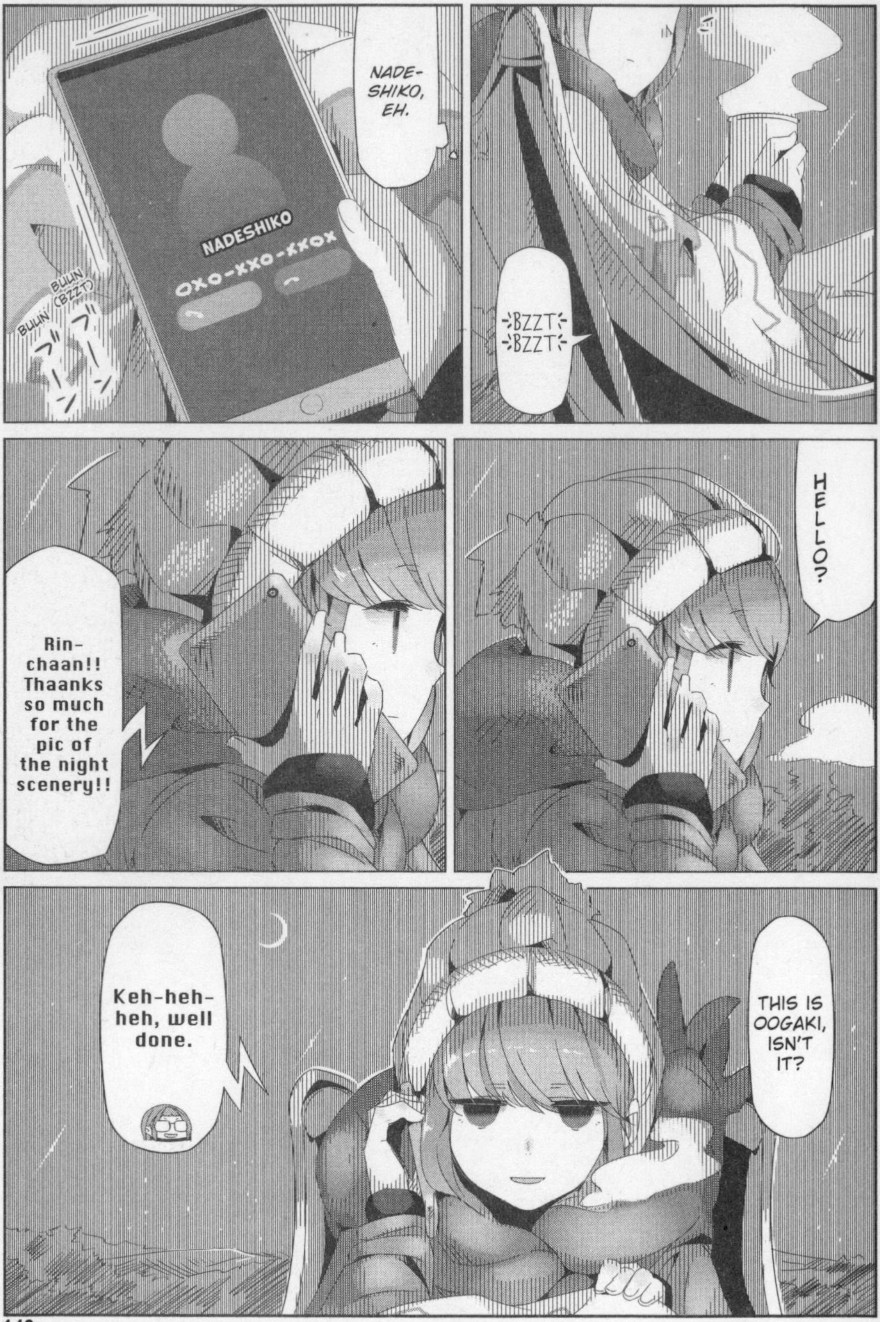

BZZT
BZZT
NADESHIKO
OXO-XXO-XXOX
BUUN BUUN (BZZT)
NADE-SHIKO, EH.
HELLO?
Rin-chaan!! Thaanks so much for the pic of the night scenery!!
THIS IS OOGAKI, ISN'T IT?
Keh-heh-heh, well done.

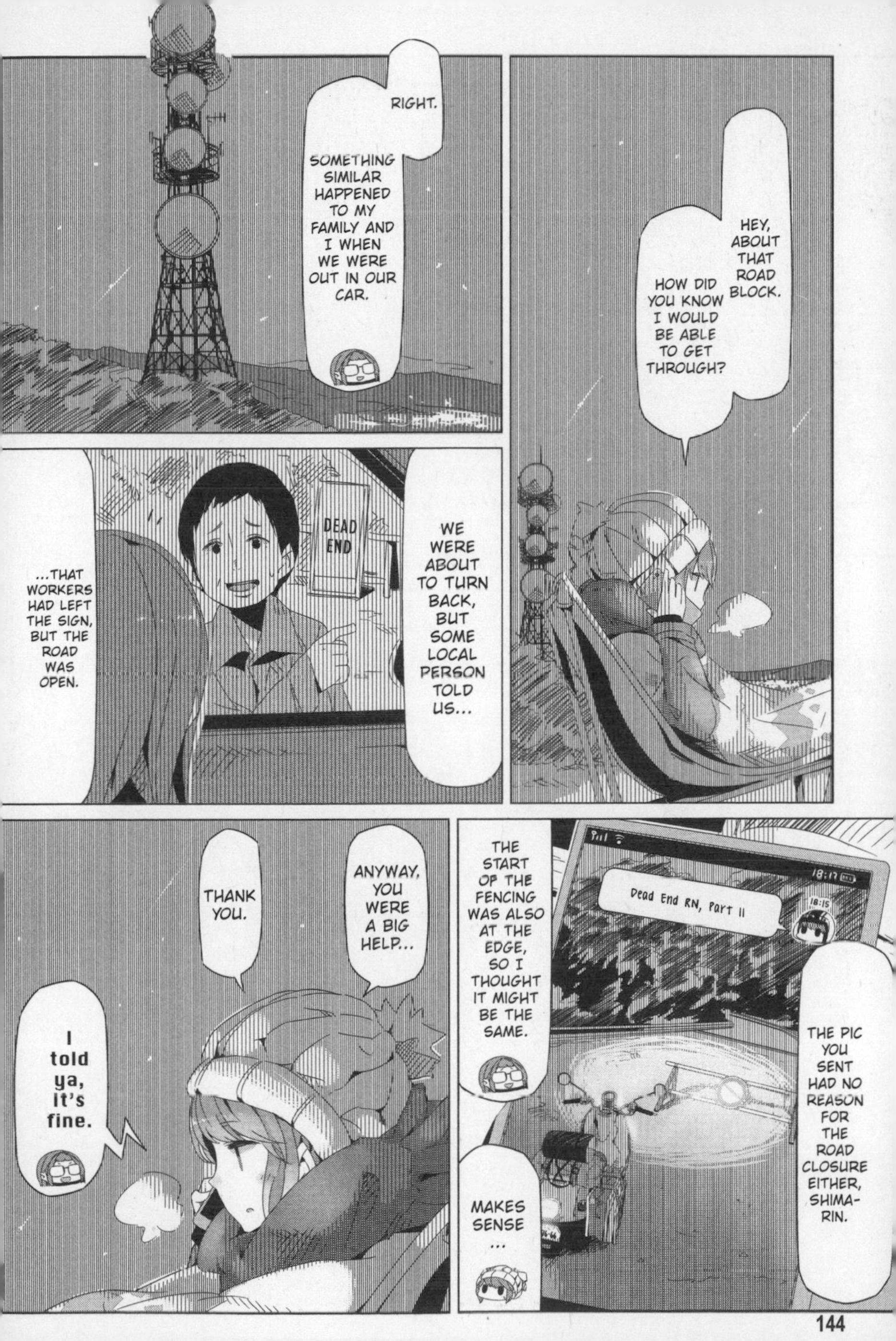
HEY, ABOUT THAT ROAD BLOCK.
HOW DID YOU KNOW I WOULD BE ABLE TO GET THROUGH?
RIGHT.
SOMETHING SIMILAR HAPPENED TO MY FAMILY AND I WHEN WE WERE OUT IN OUR CAR.
WE WERE ABOUT TO TURN BACK, BUT SOME LOCAL PERSON TOLD US...
DEAD END
...THAT WORKERS HAD LEFT THE SIGN, BUT THE ROAD WAS OPEN.
THE PIC YOU SENT HAD NO REASON FOR THE ROAD CLOSURE EITHER, SHIMA-RIN.
18:17
Dead End RN, Part II
18:15
THE START OF THE FENCING WAS ALSO AT THE EDGE, SO I THOUGHT IT MIGHT BE THE SAME.
MAKES SENSE...
ANYWAY, YOU WERE A BIG HELP...
THANK YOU.
I told ya, it's fine.

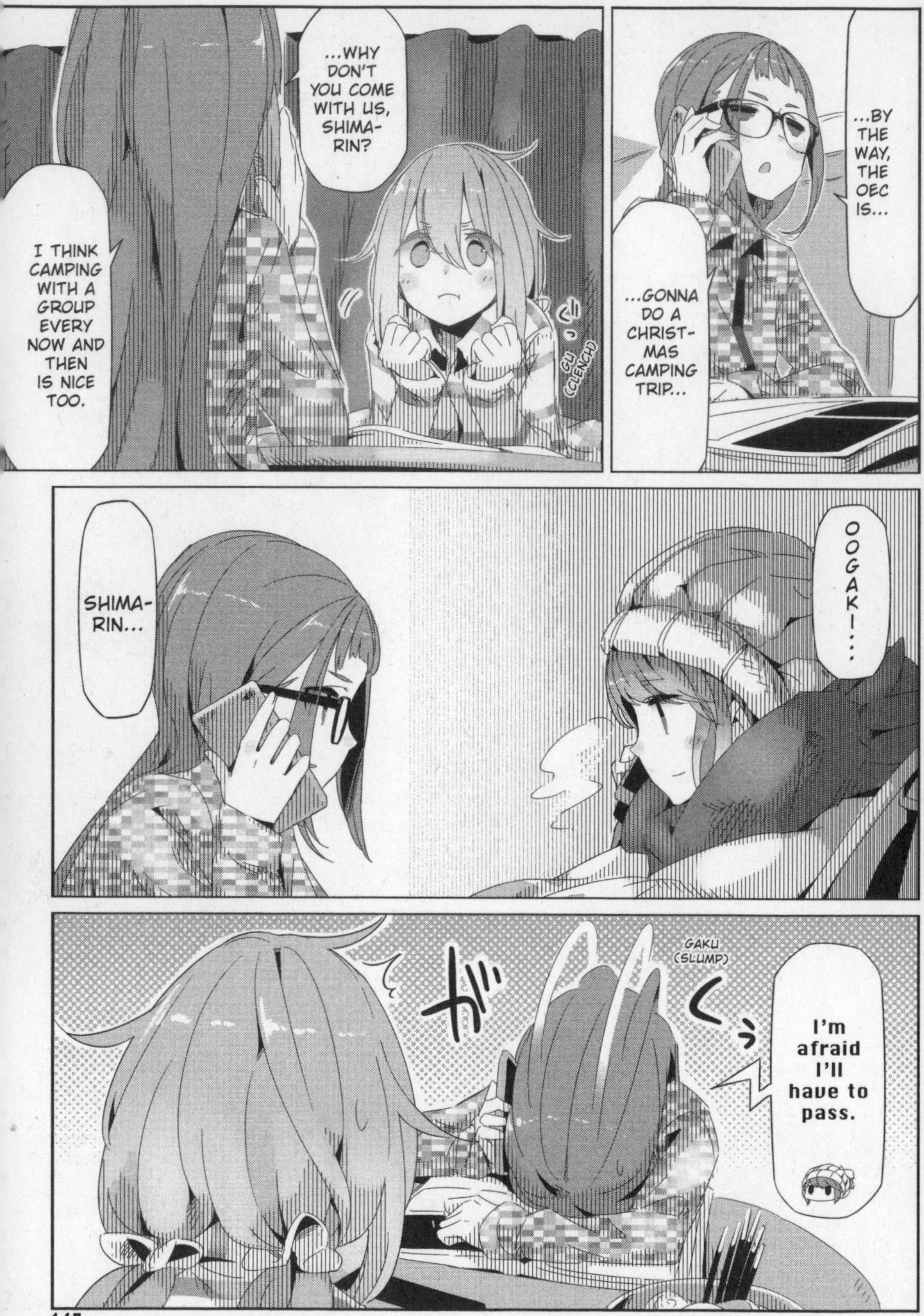
...BY THE WAY, THE OEC IS...
...GONNA DO A CHRISTMAS CAMPING TRIP...
...WHY DON'T YOU COME WITH US, SHIMA-RIN?
GU (CLENCH)
I THINK CAMPING WITH A GROUP EVERY NOW AND THEN IS NICE TOO.
OOGAKI!...
SHIMA-RIN...
GAKU (SLUMP)
I'm afraid I'll have to pass.

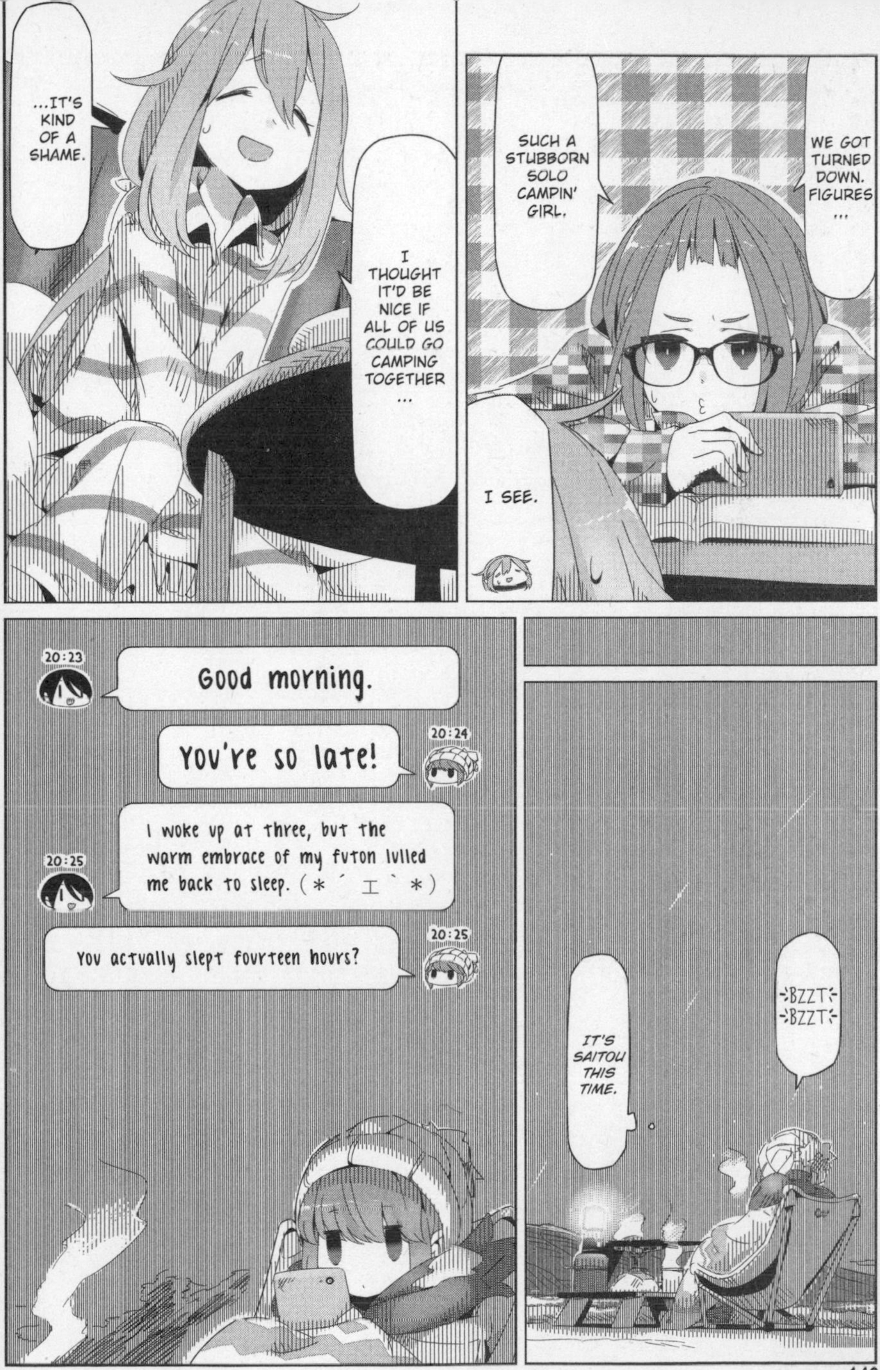
WE GOT TURNED DOWN. FIGURES...
SUCH A STUBBORN SOLO CAMPIN' GIRL.
I SEE.
...IT'S KIND OF A SHAME.
I THOUGHT IT'D BE NICE IF ALL OF US COULD GO CAMPING TOGETHER...
BZZT BZZT
IT'S SAITOU THIS TIME.
20:23
Good morning.
20:24
You're so late!
20:25
I woke up at three, but the warm embrace of my futon lulled me back to sleep. (*´エ`*)
20:25
You actually slept fourteen hours?

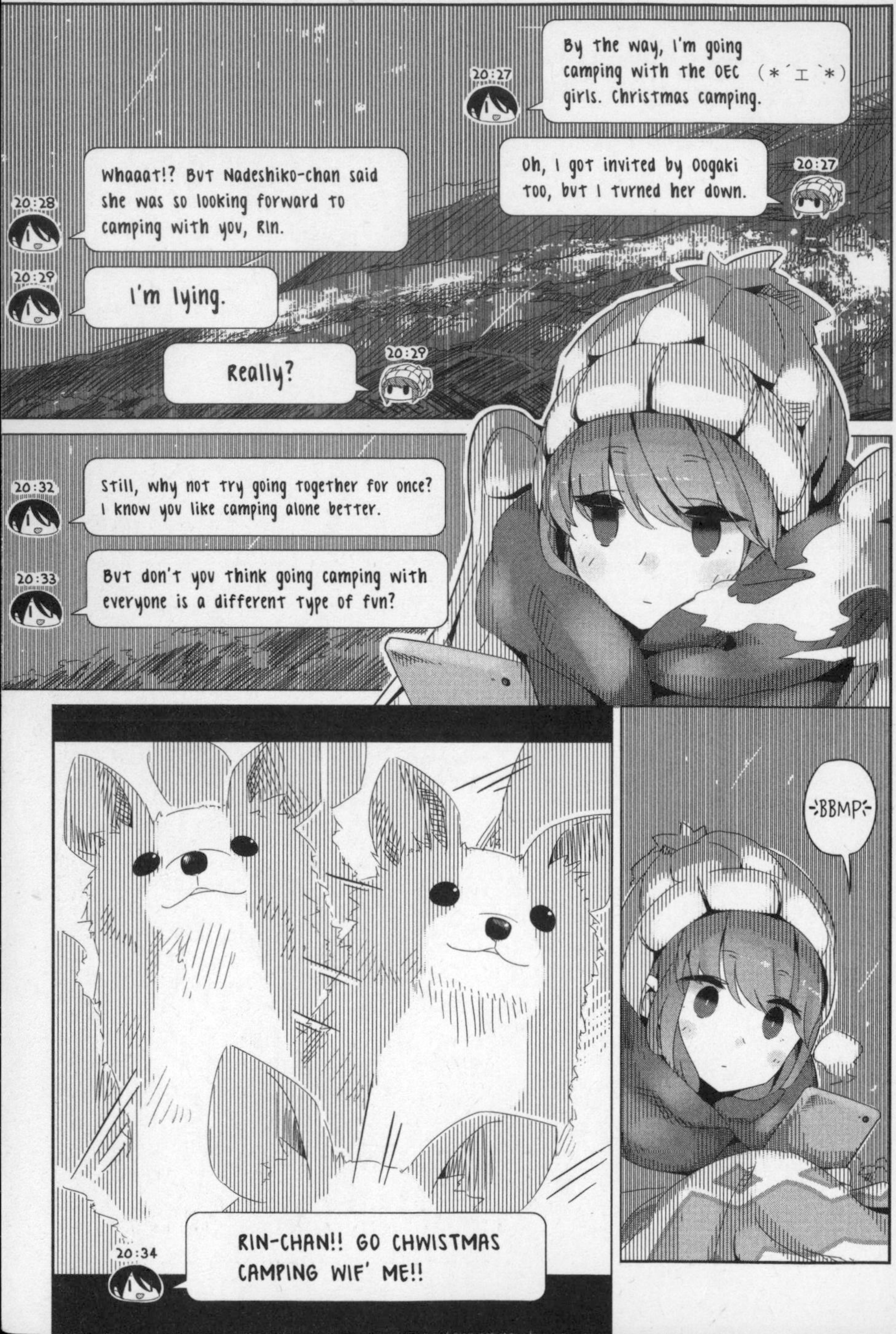
20:27
By the way, I'm going camping with the OEC girls. Christmas camping. (*´ェ`*)
20:27
Oh, I got invited by Oogaki too, but I turned her down.
20:28
Whaaat!? But Nadeshiko-chan said she was so looking forward to camping with you, Rin.
20:29
I'm lying.
20:29
Really?
20:32
Still, why not try going together for once? I know you like camping alone better.
20:33
But don't you think going camping with everyone is a different type of fun?
BBMP
20:34
RIN-CHAN!! GO CHWISTMAS CAMPING WIF' ME!!

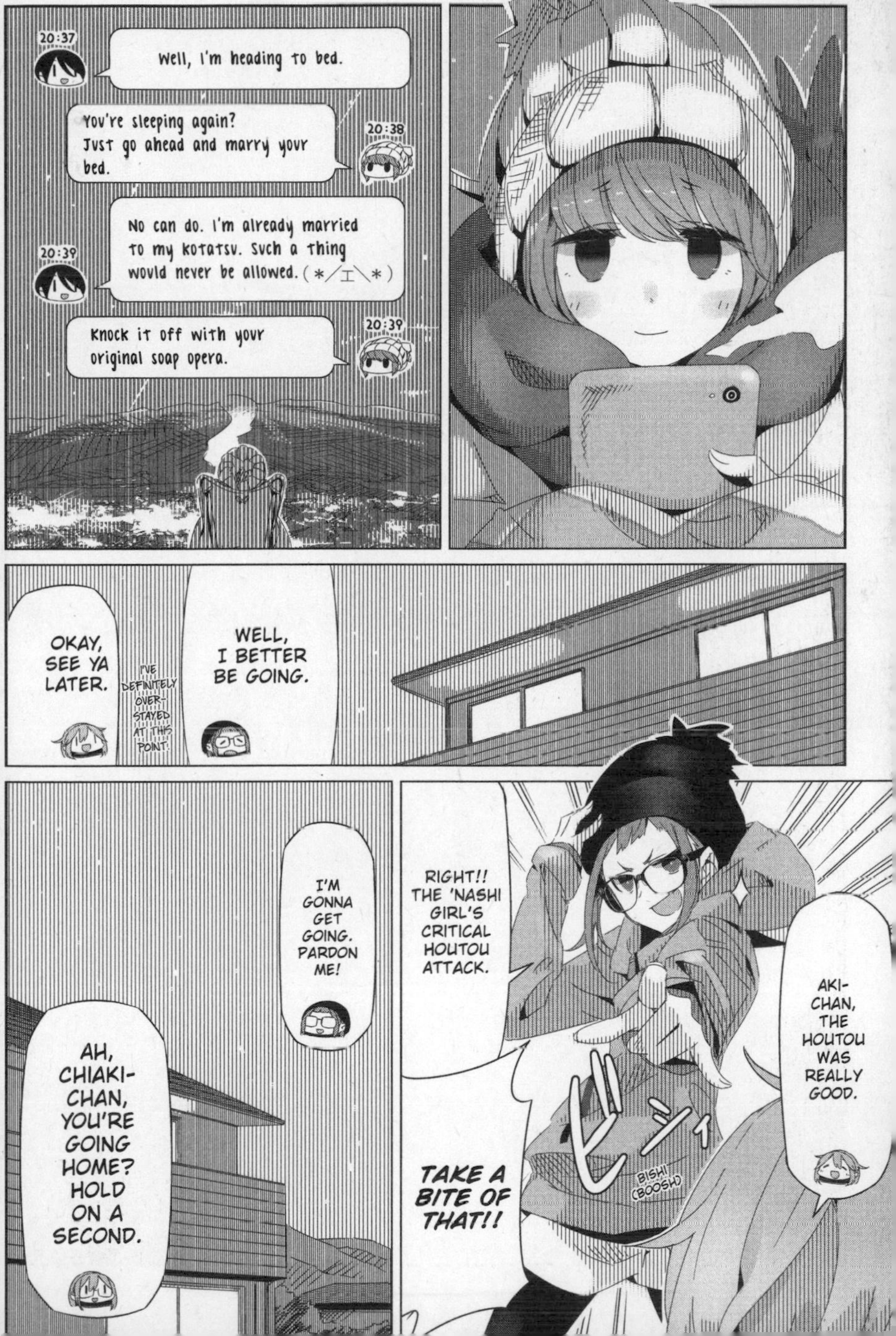
20:37
Well, I'm heading to bed.
You're sleeping again? Just go ahead and marry your bed.
20:38
No can do. I'm already married to my kotatsu. Such a thing would never be allowed. (*/エ*)
20:39
Knock it off with your original soap opera.
20:39
WELL, I BETTER BE GOING.
I'VE DEFINITELY OVER-STAYED AT THIS POINT.
OKAY, SEE YA LATER.
AKI-CHAN, THE HOUTOU WAS REALLY GOOD.
RIGHT!! THE 'NASHI GIRL'S CRITICAL HOUTOU ATTACK.
TAKE A BITE OF THAT!!
BISHI (BOOSH)
I'M GONNA GET GOING. PARDON ME!
AH, CHIAKI-CHAN, YOU'RE GOING HOME? HOLD ON A SECOND.

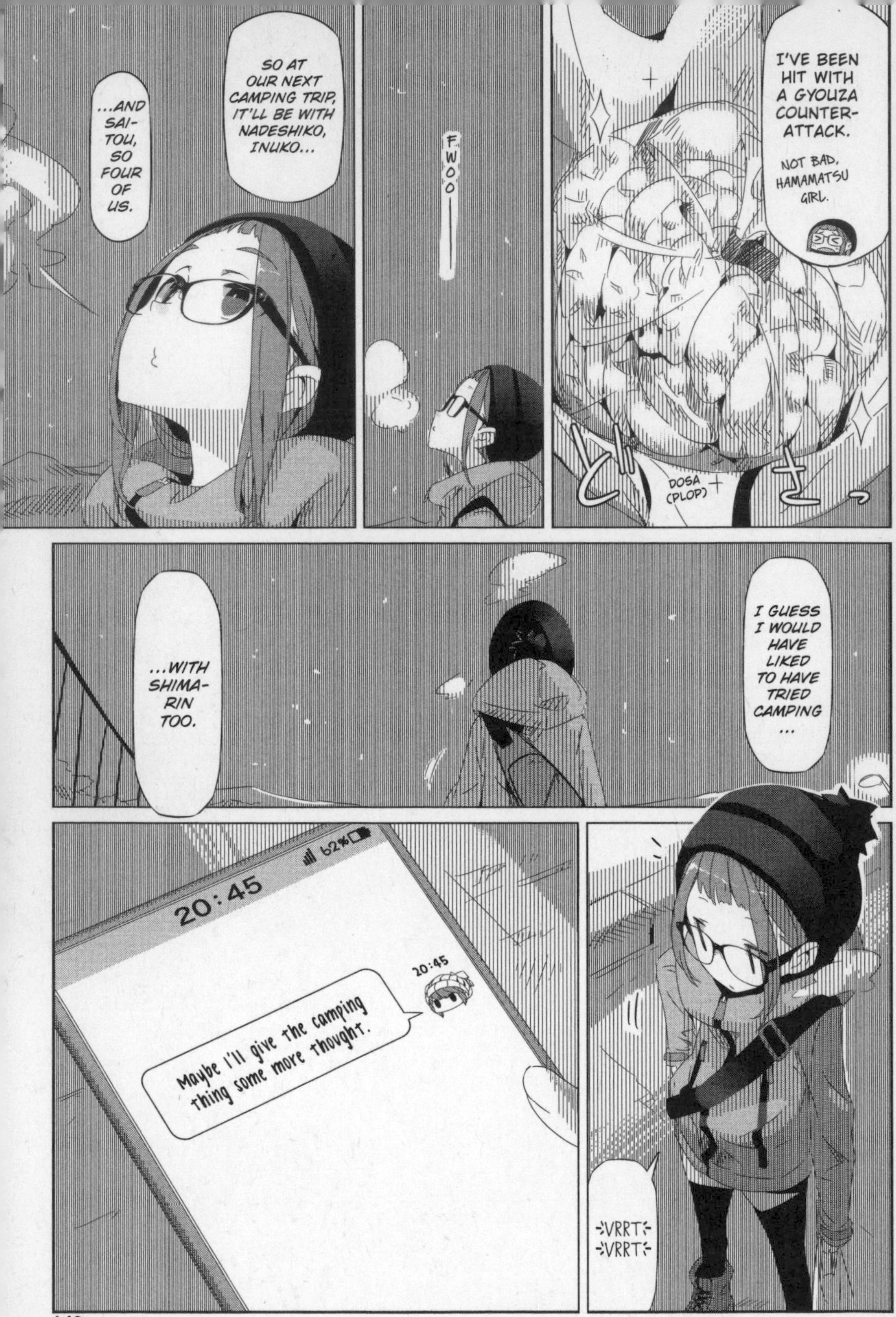
I'VE BEEN HIT WITH A GYOUZA COUNTER-ATTACK.
NOT BAD, HAMAMATSU GIRL.
DOSA (PLOP)
FWOO—
SO AT OUR NEXT CAMPING TRIP, IT'LL BE WITH NADESHIKO, INUKO...
...AND SAI-TOU, SO FOUR OF US.
I GUESS I WOULD HAVE LIKED TO HAVE TRIED CAMPING...
...WITH SHIMA-RIN TOO.
VRRT
VRRT
62%
20:45
20:45
Maybe I'll give the camping thing some more thought.

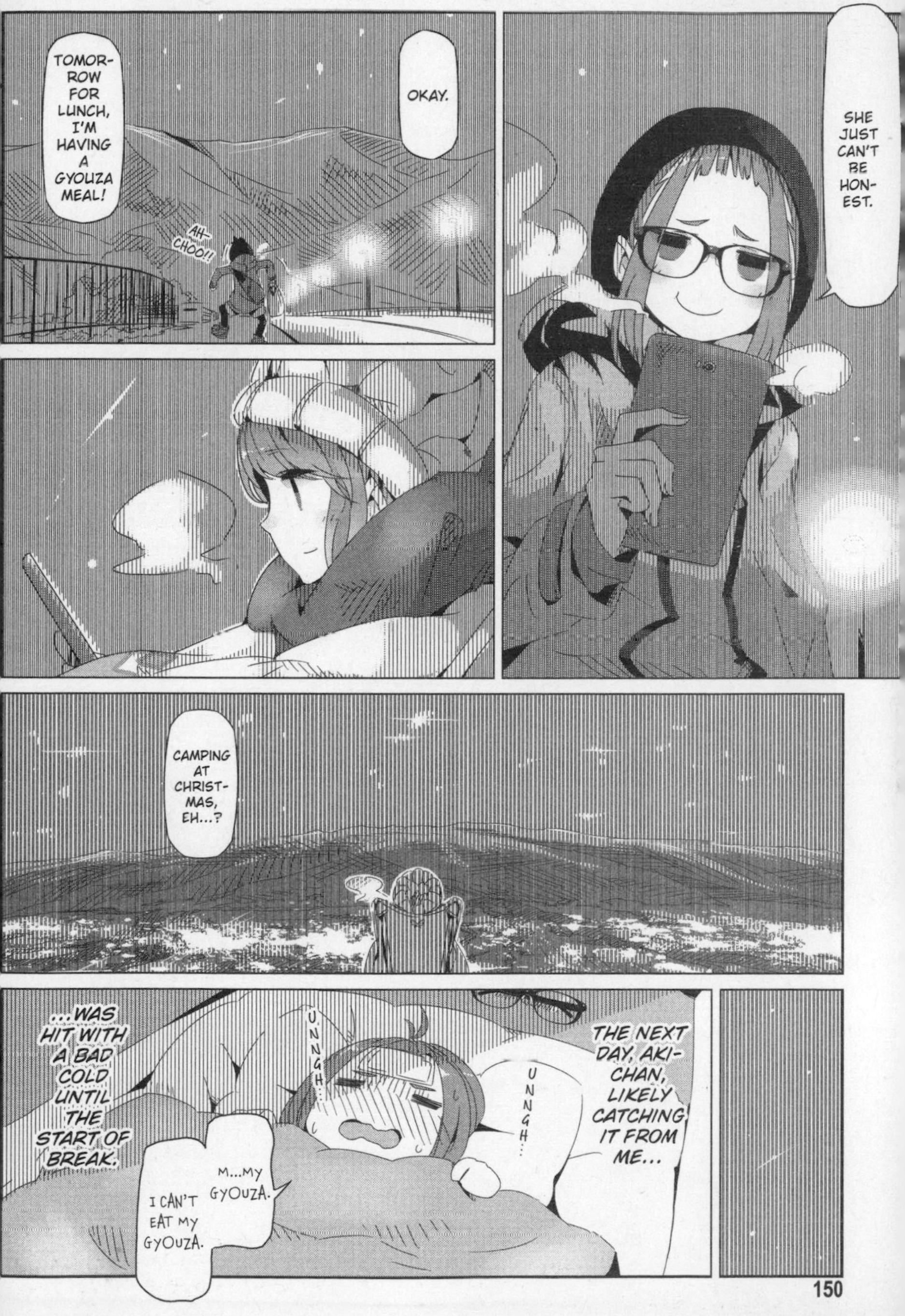
SHE JUST CAN'T BE HON-EST.
OKAY.
TOMOR-ROW FOR LUNCH, I'M HAVING A GYOUZA MEAL!
AH-CHOO!!
CAMPING AT CHRIST-MAS, EH...?
THE NEXT DAY, AKI-CHAN, LIKELY CATCHING IT FROM ME...
UNNGH...
UNNGH...
...WAS HIT WITH A BAD COLD UNTIL THE START OF BREAK.
M...MY GYOUZA.
I CAN'T EAT MY GYOUZA.

TRANSLATION NOTES

100 yen is approximately $1 USD.

PAGE 29
"Hotaru no Hikari": Meaning "light of the fireflies," it's a Japanese song to the tune of "Auld Lang Syne." The song is used in various ways, including as a tune to usher customers out of stores at closing and as a tradition on an annual Japanese New Year's Eve television special.

PAGE 38
Linear bullet train: Another name for the type of train used on the Chuo Shinkansen high-speed rail line. They utilize magnetic levitation (maglev) technology.

PAGE 46
Yashajintouge: Means roughly "Great Demon's Mountain Pass," hence why Rin finds the name so appealing.

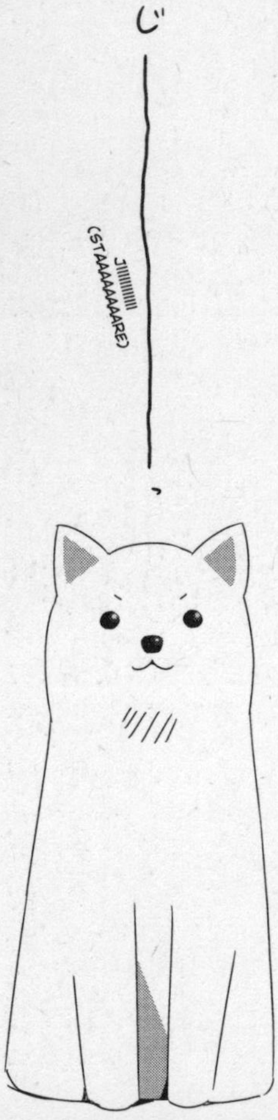
じ
JIIIIIIIIIII
(STAAAAAAARE)

PAGE 50
Making my own problem just to solve it: The Japanese version uses the term "match pump," a case of *wasei eigo*—uniquely Japanese terms based on English. It refers to lighting a match just to put it out with water.

PAGE 71
Mushroom Empire: Based on an actual place in Ina called Kinoko Oukoku (Mushroom Kingdom) where customers can buy mushroom-based products and eat mushroom-based dishes.

PAGE 76
'Nashi Girl: Short for "Yamanashi Girl," i.e. where Chiaki is from.

PAGE 85
Babyface: A pro wrestling industry term to describe good guys, the opposite would be "heels"—villainous wrestlers. Babyface is often shortened to "face."

PAGE 86
Laid-back fortunes: In Japanese, this is *yurumikuji*, a play on *yurukyara* (gentle mascots) and *mikuji* (fortune), the Japanese title for *Laid-Back Camp*, *Yurucamp*. Temples in Japan commonly sell fortunes to customers.

PAGE 99
Romen: An Ina specialty dish, it's very similar to the American Chinese version of lo mein.

PAGE 141
Chic climbing outfit: In Japanese, Rin uses the term *yama gaaru* (mountain girl), referring to girls who still try to remain fashionable while doing outdoor activities such as climbing.

PAGE 161
Glamping: A combination of "glamor" and "camping."

PAGE 172
Gold: Chiaki here is dressed as Kintarou (golden boy), a Japanese folk hero.

PAGE 173
Hospitality: The concept of *omotenashi* (roughly defined as Japanese hospitality) is vital to the country's service industry. *Omotenashi* literally means "no front," referring to a philosophy of honesty and openness toward customers.

◁ SIDE STORIES BEGIN ON THE NEXT PAGE ◁
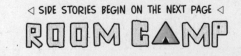

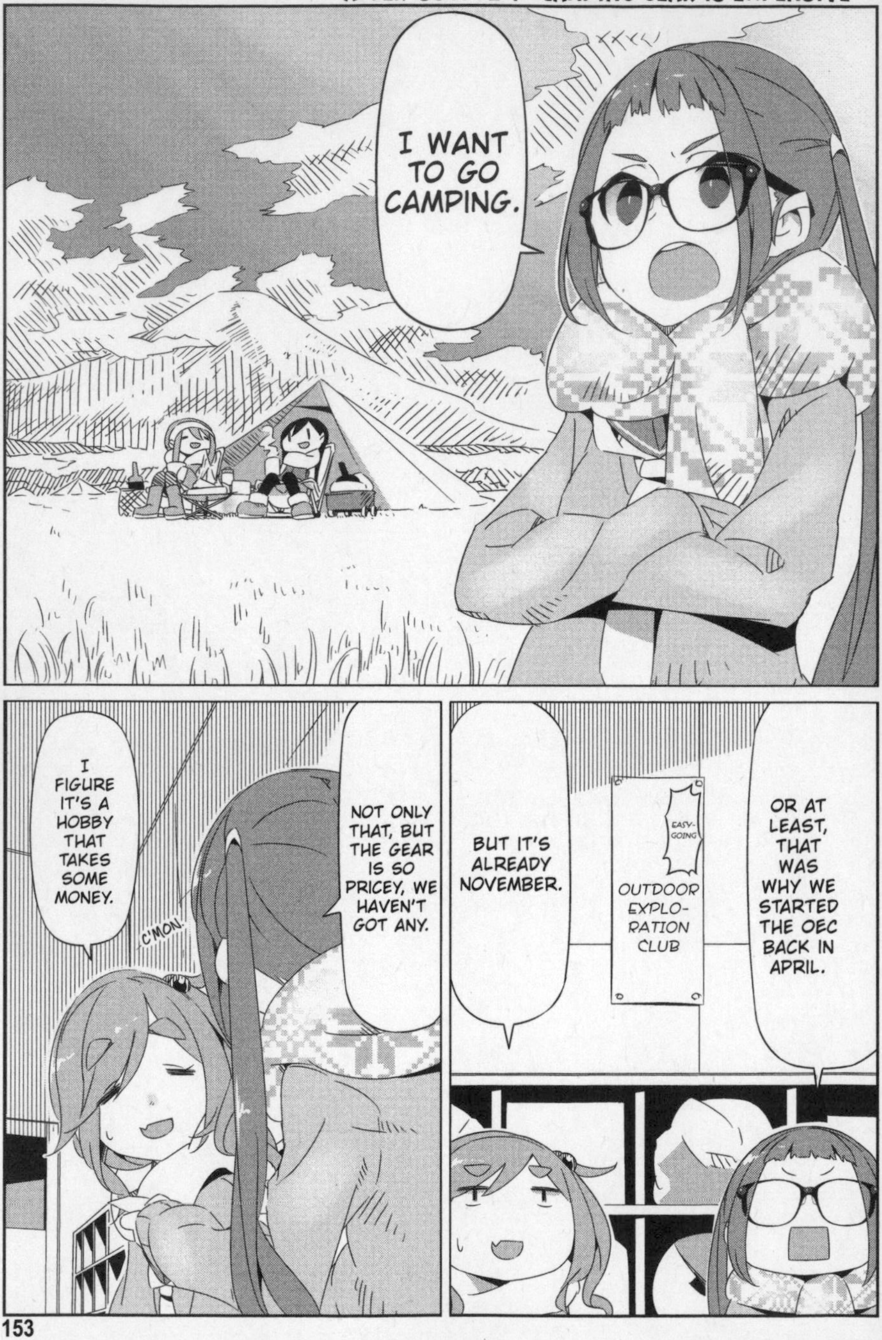
I WANT TO GO CAMPING.
OR AT LEAST, THAT WAS WHY WE STARTED THE OEC BACK IN APRIL.
EASY-GOING
OUTDOOR EXPLORATION CLUB
BUT IT'S ALREADY NOVEMBER.
NOT ONLY THAT, BUT THE GEAR IS SO PRICEY, WE HAVEN'T GOT ANY.
C'MON.
I FIGURE IT'S A HOBBY THAT TAKES SOME MONEY.

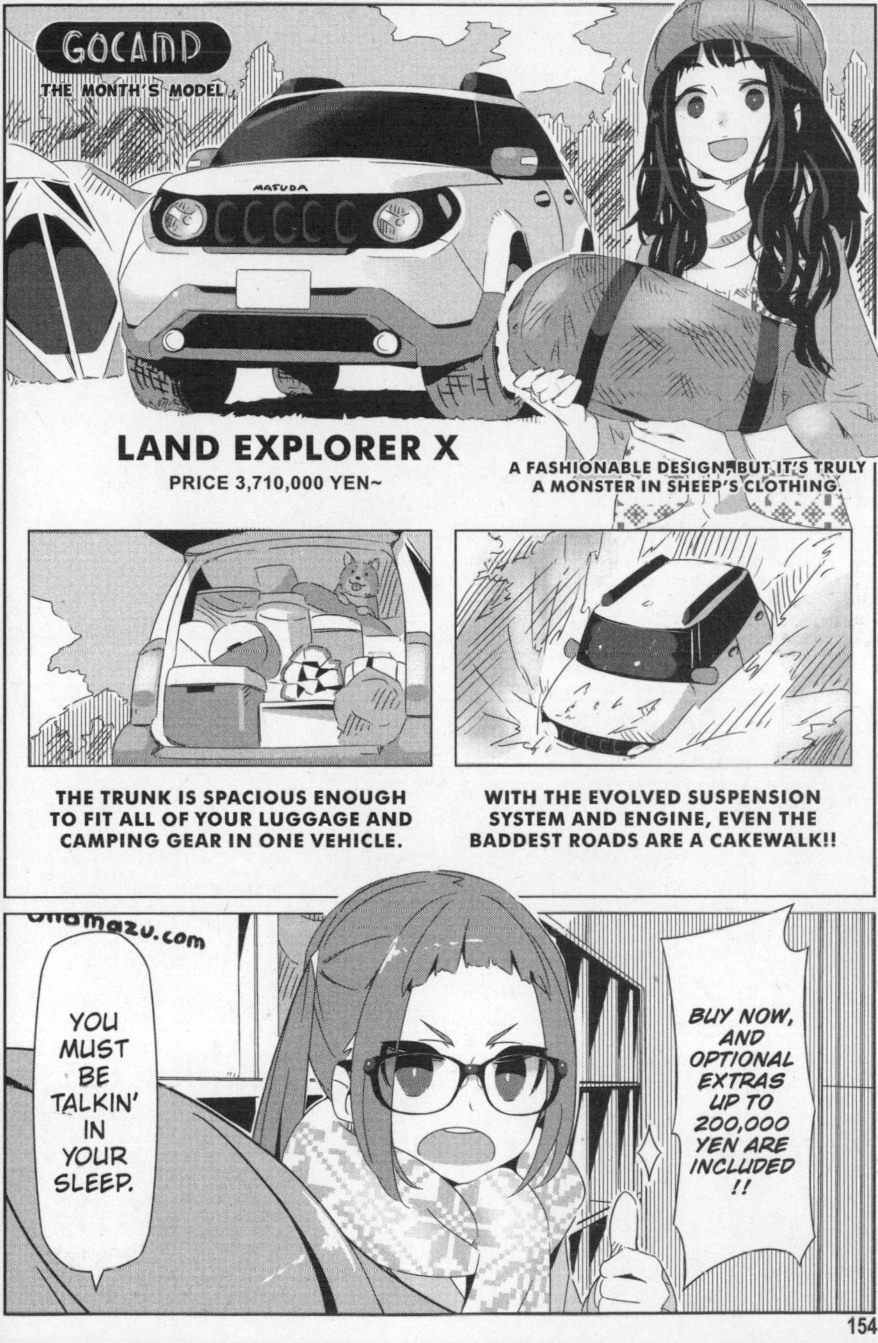
GOCAMP
THE MONTH'S MODEL
MASUDA
LAND EXPLORER X
PRICE 3,710,000 YEN~
A FASHIONABLE DESIGN, BUT IT'S TRULY A MONSTER IN SHEEP'S CLOTHING.
THE TRUNK IS SPACIOUS ENOUGH TO FIT ALL OF YOUR LUGGAGE AND CAMPING GEAR IN ONE VEHICLE.
WITH THE EVOLVED SUSPENSION SYSTEM AND ENGINE, EVEN THE BADDEST ROADS ARE A CAKEWALK!!
BUY NOW, AND OPTIONAL EXTRAS UP TO 200,000 YEN ARE INCLUDED !!
YOU MUST BE TALKIN' IN YOUR SLEEP.

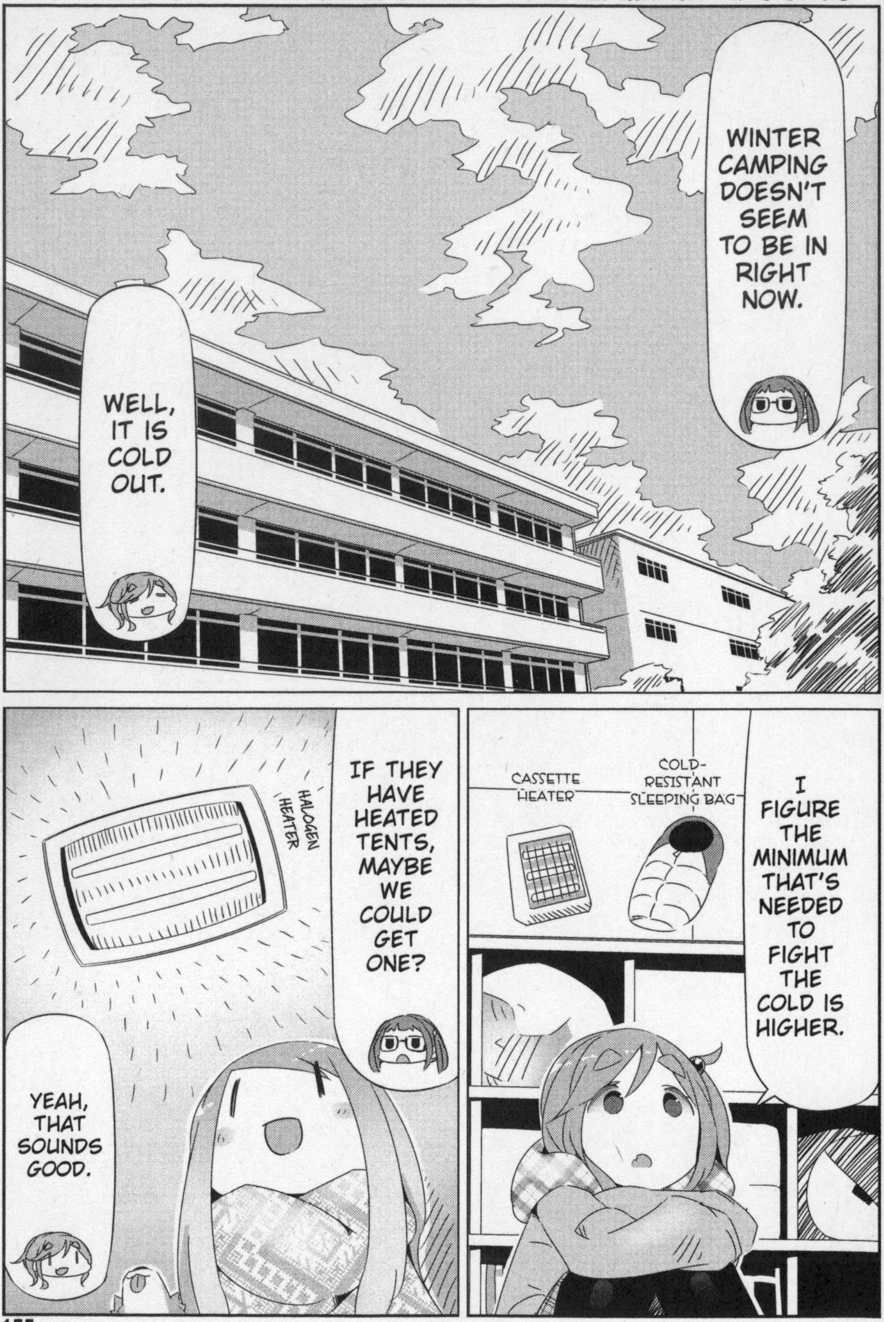
WINTER CAMPING DOESN'T SEEM TO BE IN RIGHT NOW.
WELL, IT IS COLD OUT.
I FIGURE THE MINIMUM THAT'S NEEDED TO FIGHT THE COLD IS HIGHER.
COLD-RESISTANT SLEEPING BAG
CASSETTE HEATER
IF THEY HAVE HEATED TENTS, MAYBE WE COULD GET ONE?
HALOGEN HEATER
YEAH, THAT SOUNDS GOOD.

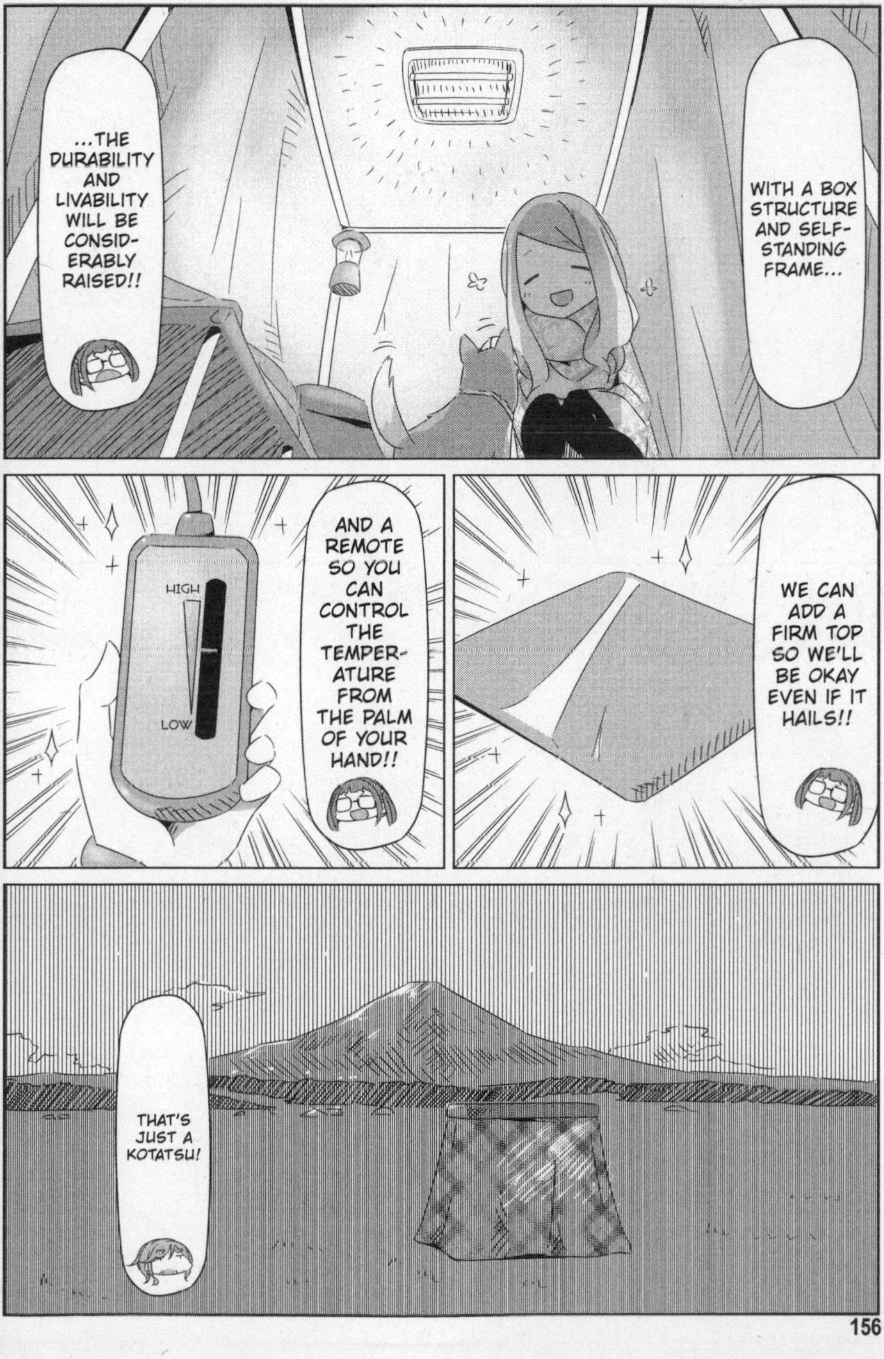
WITH A BOX STRUCTURE AND SELF-STANDING FRAME...
...THE DURABILITY AND LIVABILITY WILL BE CONSID-ERABLY RAISED!!
WE CAN ADD A FIRM TOP SO WE'LL BE OKAY EVEN IF IT HAILS!!
AND A REMOTE SO YOU CAN CONTROL THE TEMPER-ATURE FROM THE PALM OF YOUR HAND!!
HIGH
LOW
THAT'S JUST A KOTATSU!

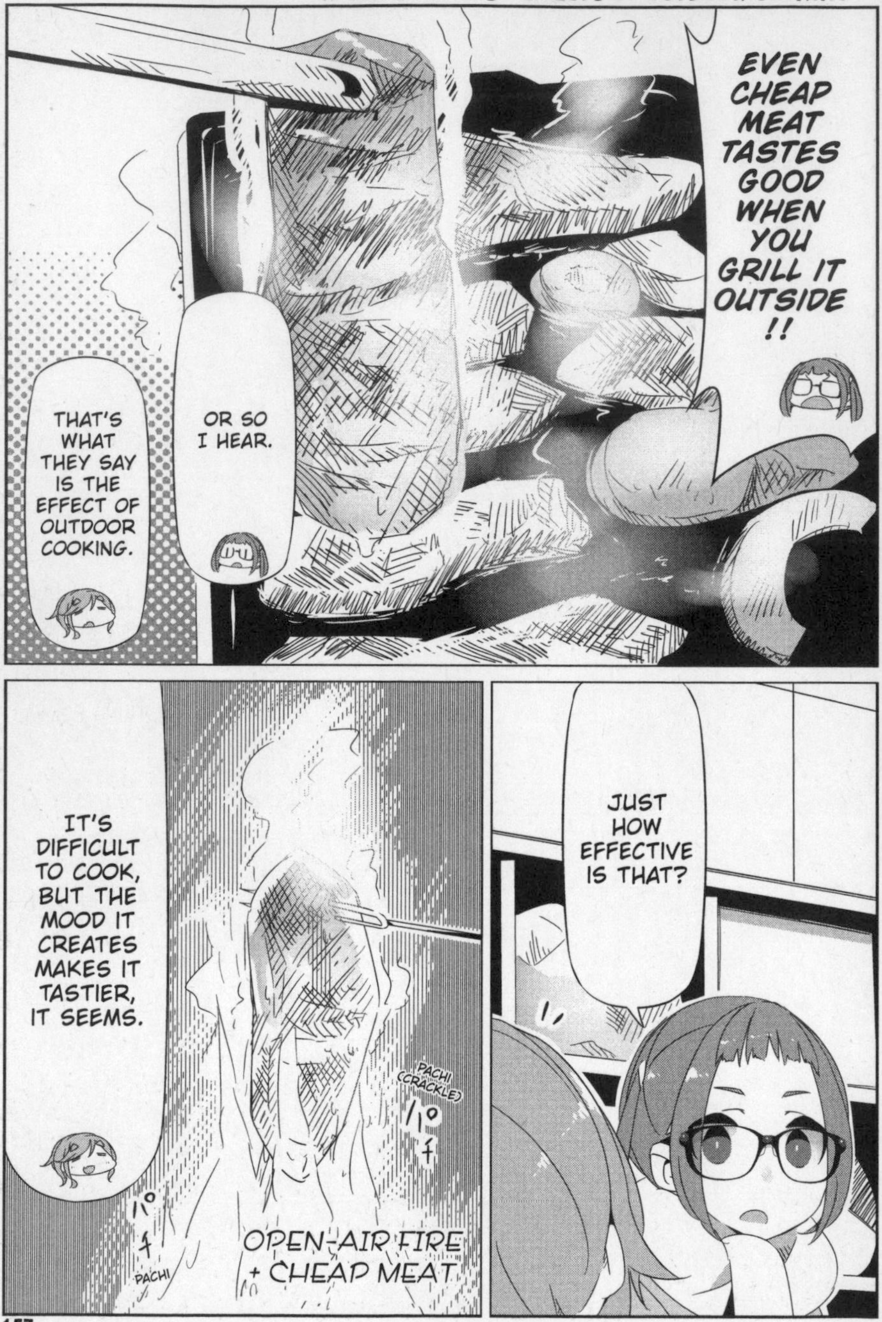
EVEN CHEAP MEAT TASTES GOOD WHEN YOU GRILL IT OUTSIDE!!
OR SO I HEAR.
THAT'S WHAT THEY SAY IS THE EFFECT OF OUTDOOR COOKING.
JUST HOW EFFECTIVE IS THAT?
IT'S DIFFICULT TO COOK, BUT THE MOOD IT CREATES MAKES IT TASTIER, IT SEEMS.
PACHI (CRACKLE)
パチ
パチ
PACHI
OPEN-AIR FIRE + CHEAP MEAT

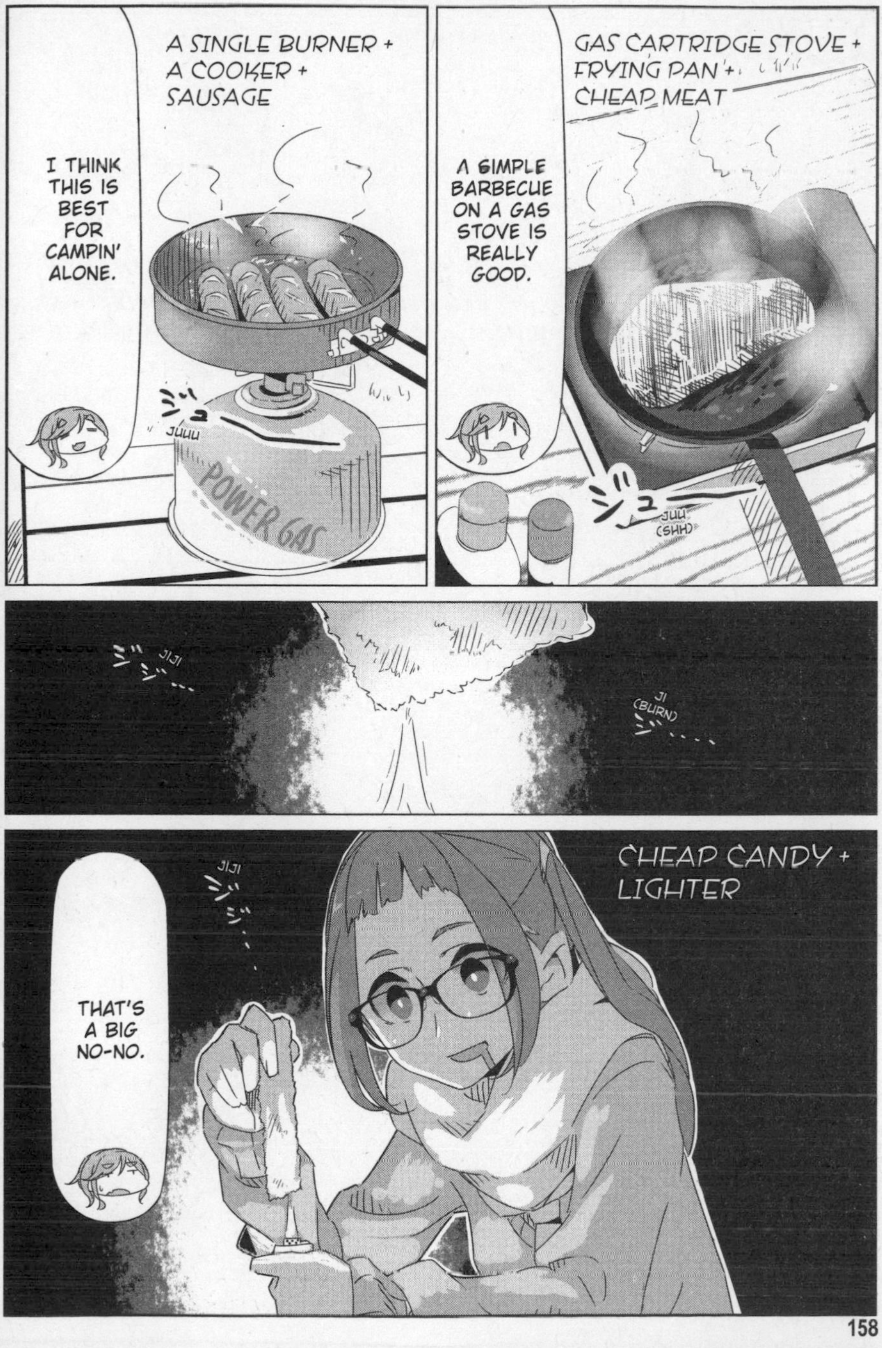
GAS CARTRIDGE STOVE + FRYING PAN + CHEAP MEAT
A SIMPLE BARBECUE ON A GAS STOVE IS REALLY GOOD.
JUU (SHH)
A SINGLE BURNER + A COOKER + SAUSAGE
I THINK THIS IS BEST FOR CAMPIN' ALONE.
JUUU
JI (BURN)
JIJI
CHEAP CANDY + LIGHTER
JIJI
THAT'S A BIG NO-NO.

AFTER-SCHOOL 4 WELCOME, NEWCOMER

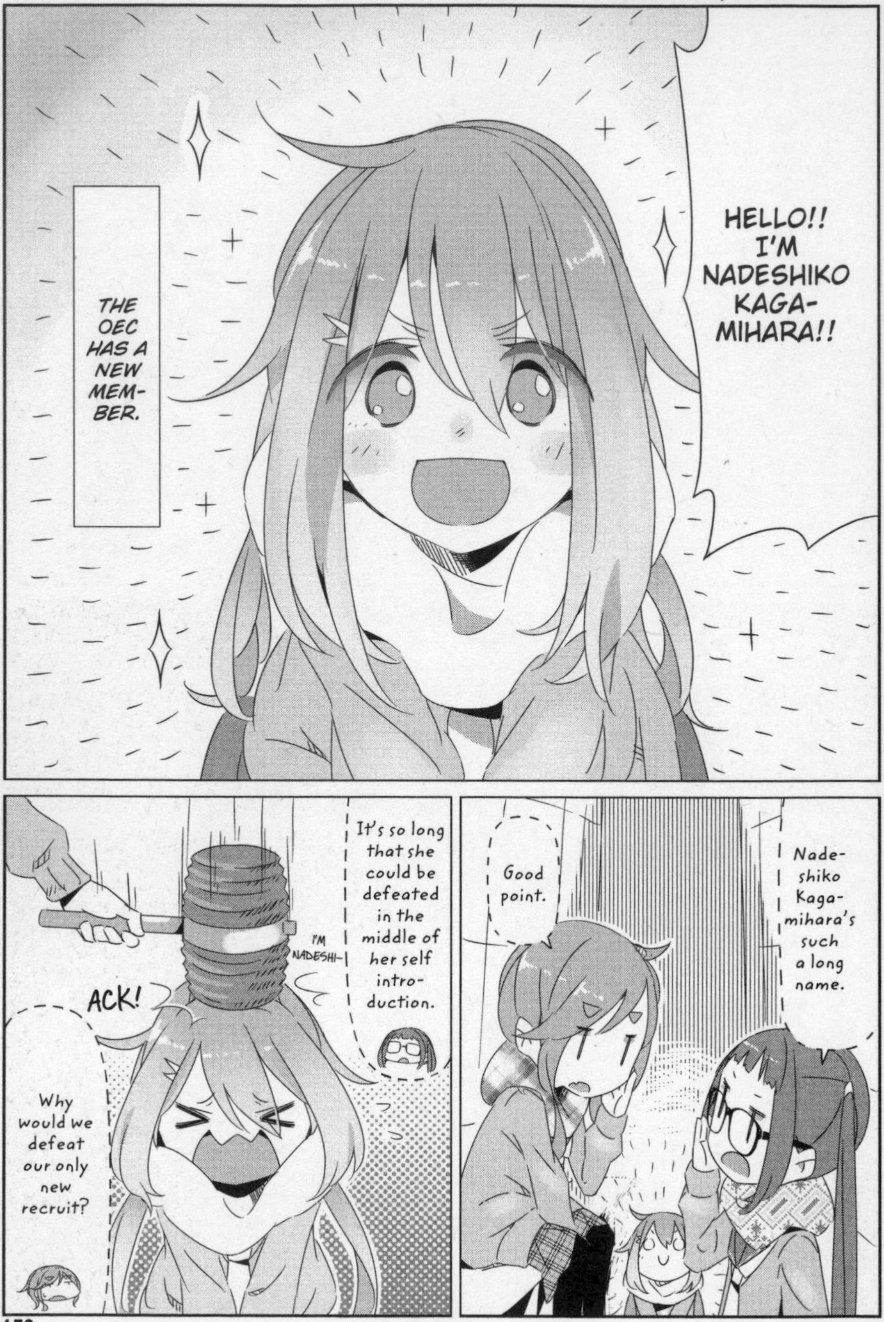
HELLO!! I'M NADESHIKO KAGA-MIHARA!!
THE OEC HAS A NEW MEM-BER.
Nade-shiko Kaga-mihara's such a long name.
Good point.
It's so long that she could be defeated in the middle of her self intro-duction.
I'M NADESHI-
ACK!
Why would we defeat our only new recruit?

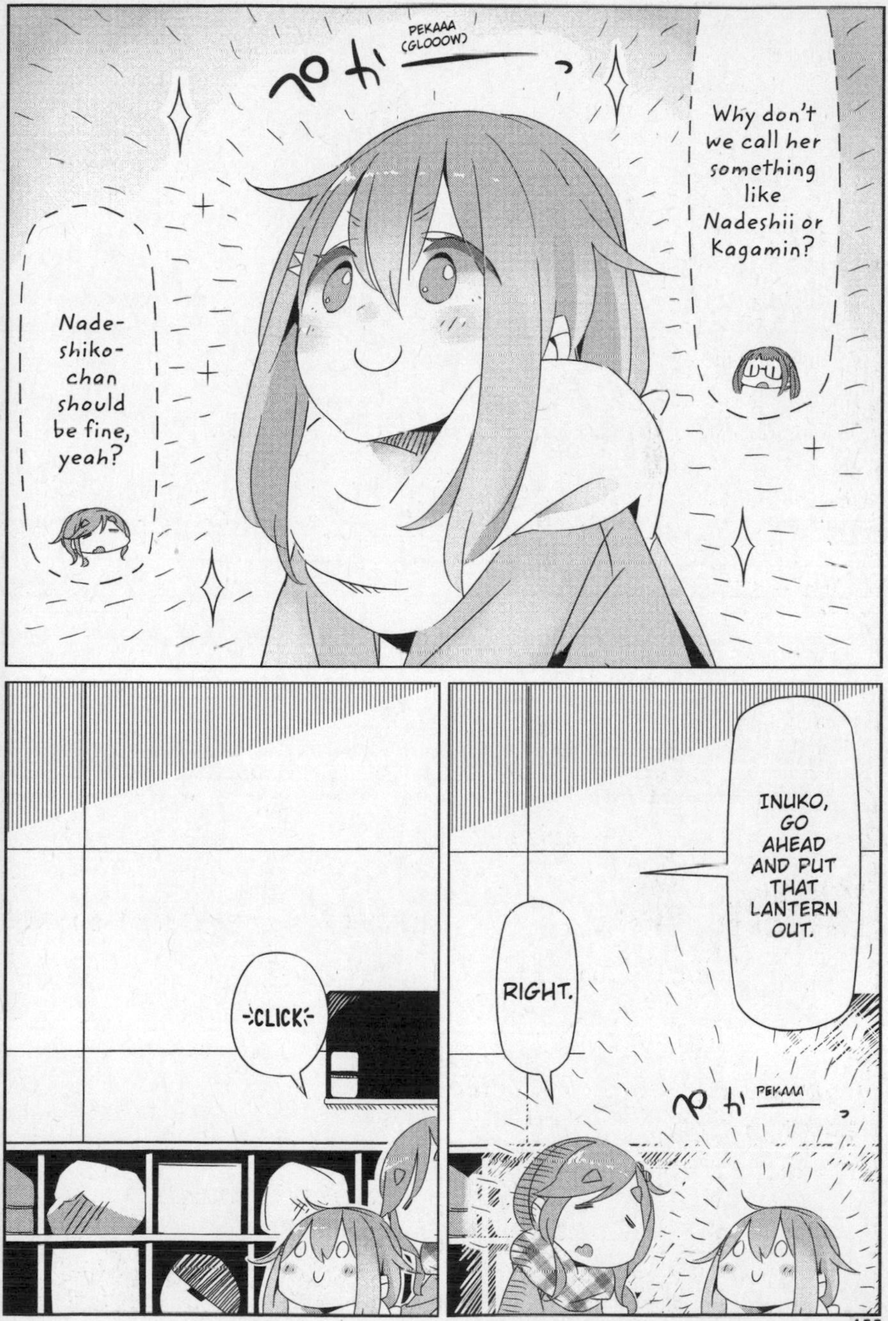
PEKAAA (GLOOOW)
Why don't we call her something like Nadeshii or Kagamin?
Nade-shiko-chan should be fine, yeah?
INUKO, GO AHEAD AND PUT THAT LANTERN OUT.
RIGHT.
PEKAAA
-CLICK-

AFTER-SCHOOL 5 WALLETS AND WISDOM

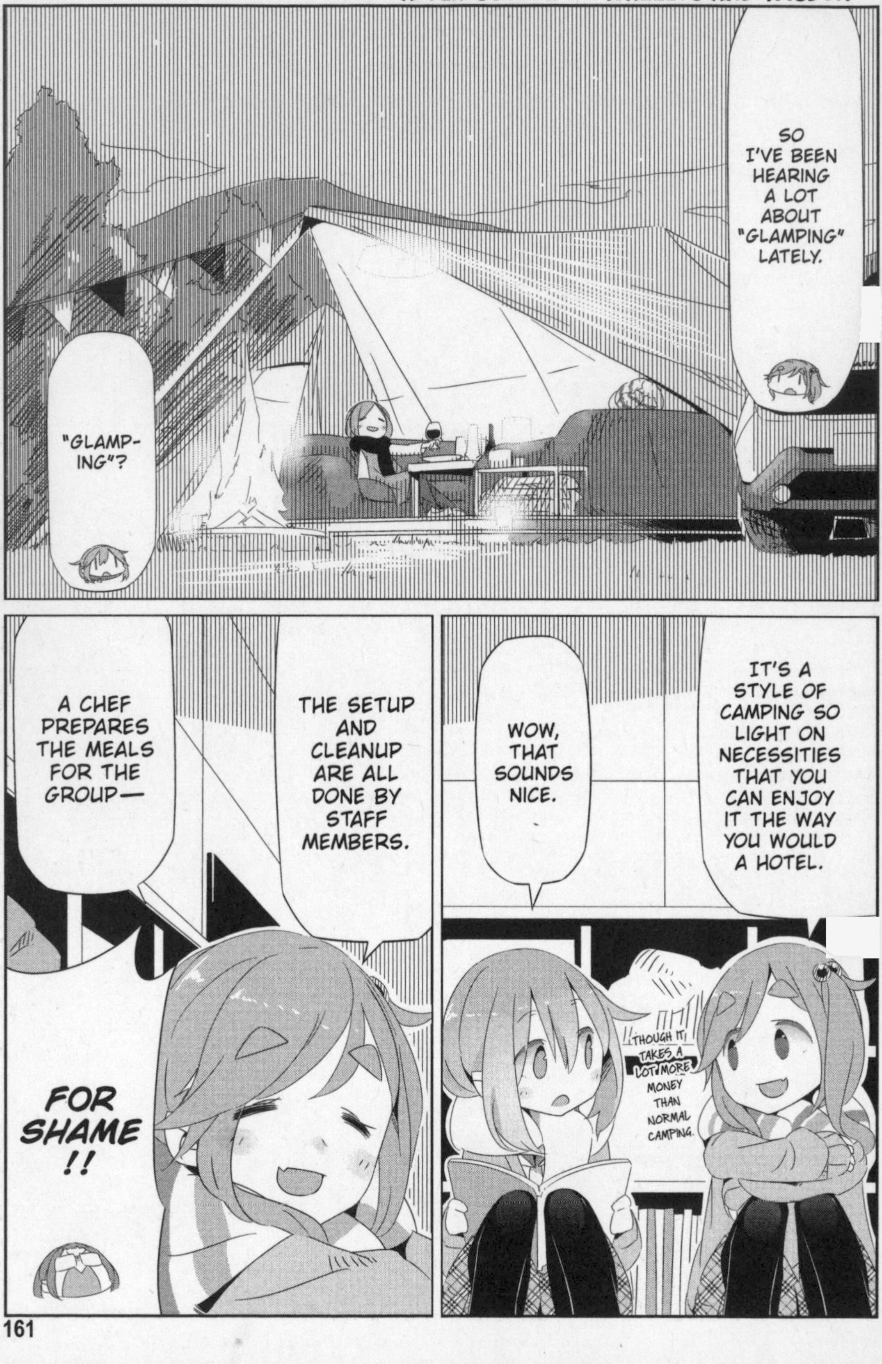
SO I'VE BEEN HEARING A LOT ABOUT "GLAMPING" LATELY.
"GLAMP-ING"?
IT'S A STYLE OF CAMPING SO LIGHT ON NECESSITIES THAT YOU CAN ENJOY IT THE WAY YOU WOULD A HOTEL.
WOW, THAT SOUNDS NICE.
THOUGH IT TAKES A LOT MORE MONEY THAN NORMAL CAMPING.
THE SETUP AND CLEANUP ARE ALL DONE BY STAFF MEMBERS.
A CHEF PREPARES THE MEALS FOR THE GROUP—
FOR SHAME !!

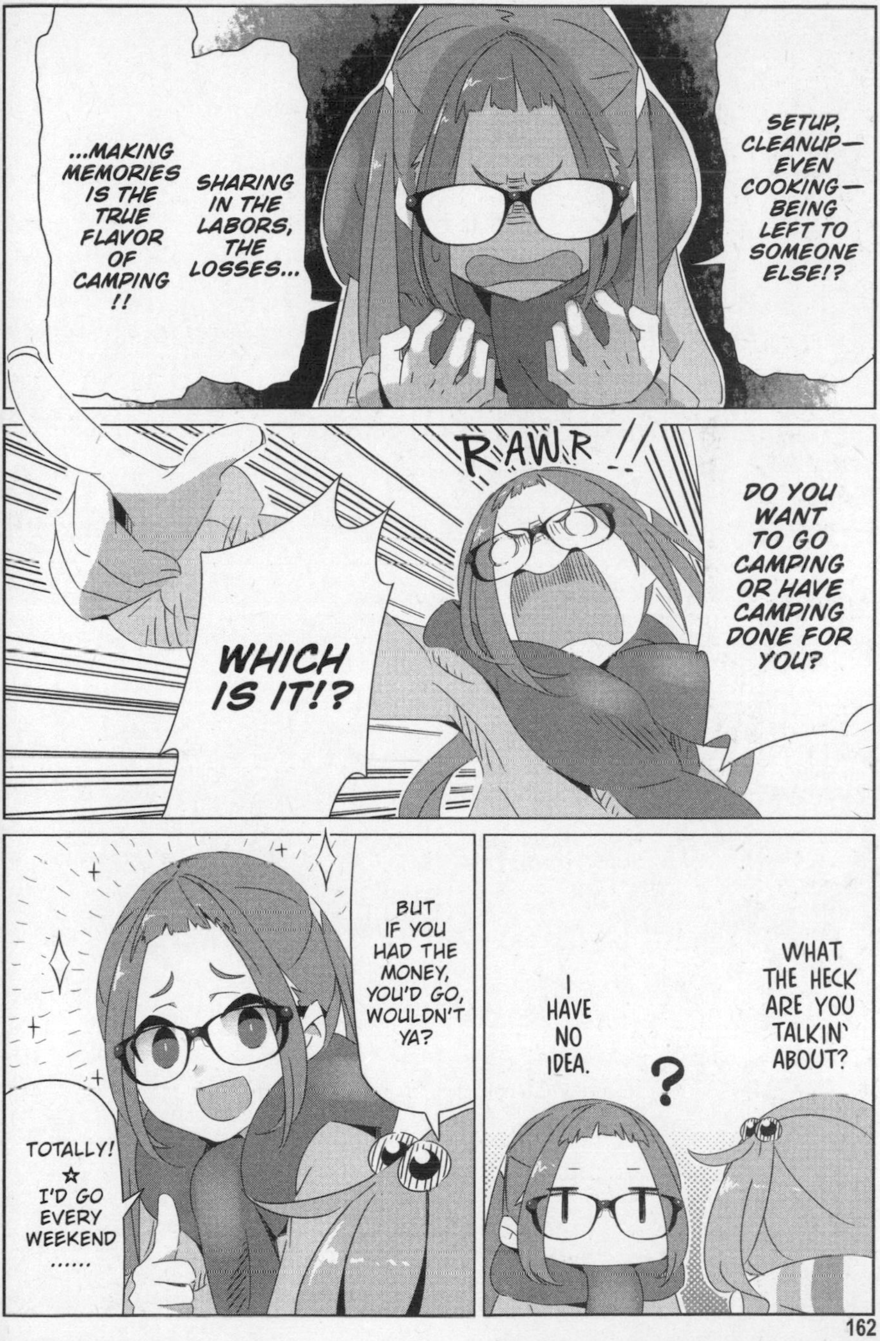
SETUP, CLEANUP— EVEN COOKING— BEING LEFT TO SOMEONE ELSE!?
SHARING IN THE LABORS, THE LOSSES...
...MAKING MEMORIES IS THE TRUE FLAVOR OF CAMPING!!
RAWR!!
DO YOU WANT TO GO CAMPING OR HAVE CAMPING DONE FOR YOU?
WHICH IS IT!?
WHAT THE HECK ARE YOU TALKIN' ABOUT?
I HAVE NO IDEA.
BUT IF YOU HAD THE MONEY, YOU'D GO, WOULDN'T YA?
TOTALLY! ☆ I'D GO EVERY WEEKEND......

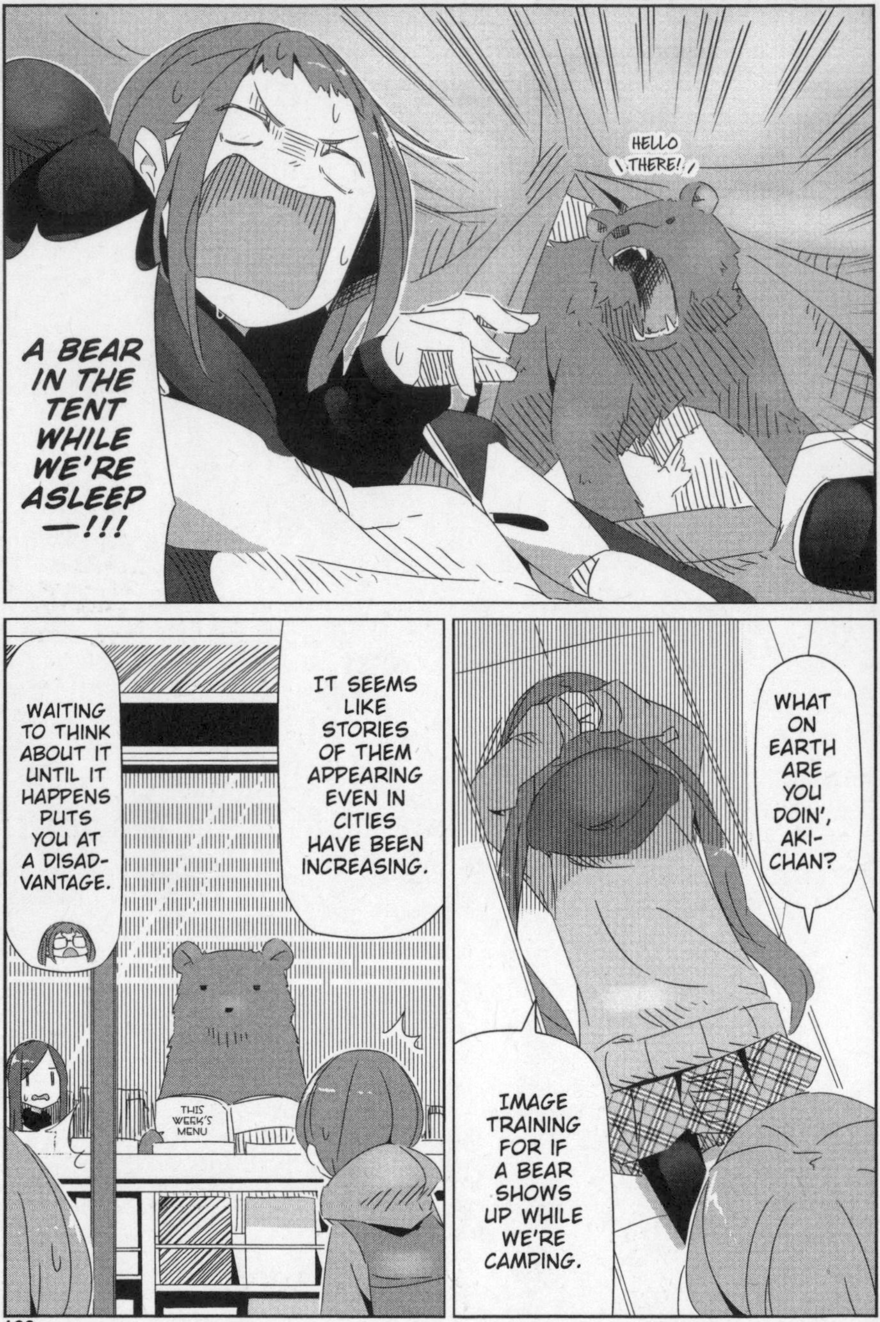
HELLO THERE!
A BEAR IN THE TENT WHILE WE'RE ASLEEP—!!!
WHAT ON EARTH ARE YOU DOIN', AKI-CHAN?
IMAGE TRAINING FOR IF A BEAR SHOWS UP WHILE WE'RE CAMPING.
IT SEEMS LIKE STORIES OF THEM APPEARING EVEN IN CITIES HAVE BEEN INCREASING.
WAITING TO THINK ABOUT IT UNTIL IT HAPPENS PUTS YOU AT A DISAD-VANTAGE.
THIS WEEK'S MENU

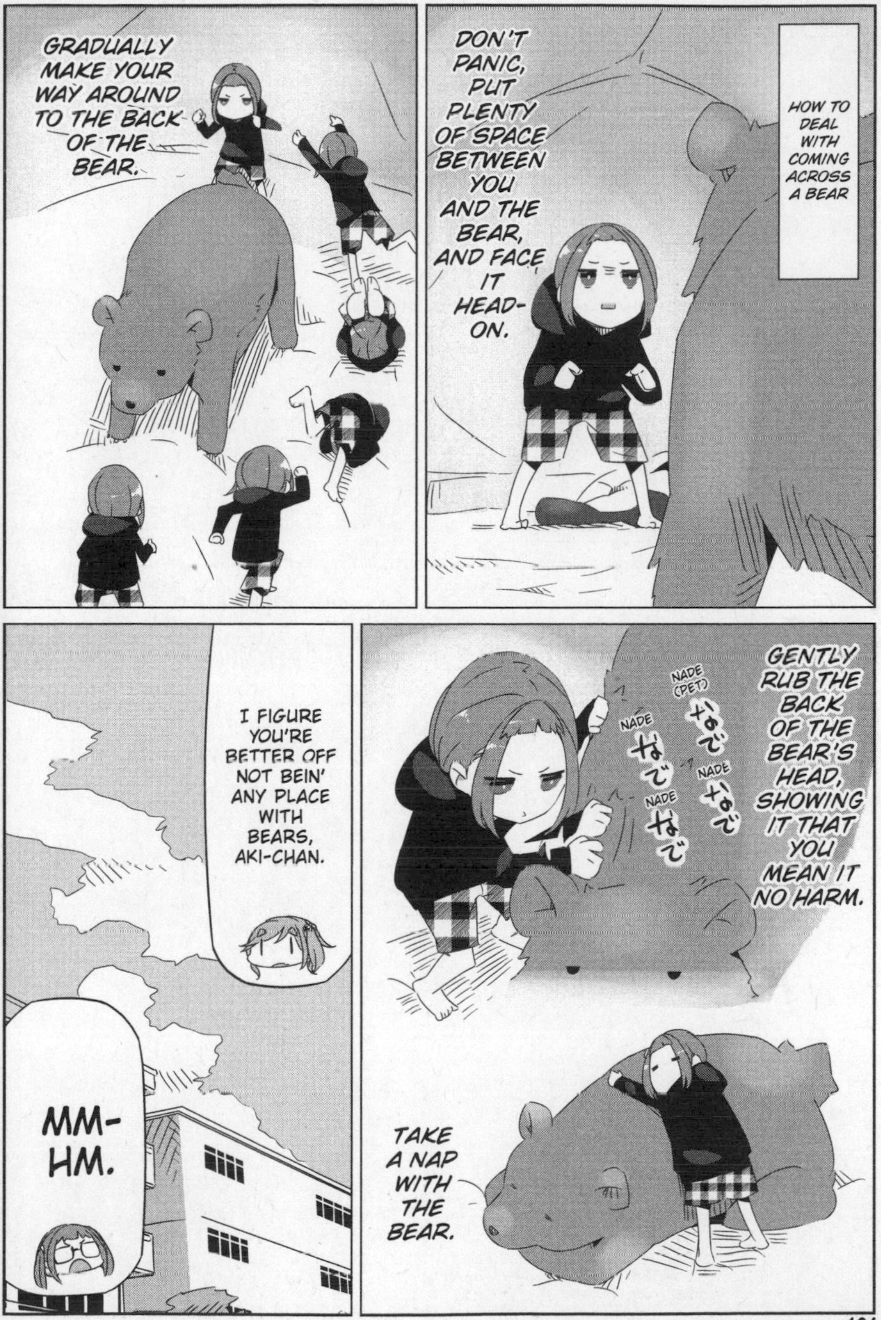
HOW TO DEAL WITH COMING ACROSS A BEAR
DON'T PANIC, PUT PLENTY OF SPACE BETWEEN YOU AND THE BEAR, AND FACE IT HEAD-ON.
GRADUALLY MAKE YOUR WAY AROUND TO THE BACK OF THE BEAR.
GENTLY RUB THE BACK OF THE BEAR'S HEAD, SHOWING IT THAT YOU MEAN IT NO HARM.
NADE (PET) なで
NADE なで
NADE なで
NADE なで
TAKE A NAP WITH THE BEAR.
I FIGURE YOU'RE BETTER OFF NOT BEIN' ANY PLACE WITH BEARS, AKI-CHAN.
MM-HM.

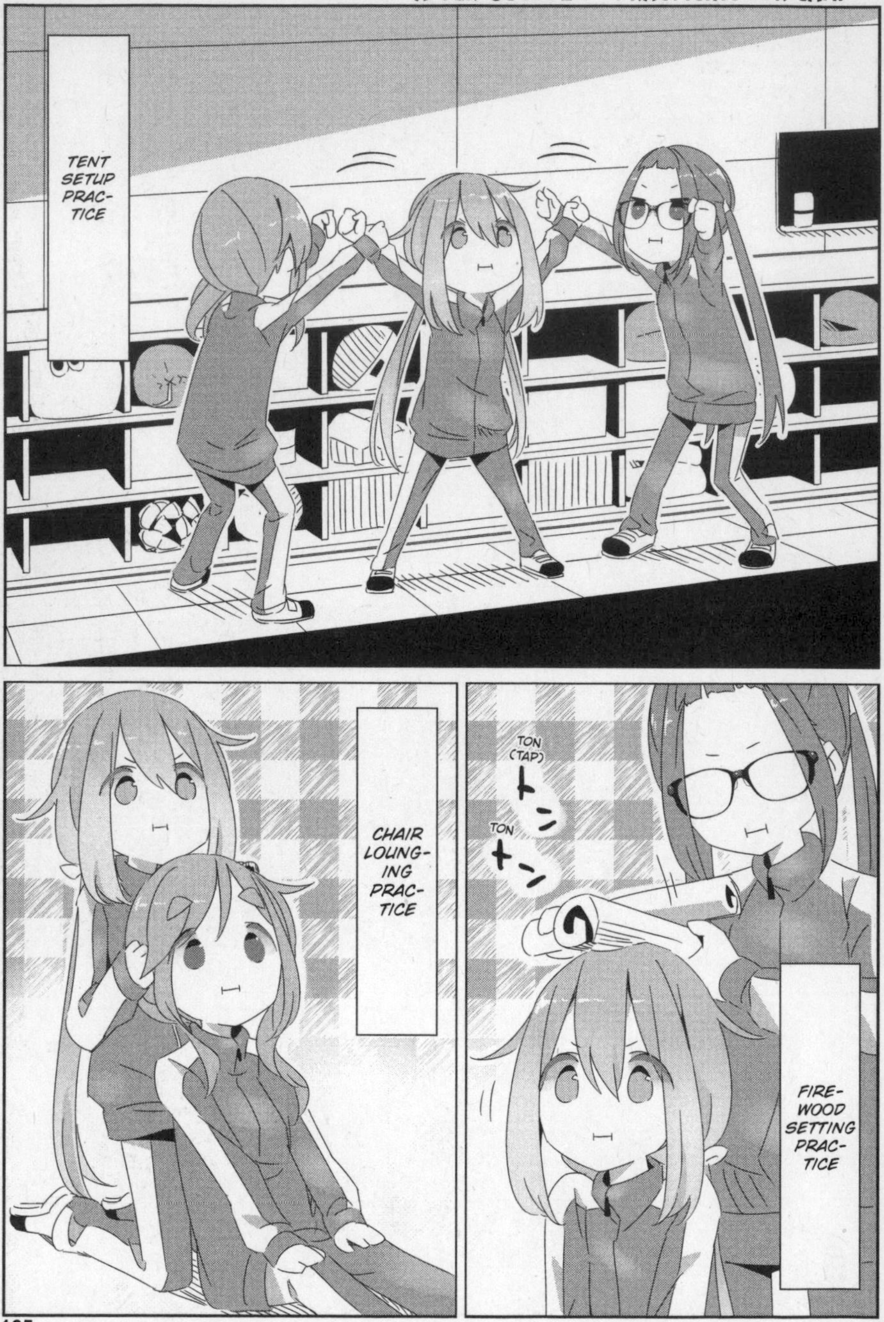
TENT SETUP PRAC-TICE
TON (TAP)
トン
TON
トン
FIRE-WOOD SETTING PRAC-TICE
CHAIR LOUNG-ING PRAC-TICE

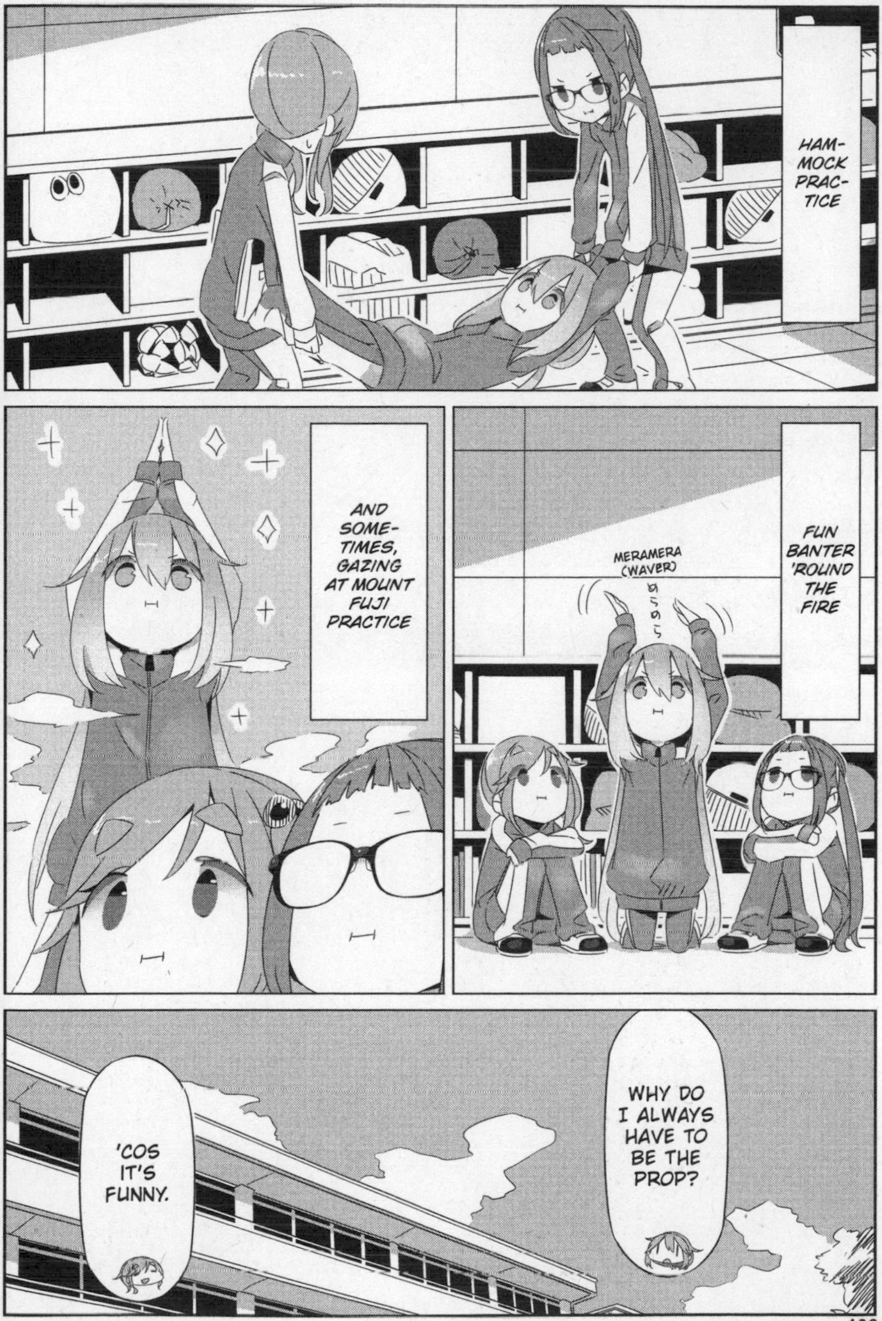
HAM-MOCK PRAC-TICE
FUN BANTER 'ROUND THE FIRE
MERAMERA (WAVER)
めらめら
AND SOME-TIMES, GAZING AT MOUNT FUJI PRACTICE
WHY DO I ALWAYS HAVE TO BE THE PROP?
'COS IT'S FUNNY.

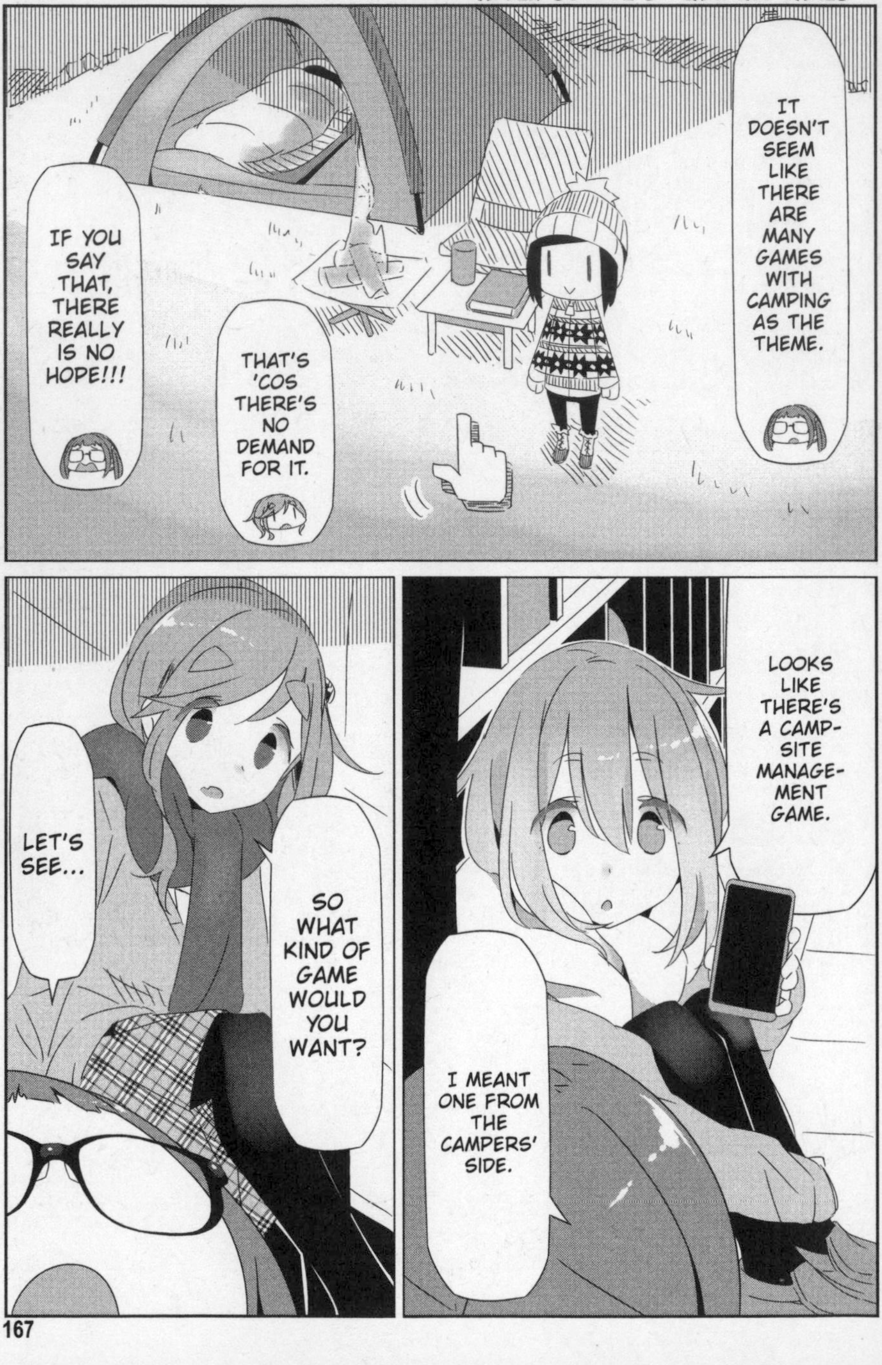
IT DOESN'T SEEM LIKE THERE ARE MANY GAMES WITH CAMPING AS THE THEME.
THAT'S 'COS THERE'S NO DEMAND FOR IT.
IF YOU SAY THAT, THERE REALLY IS NO HOPE!!!
LOOKS LIKE THERE'S A CAMP-SITE MANAGE-MENT GAME.
I MEANT ONE FROM THE CAMPERS' SIDE.
SO WHAT KIND OF GAME WOULD YOU WANT?
LET'S SEE...

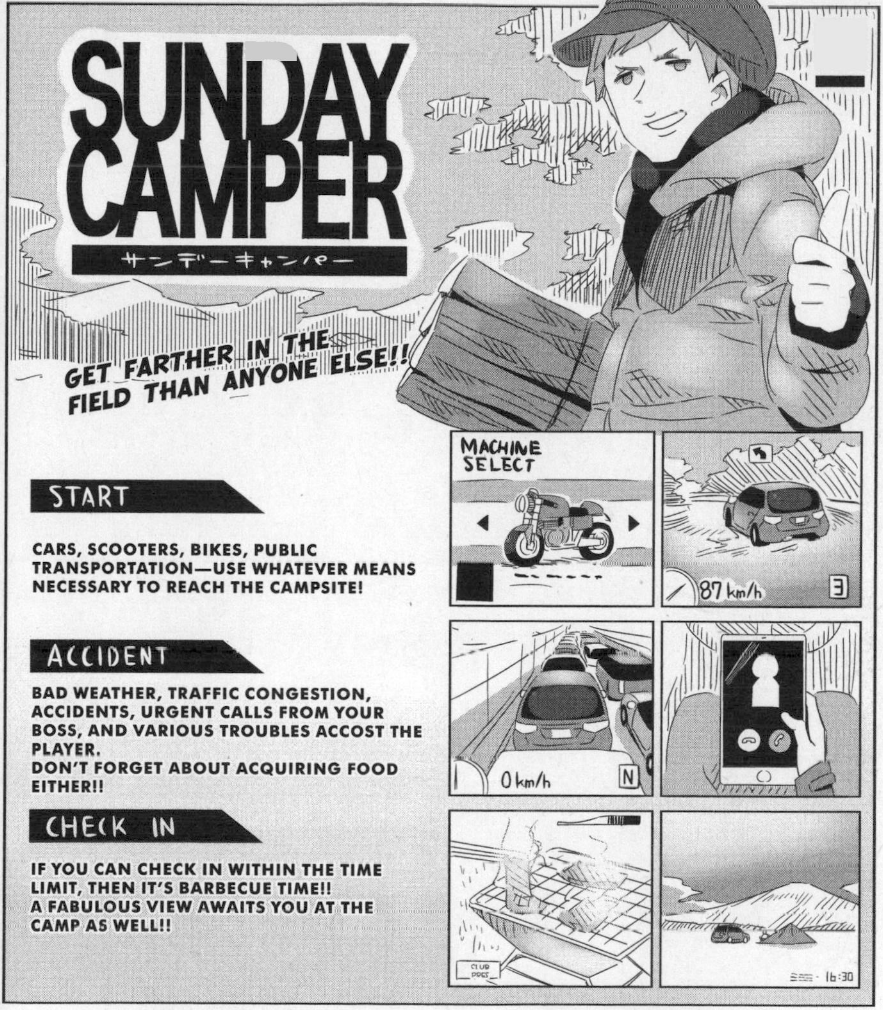
SUNDAY CAMPER
サンデーキャンパー
GET FARTHER IN THE FIELD THAN ANYONE ELSE!!
START
CARS, SCOOTERS, BIKES, PUBLIC TRANSPORTATION—USE WHATEVER MEANS NECESSARY TO REACH THE CAMPSITE!
MACHINE SELECT
87 km/h
ACCIDENT
BAD WEATHER, TRAFFIC CONGESTION, ACCIDENTS, URGENT CALLS FROM YOUR BOSS, AND VARIOUS TROUBLES ACCOST THE PLAYER.
DON'T FORGET ABOUT ACQUIRING FOOD EITHER!!
0 km/h
N
CHECK IN
IF YOU CAN CHECK IN WITHIN THE TIME LIMIT, THEN IT'S BARBECUE TIME!!
A FABULOUS VIEW AWAITS YOU AT THE CAMP AS WELL!!
16:30

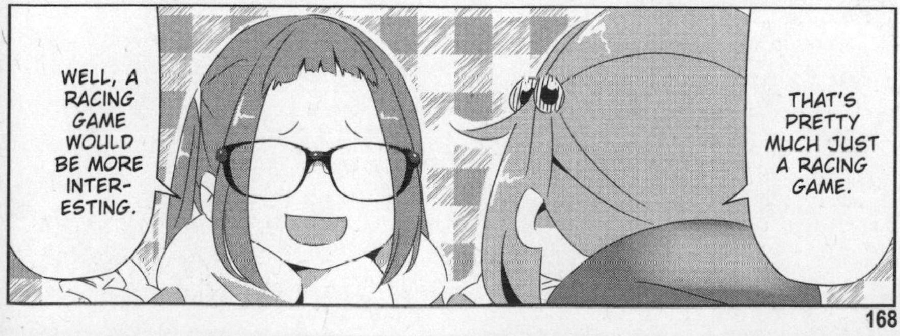
THAT'S PRETTY MUCH JUST A RACING GAME.
WELL, A RACING GAME WOULD BE MORE INTER-ESTING.

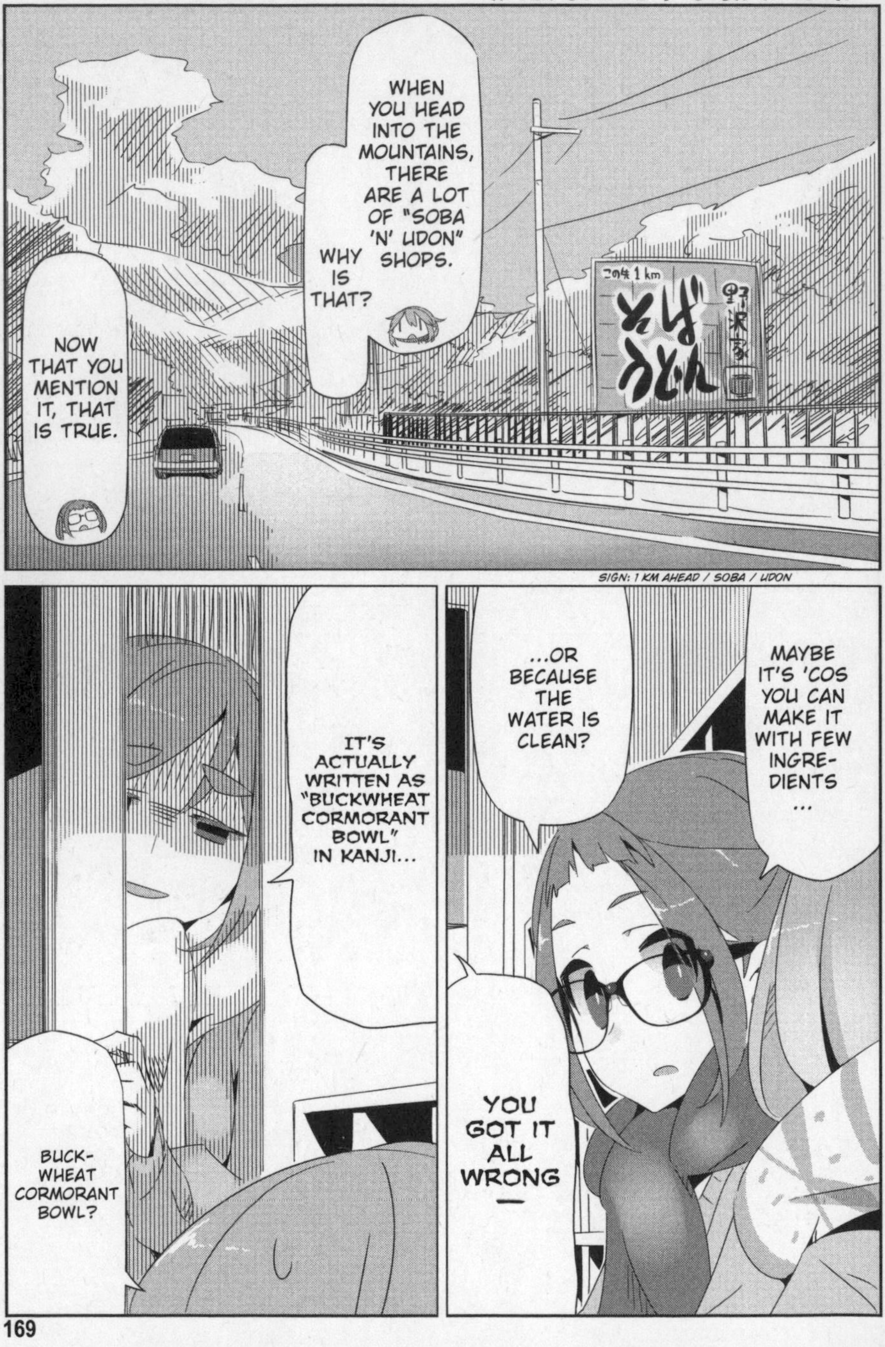
WHEN YOU HEAD INTO THE MOUNTAINS, THERE ARE A LOT OF "SOBA 'N' UDON" SHOPS.
WHY IS THAT?
この先1km
そば
うどん
NOW THAT YOU MENTION IT, THAT IS TRUE.
SIGN: 1 KM AHEAD / SOBA / UDON
MAYBE IT'S 'COS YOU CAN MAKE IT WITH FEW INGRE-DIENTS...
...OR BECAUSE THE WATER IS CLEAN?
YOU GOT IT ALL WRONG —
IT'S ACTUALLY WRITTEN AS "BUCKWHEAT CORMORANT BOWL" IN KANJI...
BUCK-WHEAT CORMORANT BOWL?

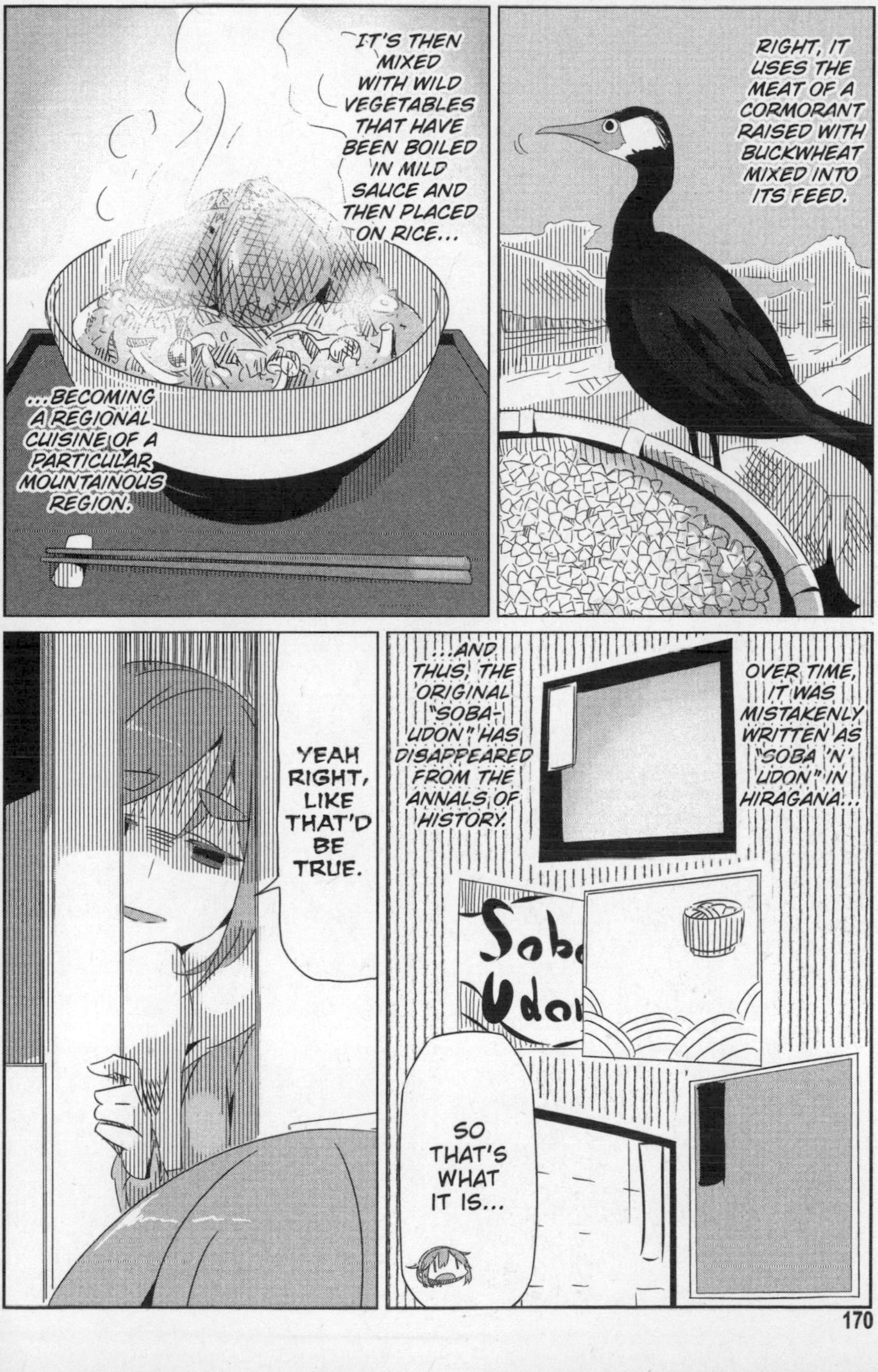
RIGHT, IT USES THE MEAT OF A CORMORANT RAISED WITH BUCKWHEAT MIXED INTO ITS FEED.
IT'S THEN MIXED WITH WILD VEGETABLES THAT HAVE BEEN BOILED IN MILD SAUCE AND THEN PLACED ON RICE...
...BECOMING A REGIONAL CUISINE OF A PARTICULAR MOUNTAINOUS REGION.
OVER TIME, IT WAS MISTAKENLY WRITTEN AS "SOBA 'N' UDON" IN HIRAGANA...
...AND THUS, THE ORIGINAL "SOBA-UDON" HAS DISAPPEARED FROM THE ANNALS OF HISTORY.
SO THAT'S WHAT IT IS...
YEAH RIGHT, LIKE THAT'D BE TRUE.

AFTER-SCHOOL 10 HANDLE WITH CARE

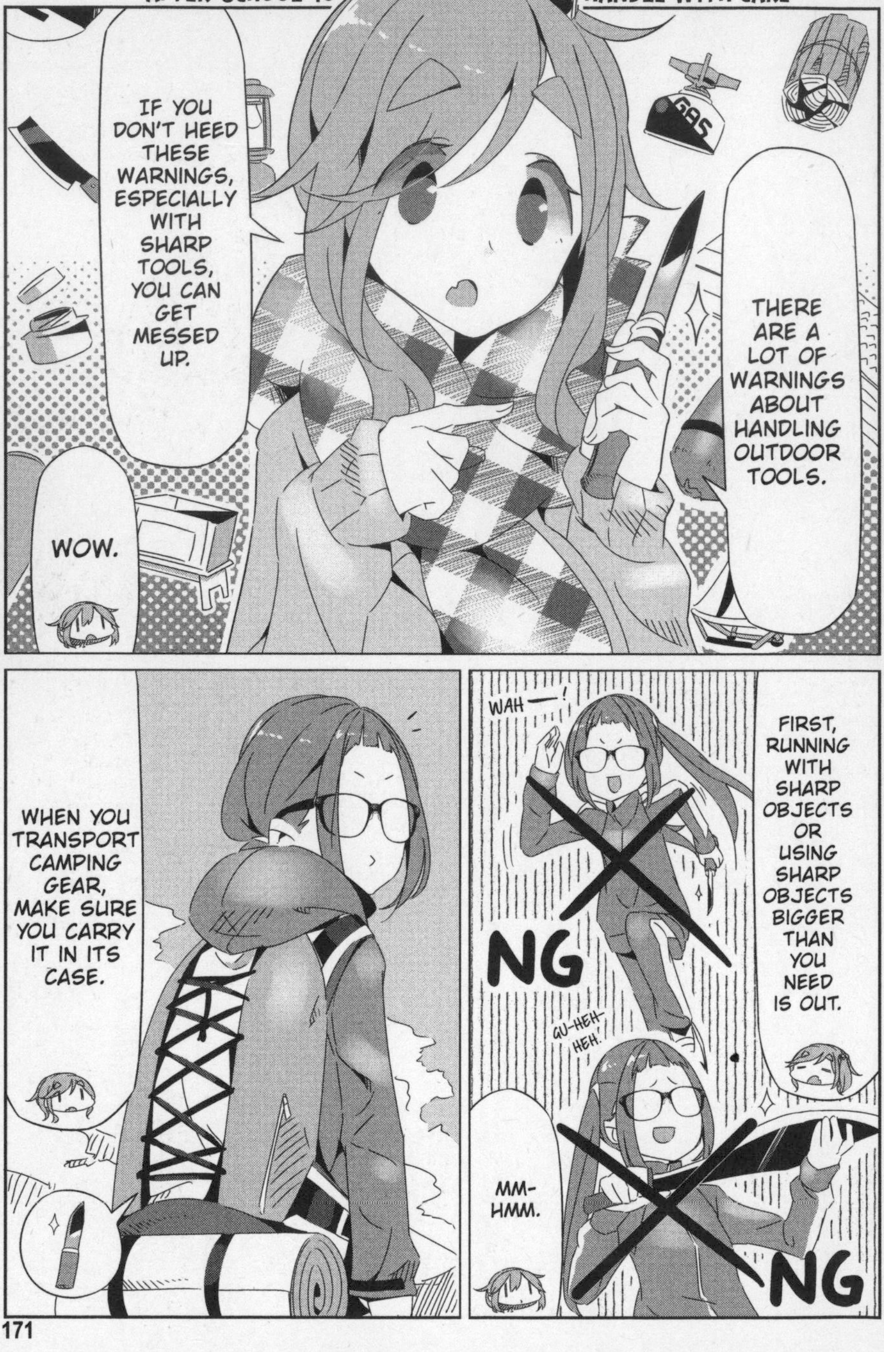
THERE ARE A LOT OF WARNINGS ABOUT HANDLING OUTDOOR TOOLS.
IF YOU DON'T HEED THESE WARNINGS, ESPECIALLY WITH SHARP TOOLS, YOU CAN GET MESSED UP.
WOW.
WAH—!
FIRST, RUNNING WITH SHARP OBJECTS OR USING SHARP OBJECTS BIGGER THAN YOU NEED IS OUT.
NG
GU-HEH HEH.
MM-HMM.
NG
WHEN YOU TRANSPORT CAMPING GEAR, MAKE SURE YOU CARRY IT IN ITS CASE.

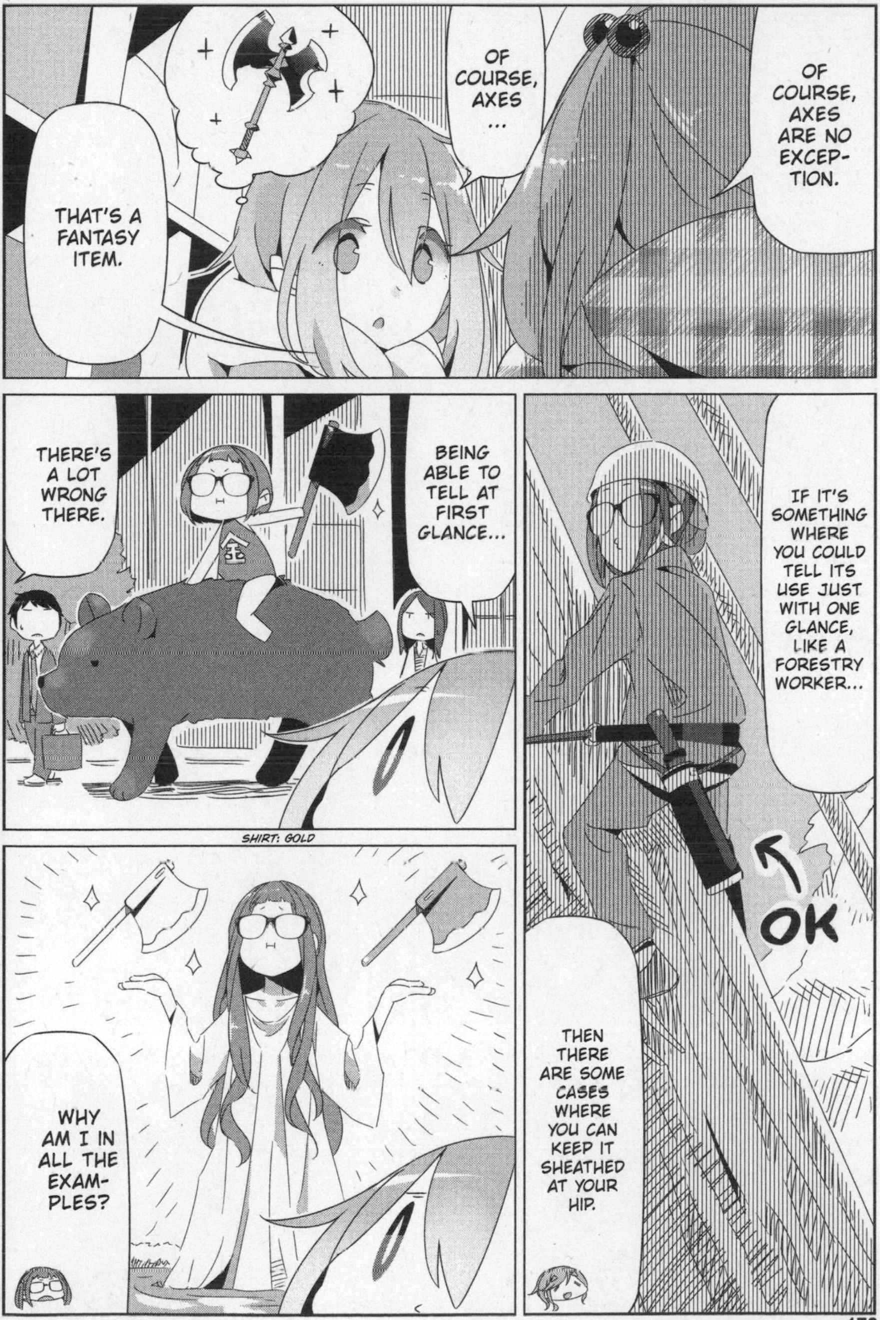
OF COURSE, AXES ARE NO EXCEP-TION.
OF COURSE, AXES ...
THAT'S A FANTASY ITEM.
IF IT'S SOMETHING WHERE YOU COULD TELL ITS USE JUST WITH ONE GLANCE, LIKE A FORESTRY WORKER...
OK
THEN THERE ARE SOME CASES WHERE YOU CAN KEEP IT SHEATHED AT YOUR HIP.
BEING ABLE TO TELL AT FIRST GLANCE...
金
THERE'S A LOT WRONG THERE.
SHIRT: GOLD
WHY AM I IN ALL THE EXAM-PLES?

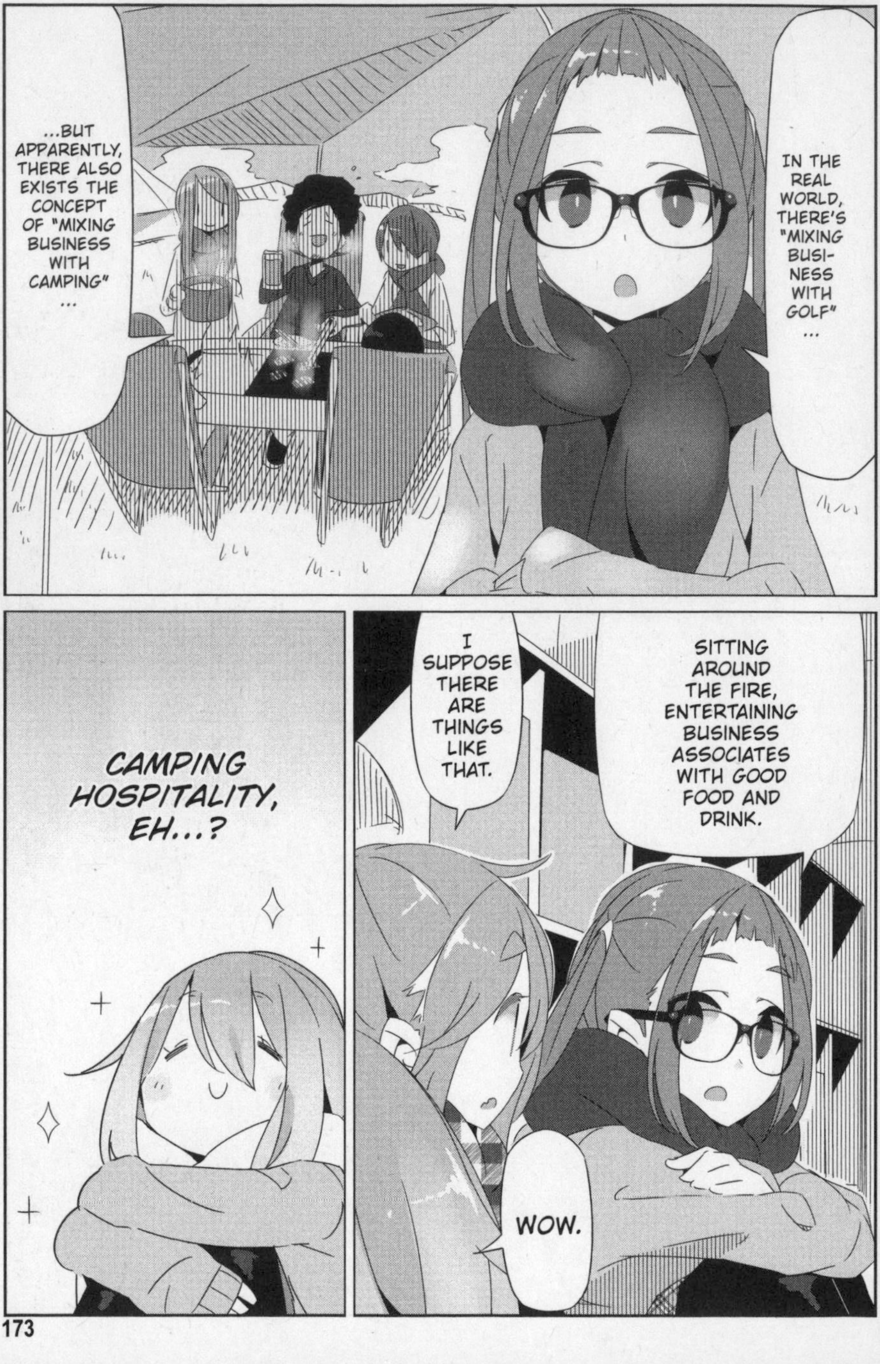
IN THE REAL WORLD, THERE'S "MIXING BUSI-NESS WITH GOLF"...
...BUT APPARENTLY, THERE ALSO EXISTS THE CONCEPT OF "MIXING BUSINESS WITH CAMPING"...
SITTING AROUND THE FIRE, ENTERTAINING BUSINESS ASSOCIATES WITH GOOD FOOD AND DRINK.
I SUPPOSE THERE ARE THINGS LIKE THAT.
WOW.
CAMPING HOSPITALITY, EH...?

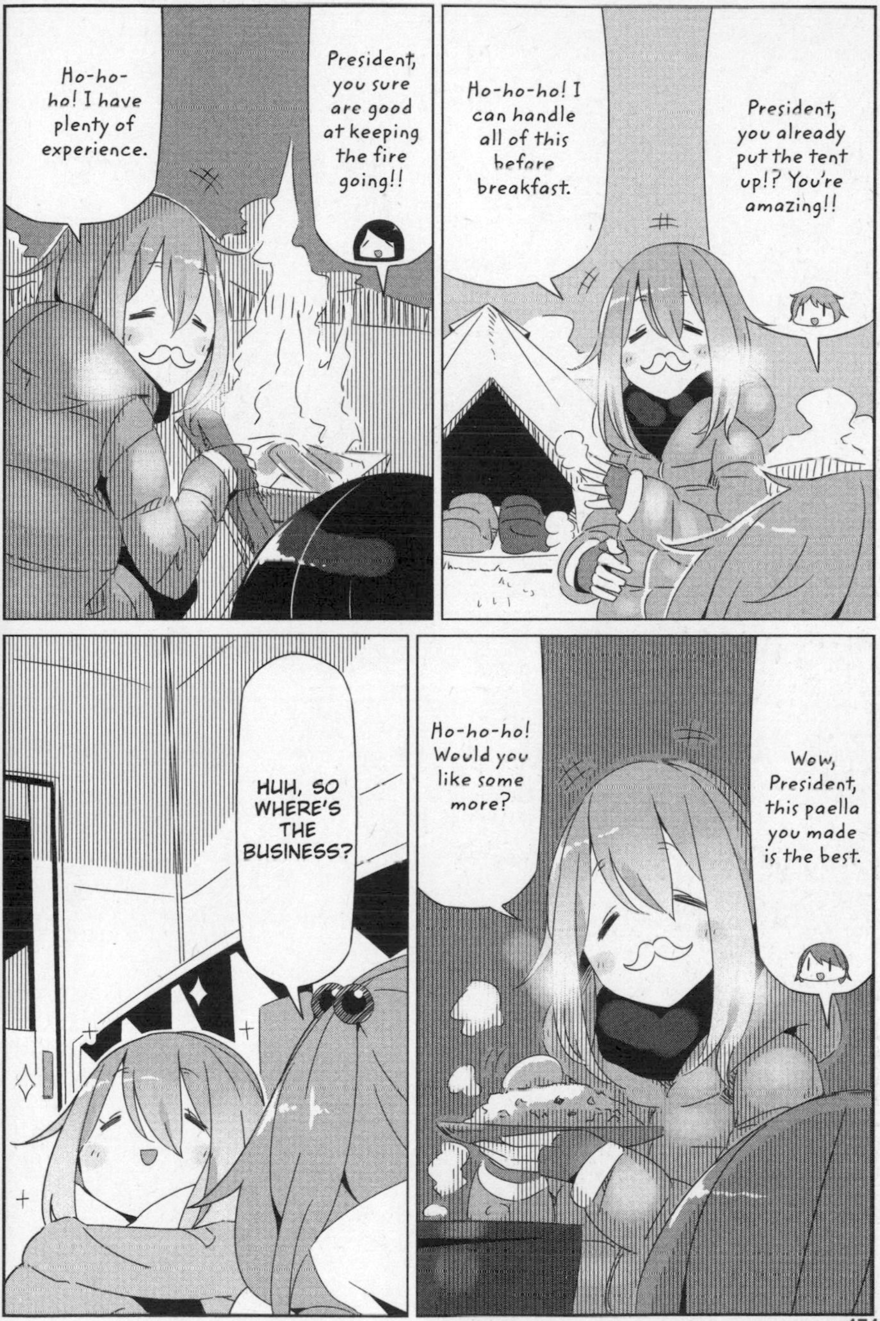
President, you already put the tent up!? You're amazing!!
Ho-ho-ho! I can handle all of this before breakfast.
President, you sure are good at keeping the fire going!!
Ho-ho-ho! I have plenty of experience.
Wow, President, this paella you made is the best.
Ho-ho-ho! Would you like some more?
HUH, SO WHERE'S THE BUSINESS?

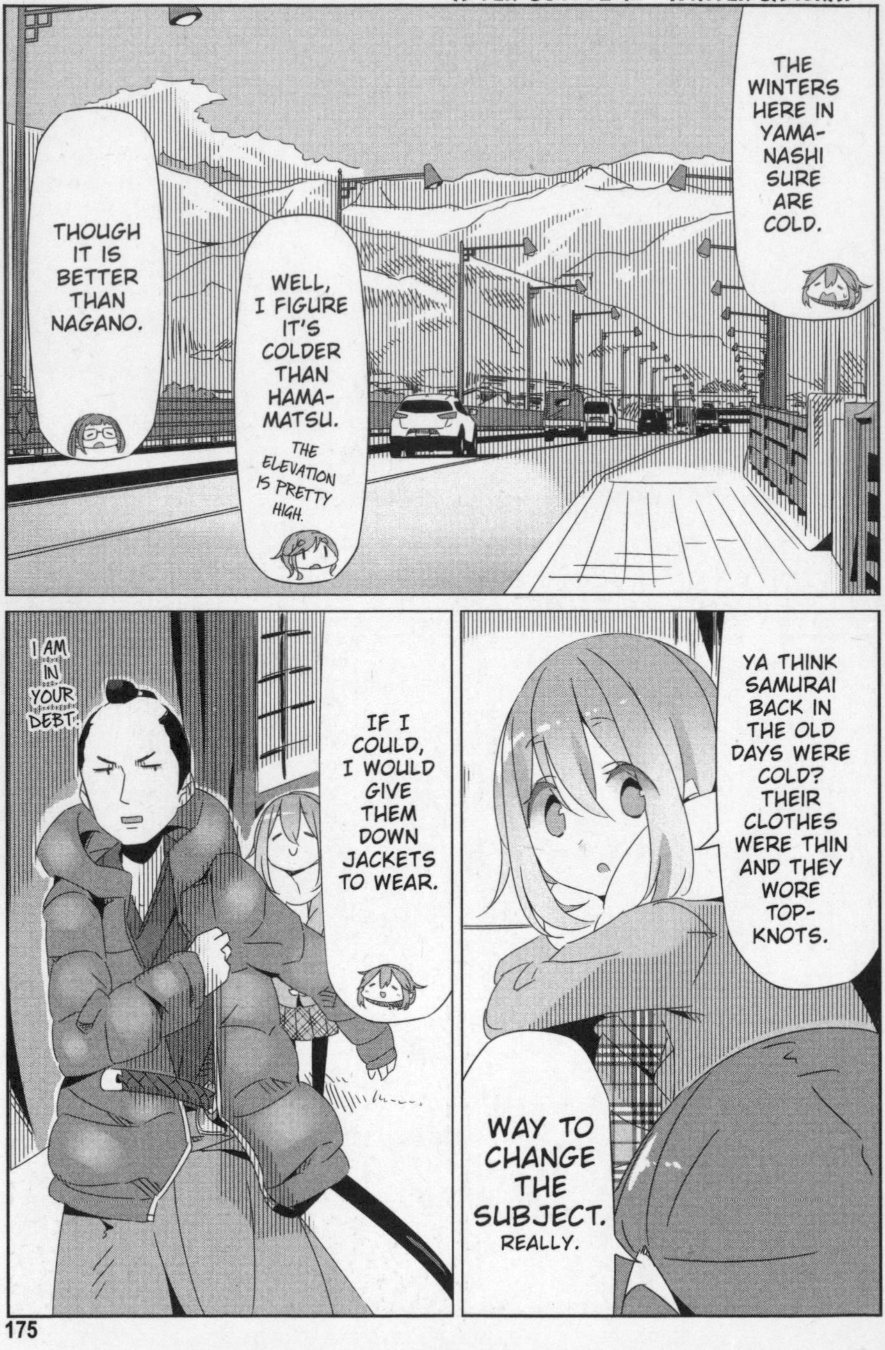
THE WINTERS HERE IN YAMA-NASHI SURE ARE COLD.
WELL, I FIGURE IT'S COLDER THAN HAMA-MATSU.
THE ELEVATION IS PRETTY HIGH.
THOUGH IT IS BETTER THAN NAGANO.
YA THINK SAMURAI BACK IN THE OLD DAYS WERE COLD? THEIR CLOTHES WERE THIN AND THEY WORE TOP-KNOTS.
WAY TO CHANGE THE SUBJECT.
REALLY.
IF I COULD, I WOULD GIVE THEM DOWN JACKETS TO WEAR.
I AM IN YOUR DEBT.

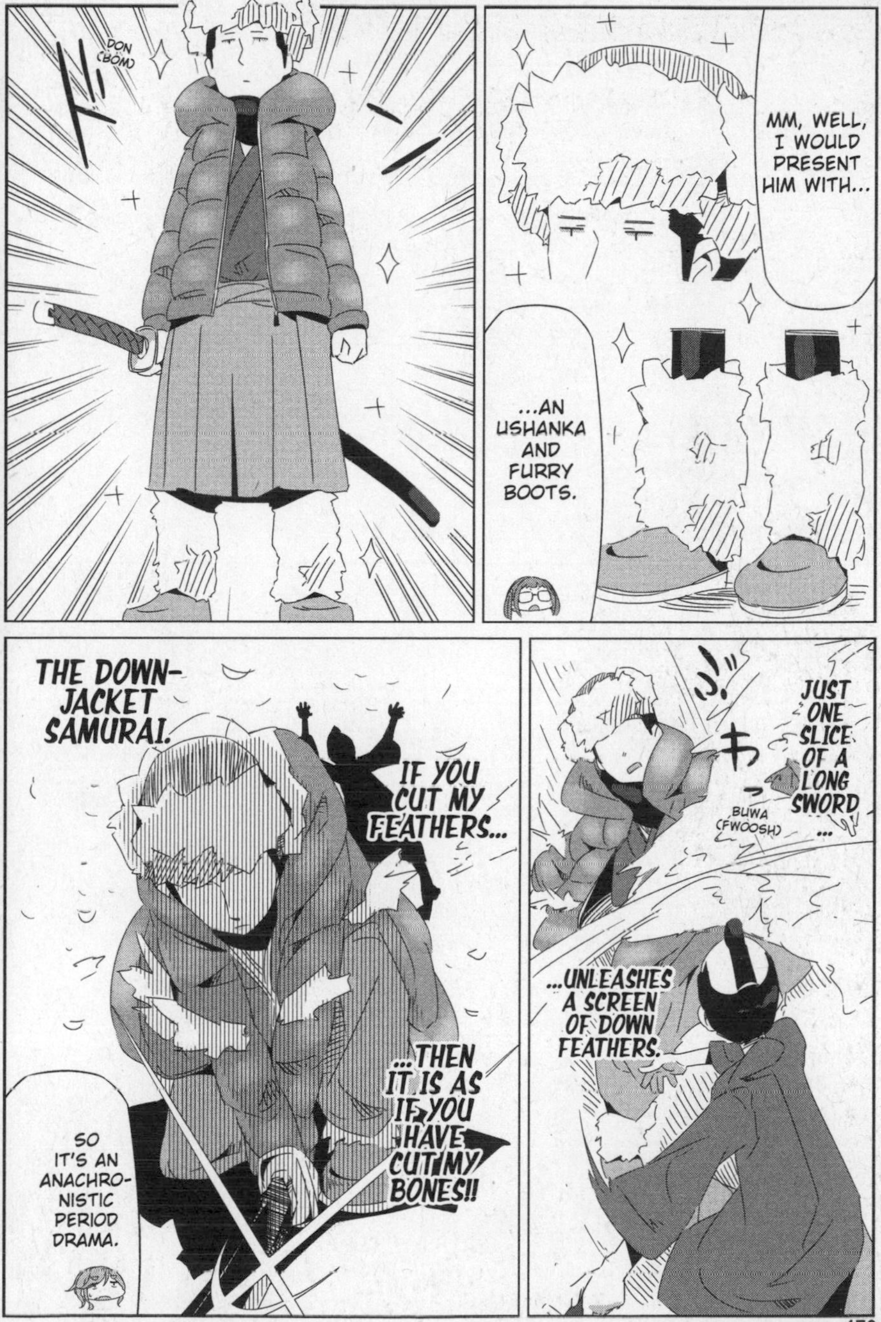
MM, WELL, I WOULD PRESENT HIM WITH...
...AN USHANKA AND FURRY BOOTS.
DON (BOM)
JUST ONE SLICE OF A LONG SWORD...
BUWA (FWOOSH)
...UNLEASHES A SCREEN OF DOWN FEATHERS.
THE DOWN-JACKET SAMURAI.
IF YOU CUT MY FEATHERS...
...THEN IT IS AS IF YOU HAVE CUT MY BONES!!
SO IT'S AN ANACHRONISTIC PERIOD DRAMA.

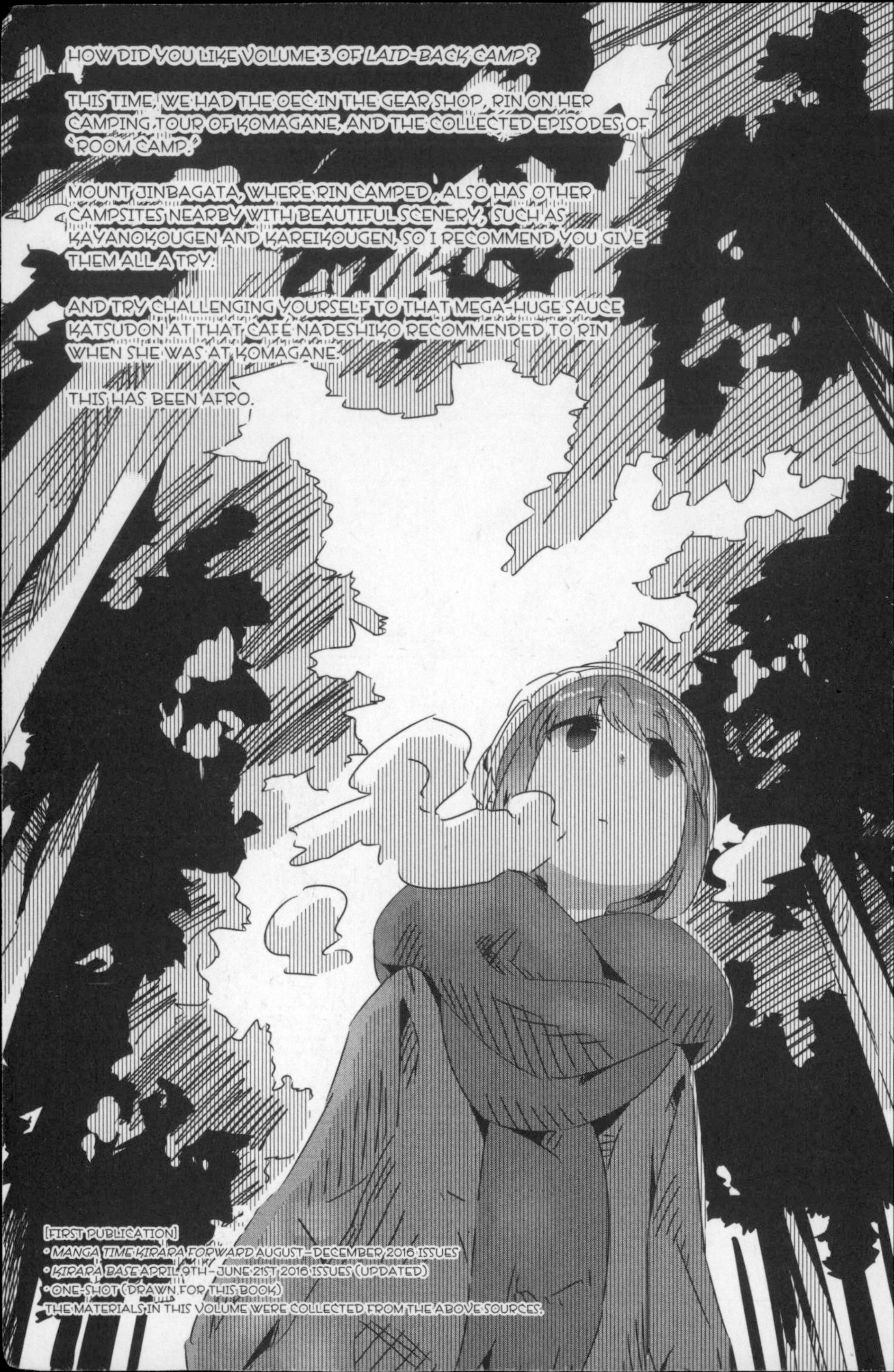

HOW DID YOU LIKE VOLUME 3 OF *LAID-BACK CAMP*?

THIS TIME, WE HAD THE OEC IN THE GEAR SHOP, RIN ON HER CAMPING TOUR OF KOMAGANE, AND THE COLLECTED EPISODES OF "ROOM CAMP."

MOUNT JINBAGATA, WHERE RIN CAMPED, ALSO HAS OTHER CAMPSITES NEARBY WITH BEAUTIFUL SCENERY, SUCH AS KAYANOKOUGEN AND KAREIKOUGEN, SO I RECOMMEND YOU GIVE THEM ALL A TRY.

AND TRY CHALLENGING YOURSELF TO THAT MEGA-HUGE SAUCE KATSUDON AT THAT CAFÉ NADESHIKO RECOMMENDED TO RIN WHEN SHE WAS AT KOMAGANE.

THIS HAS BEEN AFRO.

[FIRST PUBLICATION]
• *MANGA TIME KIRARA FORWARD* AUGUST–DECEMBER 2016 ISSUES
• *KIRARA BASE* APRIL 9TH–JUNE 21ST 2016 ISSUES (UPDATED)
• ONE-SHOT (DRAWN FOR THIS BOOK)
THE MATERIALS IN THIS VOLUME WERE COLLECTED FROM THE ABOVE SOURCES.

LAID ♦ BACK CAMP ③

Afro

Translation: **Amber Tamosaiti**

D0102643

YURUCAMP Vol. 3
© 2017 afro. All rights reserved. First published in Japan in 2017 by HOUBUNSHA CO., LTD., Tokyo. English translation rights in United States, Canada, and United Kingdom arranged with HOUBUNSHA CO., LTD. through Tuttle-Mori Agency, Inc., Tokyo.

English translation © 2018 by Yen Press, LLC

Yen Press
1290 Avenue of the Americas
New York, NY 10104

Visit us at yenpress.com
facebook.com/yenpress
twitter.com/yenpress
yenpress.tumblr.com
Instagram.com/yenpress

First Yen Press Edition: July 2018

Yen Press is an imprint of Yen Press, LLC.
The Yen Press name and logo are trademarks of Yen Press, LLC.

The publisher is not responsible for websites (or their content) that are not owned by the publisher.

Library of Congress Control Number: 2017959206

ISBNs: 978-0-316-51785-0 (paperback)
       978-0-316-51786-7 (ebook)

10 9 8 7 6 5 4 3 2 1

WOR

Printed in the United States of America